# Insurgency
# in the Modern World

## Other Titles of Interest

*Armed Struggle in Palestine: A Political-Military Analysis*, Bard E. O'Neill

*Terrorism: Theory and Practice*, edited by Yonah Alexander, David Carlton, and Paul Wilkinson

*Self-Determination: National, Regional, and Global Dimensions*, edited by Yonah Alexander and Robert A. Friedlander

*International Terrorism: An Annotated Bibliography and Research Guide*, Augustus R. Norton and Martin H. Greenberg

*Victims of Terrorism*, edited by Frank M. Ochberg and David Soskis

*Terrorism and Global Security: The Nuclear Threat*, Louis René Beres

*Terrorism and Hostage Negotiations*, Abraham H. Miller

## Also of Interest

*The Military and Security in the Third World: Domestic and International Impacts*, Sheldon W. Simon

# A Westview Special Study

## Insurgency in the Modern World
### edited by Bard E. O'Neill,
### William R. Heaton, and Donald J. Alberts

While all instances of insurgency have elements in common, the circumstances that precipitate them and the forms they take vary immensely. The editors of this book synthesize the literature on insurgency to provide an analytical framework that outlines categories of insurgent movements (secessionist, revolutionary, restorational, reactionary, conservative, and reformist), strategies (Maoist, Cuban, and urban), and factors that can have a major bearing on the outcome of insurgent conflicts. Case studies on Thailand, Oman, Angola, Guatemala, Uruguay, Iraq, the PLO, and Northern Ireland are then examined systematically in terms of the framework, facilitating the testing of extant propositions and comparative analyses of the different movements.

Bard E. O'Neill is director of studies of insurgency and revolution, and of Middle East Studies at the National War College, and is adjunct professor of political science, Catholic University; previously he was associate professor at the U.S. Air Force Academy and the University of Denver. William R. Heaton is senior research fellow at the National Defense University Research Directorate. He holds a Ph.D. from the University of California, Berkeley, and has been professor of political science at the Air Force Academy. Donald J. Alberts, programming and planning action officer of the Doctrine and Concepts Division, U.S. Air Force, has been assistant professor of political science at the U.S. Air Force Academy and is now a Ph.D. candidate in international politics at Georgetown University.

# Insurgency
# in the Modern World

edited by Bard E. O'Neill,
William R. Heaton, and
Donald J. Alberts

Westview Press / Boulder, Colorado

*A Westview Special Study*

Copyright © 1980 by Westview Press, Inc.

Published in 1980 in the United States of America by
    Westview Press, Inc.
    5500 Central Avenue
    Boulder, Colorado 80301
    Frederick A. Praeger, Publisher


Library of Congress Cataloging in Publication Data
Main entry under title:
Insurgency in the modern world.
  (A Westview special study)
  1. Insurgency. I. O'Neill, Bard E. II. Heaton, William R. III. Alberts, Donald J.
JC328.5.I57   1980           322.4'2           79-26789
ISBN 0-89158-598-2

Printed and bound in the United States of America

# Contents

# Introduction

Since the end of World War II the international system has been spared the trauma of a major war involving the great powers. Some would even argue that the continuing evolution of the means of massive destruction has made war among the major powers increasingly unthinkable. Yet, in spite of this situation, we are witnessing an escalating and seemingly unending incidence of political violence in the international community. Of the various forms of political violence, terrorism and guerrilla warfare predominate.

During the period of U.S. involvement in Vietnam, the study of insurgency and counterinsurgency reached its zenith. With the passing of the Vietnam War, interest in insurgency waned, at least as far as government and academe were concerned. Paradoxically, however, insurgency remains the principal form of conflict on our planet today. Terrorism, in particular, is having a significant impact on all societies, and it appears likely that it will be with us for some time to come. Consequently, the need for greater understanding of these forms of political violence is vital.

We have long recognized the need for a book that combines an analytical technique with a variety of case studies to illuminate and assess various movements engaged in political violence. There is, of course, a rich and variegated body of literature on the phenomenon of political violence written by both scholars and practitioners. While many of these writings are historical and descriptive, there has been an outpouring of analytical work over the past several years that has made significant contributions to our understanding of political violence. Noticeably absent, however, has been an effort to integrate the findings into a general conceptual scheme that is then applied in several cases. This book is a product of our belief that such an undertaking is particularly important for students, whether in the university or in professional military schools.

The first part of the book proposes a broad analytical framework. This framework synthesizes the many lessons and principles derived from past experience in terms of six major interrelated variables—the government role, the environment, popular support, organization, cohesion, and external support—that can be used to analyze and compare insurgencies. The framework also posits four general strategies that attract many insurgents, and compares the importance they attribute to the variables. Subsequent chapters utilize the framework to analyze cases in Northern Ireland, Thailand, Guatemala, Uruguay, Iraq, Oman, and Angola. The final section reexamines the utility of the framework in light of the case studies, makes some comparisons, and offers conclusions.

The selection of the case studies reflects our desire to provide diverse coverage in terms of their time frame, type, strategy, geographic region, and relative success or failure. Accordingly, we shall examine both past (Guatemala) and present (Angola) situations as well as revolutionary (Thailand), reformist (Iraq), and conservative (the Protestants in Ulster) groups. As far as strategy is concerned, our coverage will encompass the Maoist approach in Thailand and Oman, as well as the urban terrorist in Uruguay and Northern Ireland. Finally, the cases vary by geographic region and differ with respect to their relative success or lack thereof. From this variety, we believe a compelling argument can be made for the utility of our framework in gaining a better, more comprehensive understanding of the nature of insurgency.

We are constrained to point out what our book does not do. This is not a theory of insurgency. Past attempts to construct macro theories have tended toward tautological arguments or untestable general hypotheses. For example, political violence is often explained as failure of government to provide order or social justice; the prima facie evidence of government failure is the existence of political violence. Nor are we proposing a definitive treatise on the necessary and sufficient causes of political violence and insurgency, though, clearly, we offer evidence as to the factors associated with their development. Our framework has been designed to move beyond mere description, to identify key variables affecting the development of insurgency, suggest relationships, clarify linkages, and help provide a meaningful way to organize and interpret large amounts of data. Accordingly, we are proposing a framework and not a theory. In a practical sense, we are interested in leaving the reader with a range of important questions that should be asked about insurgency, regardless of type.

We would like to thank those many people who have assisted in the preparation of this work. We are grateful to the contributors who systematically utilized the framework in the preparation of their studies, yet retained flexibility in the presentation of their cases. A special debt is owed to our editors, students, and families. We are aware of their sacrifices during the preparation of this work, and we hope that the final result will compensate them for their patience and support.

*B.E.O.*
*W.R.H.*
*D.J.A.*

# The Contributors

Bard E. O'Neill is director of studies of insurgency and revolution and of Middle East Studies at the National War College, and is senior research fellow in the National Defense University Research Directorate. Lt. Col. O'Neill holds a Ph.D. in international relations from the University of Denver. His publications include *Armed Struggle in Palestine: A Political-Military Analysis; The Energy Crisis and U.S. Foreign Policy,* which he co-edited; and a number of articles and monographs dealing with Middle Eastern affairs.

William R. Heaton is senior research fellow in the National Defense University Research Directorate. Capt. Heaton holds a Ph.D. from the University of California, Berkeley. He is coauthor of *The Politics of East Asia* and has written extensively on East Asian affairs.

Donald J. Alberts is currently assigned to the Doctrine and Concepts Division of the Directorate of Plans, Headquarters, U.S. Air Force. Lt. Col. Alberts is a Ph.D. candidate at Georgetown University. A highly decorated combat flier in Southeast Asia, he was formerly assistant professor of political science at the USAF Academy. He has been a frequent contributor to military journals.

Vincente Collazo-Davila is currently serving as an aircraft commander of the F-111. Maj. Collazo is a graduate of the USAF Academy and holds an M.A. in international relations from the Fletcher School of Law and Diplomacy. He is a specialist in Latin American politics.

Richard MacLeod is chief, Policy and Doctrine Branch, North American Air Defense Command/Aerospace Defense Command. Lt. Col. MacLeod, who holds an M.A. from the University of Southern California, was an adviser to the Thai counterinsurgency effort as chief, Military Civic Action/Special Operations in Northeast Thailand, 1973–74.

Don Mansfield is presently assigned as an international political-military analyst at Headquarters, U.S. Air Force. Lt. Col. Mansfield holds a Ph.D. from the University of Denver, is a distinguished graduate of the Air War

College, and formerly served as chairman of instruction in the Department of Political Science at the USAF Academy. He is a specialist in and has written about international politics, comparative politics, and U.S. foreign policy.

**James A. Miller** is president of Interaction Systems, Inc., of Vienna, Virginia, which specializes in negotiation, strategic planning, and research and analysis in national security affairs. He holds a Ph.D. from American University and is a specialist on insurgency and international terrorism.

**Paul R. Viotti** is associate professor of political science at the USAF Academy. Maj. Viotti holds a Ph.D. in political science from the University of California, Berkeley. He is a specialist in international relations, comparative politics, political economy, and methodology. He has written several articles on national security topics and is currently coediting a book on comparative defense policy.

# 1
# Insurgency:
# A Framework for Analysis

*Bard E. O'Neill*

It is hardly an exaggeration to suggest that a good deal of conceptual confusion obtains in the existing corpus of literature on internal political violence. In large part, this is due to the lack of agreement on the definitions of major terms such as insurgency, revolution, guerrilla warfare, terrorism, protracted struggle, and the like. As a result, it is not uncommon to find these terms used imprecisely, indiscriminately, and, at times, interchangeably.

In view of this unhappy situation and the problems it engenders for those interested in the systematic study of internal political violence, it is imperative that the principal concepts employed in our comparative analysis of insurgency be defined as carefully as possible. Accordingly, we begin by addressing the meaning of insurgency, its relationship to the political system, and six types of insurgency. Thereafter we turn to a commentary on the political resources and forms of warfare the insurgents utilize. Once the discussion of terminology is completed, we are ready to proceed to the principal foci of the framework for analysis: the variables that have a major bearing on the outcomes of insurgent conflicts, and insurgent strategies.

## The Nature of Insurgency

Insurgency can be defined as a struggle between a nonruling group and the ruling authorities in which the former consciously employs political resources (organizational skills, propaganda, and/or demonstrations) and instruments of violence to establish legitimacy for some aspect of the political system it considers illegitimate. Legitimacy and illegitimacy refer to whether or not existing aspects of politics are considered moral or immoral (or, to simplify, right or wrong) by the population or selected elements therein. For our purposes politics is defined as the process of making and executing binding decisions for a society; therefore, all behavior associated with this enterprise comprises the "political system." On a general level, the major components of the system

1

may be identified as: the political community, the regime, the authorities, and policies. Any or all of these may be considered immoral by insurgents, and it makes a great deal of difference precisely which one is at stake.[1]

The political community consists of those who accept interacting together in a situation where binding decisions will be made for all. In the contemporary international system this is, for the most part, equivalent to the nation-state. On this very basic point, violent conflict may result from considerations of legitimacy. The current uprising in the Eritrean sector of Ethiopia is illustrative here since the insurgents reject any notion that they should be an integral part of Ethiopia. Consequently, the Eritreans have sought through violent means to separate themselves from existing arrangements and to establish a separate political community. In the United States, Great Britain, France, and Japan, by contrast, there is a general acceptance of the morality of the political community rooted in common history, tradition, and language.

Where a consensus on the morality of the political community obtains, there may be other grounds for violent internal conflict. For instance, there can be considerable discord over the salient values and structures that provide the basic framework within which binding decisions and policies are made. Thus, while the Marxists in Afghanistan accepted the political community, they used violence to expunge the traditional political values and patrimonial structures of the regime in order to replace them with a system in which binding decisions would be made within the framework of a one-party regime, in which the value of equality would replace ascriptive values that reflect private and aristocratic interests.

On another level some groups may grant legitimacy to the regime but reject the specific individuals in power. This is exemplified by coups in which insurgents seize the key decision making offices without changing the regime of their predecessors. Besides the well-known Latin American cases of the 1950s, one could point to the 1970 overthrow of the Sultan of Oman, Said bin Taimur, by his son Qabus in this regard.[2]

Finally, violence may be used by nonruling groups in an effort to change existing policies that they believe have prevented them from acquiring their fair share of the collective political and economic product. One example is the terminal phase of the recent insurgency in the Sudan, where the blacks in the south demanded a change in policies to enable them to obtain a greater share of the political and economic benefits in society. Another is provided by the periodic attempts by Muslim and Druse elements in Lebanon to redress the perceived maldistribution of political and economic assets that clearly favors the Christian community.

The important thing to remember up to this point is that insurgency is essentially a political legitimacy crisis of some sort. The first task of the analyst, therefore, is to ascertain exactly what the issue is. In seeking an answer to this question, it is useful to carefully examine the articulated long-term aims of the insurgents.

By focusing on the ultimate goal of the insurgents and relating it to the aspects of politics discussed above, one can identify six types of insurgent movements: secessionist, revolutionary, restorational, reactionary, conservative, and reformist. *Secessionist* insurgents, such as the aforementioned Eritreans in Ethiopia, reject the existing political community of which they are formally a part; they seek to withdraw from it and constitute a new autonomous political community. *Revolutionary* insurgents seek to impose a new regime based on egalitarian values and centrally controlled structures designed to mobilize the people and radically transform the social structure within an existing political community (e.g., Marxist insurgents).[3] While *restorational* insurgent movements also seek to displace the regime, the values and structures they champion are identified with a recent political order. In this case the values are ascriptive and elitist while the structures are oligarchical ones that have little or no provisions for mass participation in politics. The National Front for the Rescue of Afghanistan and Sultan Ali Mirrah's Afar Liberation Front in the Haoussa region of Ethiopia are contemporary manifestations of this type. Historical examples are provided by noncommunist partisans in Europe during World War II. Although *reactionary* insurgents likewise seek to change the regime by reconstituting a past political order, their repristination relates to an idealized, golden age of the distant past in which religious values and authoritarian structures were predominant. The Moslem Brotherhood in Egypt and other Arab countries, which seeks to recreate the flowering Islamic society of centuries ago, is a case in point. *Conservative* insurgents, on the other hand, seek to maintain the existing regime in the face of pressures on the authorities to change it. This type of insurgent movement was exemplified in the early 1970s by Protestant organizations in Ulster that wished to retain the regime in Northern Ireland that they saw as threatened by the Irish Republican Army, Catholic moderates, the Irish Republic, and "British capitulationists."[4] Finally, *reformist* insurgents, such as the Kurds in Iraq and the Anayanya guerrillas in the southern Sudan, have attempted to obtain more political, social, and economic benefits without necessarily rejecting the political community, regime, or authorities. They are primarily concerned with policies that are considered discriminatory.[5]

To accomplish their objectives, insurgent movements use political resources and instruments of violence against the ruling authorities. As far as political resources are concerned, organization is the critical dimension. This can be one of two types: *conspirational*, where small elite groups carry out and threaten violent acts; or *internal warfare*, where insurgent elites attempt to mobilize large segments of the population on behalf of their cause.[6] While internal warfare is the most familiar to students of insurgency, because of the well-known Vietnamese, Cambodian, Chinese, Algerian, and Portuguese colonial conflicts, there are also ample cases of conspiratorial insurgencies, such as those led by the Bolsheviks in Czarist Russia, the Red Army in Japan, and the Moslem Brotherhood in Egypt. Since some conspiracies gradually evolve into internal wars, the two are best viewed as ends of a continuum between which there are many intermediate cases.

In conspiracies the organizational effort necessary for coordinating both violent and nonviolent activity is not as demanding as in an internal war setting, since there is far less concern with linking the insurgency to the mass population. This neglect of the population, however, often renders such groups impotent and, hence, has provided one of the key issues dividing insurgent strategists.

Turning to the violent aspect of insurgency, one can identify different *forms* of warfare. A *form* of warfare may be viewed as one variety of organized violence emphasizing particular armed forces, weapons, tactics, and targets. Naval blockades, ground combat, air campaigns, and guerrilla operations are forms of warfare. Three forms of warfare have been associated with insurgent conflicts: terrorism, guerrilla war, and conventional warfare.[7]

*Terrorism*, a form of insurgent warfare conducted either by individuals or very small groups, involves the use of systematic, arbitrary, and amoral violence—for example, murder, torture, mutilation, bombing, arson, kidnapping, and hijacking—in order to achieve both long- and short-term political aims. Unlike conventional soldiers and guerrillas, terrorists direct their operations primarily against unarmed civilians rather than enemy military units or economic assets.[8] Although such terrorism has generally occurred within the borders of the political system whose community, regime, authorities, or policies have become the target of insurgent violence, there has been an increasing tendency over the past several years to strike at targets outside such boundaries. Since these acts are carried out by autonomous, nonstate actors, they have been referred to as transnational terrorism so as to distinguish them from similar behavior on the part of individuals or groups controlled by sovereign states (international terrorism).[9]

The long-term goal of terrorism has been not so much the desire to deplete the government's physical resources as it has been to erode its psychological support by spreading fear among officials and their domestic and international supporters. Though the general purpose of terrorism has been to alter the behavior and attitudes of specific groups, this has not excluded the simultaneous pursuit of more proximate objectives, such as extracting particular concessions (e.g., payment of ransom or the release of prisoners), gaining publicity, demoralizing the population through the creation of widespread disorder, provoking repression by the government, enforcing obedience and cooperation from those inside and outside the movement, fulfilling the need to avenge losses inflicted upon the movement, enhancing the political stature of specific factions within an insurgent movement, and undermining policies of rival insurgent groups.[10] Since the particular aims being pursued will vary from incident to incident (even in the case of actions that are similar), great care must be exercised in generalizing about terrorist acts.

Julian Paget has characterized *guerrilla warfare* as a form of warfare based on mobile tactics used by small, lightly armed groups who aim to harass their opponent rather than defeat him in battle.[11] Guerrilla warfare differs from terrorism in that its primary targets are usually the government's armed forces, police, or their support units and, in some cases, key economic targets, rather than unarmed civilians.[12] As a consequence, guerrilla units are larger than terrorist cells and tend to require a more elaborate logistical structure as well as base camps. Like terrorism, however, guerrilla warfare is a weapon of the weak; it is decisive only where the government fails to commit adequate resources to the conflict. In many cases it has been necessary to accompany guerrilla warfare with other forms of violence or to evolve mobile conventional warfare (the direct confrontation of large units in the field) in order to achieve success.

Whether or not an insurgent organization will have to move to the familiar conventional warfare mode is, in part, related to whether or not the insurgency is auxiliary or independent in nature. In the former case, suggests Otto Heilbrunn, the insurgents pursue only tactical aims, for they do not have to defeat the enemy; a regular army will be charged with that mission (e.g., Yugoslavia in World War II). Independent insurgent movements, on the other hand, have strategic aims, because they often must regularize their forces in order to be successful on their own. Even if regularization of forces is unnecessary, the independent insurgent movement must still rely largely on its own capabilities if it is to succeed.[13]

## Major Analytical Variables

In their quest for victory, insurgents have devised various strategies intended to maximize the effectiveness of political techniques and violence. These strategies can be differentiated by examining the relative importance they ascribe to six general variables—popular support, organization, cohesion, external support, the environment, and the effectiveness of the government.[14] Since these variables have a major impact on the outcome of insurgencies, they will constitute the criteria for assessing the political and military achievements, as well as strategies, of the insurgent groups in the case studies.

### Popular Support

For many insurgent leaders, popular support is an overriding strategic consideration. In the words of Mao Tse-tung, "the richest source of power to wage war lies in the masses of the people."[15] The significance attributed to civilian support can be understood by viewing it as a means to offset advantages the government possesses by virtue of its control of the administrative apparatus of the state and, most specifically, the army and police. Since insurgents know they would risk destruction by confronting the government forces in direct conventional engagements, they opt instead to erode the strength and will of their adversary through the use of terrorism and/or guerrilla warfare, which are designed to not only increase the human and material cost to the government, but also to demonstrate its failure to maintain effective control and provide protection within the country. Eventually, according to insurgent logic, the government will grow weary of the struggle and seek to prevent further losses by either capitulating or negotiating a settlement favorable to the insurgents.

For the purposes of this study, popular support is divided into two categories: active support and passive support. The latter includes individuals who merely sympathize with the aims and activities of the insurgents, while the former encompasses those who are willing to risk personal sacrifices on behalf of the insurgents. In the active support category are individuals who provide insurgents with supplies, intelligence information, shelter, concealment, liaison agents, and who, in some cases, carry out acts of disobedience or protest, all of which may bring severe punishment by the government. Although most discussions of popular support tend to emphasize active support, passive supporters are important in the sense that, at a minimum, they are not apt to betray or otherwise impede the insurgents.

In focusing on the need for active and passive support from the masses, insurgents do not neglect the vital role of the intelligentsia, since it is the principal source for recruitment of both high- and middle-level leadership positions (e.g., commanders of guerrilla units and terrorist networks, and political cadres).[16] The importance of the intellectuals has been noted by Ted Robert Gurr, who points out that their desertion from the government has repeatedly been a harbinger of revolution.[17]

It has been argued that community support and security are "safeguarded best when the native population identifies itself spontaneously with the fortunes of the guerrilla movement."[18] However, since spontaneity is often lacking, the insurgent movement must actively proselytize the people. Generally, insurgents will employ one or several of the following methods to gain the desired support and recruits: (1) charismatic attraction, (2) esoteric appeals, (3) exoteric appeals, (4) terrorism, (5) provocation of government counterterrorism, and (6) demonstration of potency. All of these, in one way or another, aim at convincing the people to render support because the insurgent's goal is both just and achievable.

In certain cases, assertive individuals emerge as the clearly identifiable leaders of insurgent movements. When such men are also blessed with oratorical skills and dynamic, forceful personalities, they frequently are able to motivate others to join their cause by virtue of their example and per-suasiveness. This is especially true in political communities where a tradition of heroic leadership is highly valued (e.g., the Arab states). While the process of "great men" inspiring sizeable numbers to follow them may unfold somewhat naturally and unconsciously, in certain instances the insurgent movement may deliberately encourage a cult of personality in order to attract adherents. Whatever the case, the individual leader becomes the principal reason why some people support insurgent movements. This phenomenon, which we refer to as *charismatic attraction*, has been exemplified by Mao Tse-tung, Fidel Castro, and Lenin, to name but a few. Although in the absence of survey data it is impossible to specify how many people joined their causes because of charismatic attraction as opposed to other factors, we do know from the many accounts of the insurgencies led by these men that the force of their personality was important. It is conceivable that more precise data could be obtained for contemporary cases by using current political science tech-niques such as survey research. The major problem, of course, is acquiring ac-cess to the insurgent rank and file. In view of this the analyst must be alert to the possible importance of charismatic attraction in the case he is in-vestigating.[19]

A second means of obtaining popular support that is frequently, though not invariably, associated with charismatic leadership is an emphasis on *esoteric appeals*. Directed primarily at the intellectual strata (broadly defined), esoteric appeals seek to clarify the situation by placing it in an ideological or theoretical context that orders and interprets political complexities. In the words of Gabriel Almond:

> An ideology imputes a particular structure to political action. It defines who or what the main initiators of action are, whether they be individuals, status groups, classes, nations, magical forces, or deities. It attributes specific roles to these actors, describes their relationships with one another, and defines the arena in which actions occur.[20]

Marxist revolutionaries, for example, have found that Lenin's exegesis on im-perialism has powerful intellectual attraction in third world countries because it provides a coherent, logical, and all-encompassing explanation of the pov-erty, illiteracy, and oppression that characterize the political and social milieu. Furthermore, by pointing a finger at indigenous feudal or capitalist classes and their links with external imperialist elements, it provides an identifiable target for the frustrations of the intellectuals, many of whom are either unemployed or underemployed.[21] Although Almond has suggested that ideology is rarely perceived by persons at the point of admission to political movements, one must still account for those few who do respond to ideological incantations.[22] This is especially important in circumstances where members of the educated strata join one insurgent group, in lieu of its rivals, because it is more ideologically oriented and intellectually compelling.

Even though the esoteric appeal is primarily directed at the intellectuals, it is also related to support of the masses, because the latter often need their discontent focused on a real villain if they are to be galvanized for action. One of the functions of ideology, the identification of friend and foe, meets this need. Indeed, identifying the source of frustration and grievances is important because as Gurr notes, "discontented people act aggressively only when they become aware of the supposed source of frustration, or something or someone with whom they associate frustration." Moreover, doctrinal rationalizations for violence can themselves intensify discontent by increasing expectations and defending violence as a means to their attainment. This, of course, presupposes that there are extant grievances – the exoteric dimension – because "men's susceptibility to these beliefs is a function of the intensity of their discontent."[23]

*Exoteric appeals* focus on concrete grievances of both the intelligentsia and the masses. In the case of the former, the aforementioned employment issue can be exploited, whereas for the latter, emphasis is directed to more mundane matters, such as corruption and repression by local officials as well as the need for food, land reform, jobs, medical assistance, and the like.[24] If they are successful in achieving their goal, the insurgents promise that such problems will be effectively resolved.

In those situations where external nations either impose their authority directly (imperialism), exert tremendous influence through international economic networks (neoimperialism), or intervene in support of the local authorities, the insurgents will frequently merge powerfully enticing nationalist themes with esoteric and exoteric appeals. Relying on a formulation such as Lenin's theory of imperialism, they will identify the external enemy as the source of national deprivations. For many intellectuals this, again, provides both a cogent explanation and target, while for the masses it is presented in such a way as to provide a simplified explanation and a target.[25]

Where esoteric and exoteric appeals are unsuccessful, because of effective government action and/or environmental disadvantages, the insurgents may turn to *terrorism*. In this context, the purpose of terrorist acts is to obtain popular support by demonstrating the government's weaknesses compared to insurgent strength.[26] Whether or not the insurgents will be successful in this undertaking depends substantially on two factors: the target of terror and the duration of terrorist campaigns.

With respect to the target, if terror is aimed at individuals or groups disliked by the people, it can facilitate the identification of the insurgents with oppressed and exploited elements. By manipulating resentment (based on grievances), and using selective terror against hated individuals and groups, the insurgents may well be able to increase popular support. Such was the case in the Cypriot insurrection against the British, according to Paget. On the other hand, if, at the outset, potential support is low, terror can create hostility toward the insurgents.[27] In any case, terrorism can end up alienating potential domestic and international supporters if it becomes indiscriminate and unduly prolonged.[28]

As far as transnational terrorism is concerned, there is little evidence to suggest that it has been considered a significant means of acquiring popular support. Indeed, if anything, the decision to engage in transnational terrorism generally is associated with an inability to operate internally which, in turn, is closely related to exiguous domestic support.

A fifth means which the insurgent utilizes in winning popular support is "catalyzing and intensifying counterterror which further alienates the enemy from the local population."[29] In other words, the guerrillas seek to provoke arbitrary and indiscriminate government reprisals against the population that will increase resentment and win the insurrectionary forces more adherents and support. The success of such an insurgent ploy will be determined largely by the nature of the government response and ethnic considerations. A widespread violent reaction by the government similar to that of the Pakistani Army in Bangladesh in 1971 would appear to effect more resentment and hatred than, say, such nonviolent actions as curfews and resettlement. While ruthless methods by the government might restore law and order in the short run, the long-term effect may be, as Richard Clutterbuck suggests, to provide the seeds for further insurgency.[30]

Race or ethnicity is a complicating factor. Jerry Silverman and Peter Jackson have argued that ethnic solidarity between the people and insurgents may be important in terror-counterterror situations, since it can cause the population to forgive insurgent excesses but not those of the government.[31] However, in light of the fact that this analyst found situations in Vietnam where the people reacted to American air and artillery strikes by blaming the revolutionary provocateurs, the ethnic factor cannot be considered foolproof. Nevertheless, on balance, it seems sound and suggestive.

The final technique the insurgent employs to establish popular support—demonstration of potency—has two dimensions: meeting the needs of the people through social services and a governing apparatus, and obtaining the military initiative. The former aspect demonstrates not only the reality of the insurgent's presence, but the corresponding government failure to deal with shadow government political cadres. Besides governing, guerrilla political operators normally seek to meet some of the people's basic needs and cooperate with them in such affairs as harvesting crops, building schools, and so forth.[32] Quite often the extension of such aid to the people will be the first step in involving them with the insurgent movement, either actively or passively. This would seem to be especially true in those contexts where the regime has been delinquent in responding to popular demands.

The second means of demonstrating potency—gaining the military initiative—is designed, in part, to create the impression that the insurgency has momentum and will succeed. A number of writers have stressed the importance of initiative to the guerrillas because, in addition to winning adherents for the movement, it boosts and sustains morale within insurgent organizations. "Units that are active and successful in the accomplishment of assigned missions build up a high esprit de corps and attract followers; success is contagious." Putting it another way: "no guerrilla movement in the field can afford to remain inactive for long; by so doing, it loses its morale and sense of purpose."[33]

In his quest to gain the initiative, the insurgent has at his disposal a flexible arsenal—ambushes, sabotage, kidnapping, assassination, mass attacks, etc. In order to employ such diverse methods effectively, however, the insurgent must have a coordinated strategy, a requisite that involves another major criterion, cohesion. Although the question of cohesion will be discussed in a separate section, a few comments about its relationship to popular support are necessary at this point. Of special significance is the reality that an insurgent movement with competing centers of loyalty will not only raise command and control problems that undercut military operations and initiative, but will lead some potential supporters to believe the resistance is in a state of confusion. As a result, the corresponding image of weakness may dissuade many from joining. Moreover, violent conflict among insurgent groups will undoubtedly sap the movement's overall strength, divert it from the main enemy, and deny it a positive image in the people's eyes. The spectacle of various guerrilla organizations criticizing (if not shooting at) each other in order to enhance their stature is bound to be bewildering to those being proselytized.

Military initiative will require continuous victories. Since the guerrilla is usually weak at the outset of hostilities, these may be only small successes, but such tactical self-sacrifice at the beginning may be necessary for eventual victory.[34] Local victories in guerrilla war, however, are heavily dependent on popular support, hence initiative and popular support are interdependent.

Initiative will require freedom of action. In Mao's words, "Freedom of action is the very life of an army and once this freedom is lost an army faces defeat or annihilation."[35] Although freedom of action is normally associated with operations in the target country, there are circumstances in which it is related to sanctuaries outside the country being contested. These sanctuaries, which involve the external support factor, are of great importance if, during the incipient stages of the conflict, the resistance movement has difficulty operating within the target country's borders. In such circumstances the attitude of contiguous states will assume a major role in the conflict for, in a sense, the territory of such states constitutes the insurgent's last fallback position. One should not conclude from this, however, that guerrillas can indefinitely operate from outside the target state. At some point they must organize the population and establish an internal popular base. Douglas Hyde, for instance, has called attention to the fact that guerrillas from Sarawak found that operating from bases across the border in Indonesia had a deleterious effect on the revolutionary movement, because it prevented direct and continuous contacts between leaders and the guerrillas in Sarawak. As a result, the insurgents had to make an effort to set up bases in Sarawak itself.[36]

A final aspect of initiative that deserves mention is what Hyde calls the dramatic gesture. This tactic, which involves terrorist acts such as kidnapping and hijacking, is employed by the insurgents in order to convince world and domestic opinion that they are not just rabble, but are active and fighting for a worthwhile goal.[37]

To summarize, popular support is often crucial for the success of an insurgency. In order to acquire it, the insurgent movement may rely on charismatic attraction, esoteric and exoteric appeals, terrorism, provocation of counterterrorism, demonstrations of potency, or some combination thereof. The orchestration of such a campaign is quite complex, and its outcome can be heavily influenced by other major variables considered in this chapter, most especially government response and the insurgents organizational dexterity.

## Organization

Organization is a major factor enabling insurgents to compensate for the material superiority of their opponents. Indeed, when scholars emphasize the point that insurgency is more a political phenomenon than a military one, they usually have in mind the great amount of effort insurgents devote to organization, either on the elite level, if it is a conspiracy, or the mass level, if it is an internal war. When examining an insurgent organization, three structural dimensions—scope, complexity, and cohesion—and two functions—provision of instrumental services and establishment of channels for expressive protest—are of primary interest.[38] Given the particular salience of cohesion in so many cases, it will be treated as a major factor and discussed in a separate section below.

*Scope* refers to the number of people who either play key roles in the movement (terrorists, guerrillas, and political cadres) or provide active support.
How many will be controlled by the insurgent movement is partially a function of complexity and cohesion. If an insurgent organization perceives a need
to augment its membership, it will normally increase its level of differentiation
or complexity, and—through the efforts of its political cadres—penetrate
hamlets, villages, and cities, especially in contested areas (i.e., areas in which
neither the government nor insurgents have firm control). Insurgents often
create what Bernard Fall called parallel hierarchies to compete with government institutions. The parallel hierarchy can take two forms: penetration of
the existing official administrative structures by subversive agents, or creation of autonomous insurgent structures designed to take over full administrative responsibility when military-political conditions are deemed appropriate.
The importance of this type organization is well-known to students of World
War II partisan movements and the two Vietnam conflicts. Moreover, in
order to broaden its support base, the insurgent organization may go beyond
the government structures it seeks to imitate by creating functional aux-
iliaries—such as youth groups, peasant organizations, workers' groups, and
women's organizations—and by arranging tactical alliances with other independent groups that oppose the government. When this is done the new
entity is frequently referred to as a front.[39] The effectiveness of winning
adherents by increasing the differentiation of the organization is exemplified
by the Huk movement in the Philippines, where many joined front organizations, often without even knowing party aims.[40]

In the early stages of an insurgency, the viability of parallel hierarchies in
government-controlled areas is usually precarious. While organizational structures exist in the guerrilla-controlled base area, the aim of the insurgent is to
spread them to partially controlled government regions. The first step in this
undertaking is the formation of small, secretive cells to assess the insurrectionary potential of the people and recruit followers and supporters. Should
the insurgents fail to establish cells, more sophisticated organizational
development will remain nothing more than wishful thinking.

In addition to the differentiation of political structures, insurgents—
especially those engaged in a protracted armed struggle—may diversify their
military organization by creating logistics units, terrorist networks, and guerrilla forces, with the last-mentioned divided between full-time and part-time
fighters. The full-time guerrillas, operating from secure bases, attack government military units and installations on a continuous basis and constitute a
nucleus for a regularized force in the event the movement progresses to
mobile-conventional warfare. The part-time or local guerrillas, on the other
hand, stay in their communities and provide a number of invaluable services,
such as collecting intelligence, storing supplies, and providing a coercive arm

to protect the political organizers. In addition, the local guerrillas can attach themselves to main force units for local attacks either as combatants or as scouts and guides.[41]

The effective functioning of both parallel hierarchies and military units may itself convert people by simply demonstrating the insurgent's ability to control an area in defiance of the government (a linkage of demonstration of potency and organization). Such differentiation is particularly important in situations where the regime is reasonably strong.

By increasing the complexity of their organization, the insurgents will be better able to perform the instrumental and expressive functions that attract adherents. On the individual level, participation can yield material benefits, if the organization has the resources, and it can generate a good deal of psychological satisfaction by virtue of the new sense of identity and self-worth that is generated by the perception that one is engaged in a sublime common endeavor. Although external support and control of base areas by dissidents facilitate meeting material needs, most dissident organizations lack the capability to fully meet economic demands. To compensate, great stress is placed on psychosocial requirements for status, communality, ideational coherence, and expression of hostility.[42]

*Cohesion*

The third major variable that affects the fortunes of insurgencies is cohesion. Indeed, many experts and practitioners have stressed the importance of unity within insurgent ranks. John J. McCuen, for example, contends that unifying the effort is the basic principle behind all effective revolutionary strategy, planning, tactics, and organization. "This has been so ever since 1902 when Lenin's *What Is To Be Done?* made revolution into a science."[43] Though the conduct of operations and authority may be delegated to local leaders, a general headquarters is necessary to provide the common political sense of direction, integrated strategy, and discipline. As Mao pointed out in *The Strategy of Partisan Warfare,* "without centralized strategic command the partisans can inflict little damage on their adversaries, as without this, they can break down into roaming, armed bands, and then find no more support by the population."[44]

Although unity is usually important for insurgent movements, its absence has not always resulted in failure. Despite ideological divisions and internecine violence within the Algerian revolutionary ranks and between the Tito and Mihailovitch factions in Yugoslavia, both insurgent groups achieved their political goals. But in each case other major developments offset the lack of cohesion. In Algeria it was a breakdown of French resolve to stay on, despite the fact the military aspect of the insurrection was brought under control, that enabled the National Liberation Front to succeed; while in Yugoslavia it was the thrust of the allied armies (an external support input) that defeated the Germans and thereby created a power vacuum in the country. It seems therefore, that if the regime loses its will, or if outside forces intervene in a substantial way, insurgent disunity need not be a critical failing. On the other hand, where the regime is strong, insurgents court disaster by fighting among themselves and failing to coordinate their efforts.

In order to achieve unity, insurgent movements stress common attitudes, sanctions, and organizational schema. While ideology can be a basis for cohesion—because it provides members of an insurgent movement with shared values and orientations toward the political world—it can be a double-edged sword in cases where the insurgent movement contains rival factions, each of which has a different ideology. Under such circumstances, ideology militates against cohesion and may even lead factions to split from the movement and reconstitute themselves as separate groups.

Organizational formats are also important in establishment of cohesion, and there are three general possibilities here: control by the politicians, control by the military, and independent political and military commands. Even though each organizational scheme is partially aimed at unifying insurgent forces, rival movements may continue to exist and operate. Where this happens, the insurgents may attempt to coordinate activity by creating a unified command for a particular operation, by arriving at a division of labor among various groups, or by establishing a unified command for all operations. Of the three possibilities, the idea of a unified command is most effective, since it is more conducive to giving the insurgents an overall strategy and for dealing with the ideological, tactical, and personal differences that divide the movement in the first place. For a unified command to be successful, however, rival organizations must agree to subordinate parochial interests to the overall interests of the movement, as defined by the unified command. But, if the unified command's decisions are to be considered authoritative and legitimate, competing groups must reach a prior consensus on the mechanics of the decisionmaking process and methods for invoking sanctions against deviationists.

*External Support*

Perhaps the most publicized aspect of insurgent strategy is the frequent stress on external support as yet another means to offset the government's advantages.[45] Indeed, all one has to do is pick up a newspaper or listen to television news broadcasts to become acquainted with countless examples, such as Soviet and Chinese aid to various insurgent groups, the People's Democratic Republic of the Yemen's support for the Popular Front for the Liberation of Oman, Algeria's assistance to the Polisario insurgents in the former Spanish Sahara, and so forth. Just how important such support is and precisely what it consists of merits closer examination.

One way to disaggregate the general phenomenon of external support is to divide it into four categories: moral, political, material, and sanctuary. *Moral* support is least costly and risky for a donor, for all it involves is public acknowledgment that the insurgent movement is just and admirable. *Political* support advances a step further, since the donor nation actively champions and supports the strategic goal of the insurgent movement in inter-national fora. Both of these types of intangible support can be effective against a wavering government that must, as the French found in Algeria, bear the additional burden of international pressure and censure. Of the two, political support clearly is most desirable because its payoffs are more con-crete (in the sense that it may encourage additional uncommitted nations to render support in some or all categories). One final point here: external states are not the only source of political and moral support. In colonial contexts in-surgents will seek to obtain backing from dissident groups in the mother coun-try (e.g., the Algerian and Vietnamese relations with the French left and peace groups).

In contrast with moral and political support, *material* assistance is more con-crete and risky for an outside power. Consisting of such things as money, weapons, ammunition, medical supplies, food, training, and perhaps even the provision of military advisors, fire support, or combat units, it becomes par-ticularly important as the insurgents increase the scale and intensity of violence, since such a development usually necessitates greater logistical in-puts (e.g., the Viet Cong after 1965). Before this period, the insurgents may rely on the populace, nongovernmental arms merchants, or materials seized from the government for their sustenance.

When insurgents conclude that external logistical inputs are essential, the role of sympathetic major powers can be very important. As a result, in-surgent leaders will expend great efforts to persuade them to provide material assistance. Yet, success in this endeavor is not the end of the story, for in some cases the provision of aid may be dependent on third parties who con-trol overland transportation routes. In light of this, the attitude of states con-tiguous to the area being contested is vital. A positive response on their part will facilitate the flow of materials; a negative reaction may neutralize the en-tire effort.

Besides facilitating the supply flow or actually making materials available to the insurgents, external states may be important as *sanctuaries* in which guer-rillas can be trained, arms stockpiled, operations planned, leadership secured, and perhaps a provisional government established. While both sanctuaries and material aid are usually more important in the terminal stages of an in-surgency, there are circumstances that can make them indispensable early in the struggle. Such may be the case in situations wherein the insurgents are unable to establish a secure base in the target country and lack popular support. With such an inauspicious start, the insurgents are literally forced to rely on adjacent countries, for, at the minimum, security and freedom of movement must be guaranteed if the insurgents are ever to establish bases, organize the people, and obtain popular support and commitment. The Sarawak insurgency, which relied on bases in Indonesia during its infancy, is an example here, as is the current situation in Spanish Sahara.[46]

When seeking to obtain support in the international system, the insurgents must first attract attention from outside states or groups. One way of doing this is to use dramatic gestures such as kidnappings or skyjackings. Normally, however, such acts must be followed by more substantial actions in order to gain respectability. In this connection, military successes against the regime, backed by good organization and demonstrable popular support, are crucial. In contradistinction, a poorly organized, disunited guerrilla movement with little popular backing is unlikely to attract significant external support.

While the types of external support discussed thus far are very often important to the fortunes of insurgent movements, there have been cases where only low-level outside help has been sufficient. In these instances one usually finds the insurgents have benefitted from a favorable position vis-à-vis other major factors (e.g., a weak regime or substantial popular support). A case in point would be the Castro revolution in Cuba, during which the insurgents did not have a contiguous friendly country to function as a sanctuary or logistics area, although they did receive some arms via flights from Mexico, Venezuela, and the United States. Since the government was inept, corrupt, and unresolved, and the army demoralized, this level of aid was sufficient to topple the Batista regime and to obviate the need for a protracted guerrilla war along the lines of the Chinese and Vietnamese models.

### Environment

The fifth major variable used to assess an insurgency is environment. Among other things, this encompasses terrain, climate, the road and communications network, ethnicity, religion and culture, size of the country, and the quantity and distribution of the people.

Rugged terrain—vast mountains, jungles, swamps, forests, and the like—is usually related to successful guerrilla operations, because it hinders movement by government troops and provides inaccessible hideouts for the guerrillas' main bases. The triple-canopied jungles of Indochina, which were an invaluable asset to the forces of Ho Chi Minh in two wars, are an example of excellent terrain for guerrilla operations and the establishment of base areas. Although deserts sometimes have proven to be advantageous for guerrilla operations—one such case being the Arab revolt led by the legendary T. E.

Lawrence from 1916–18 – the advent and development of air surveillance and air attack have made guerrillas more susceptible to detection and destruction in their environs. Yet, as the activity of the Polisario insurgents in the Spanish Sahara in 1977–78 has shown, deserts are not completely inhospitable, especially when they are expansive and the adversary has only a marginal air force capability.[47]

Along with the composition of the terrain, one must consider its extensiveness. If favorable areas for guerrilla operations and bases are small, they can be easily isolated and penetrated; if the area, on the other hand, is vast and guerrillas take advantage of this by expanding their area of operations, government administration will be complicated, firepower concentration reduced, and supervision of the populace made more difficult. Considerations such as these led Mao to view a vast countryside as a sine qua non of successful protracted war.[48]

Although a lack of favorable terrain can be a debit on the insurgent balance sheet, there are cases (the 1945–48 Jewish insurrection in Palestine, for instance) where it was overcome. The key here appears to be a weak or wavering government that is prone to capitulate early when faced with sustained violence. Where the government is able to pursue the conflict, favorable terrain becomes crucial to the insurgent side.

The importance of terrain is accented by Heilbrunn, who suggests that geography is the main consideration in the establishment of the guerrilla bases that he believes are necessary for the insurgent success. It is in the base area that the guerrillas first establish the parallel hierarchy that rules the population and from which they will seek to expand into areas partially controlled by the government. Nevertheless, as important as such base areas usually are, there are cases where they may be dispensable. Thus, Heilbrunn argues that, where popular support is high and the army is demoralized or in sympathy with the insurgents, bases may not be important because the government will collapse without a long struggle. If these conditions are reversed, a prolonged war will be necessary, and in that situation bases will be required to wear down the enemy.[49]

The relationship of climate to guerrilla success has not received the attention terrain has in the writings on insurgency. Perhaps this is because climate can favor both the regime and insurgents. Severe weather, for example, can hinder both guerrilla and government movement and increase the logistical needs of both. In the Vietnam conflict, the North Vietnamese campaigns frequently coincided with weather conducive to the movement of supplies, while bad climatic conditions often brought lulls in fighting. Yet in military actions the Viet Cong used poor weather to advantage because it hampered government air support. Severe weather may also benefit the guerrillas by preventing government attacks during periods when the revolutionary side has to regroup and reorganize. All told, however, climate is difficult to isolate and define as crucial to insurgent success.

An aspect of environment that seems to have more bearing on the fortunes of an insurgency than weather is the state of the transportation- communications network. Suffice to say, if the road communications system is highly developed and extensive, regular government forces are favored because their mobile units can move about expeditiously and make better use of their technological superiority. On the other hand poor roads and communications favor the guerrilla side. Gurr comments on this point as follows:

> Guerrilla war is common in underdeveloped countries because of poor transportation and communication networks and the isolation of rural areas, which facilitate guerrilla incursions. Free access to rural people enables guerrillas to propagandize, control, and secure support from them. . . . Given the technological capabilities of the best-equipped modern military forces, the terrain that offers the most effective physical protection for the guerrillas must be mountainous, without roads or tracks, and almost continuously cloud-covered.[50]

Demographic factors also have an impact on an insurgency. Where the population is small and concentrated, it is easier for the government to control the people and sever their links with the guerrillas. The location of the majority of the people in cities does not appear as favorable to insurgent movements as the situation in which they are concentrated in rural areas, although, as noted later, some contemporary insurgent strategists believe otherwise. If a society is highly urbanized, the government can control and monitor the people and prevent the establishment of guerrilla bases. But, if the government is weak and the insurgents have a significant degree of international support, it is possible some of the tactical aims of the insurgents may be achieved. An example is Palestine, where Jewish terrorism combined with pro-Zionist currents in the international arena to force a British retreat. When the authorities demonstrate both the resolution and competence to combat the insurgent threat, thus forcing the insurgents to opt for protracted warfare, an urban environment, although conducive to terrorist activities, hardly suffices; a rural, underdeveloped society, on the other hand, is more promising.

Societal cleavages such as ethnicity, religion, and language may be helpful to dissident elements. This would seem to be especially true where the majority of the population is from the same ethnic, religious, and/or language group as the insurgents, whereas the authorities are not.[51] Although the colonial systems are classic examples of this, it may also be true in independent states ruled by minority factions, because of the tendency of individuals to sympathize with kinsman rather than outsiders. Nevertheless, as the first In-dochina war shows, it requires an assiduous political effort to actualize the potential inherent in such circumstances.

As the preceding discussion indicates, in situations where the government dis-plays the ability and willingness to resist and the military is not demoralized, the insurgent movement must prepare itself to wage a prolonged conflict. In that case, it will be necessary for the insurgents to effectively organize the population, unify the movement, obtain external support, and exploit what advantages the environment has to offer, if they are to have any hope of succeeding.

One conclusion that seems inescapable after considering the first five variables is that government's response is the pivotal variable in insurgent conflicts, because where its response is poor or uneven the insurgents can tolerate shortcomings in popular and external support, organization, cohesion, and the environment. Conversely, where the government manifests strength, such failings can spell defeat. Hence, since it is so important, the government response must be examined in some detail.

*The Government Role*

Professor Walter Sonderland has argued that the government's response to an insurgent challenge is the major variable determining the outcome of an in-surrection. As he put it: "As soon as the challenge is in the open the success of the operations depends not primarily on the development of insurgent strength, but more importantly on the degree of vigor, determination and skill with which the incumbent regime acts to defend itself, both politically and militarily."[52]

Carrying his argument a step further, one might suggest that whether a given insurgency can succeed by confining itself to low-level activity or will have to take on the dimensions of a protracted internal war is largely deter-mined by the nature of the government and its responses to the incipient ac-tions of the insurgents. Because of this, the counterinsurgency aspects merit closer and extended examination.

Governments facing an insurrection may confront one or more of the political challenges or forms of violence discussed earlier, namely: (1) propaganda-organizational activity, (2) terrorism, (3) guerrilla warfare, and (4) mobile-conventional warfare.[53] Since each type of threat involves different techniques and poses a unique problem for the government, effective and ap-propriate countermeasures are heavily dependent upon the willingness and ability to differentiate among them. This is because each type of insurgent threat compels the government to emphasize a particular facet of counterin-surgency. McCuen has pointed out that to cope successfully with the organizational challenge the government will have to stress civic action, administration, and low-level police activity, whereas a terrorist threat will necessitate intensified police work. Guerrilla warfare calls for a low-level military response, while mobile-conventional warfare will require conventional operations by the military.[54]

The creation and implementation of a counterinsurgency program along these lines is complicated by the fact that, in practice, insurgent threats not only overlap and are cumulative, but they often vary in regions of the country being contested. In view of this, an effective government response is associated not with a single purpose strategy applied indiscriminately in all sectors, but rather with the adoption of a flexible policy that coordinates a variety of countermeasures in different areas, depending on the nature of the threats. For example, it would be a mistake for a government facing a substantial mobile-conventional threat in one sector and low-level guerrilla activity in another to extend its search and destroy operations against conventional formations to the guerrilla area, inasmuch as such a move would constitute a costly, and perhaps counterproductive, overreaction. The reason for this is that guerrillas can easily blend back into the population, and thus raise the possibility of regular military units striking out against the people, many of whom may be quite innocent. Past experience suggests that under such circumstances it is more appropriate to conduct mobile-conventional operations in one area and patrols in the other.

The execution of a multifaceted and sophisticated counterinsurgency program obviously requires coordination of political, administrative, military, police, and intelligence efforts; this is essential if the various counterinsurgency agencies are to avoid working at cross purposes. The problem here, however, is that optimal organizational conditions—i.e., an effective existing administration, a tradition of civilian primacy, and an adequate number of good leaders—are often missing; in fact, their very absence may be one of the reasons for the insurgency.[55] While the question of civilian leadership is perhaps the most difficult to resolve in the short term, improvements can be made in the areas of administration and leadership recruitment and training.

A critical ingredient for an effective government organizational effort is the provision of a common purpose and policy guidelines for its officials. This, in turn, places a premium on the articulation and communication of an overall program for the future.[56]

Since the national program is also instrumental in gaining the support of the population, ascertaining the people's aspirations—which vary from one insurrection to another and from one region to another within the same country—becomes important. Land reform, for instance, may be a basic grievance in some circumstances but not in others. History provides a number of cases sustaining the proposition that benevolent treatment of the population and reforms designed to meet the basic needs of the people can go a long way toward undermining support for the insurgents.

The behavior of the German administration in the Ukraine during World War II was a striking example of the government's being its own worst enemy, especially since the Ukrainians had no love for Stalin and seemed ready to help the Germans. As it happened, German exactions against and repression of the Ukrainians eventually turned the latter against the Third Reich. Benevolent administration and effective reforms, which were carried out by the Germans in other sectors and which proved effective in harnassing popular support, were few and far between and were undercut by general Nazi policies.[57]

A classic case of the government's gaining popular support would be the actions of the Philippines regime aginst the Huks. In that instance, Ramon Magsaysay's election to the presidency led to a number of social and military reforms that mobilized popular support and combined with the use of force against the insurgents to bring victory.[58]

Devising a program to satisfy the grievances of the population is, of course, no easy undertaking, especially for a developing nation with a paucity of resources. In light of this, it is frequently necessary for the governments of such states to seek economic assistance from external sources. Demands for redistribution of existing economic or political power, on the other hand, are largely internal matters that can be accommodated by the government from within, albeit not without political resistance from privileged classes or groups.[59]

The most difficult demand for a government to meet is that it abdicate in favor of insurgent rule at the central level. Nevertheless, since popular support for an insurgent organization with such a totalistic objective is usually based on lesser socioeconomic needs, the government can seek to undercut the basis of such support by attenuating the concrete grievances of the masses. In other words, the material demands of the people are distinguished from the political power aims of the insurgent leadership. While the government cannot accommodate the latter, it may well be able to deal with the former, and by so doing, deprive the insurgent movement of its main source of strength and resources—the people.

Clearly, it will be more difficult to design an effective counterinsurgency program in colonial situations where not only the insurgent leadership but also the people are motivated by the nationalist aim of independence. Faced with such circumstances some regimes have sought to contain the situation by improving the well-being of the population in the hope that the latter would support the existing political order in return for short-term benefits. Where the population is divided into rival ethnic groups, the government may also seek to sustain or exacerbate societal cleavages in order to keep the insurgent movement divided (the well-known strategy of divide and rule).

The execution of a general program to deal with the needs of the people depends upon an effective administration, staffed by local personnel if possible.[60] History is replete with cases wherein governments forfeited their presence to insurgent forces that were quick to exploit the administrative vacuum by establishing their own organizational apparatus, however rudimentary. The initial British inattention to the Chinese squatters in areas bordering the jungles during the Malayan Emergency exemplifies this point.

An essential component of any organizational effort by a government is forging a sense of loyalty between itself and the people. To facilitate this task, potential groups and leaders that can serve the government and provide personnel for the auxiliary police and militia forces are identified and organized. The role of the police and militia is to isolate the people from infiltrators, prevent exactions from being made on the people by the insurgents, and provide security against terrorism and low-level guerrilla operations. In view of the fact that most people place the highest value on individual security, the government's success in gaining their cooperation has been closely associated with its ability to provide personal protection.

Along with the political and administrative action outlined above, effective counterinsurgency invariably involves a number of security measures—detention without trial, resettlement of sections of the population, control of the distribution of food, curfews, restrictions on movement, the issuance and checking of identification cards, and the imposition of severe penalties for the carrying of unauthorized weapons—in order to separate the population from the insurgents. While such sanctions may be undesirable from an ideal or moral standpoint, they have proven effective, especially when applied consistently, fairly, and judiciously.[61]

Resettlement, for example, has sometimes been used to sever the links between the insurgents and the populace, particularly when terror and/or guerrilla attacks persisted and were attributed, at least partially, to support rendered the insurgents by portions of the population. Civic action and political organization have been extremely important during resettlement; indeed, they are often viewed as concomitants of that technique. The Briggs Plan for moving the Chinese squatters in Malaya, the Kitchener resettlement scheme during the Boer War, and the relocation program during the Mau Mau uprising are examples where transpositioning segments of the population was instrumental in denying insurgents support of the population. Conversely, the resettlement carried out by the regime of Ngo Dinh Diem in South Vietnam failed, largely because it was overextended, too rapid, procedurally deficient, and inadequately supported by the police establishment.[62] Much of the same was true of the Rhodesian government's ill-fated "protected villages" during the mid-1970s.

Whenever the government invokes security measures directed at individuals or the collectivity, it can expect the insurgents to make use of the legal structure in an attempt to portray the regime as a violator of civil and human rights, and to protect their personnel. Essentially, the insurgents will seek to have those under detention treated as peacetime offenders. This ploy, which will make it even more difficult for the government to avoid alienating the population, is another reason for imposition of such measures in a judicious and limited manner.

A primary requisite for fair security measures is accurate information about the insurgent organization, including the identification and location of its members and intended activities. Traditionally, the easiest way for the government to obtain the necessary information has been the creation of effective rapport with the people by means of good administration and prudent and diligent police work. This, in turn, has required well-trained interrogation experts, who can minimize violence by knowing the right questions to ask, and agents who can penetrate the insurgent apparatus.[63]

Since insurgents themselves are a potential valuable source of intelligence, their treatment by government forces is important. While it is unlikely members of the hard core will defect, it is possible that less dedicated insurgents may be induced to surrender, especially if insurgent prospects are not bright. Psychological warfare efforts designed to increase the number of defectors by promising them amnesty, security, and material benefits have often been used to exploit such situations.

As far as military measures designed to deal with insurgent threats are concerned, there are a number of prescriptive propositions based on previous cases.

McCuen, for instance, argues that to cope with an insurgent organizational threat and the low-level terrorism and sporadic guerrilla attacks which often accompany it, the military must be oriented toward population contact. Armed units should be positioned in a large number of small posts, allowing for protection of and mixing with the local people. If there is a small-scale guerrilla threat, the territorial defense force must make extensive use of ambushes and patrols in an effort to intercept insurgent bands. Moreover, the government ordinarily must provide backup mobile air, naval, and ground forces to assist ambush patrols that engage the enemy, and to conduct harassment operations against insurgent units in underpopulated hinterlands. But, in no case can the mobile forces be considered a substitute for territorial defense forces.[64]

Where the insurgent movement has been able to mount a substantial internal terrorist campaign, the government must consolidate its own areas and then, operating from these secure bases, seek to destroy the political-military structures of the insurgent organization by locating and detaining its members. Police forces that have received quasi-military training for operations in the contested areas and the hinterlands can concentrate on this while lesser duties are performed by the auxiliary police.[65]

If transnational terrorism becomes a threat to officials and civilians abroad, the government may resort to a combination of defensive and offensive measures. Defensively, the government can take steps to enhance the security of embassies, consulates, airline offices, airliners, and the like by assigning armed guards to them, cooperating with national and international police and intelligence agencies, and providing information on personal security measures for individuals located in areas outside the country. Offensively, it can undertake intensive diplomatic efforts to acquire international support for antiterrorist sanctions. In the event such steps prove unsatisfactory, the government may consider punitive military attacks against countries that provide sanctuary for terrorists and special operations against insurgents located in such countries. Violent ripostes in third countries, however, risk international opprobrium and an expansion of war. Despite this, as the Israelis demonstrated in 1970–73, they may be successful in blunting an upsurge in transnational terrorism.[66]

When insurgents have begun to conduct large-scale *guerrilla* actions, the government normally faces a more serious threat. In response, it must first consolidate the areas it does hold, and then gradually expand from those areas with the objectives of gaining control of the population, food, and other resources, while inflicting losses on guerrilla units and defending vital lines of communication. An essential component of the antiguerrilla campaign is a nomadic territorial offensive that emphasizes the use of sophisticated detection technology, patrols, attacks, and ambushes by small dispersed units during both day and night hours. Once an area has been cleared of guerrilla bands, experience counsels that the government should establish an administrative presence, if only initially by civic action teams.[67]

To further deprive the guerrillas of the initiative, the government can employ mobile forces, commandos, airpower, and artillery to harass insurgents in remote and thinly populated hinterlands where they are likely to have established bases. Eventually these areas should also be organized by the government. If forbidden zones (i.e., areas that can be fired into at will) are to be created, experience suggests great care be taken to assure innocent civilians are not located in them, otherwise such military actions may create more insurgents than are eliminated.

If the government finds itself confronted by *mobile-conventional* warfare, it is near defeat, a reality that may require a call for outside assistance. McCuen argues the first countermove by the government should be to consolidate base areas, even if this means sacrificing large areas of the country. After securing base areas and expanding from them, mobile strike forces are used against insurgent bases in the same manner as the assaults on the Greek guerrilla strongholds during the Greek civil war. If the government is lucky, the guerrillas may choose to defend their bases, thus violating a cardinal guerrilla principle that warns against engaging a superior force. In the event insurgents decide to revert to guerrilla warfare, the government should respond likewise, taking appropriate steps summarized above.[68]

If the government concludes sanctuaries across the border are playing an important role in sustaining the insurgent activities at any time, it can at-tempt to create a *cordon sanitare*. Should jungle and mountain terrain make this task impossible or difficult, the government may opt to establish forbid-den zones, conduct a nomadic territorial offensive, implant detection devices, build barriers, infiltrate counterguerrillas across the border, or directly strike the sanctuary country. Since the last-mentioned tactic can be a casus belli that might widen the conflict, the government must weigh its aims, possible costs, and risks carefully.[69]

Although the insurgent threat is largely a political-administrative one, this does not mean military success is unimportant. Besides inflicting material and personnel losses on the insurgent movement, and in some cases forcing the in-surgent from familiar operating terrain, military victories can enhance govern-ment morale, undermine the insurgent image, and impress the population. It must be remembered the insurgents are trying to establish an image of strength in order to convince the people they will succeed; when most of the victories go to the government side, the insurgents' credibility suffers.

One caveat here, however. If military victories are achieved at the expense of the local population—in terms of casualties and property losses—they may prove to be counterproductive in that the alienation engendered may increase the ranks of the disaffected. This leads to the inexorable conclusion that all military operations must be planned and executed in such a way as to minimize civilian losses, for as Richard Clutterbuck has pointed out, one misplaced bomb or artillery shell can undo countless hours of political effort.[70]

In summary, the government faced with an insurgency must combat four different types of threat with four different types of response. Insurgent organizational and propaganda efforts must be countered by both government counterorganization and psychological warfare actions and police operations designed to uncover insurgent political cadres; terrorism must be countered by security measures and intensified police and intelligence operations; guer-rilla warfare must be dealt with by low-level military action (the nomadic territorial offensive) that puts a premium on small unit patrolling, mobile op-erations against hinterland guerrilla bases, and the defense of vital lines of communication; and mobile-conventional warfare must be neutralized by con-ventional military operations on the part of the government's mobile units. Furthermore, the government must be prepared to deal with all of these threats simultaneously.

Regardless of how one looks at it, the effort required by a counterinsur-gency program is substantial. The demands in terms of morale, patience, and determination become greater as the insurgent movement progresses. To be successful, the counterinsurgency forces need the firm backing of their government and people. Whether or not such support is forthcoming will be partially determined by the strategy the regime uses and the way it is implemented. Indicators that things are not going well are serious dissent supporting the insurgent objective (explicitly or implicitly), desertions from government forces, general lack of combativeness, a poor job of local law enforcement, guerrilla operations carried out by increasingly larger units, lack of information from the people, and a low surrender rate. Conversely, the opposite of each of these indicators would suggest the government is succeeding.

As the foregoing commentary suggests, an effective counterinsurgency effort depends primarily on the political and military adroitness of the government. Although moral, political, and material support from friendly states may be an important asset to the government in specific cases, there is always a danger, as the United States found in Vietnam, of overreliance and a failure on the part of indigenous authorities to fulfill their responsibilities. When this occurs, the outside power may end up assuming the major burden of the conflict, especially in the military area, while the essential political tasks necessary to undercut the insurrection are either not performed or poorly effectuated.[71]

Where threatened governments eschew an inordinate reliance on external powers and where they devise and apply the types of programs suggested earlier, insurgents will have little chance of success. Moreover, even if the government does a mediocre job, it may still succeed, depending upon how insurgents perform in relation to other major criteria for successful insurgency. Which of those factors is important and how the insurgents will perform is, in large part, a function of the particular strategy they adopt, the final consideration in this chapter.

## Insurgent Strategies

There are a myriad of insurgent strategies in the real political world. In terms of conceptual sophistication such schema range from the carefully articulated to the inchoate. We shall focus on four general patterns of strategic thought that have attracted many adherents: the Leninist, Maoist, Cuban and urban. It should come as no surprise, by the way, that proponents have proclaimed the widespread, if not universal, applicability of each.

### The Leninist Strategy

Those insurgents who adhere to a Leninist strategy believe that a small, tightly knit, disciplined, and highly organized conspiratorial group that has obtained support from major discontented social groups—such as the military and working class—provides the most effective means for achieving the goal of the movement. For the most part, insurgent activity takes place in those ur-ban centers with the major concentrations of political and economic power. While the purpose is normally revolutionary, there is no logical incompatibil-ity with the other types of insurgent goals discussed earlier. The Leninist ap-proach assumes a government that is alienated from its population; hence, it will capitulate when confronted by low-level terrorism, subversion of the military and police, and the final seizure of radio stations, government offices, and other state institutions. However, where the regime and authorities re-tain substantial legitimacy and exercise effective control over structures such as the army and police, this strategy does not appear promising as far as revolutionary goals are concerned, a fact which partially explains the ten-dency of many communist parties in relatively stable states like France, Italy, and Portugal to opt for political participation. Prospects are similarly unen-couraging where the regime is threatened by other types of insurgents (reac-tionary, restorational, and secessionist). Nevertheless, a Leninist approach might prove successful where the aims are reformist or conservative, because under such circumstances the insurgents are interested in either maintaining the regime or changing policies rather than seizing the reigns of political power. The reasoning here is that since the regime and authorities are not threatened they may choose to cut their losses by making the necessary political concessions.

As far as the five strategic factors are concerned, political organization is clearly the most important. In practical terms, this means a limited group of activists; there is no intention to mobilize the general populace within the framework of a shadow government. At best, one might find ad hoc workers' councils or other such groups whose purpose is to proselytize selected segments of the populace via exoteric appeals. If they are successful in this undertaking, the insurgents will have a reservoir of supporters who will engage in demonstrations and riots chosen by the leadership.

The elite cadre of such a movement is often recruited on the basis of esoteric and/or exoteric appeals. The former, in particular, looms very signifi-cant in revolutionary movements. Although there may be limited violence (usually some form of terrorism), primary importance is not accorded terror tactics, provocation of government counterterror, or guerrilla warfare. Thus, it is not surprising that external support receives but moderate emphasis. This is not meant to suggest, however, that moral and political backing—as well as financial inputs and limited crossborder sanctuaries—are unwelcome. To the contrary, they may be quite helpful, but, in the final analysis, they are secondary assets. Indeed, there is simply no gainsaying the fact that the quintessential aspect of Leninist strategy is conspiratorial organization combined with active support from selected social groups.

## The Maoist Strategy

No doubt the most elaborate insurgent strategy is articulated by Maoist theoreticians who ascribe great significance to popular support, extensive organizational efforts, and the environment as resources necessary for a prolonged conflict with an enemy perceived as being in a superior position prior to hostilities. What is more, the Maoist approach is, par excellence, a sequential strategy—i.e., it unfolds in distinct steps, each of which is designed to partially achieve the goal and is dependent on the outcome of the step before it. Both scholars and practitioners have identified these steps or "stages" as political organization-terrorism, guerrilla warfare, and mobile-conventional warfare.

In the organizational stage, cellular networks are created around which the guerrilla builds political-propaganda groups to win popular support and trains teams of terrorists to engage in selective intimidation of recalcitrant individuals. At this point, fronts may be organized along with pressure groups and parties in order to facilitate the acquisition of popular support. Simultaneously, insurgents usually try to infiltrate enemy institutions; foment strikes, demonstrations, and riots; and perhaps carry out sabotage missions.[72]

During the first stage, the insurgents stress esoteric and exoteric appeals as well as the social services and mutual help aspects associated with demonstrations of potency. One key objective at this time is the recruitment of local leaders who, once in the organization, will then go forth and attempt to detach the people from the government.

In order to institutionalize support, insurgents begin to construct parallel hierarchies. If the regime fails to react it will lose by default; if it responds successfully the insurgents may suffer a fate similar to that suffered by the Tudeh insurgents in Iran.[73]

Terrorism during this period serves many functions, including acquisition of both popular and external support. It may be very significant where the insurgent organization and/or terrain are insufficient for guerrilla warfare. In situations where regime strength has been the key reason for the use of terror, the insurgent movement is worse off than where organizational deficiencies are the problem. Organizational failings can conceivably be rectified and the insurgency may then evolve toward guerrilla warfare.

Guerrilla warfare is the second stage in the Maoist scheme. The earliest part of this stage is characterized by armed resistance carried out by small bands operating in rural areas where terrain is rugged and government control weak. If the guerrillas face significant government opposition, they have the option of reverting to stage one. Considerations most likely to be involved in the decision-making calculus are: vitality of the incumbent regime, its projected capability against guerrilla warfare, and external political-military factors.

The insurgent aim in the incipient part of stage two is to isolate the people from the government. The organizational apparatus established in stage one begins to supply small guerrilla units and full- and part-time personnel play a more prominent role. Yet, during the early part of stage two, there is still a lack of organization above village level, and groups operate from shifting and remote bases. Militarily, actions in early stage two are small hit-and-run attacks against convoys, military and economic installations, and isolated outposts. These scattered attacks are intended to goad the enemy into adopting a static defensive posture that stresses the dispersal of forces in order to protect many potential targets.[74]

If there is satisfactory progress during the early phase of stage two, insurgents normally move into the second half of that stage and expand their organization in the regions they control. In addition, regional forces emerge, which, along with the full-time forces, enable the insurgents to join villages together into a political network that constitutes a major base area. At this point the guerrillas step up the mobilization of the population by exploiting and satisfying (as best they can) popular aspirations. Meanwhile, there is usually a stress on ideology which is designed to supplant whatever type legitimacy sustains the existing regime.[75]

During stage two the parallel hierarchy is more visible than during stage one. Besides resembling the state apparatus, it also includes auxiliary organizations controlled by revolutionary cells linked to the central political structure. Moreover, a government-in-exile may be created.[76]

The organizational evolution in late stage two includes the establishment of arsenals, arms production facilities, and hospitals. The logistics operation encompasses activities that range from procurement of basic foodstuffs and war supplies to acquisition of material aid from external sources. Once base areas are set up, the delivery of supplies from nearby friendly states becomes less risky and more likely.

In the military realm, recruitment of full-time guerrillas, establishment of an extensive reserve system, and creation and training of regular army units are emphasized. If voluntary recruits are insufficient, there may be abductions. Since abductees often make poor fighters, voluntary enlistments are stressed.

Three operational levels often comprise the military organization in late stage two: regional, district, and local. The regional troops, the best armed and trained, form the strike forces that are the backbone of the movement. At the next level, the district battalion is led by full-time cadres, though the subordinate companies are themselves composed of part-time soldiers. Local forces are made up of both full- and part-time guerrillas with the latter predominant. All three levels are coordinated by a central headquarters in pursuit of common military and political objectives.

Even though the parallel hierarchy and military organization may be relatively secure in late stage two, the guerrillas usually do not elect to fight positional battles or even defend their base areas. Instead, the insurgents avoid large government sweeps and patrols in order to demonstrate the government's inability to destroy them and to contrast the regime's ephemeral authority with the guerrillas' permanence.[77]

While base areas are being constructed, the insurgents will continue to establish bands and send agents into contested or government controlled areas with the purpose of implanting new cells, networks, and bands in these sectors. A major effort is made to deceive the government in the hope its response will be tardy, insufficient, and tactically misdirected. Military actions in stage two are basically large-scale guerrilla attacks carried out from secure base areas. In addition to operations designed to acquire additional supplies and reduce areas of government control, armed propaganda teams are dispatched to further undermine the enemy. Considerable attention is devoted in the terminal period of this stage to seizing and securing large areas and preparing the physical battlefield for mobile-conventional warfare. Thus, military considerations receive as much attention as political calculations when it comes to target selection.[78]

The third and final stage of a Maoist-type insurgency is civil war, characterized by regularization of guerrilla forces and mobile-conventional warfare. The objective at this point is displacement of the regime and authorities. Regular units conduct conventional operations, with small bands supporting the main effort in an ancillary role. Ordinarily, external support is important at this time, unless the regime has totally collapsed from within.[79]

It should be readily apparent from the preceding discussion that the Maoist insurgent strategy is a multifaceted one which emphasizes several interrelated elements: popular support, organization, and the environment. Whereas the first two factors can be directly affected by the conscious decisions and skills of the insurgents, the environment is a given to which the latter must adapt. Through a combination of propaganda efforts and organizational dexterity, the insurgents prepare the people for prolonged conflict with the government and, once conflict has commenced, sustain and gradually expand their support to the point where they control the countryside, thereby isolating the urban centers. Since such an enterprise requires flexibility and coordinated efforts on the part of many activists, it is vulnerable to government psychological, organizational, and military-police countermeasures at many points. In a very real sense, the outcome will be determined by the side manifesting superior political and military skills, as well as emotional commitments. Despite copious external inputs to both parties, in the final analysis it was these ingredients that prevailed in China, Cambodia, and Vietnam.

Environmental characteristics are also important in the Maoist strategy. In the three cases just mentioned, the insurgents were able to build and expand their organization and base of popular support in relative security because of favorable topographical and demographic patterns. By contrast, if the contested country is small and relatively open, if the population is concentrated in a few areas that can be isolated, and if the road and communications systems are developed, the insurgents will find it very difficult to organize and gain support.

External support has a rather ambiguous place in the framework of Maoist strategy. Although self-reliance is said to be the overriding consideration, in practice, moral, political, material, and sanctuary support have played key roles, especially in offsetting similar assistance to the government.

### The Cuban Strategy

An alternative to the Maoist protracted warfare strategy is provided by the Cuban model. Che Guevara, a much publicized figure in insurgent folklore, opened his book, *Guerrilla Warfare,* with the following comments:

> We consider that the Cuban revolution contributed three fundamental lessons to the conduct of revolutionary movements in America. They are:
> 1. Popular forces can win a war against the army.
> 2. It is not necessary to wait until all the conditions for making revolution exist; the insurrection can create them.
> 3. In underdeveloped America the countryside is the basic area for armed fighting.[80]

While one may debate the originality of points (1) and (3), the second claim merits attention because Guevara seems to give more scrutiny to the initial phase of insurgency than does Mao. John Pustay has suggested one reason for this may be that Castro and Che had to start by recruiting at the grass-roots level, whereas Mao did not have to start from scratch. In his words:

> Castro, Guevara, and their eleven cadre men, on the other hand, were forced to form guerrilla insurgency units by drawing upon recruitment sources at the grass-roots level. They had to start essentially from nothing and build a revolutionary force to achieve victory. It is reasonable, therefore, for Guevara to discuss in detail the initiatory steps in creating a viable guerrilla force. Of priority is the assembly of revolutionary leaders and cadre guerrilla fighters in exile or in some isolated spot within an object country "around some respected leader fighting for the salvation of his people." Guevara then calls for elaborate advanced planning, for the advanced establishment of intelligence networks and arsenals, and above all for the continued maintenance of absolute secrecy about

the potential insurgency until overt resistance is actually initiated. Thus Guevara fills in the details, overlooked by Mao and only slightly covered by Giap, of the initiatory phases of the first general stage of Maoist insurgency warfare.[81]

While one may interpret this as little more than an effort by Che to refine and elaborate the Chinese leader's scheme, a closer look at the Cuban case reveals substantive divergences from the Maoist strategy.

It was Guevara's contention that insurgent leaders did not have to wait for the preconditions of insurgency to appear, since they could act to catalyze existing grievances required for positive action. Thirty to fifty men, he believed, were adequate to start an armed rebellion in Latin American countries, given "their conditions of favorable terrain for operations, hunger for land, repeated attacks upon justice, etc."[82] In other words, Guevara was arguing that the mere fact of taking up arms in situations where grievances existed would create suitable conditions for revolution.[83] One of the major characteristics of the Cuban revolution, according to Regis Debray, was rejection of the idea of subordinating the guerrilla force to the party in favor of placing primary emphasis on the army as the nucleus of the party. Putting it another way, he suggested the guerrilla force was a political embryo from which the party could arise. Whereas Mao stressed the leading role of the party and the need for political preparation before military struggle, Debray argued the Cuban case made it clear that military priorities must take precedence over politics. "Psychological warfare," he asserted, "is effective only if it is introduced into war itself."[84]

Debray contended it was an old obsession to believe revolutionary awareness and organization must and can, in every case, precede revolutionary action. Rather than wait for the emergence of an organization, it is necessary to proceed from what he calls the guerrilla *foco*, nucleus of the popular army. This *foco* was referred to as "the small motor" that sets "the big motor of the masses" in action and precipitates formation of a front, as victories of the small motor increase.[85] Debray's belief in the widespread applicability of this strategy was obvious in his remarks that:

> The Latin American revolution and its vanguard, the Cuban revolution, have thus made a decisive contribution to international revolutionary experience and to Marxism-Leninism.
>
> *Under certain conditions, the political and the military are not separate, but form one organic whole, consisting of the people's army, whose nucleus is the guerrilla army. The vanguard party can exist in the form of the guerrilla foco itself. The guerrilla force is the party in embryo.*
>
> This is the staggering novelty introduced by the Cuban Revolution.[86]

For insurgents who see the Cuban experience as analogous to their own situation and believe the Vietnamese and Chinese models are inapplicable because of unfavorable circumstances—poor chances of substantial external support and a small country—there is another way, the way of Fidel, wherein the key ingredients are violence in the form of small to moderately sized guerrilla attacks, limited organization, popular support, and—perhaps most important—a weak government. Indeed, it is questionable whether Castro could have achieved his aims if the Batista government had not been in a state of profound decay.[87] As a matter of fact, in any of the types of insurgency that threaten either the political community or regime, a reasonably strong government could be expected to take resolute steps to eradicate the insurgents. On the other hand, where conservative or reformist insurgents are operating, the Cuban approach might prove effective even in the face of a strong government, for the latter might decide to reduce its losses by initiating policy changes that do not threaten the integrity of either the political community or the regime.[88]

### Urban Strategy

A fourth strategy, which many insurgents in the 1960s and 1970s have found attractive, is the urban terrorist model (sometimes referred to as the urban guerrilla model). As in the case of the Maoist and Cuban schemes, emphasis is placed on popular support and erosion of the enemy's will to resist, rather than on defeating the enemy in classical military engagements. Unlike the Maoist and Cuban examples, the locus of conflict during initial phases is in the cities rather than in the countryside, because of the assumption that the increased size and socioeconomic differentiation of urban centers make them especially vulnerable to terrorism and sabotage. Closely related to this is the notion that the concentration of people in the cities renders government assets, such as aircraft, artillery, mortars, and the like, unusable.

The essential strategy of the urban terrorist, according to the late Carlos Marighella, one of its foremost proponents, is to "turn political crisis into armed conflict by performing violent actions that will force those in power to transform the political situation of the country into a military situation." That will alienate the masses who, from then on, "will revolt against the army and the police and thus blame them for this state of things."[89] To effectuate this transformation, urban terrorists stress organization, propaganda, and terrorism as techniques. Organizationally, they rely on small cells, with a link man in each. Although this has the advantage of limiting exposure and police penetration, it severely undercuts the insurgent ability to mobilize significant sectors of the population.[90] The aim of terrorism is to create havoc and insecurity, which will eventually produce a loss of confidence in the government.

For such a strategy to be successful, however, it would seem the regime would already have to be on the brink of collapse. It is not surprising, therefore, that Marighella himself acknowledged the function of urban terrorists was to tie down government forces in the cities so as to permit the emergence and survival of rural guerrilla warfare, "which is destined to play the decisive role in the revolutionary war."[91] Accordingly, the major question is how effective urban terrorism is in undermining the government and in gaining popular support, not whether urban terrorism alone can be successful. And this, in turn, brings us back not only to the Maoist and Cuban examples, but to the criteria for successful insurgency discussed earlier.[92]

The perceived need to transfer the conflict to the rural areas stems from the belief that widespread popular support will be required to defeat an adversary that controls the state apparatus and that is unlikely to remain passive in the face of a challenge to the political community or the regime.[93] Although such reasoning certainly makes a good deal of sense, it overlooks the possibility that urban terrorism might serve the aims of reformist and conservative insurgents quite well. Again, the point to be made is that it is easier for the authorities to make the concessions when demands focus on maintenance of the regime or on alteration of policy outputs, rather than displacement of the regime and authorities.

## Concluding Note

It is obvious at this point that insurgency is a complex and multifaceted phenomenon, having wide variations with respect to the specific goals and strategies. In order to cope with the analytical difficulties inherent in such a situation, several factors which can have a major bearing on the outcome of insurgent conflicts were identified: namely, popular support, organization, cohesion, external support, environment, and the government role. Each of these was then discussed in some detail. Finally, it was suggested that the salience of individual factors could be ascertained by reference to the importance ascribed to them in different strategic contexts.

Commencing with Chapter 2, several insurgent movements will be analyzed in terms of their goals and the factors that their strategies suggest are vitally important. In each undertaking, the most relevant portions of the framework for analysis will naturally receive greater and more explicit emphasis than other sections.

## Notes

1. On the questions of legitimacy and parts of the political system see Charles F. An-

drain, *Political Life and Social Change* (Belmont, California: Duxbury Press, 1971), pp. 137–144; David Easton, *A Systems Analysis of Political Life* (New York: John Wiley and Sons, 1965), pp. 171–219.

2. Military coups fall within the broad scope of our definition. Even though those who engineer coups occupy supportive roles in the political system, they are not, strictly speaking, part of the "ruling authorities." Indeed, one of the reasons for coups is to seize control of the highest offices or create new ones.

3. The term revolution, as used in this book, refers primarily to political revolution. Whether or not it will be followed by a social revolution that drastically alters the class stratification system will depend upon subsequent actions by the new revolutionary elite and the response to those actions. The importance of value changes and the relationship between values and structures is the principal focus of Chalmers Johnson's *Revolutionary Change* (Boston: Little, Brown, 1966), a seminal work on the application of systems theory to revolution. For a comparison and evaluation of the explanatory power of Johnson's work vis-à-vis several other approaches see Walthraud Q. Morales, *Social Revolution: Theory and Historical Explanation* (Denver, Colorado: The Social Science Foundation and Graduate School for International Studies Monograph Series in World Affairs, Denver University, 1973).

4. Some scholars have analyzed conservative insurgents within the context of "vigilantism"—i.e., acts or threats of coercion, conducted by individuals and groups seeking to defend the existing order against subversion, which transgress the accepted normative restraints on coercion in a polity. See H. Jon Rosenbaum and Peter C. Sederberg, "Vigilantism: An Analysis of Establishment Violence," *Vigilante Politics*, eds. H. Jon Rosenbaum and Peter C. Sederberg (Philadelphia: University of Pennsylvania Press, 1976), pp. 4–5. The concept vigilantism is broader than our category of conservative insurgents in that it encompasses coercion that receives support from the ruling authorities whereas we are interested only in cases where it is applied by autonomous groups. Otherwise put, we concentrate on insurgent vigilantism.

5. While the Kurds at one time had a secessionist goal, their demands during the recent and ill-fated round of fighting were essentially reformist (to wit, increased revenues from oil, more social services, and a substantial degree of political autonomy within the framework of Iraq).

6. On this distinction see Ted Robert Gurr, *Why Men Rebel* (Princeton: Princeton University Press, 1970), pp. 10–11.

7. Samuel P. Huntington, "Guerrilla Warfare in Theory and Policy," *Modern Guerrilla Warfare*, ed. Franklin Mark Osanka (New York: The Free Press of Glencoe, 1962), p. xvi; Arthur Campbell, *Guerrillas* (New York: The John Day Company, 1968), p. 3.

8. The systematic, arbitrary and amoral attributes of political terrorism are analyzed cogently by Paul Wilkinson, *Political Terrorism* (New York: John Wiley and Sons, 1974), pp. 14–18.

9. See United States Central Intelligence Agency, *International and Transnational Terrorism: Diagnosis and Prognosis*, Research Study (Washington, D.C.: The Central Intelligence Agency, April 1976), pp. 8–9. The University of Oklahoma Study Group on Terrorism subsumes both international and transnational terrorism within a broader

category which it calls nonterritorial terrorism. See Charles Wise and Stephen Sloan, "Countering Terrorism: The U.S. and Israeli Approach," *Middle East Review*, Spring 1977, p. 55.

10. On terrorist aims see Brian Jenkins, "International Terrorism: A Balance Sheet," *Survival*, July/August 1975, pp. 158–160; Bard E. O'Neill, "Towards a Typology of Political Terrorism: The Palestinian Resistance Movement," *Journal of International Affairs*, Spring/Summer 1978, pp. 35–37 and 42. Although much attention has been paid to terrorism since the upsurge of its international and transnational variants in the late 1960s and early 1970s, the construction of a reasonably precise, general definition agreeable to most or all scholars has remained elusive. For a representative sampling of more recent attempts to grapple with the definitional problem see Wilkinson, *Political Terrorism*, pp. 9–31; David Fromkin, "The Strategy of Terrorism," *Foreign Affairs*, July 1975, pp. 692–693; H. Edward Price, Jr., "The Strategy and Tactics of Revolutionary Terrorism," *Comparative Studies in Society and History*, January 1977, pp. 52–53; Jay Mallin, "Terrorism As a Military Weapon," *Air University Review*, January–February 1977, p. 60; Central Intelligence Agency, *International and Transnational Terrorism: Diagnosis and Prognosis*, pp. 8–9; Jordan J. Paust, "A Definitional Focus," *Terrorism: Interdisciplinary Perspectives*, eds. Yonah Alexander and Seymour Maxwell Finder (New York: The John Jay Press, 1977), pp. 19–25; and Martha Grenshaw Hutchinson, "The Concept of Revolutionary Terrorism," *The Journal of Conflict Resolution*, September 1972, pp. 383–385. The last mentioned is a particularly admirable effort to carefully define terrorism, albeit only in its revolutionary variation.

11. Julian Paget, *Counter-Insurgency Campaigning* (New York: Walker and Company, 1967), p. 15.

12. This definition is similar to the one used by Robert B. Asprey in his two-volume work, *War in the Shadows* (New York: Doubleday and Co., Inc., 1975). Whereas Asprey identifies the target of the small-scale attacks as "orthodox military forces" (p. xi. volume one), we have expanded it to include police and key economic targets.

13. Otto Heilbrunn, *Partisan Warfare* (New York: Frederick A. Praeger, 1962), pp. 39 and 160.

14. The cohesion and organization factors are sometimes treated as one variable. Since both can be very important in particular cases, they will be treated separately herein. For a similar listing of strategic factors see Virgil Ney, "Guerrilla Warfare and Modern Strategy," *Modern Guerrilla Warfare*, pp. 25–38.

15. *Selected Military Writings of Mao Tse-Tung* (Peking: Foreign Language Press, 1963), p. 260.

16. For an analysis of the role and traits of the intelligentsia in the third world see Harry J. Benda, "Non-Western Intelligentsias As Political Elites," in *Political Change in Underdeveloped Countries*, ed. John H. Kautsky (New York: John Wiley and Sons, 1967), pp. 235–251. On their role in insurgencies see David A. Wilson, *Nation Building and Revolutionary War* (Santa Monica, California: The RAND Corporation, September 1962), p. 7; Gil Carl Alroy, *The Involvement of Peasants in Internal Wars* (Princeton: Center of International Studies, Princeton University, Research Monograph Number 24, 1966), pp. 16–19.

17. Gurr, *Why Men Rebel*, p. 337.

18. Ney, "Guerrilla Warfare," p. 34.

19. Suggestive analyses of the psychological foundations of the leader-follower relationship may be found in Bruce Mazlish, *The Revolutionary Ascetic* (New York: Basic Books, Inc., 1976), especially pp. 22–43; E. Victor Wolfenstein, *The Revolutionary Personality* (Princeton, New Jersey: Princeton University Press, 1967), pp. 174–239. Both Mazlish and Wolfenstein limit their focus to revolutionary leaders. For a more general and historical examination of the leader, which distinguishes between eventful and event-making man, see Sidney Hook, *The Hero in History* (Boston: Beacon Press, 1943), pp. 151–183.

20. Gabriel A. Almond, *The Appeals of Communism* (Princeton: Princeton University Press, 1954), p. 62. On the basic distinction between esoteric and exoteric appeal see Almond, pp. 65–66 and Morris Watnick, "The Appeal of Communism to the Underdeveloped Peoples," in *Political Change in Underdeveloped Countries*. The same dichotomy is implicit in Peter Van Ness, *Revolution and Chinese Foreign Policy* (Berkeley, California: University of California Press, 1970), pp. 118–119; Gurr, *Why Men Rebel*, p. 195.

21. V. I. Lenin, *Imperialism: The Highest Stage of Capitalism* (New York: International Publishers, 1969), pp. 1–128. Other aspects of Leninist thought, such as the leading role of the intellectuals within the revolutionary party, enhance its attractiveness for many intellectuals. See John H. Kautsky, *Communism and the Politics of Development* (New York: John Wiley & Sons, 1968), p. 77.

22. Almond, *Appeals of Communism*, p. 65.

23. Gurr, *Why Men Rebel*, p. 205; quotes from pp. 199 and 198 respectively.

24. A striking passage on the manipulation of mass grievances can be found in Mao Tse-tung, "On Methods of Leadership," *Selected Works*, Vol. IV (New York: International Publishers, 1958), p. 113.

25. Thomas H. Greene has argued that "an ideology that appeals to national identity is the most powerful symbolic means of mobilizing revolutionary support." See his penetrating *Comparative Revolutionary Movements* (Englewood Cliffs, New Jersey: Prentice-Hall, 1974), p. 52. Also see Carl Leiden and Karl Schmitt, *The Politics of Violence* (Englewood Cliffs, New Jersey: Prentice-Hall, 1968), pp. 107–108.

26. The impact of terrorism has led some scholars and practitioners to contend terror is the most powerful weapon for establishing community support. Roger Trinquier, for example, calls it the principal weapon of modern warfare (revolutionary warfare) and suggests that by making the people feel insecure it causes them to lose confidence in the government and to be drawn to the guerrillas for protection. See Roger Trinquier, *Modern Warfare* (New York: Frederick A. Praeger, 1964), pp. 16–17. It has been argued that the Chinese Communist ability to get popular support without large-scale terror is atypical, because most insurgencies start without the degree of popular backing that Mao had and therefore must resort to terror. See, for example, Brian Crozier, *The Study of Conflict* (London: The Institute for the Study of Conflict, October 1970), p. 7.

27. Jerry M. Silverman and Peter M. Jackson, "Terror in Insurgency Warfare," *Military Review*, October 1970, pp. 62–64; Paget, *Counterinsurgency Campaigning*, p. 65.

28. Silverman and Jackson, "Terror in Insurgency Warfare," pp. 64–67. Richard L. Clutterbuck in *The Long, Long War* (New York: Frederick A. Praeger, 1966),

p. 63, cites an example of the ineffectiveness of terror in the Malayan case in the fall of 1951 where the Malayan Communist party realized that intimidation was not gaining popular support and, therefore, issued a directive proscribing attacks on innocent people.

29. J. K. Zawodny, "Unconventional Warfare," in *Problems of National Strategy*, ed. Henry A. Kissinger (New York: Frederick A. Praeger, 1965), pp. 340–341. Peter Braestrup, "Partisan Tactics – Algerian Style," *Modern Guerrilla Warfare*, p. 393, argued that such was the case with the French in Algeria; see also Bernard B. Fall, *The Two Viet-Nams* (2nd rev. ed., New York: Frederick A. Praeger, 1967), pp. 348–352.

30. Clutterbuck, *The Long War*, pp. 178–179.

31. Silverman and Jackson, "Terror in Insurgency Warfare," p. 67.

32. On the political aspects see the depiction of the agent's role in Andrew R. Molnar, James M. Tinker, and John D. LeNoir, *Human Factors Considerations of Underground in Insurgencies* (Center for Research in Social Systems, The American University, December 1966), p. 109; also see Vo Nguyen Giap, *People's War People's Army* (New York: Bantam Books, 1968), p. 50.

33. George B. Jordan, "Objectives and Methods of Communist Guerrilla Warfare," *Modern Guerrilla Warfare*, pp. 404 and 409; Paget, *Counter-Insurgency Campaigning*, p. 22.

34. Edward L. Katzenbach, Jr., and Gene Z. Hanrahan, "The Revolutionary Strategy of Mao Tse-tung," *Modern Guerrilla Warfare*, pp. 144–145.

35. Mao Tse-tung, "On Protracted War," *Selected Works*, Vol. II (London: n.p., 1954), p. 211ff., quoted in Heilbrunn, *Partisan Warfare*, p. 45.

36. Douglas Hyde, *The Roots of Guerrilla Warfare* (Chester Springs, Pa.: Du Four Editions, 1968), pp. 86–88. He also cited his conversations with Huk leaders in the Philippines who said that government ability to sever the leaders from the rest of the movement was a key reason for their downfall.

37. Ibid., pp. 36–37 and 43.

38. See Gurr, *Why Men Rebel*, pp. 274–316, for an expanded discussion of the structural and functional aspects of organizations.

39. The commentary on auxiliary organizations, like that on parallel hierarchies, is extensive. See, for example, Fall, *The Two Viet-Nams*, p. 134; Hyde, *The Roots of Guerrilla Warfare*, p. 34. An especially good source for the treatment of the role of auxiliary organizations is Douglas Pike, *Viet Cong* (Cambridge: M.I.T. Press, 1966), Chapters 6 and 10.

40. Tomas C. Tirona, "The Philippine Anti-Communist Campaign," *Modern Guerrilla Warfare*, p. 204.

41. On the question of military differentiation, see Ney, "Guerrilla Warfare," pp. 35–36; Heilbrunn, *Partisan Warfare*, p. 25; Pike, *Viet Cong*, ch. 13; Anthony Crockett, "Action in Malaya," *Modern Guerrilla Warfare*, p. 310; Brooks McClure, "Russia's Hidden Army," *Modern Guerrilla Warfare*, p. 90; James E. Dougherty, "The Guerrilla War in Malaya," *Modern Guerrilla Warfare*, p. 302.

42. Gurr, *Why Men Rebel*, pp. 297–301.

43. John J. McCuen, *The Art of Counter-Revolutionary War* (Harrisburg, Pa: Stackpole Books, n.d.), p. 69.

44. Cited in George B. Jordan, "Objectives and Methods of Communist Guerrilla Warfare," *Modern Guerrilla Warfare*, p. 404. See also p. 407.

45. Many writers cite the significance of external material aid. See for instance, Ney, "Guerrilla Warfare," pp. 31–32; Gurr, *Why Men Rebel*, pp. 269–270; Frank Trager, *Why Vietnam* (New York: Frederick A. Praeger, 1966), p. 77; and Bernard B. Fall, *Street Without Joy* (Harrisburg, Pa.: Stackpole, 1963), p. 294.

46. Hyde, *The Roots of Guerrilla Warfare*, pp. 86–88.

47. Numerous observers have noted the ability of the Polisario insurgents to con-duct guerrilla attacks in the desert. See, for instance, Marvine Howe, "Saharan Guer-rillas Roam Freely in Territory Ceded to Moroccans," *The New York Times* (hereafter *NYT*), March 15, 1977; Don A. Schanche, "Sahara Desert," *The Washington Post* (hereafter *WP*), May 29, 1977 and "Sahara War Strains Morocco," *WP*, May 30, 1977; Associated Press Dispatch, "20,000 Desert Fighters Seize Control of Vast No-Man's Land in Northwest Africa," *Los Angeles Times*, November 15, 1977; and *The Age* (Melbourne), August 3, 1978.

48. On this point see Mao Tse-tung, "On Protracted War," *Selected Military Writings of Mao Tse-tung* (Peking: Foreign Language Press, 1963), pp. 200–201; A. H. Shollom, "Nowhere Yet Everywhere," in *Modern Guerrilla Warfare*, p. 19; C.E.S. Dudley, "Subversive Warfare–Five Military Factors," *The Army Quarterly and Defence Journal* (U.K., July 1968), p. 209.

49. Heilbrunn, *Partisan Warfare*, pp. 44–45.

50. Gurr, *Why Men Rebel*, pp. 363–364.

51. The relationship between primordial cleavages and insurgent fortunes is ex-tremely complicated. Where insurgent organizations draw their support from ethnic minorities, for example, they may establish a popular base sufficient for terrorism or guerrilla warfare. Whether this will enable them to achieve their aims depends in large part on the nature of the aims. If the insurgents have a revolutionary goal which will re-quire them to gain support from other communities, the initial reliance on minorities may not be equal to the task. Reformist insurgents, on the other hand, may find a minority base of support adequate for limited violence. Since the reformist goals do not challenge the regime or the authorities, the latter may decide on a conciliatory ap-proach rather than continued conflict.

52. Walter C. Sonderland, "An Analysis of the Guerrilla Insurgency and Coup D'Etat as Techniques of Indirect Aggression," *International Studies Quarterly*, De-cember 1970, p. 345.

53. McCuen, *Counter-Revolutionary War*, pp. 30–40.

54. Ibid., pp. 43–44.

55. Ibid., pp. 71 and 181–182.

56. Ibid., pp. 58–59 and 96.

57. Arthur Campbell, *Guerrillas*, pp. 73–89. See also from *Modern Guerrilla War-fare*: Frederick Wilkins, "Guerrilla Warfare," pp. 10–11; Walter D. Jacobs, "Irregular Warfare and the Soviets," p. 61; Brooks McClure, "Russia's Hidden Army," pp. 96–97; Ernst von Dohnanyi, "Combatting Soviet Guerrillas," pp. 102–105.

58. See from *Modern Guerrilla Warfare*: Kenneth M. Hammer, "Huks in the Philip-pines," p. 102; Boyd T. Bashore, "Duel Strategy for Limited War," pp. 193–196 and

199–201; Tomas C. Tirona, "The Philippine Anti-Communist Campaign," pp. 206–207.

59. The decision of the Sudanese government to meet demands of rebels from the three southern provinces for greater autonomy is an example of a regime terminating an insurrection by agreeing to reallocate political-economic power. See *NYT*, February 28, 1972.

60. In situations where the installation of the regular administrative apparatus is impossible in the short run because of a paucity of resources and trained personnel, the government should use civic action teams to help meet the needs of the population and to establish a government presence. On civic action, see Heilbrunn, *Partisan Warfare*, p. 157; Paget, *Counter-Insurgency Campaigning*, p. 178; Hyde, *The Roots of Guerrilla Warfare*, pp. 44–45. If it is possible, local administrators, as well as police and militia personnel, should be drawn from the local population. One advantage is that the additional frictions and suspicions that emerge when a group interacts with elements they consider foreign will be avoided. Moreover, there is also a military advantage, since use of local people will free regular and regional troops for operations against guerrilla units and bases.

61. In other words, each law must be enforceable, fairly applied, and must avoid falling unfairly on particular groups in the population. For a discussion of regime coercive measures, see Gurr, *Why Men Rebel*, pp. 236–259; Sir Robert Thompson, *Defeating Communist Insurgency* (New York: Frederick A. Praeger, 1966), p. 53; Charles Wolf, Jr., *Insurgency and Counter-Insurgency: New Myths and Old Realities* (Santa Monica: The RAND Corporation, July 1965), pp. 4 and 22. Thompson argued harsh security measures could be followed only in areas within the scope of government control. If they were sporadically applied in areas under insurgent control, the people would have little choice but to support the insurgents. Arguing along similar lines, others have suggested if collective sanctions are to be morally acceptable, they must be implemented in a context within which the government can provide security against insurgent reprisals. See Heilbrunn, *Partisan Warfare*, pp. 151–158; Paget, *Counter-Insurgency Campaigning*, p. 169; Campbell, *Guerrillas*, pp. 232–233; Trinquier, *Modern Warfare*, pp. 43–50.

62. On the question of resettlement and its successes and failures, see Clutterbuck, *The Long War*, pp. 56–63 and 66–72; Campbell, *Guerrillas*, pp. 36, 148 and 218; Paget, *Counter-Insurgency Campaigning*, p. 36; Heilbrunn, *Partisan Warfare*, pp. 36 and 153; McCuen, *Counter-Revolutionary War*, pp. 231–234.

63. Trinquier, *Modern Warfare*, pp. 23–27 and 25–38; Campbell, *Guerrillas*, p. 300 and 232; Paget, *Counter-Insurgency Campaigning*, p. 164; Clutterbuck, *The Long War*, pp. 95–100.

64. McCuen, *Counter-Revolutionary War*, pp. 119–124 and 166–181. French mobile operations in the Atlas Mountains in Algeria are cited by McCuen as models that might be emulated. Moreover, he suggested the counterorganization of native tribes could prove useful in some underpopulated areas, the French experience with the Moi and Thai in Indochina being examples.

65. Ibid., pp. 128–142.

66. On the Israeli countermeasures against terrorism see Bard E. O'Neill, *Armed*

*Struggle in Palestine* (Boulder, Colorado: Westview Press, 1978), pp. 86–89. Christopher Dobson, *Black September* (New York: MacMillan Publishing Co., Inc., 1974), pp. 110–133; David B. Tinnin and Dag Christensen, *The Hit Team* (New York: Dell Publishing Company, 1976).

67. O'Neill, *Armed Struggle*, pp. 195–231; Hyde, *The Roots of Guerrilla Warfare*, pp. 94–95; Clutterbuck, *The Long War*, p. 176.

68. McCuen, *Counter-Revolutionary War*, pp. 235–245; 258–309.

69. Ibid., pp. 240–249; Trinquier, *Modern Warfare*, pp. 101–103. Trinquier favored using counterguerrillas drawn from the population of the sanctuary country. That he may have overestimated the possibilities here was suggested by Bernard Fall in the Foreword to Trinquier's book.

70. Clutterbuck, *The Long War*, p. 161.

71. For an excellent and balanced analysis of the dilemmas associated with assistance to governments by outside powers see Douglas S. Blaufarb, *The Counterinsurgency Era* (New York: The Free Press, 1977).

72. McCuen, *Counter-Revolutionary War*, p. 31.

73. John S. Pustay, *Counterinsurgency Warfare* (New York: The Free Press, 1965), pp. 54–59.

74. Ibid., pp. 59–71; McCuen, *Counter-Revolutionary War*, p. 33.

75. Pustay, *Counterinsurgency Warfare*, pp. 71–72; McCuen, *Counter-Revolutionary War*, p. 34.

76. Gurr, *Why Men Rebel*, pp. 294–295; Pustay, *Counterinsurgency Warfare*, pp. 36 and 72; McCuen, *Counter-Revolutionary War*, pp. 34–35.

77. Pustay, *Counterinsurgency Warfare*, pp. 72–74; McCuen, *Counter-Revolutionary War*, pp. 34 and 36.

78. Pustay, *Counterinsurgency Warfare*, pp. 75–76.

79. Ibid., pp. 76–78; McCuen, *Counter-Revolutionary War*, pp. 37–40.

80. Che Guevara, *Guerrilla Warfare* (New York: Vintage Books, 1961), p. 1.

81. Pustay, *Counterinsurgency Warfare*, p. 112.

82. Guevara, *Guerrilla Warfare*, p. 112.

83. Crozier, *The Study of Conflict*, p. 7.

84. Regis Debray, *Revolution in the Revolution*, trans. Bobbe Ortiz (New York: Monthly Review Press, 1967), pp. 20–21, quote p. 85; Crozier, *The Study of Conflict*, p. 8.

85. Debray, *Revolution in the Revolution*, pp. 83–84.

86. Ibid., p. 106. Italics are from Debray. Despite Debray's claims, the idea of military action preceding popular support was already present in the literature on insurgency. It was one of several posssibilities raised by Ximenes in "LaGuerre revolutionarie et ses donnes Fundamentales," *Revue Militaire d'Information*, February–March 1957, pp. 9–29.

87. For a succinct account of the differences between the Maoist and Debray schemes see Arthur Jay Klinghoffer, "Mao or Che? Some reflections on Communist Guerrilla Warfare," *Mizan*, March–April 1969, pp. 94–99.

88. On the failure of Castroism in Latin America see Blaufarb, *The Counterinsurgency Era*, pp. 280–286.

89. Carlos Marighella, "On Principles and Strategic Questions," *Les Tempes*

*Modernes* (Paris), November 1969.

90. Robert Moss, *Urban Guerrilla Warfare,* Adelphi Paper No. 79 (London: The International Institute for Strategic Studies, 1971), p. 3.

91. Carlos Marighella, "Minimanual of the Urban Guerrillas," Appendix, Moss, *Urban Guerrilla Warfare,* p. 26.

92. The rural-urban linkage within the framework of a protracted war of liberation is perhaps best illustrated in the writings of Abraham Guillen, one of the major revolutionary thinkers in Latin America. See *Philosophy of the Urban Guerrilla,* ed. and trans. Donald C. Hodges (New York: William Morrow and Co., 1973), pp. 229–300. Although Guillen allows for the possibility of a Leninist type of takeover under certain conditions, the essential thrust of his argument concentrates on prolonged conflict. Guillen, it should be noted, focuses on Latin America. While he believes that armies of liberation must be created in each country, he contends that they must be a part of a larger continental strategic command which can orchestrate the liberation of all Latin America.

93. For succinct, incisive critiques of the urban terrorist approach see Anthony Burton, *Revolutionary Violence* (New York: Crane, Russak and Co., 1978), pp. 130–144; Walter Laqueur, *Guerrilla* (Boston: Little, Brown and Co., 1976), pp. 403–404.

ATLANTIC
OCEAN

Malin Head

Portrush  Ballycastle

NORTH CHANNEL

ARAN
ISLAND

LONDONDERRY
LIFFORD

Ballymena

Larne

Donegal

NORTHERN  IRELAND

Donaghadee

Killybegs

OMAGH

Belfast

Ballyshannon

Portadown

ENNISKILLEN

DOWNPATRICK

SLIGO

ARMAGH

Kinsale

Newry

Killala

CARRICK
ON SHANNON

CAVAN

DUNDALK

CASTLEBAR

Kingscourt

CLARE ISLAND

Drogheda

Westport

Claremorris

ROSCOMMON

LONGFORD

Clifden

MULLINGAR

TRIM
Enfield

IRISH
SEA

Athlone

GALWAY

Athenry

DUBLIN

ARAN
ISLANDS

TULLAMORE

KILDARE

WICKLOW

I R E L A N D

MARYBOROUGH

CARLOW

Arklow

ENNIS

Killaloe

Kilkee

KILKENNY

Enniscorthy

Kilrush

LIMERICK

Loop Head

Foynes

Cashel

Ballybunnion

CLONMEL

WEXFORD

TRALEE

Castleisland

Mallow

WATERFORD

Carnsore
Point

Dingle

Dingle Bay

Dungarvan

Hook
Head

Cahersiveen

CORK

Youghal

Macroom

Queenstown

Kinsale  Crosshaven

Clonakilty

Courtmacsherry

Dursey Head

Baltimore

ATLANTIC OCEAN

SAINT  GEORGE'S  CHANNEL

0        25        50 Miles
0        25        50 Kilometers

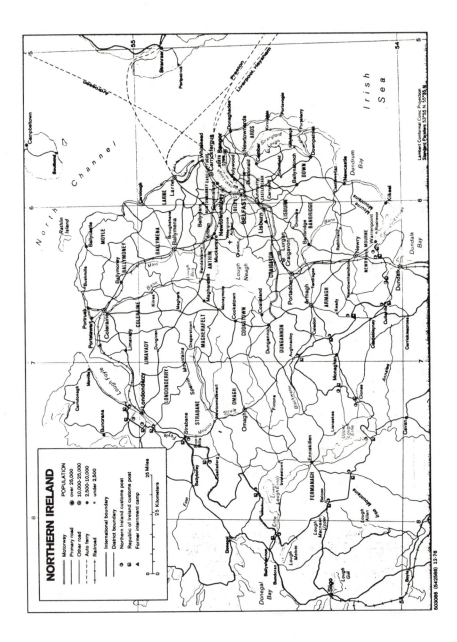

**NORTHERN IRELAND**

POPULATION
- ⊙ over 25,000
- ⊙ 10,000–25,000
- • 2,500–10,000
- • under 2,500

══════ Motorway
─────── Primary road
─────── Other road
- - - - - Auto ferry
+−+−+− Railroad

─ · ─ · ─ International boundary
─────── District boundary
⊙ Northern Ireland customs post
▣ Republic of Ireland customs post
▲ Former internment camp

0    25 Miles
0    25 Kilometers

503086 (542586) 12-76

Lambert Conformal Conic Projection
Standard Parallels 53°55′N 55°55′N

# The Irish Republican Army and Northern Ireland

*Don Mansfield*

*The Scots (originally Irish, but by now Scotch) were at this time inhabiting Ireland, having driven the Irish (Picts) out of Scotland; while the Picts (Originally Scots) were now Irish and vice versa. It is essential to keep these distinctions clearly in mind (and verce visa).[1]*

*The following is attributed to an Israeli diplomat—he was brought up in Northern Ireland and one day, as a boy, he was cornered by an aggressive looking street gang. "Are you Protestant or Catholic?" they asked him ominously. With relief he was able to reply, "I'm a Jew." "Yes, yes," was their retort, "But are ye a Protestant Jew or a Catholic Jew?"*

## Introduction

The Northern Ireland situation is distinctive for its complexity and intractability. The first quote helps to illustrate the complexity of the problem. Ireland's past is very nearly its present; the troubles of the past keep recurring. It is quite impossible, therefore, to understand the current problems in Northern Ireland without setting the historical scene at length. Three themes are of enduring significance in Irish history. The first is that the people of the island have never shared a single national identity; the second, that there has never been a time when all the people of Ireland have been effectively governed by an authority they fully accepted as legitimate; and the third, that religion has divided rather than united the people of Ireland.[2]

This last theme, vividly illustrated in the second quote above, helps to explain why the situation is so intractable. Religion has been central to political conflict in Ireland since the sixteenth century. There are two distinct communities in Northern Ireland—Protestant and Catholic—each with its own

An earlier version of this chapter was coauthored with Anthony C. Rogerson.

set of traditions, culture, and political loyalties. The smaller of these two communities, the Catholics, has suffered from a number of discriminatory measures since the division of Ireland in 1921. Seeking reunification with the Republic of Ireland as a solution to the injustice of their situation, the majority of Catholics have sought to achieve this goal through a moderate, political approach. The more militant Catholics, however, have supplied successive generations of volunteers to the Irish Republican Army, which seeks to bring about unification by force.

The principal purpose of this study of the Irish Republican Army (IRA) in Northern Ireland is to illustrate important aspects of modern urban insurgency and terrorism. If modern events such as hijackings, political assassinations, and kidnappings are not just temporary aberrations, then we have to face the fact that even in the well-established industrial nations terror and insurgency are becoming increasingly everyday facts of life. The Northern Ireland problem, with its spillover in bomb attacks elsewhere in Britain, can teach us much about what to expect from urban terror and insurgency. The cause of the conflict is unique but the methods are part of an international inventory.

### History and Environment

That the conflict in Northern Ireland has been a never-ending one is beyond dispute. What is subject to question, however, is when it began. To some the starting point is 1968, when the civil rights demonstrations erupted; to others the point is 1922, when Ulster and the Irish Free State, as the Republic of Ireland was then called, decided to go their separate ways; and to still others — perhaps most — the origin of the troubles can be traced back to 1690, the date of the Battle of the Boyne, or even to 1603, the year of the "flight of the Earles" and the start of the Ulster plantation.[3] Because each of these dates is important, a brief analysis of Irish history is necessary if a complete understanding of the struggle is to be obtained.

Ireland (the whole island) is approximately the size of West Virginia and has a total population of four and a half million. Six of Ireland's northern counties (corresponding to two-thirds of the historic province of Ulster) are an integral part of the United Kingdom. Northern Ireland, as it is called, has a population of approximately one and a half million. The rest of the island is the independent Republic of Ireland, or Eire, with an area four times that of Northern Ireland and a population twice as large. For centuries now the northern counties have been different from the rest of Ireland, above all with respect to their inhabitants.

The northeastern edge of Ireland is only a few miles from the Scottish coast and in the early years of the seventeenth century Scots settled in the area.

These Scots brought with them many different cultural traits compared to the native, or "Irish," Irish. This helps to explain why it is frequently asserted that the Protestants of Northern Ireland belong to a race different from that of the rest of the Irish. It also illustrates why the Irish problem is as much a problem of different nationalities as of different religions.

## History of Conflict: 1603 to 1968

"Ireland would not be the problem country that it is if it had ever been properly conquered."[4] Ireland's history is one of a series of attempts at colonization and conquest, none of them completely successful and each one contributing a new element to the general confusion. Her history is also one of bloodshed.

During the sixteenth century, England extended its authority over Ireland, and by 1607 the conquest was completed by James I. However, although England had become Protestant (and the same metamorphosis was prescribed for Ireland), the native Irish remained Catholic. Indeed, the fact that the ruling English were Protestant only confirmed the Irish in their attachment to the Roman Church.

Following their defeat by James I, the Earls of Tyrone and Tyrconnell chose to exile themselves from Ireland and handed their Ulster lands over to English and Scottish settlers. The most important plantation in Ulster history was begun. Many of the "Irish" Irish were driven into the poorer lands in the south and west. Thus Northern Ireland firmly attained the characteristics it has today—largely Protestant and closely aligned to the rest of Britain.

Twice more during the seventeenth century Ireland was to experience large-scale warfare, and on both occasions the Irish chose the losing side, a choice dictated by religion. They supported Charles I against Cromwell and James II against William of Orange.

During the civil war in England in 1664, the Catholic Irish massacred many of the Protestant settlers in Ulster. After Cromwell won the civil war he put down the rebellion in Ireland with great ferocity and it was the Catholics' turn to be massacred. Cromwell's campaign was extensive and left lasting grievances in the hearts of the "Irish" Irish. However, their cause looked to be improving when the Catholic James II came to the English throne in 1685 and anti-Catholic laws were discontinued. But in 1688, the English Parliament invited William of Orange to become king in place of the "too Catholic" James. The "Irish" Irish rose on behalf of King James. The Protestants stood firm for King "Billy" and took their stand at Londonderry.[5] For fifteen weeks the defenders of Londonderry held out against successive attacks by the Catholic army, until an English ship broke into the harbor to raise the siege. The Orange Order derives much of its mythology from this period and the defenders ("apprentice boys") of Londonderry are its legendary heroes.

William of Orange also won victories at the Boyne, Anghrim, and Limerick, all of them entering the folklore of both Protestants and Catholics in Ireland, so that even today they continue to stir bitterness and division. The defeat of the "papists" at the Battle of the River Boyne in 1690 has long been the central celebration of the Orange (Protestant) calendar, marked by annual processions and vituperative speeches each July 12; while on August 12 the "apprentice boys" of Londonderry reenact the gallant defense of that city in 1689. This is not to suggest that the conflict in Northern Ireland is a bizarre survival from the seventeenth century, without relevance to the modern age.[6] Nevertheless, the conflict today is made worse by the atavistic memories of the past—memories which are kept alive on both sides by parades and slogans.

The Protestant victory was buttressed by a series of anti-Catholic laws but Ireland was not completely divided on Catholic and Protestant lines. For awhile Presbyterians also suffered discriminatory legislation, as the power lay in Church of England hands, and toward the end of the eighteenth century Presbyterians and Catholics found a common cause in demands for reform, which were sparked by the French Revolution. Unfortunately, this relatively nonsectarian period in Irish history did not last long and the Protestant founding of the Orange Order in 1795—to preserve their political, social, and economic ascendancy—was a bad omen for the future.

In 1800, the Union with Ireland Act was passed by the British Parliament, thereby abolishing the Irish Parliament and uniting England and Ireland. At first Catholics looked favorably upon the act, since they viewed union as the only way of removing the religious hatred and intolerance that the Orange Order had revived in the period immediately preceding union and the most promising way by which the Catholics might obtain political power. It was not until much later that the Catholics realized that the act really left a small caste in control and enabled the Protestant minority to retain its dominance over the Irish people.[7]

Nevertheless, despite Orangism and union, Catholics and Protestants lived together in relative peace until 1829, when Catholics were allowed to become members of the British Parliament. Now, led by the chief proponent of the act, Daniel O'Connell, the Catholics began to press for independence from Britain. Protestants, who would clearly be a minority in an independent Ireland, supported union with the rest of Britain. The lines were being drawn for the twentieth-century conflict. Sectarian riots began to be common.

Pressure for Irish independence from Britain grew during the last part of the nineteenth century and became an increasingly significant factor in British parliamentary affairs. In the late 1880s, Gladstone's two bills to grant Home Rule to Ireland were defeated, but in 1914 the Third Home Rule Bill was finally passed. By this time the final division of Ireland into northern and southern camps was painfully obvious. The Protestant Ulstermen threatened armed rebellion if the act was put into force. In 1912 the Ulster Volunteer Force was formed and a half million Ulstermen signed a pledge to defeat Home Rule by all means which might prove necessary.

The outbreak of World War I in 1914 put a temporary stop to the Home Rule Bill. It was decided to delay the bill's effective date until the cessation of hostilities. To the Irish the delayed effective date was simply Britain's way of offering Home Rule with one hand and taking it away with the other. Rather than wait for the war to end and for Britain to focus her attention and military might on Ireland, a handful of Irishmen decided to take advantage of Britain's indisposition and force Ireland's independence. The uprising, led by James Connolly and Padraic Pearse, was brutally crushed. But even though the 1916 Easter Rising in Dublin was a total failure militarily, it had political advantages because it made martyrs of the men who led it. Furthermore, the Rising moved the Catholic Irish toward the rebel Sinn Fein (Gaelic for "ourselves alone") party, which sought independence for Ireland.[8]

In 1918 Sinn Fein won overwhelming control of the seats allotted to Ireland in the British Parliament. In lieu of taking their seats at Westminster, however, the 73 elected Sinn Fein members met in January 1919 to set up their own parliament in Dublin and declare their jurisdiction over Ireland. Three months later, Eamon De Valera was elected president of the Irish Republic.

No sooner was the republic announced than Britain stepped in to reassert its control. To counter British actions, the IRA in 1920 initiated a campaign of guerrilla warfare. Led by Michael Collins, the IRA struck effectively at British operations.[9]

In response to the IRA attacks, Britain countered with both increased army actions and a repressive irregular force known as the Black and Tans. Contrary to IRA legends the British forces were not defeated in the guerrilla campaign of 1919–21. However, with world opinion against her, Britain became weary of the whole affair and looked for a solution. This came with the new Government of Ireland Act of 1920. The unionists in the north reluctantly accepted the compromise by which Ireland was given two parliaments subordinate to the one at Westminster—one in Belfast for six of the nine counties of Ulster and one in Dublin for the rest of the country. In theory the act aimed at the eventual unification of the whole of Ireland.[10] So, by statute, the historical division between north and south was made legal.

The subsequent elections in Ulster in 1921 produced an overwhelming unionist majority over the Sinn Fein and the unionists have remained in power ever since. Northern Ireland took on the status of a province of the United Kingdom—self-governing in internal matters but subject to control from London in external affairs and defense.

In the south the Sinn Fein dominated the new parliament. In late 1921, after months of negotiation, this body accepted Britain's offer that the Irish Republic become a dominion of the British Empire, like Canada. Many of the southern Irish, however, were not prepared to accept even this link with Britain and civil war broke out between the Irish—a struggle even more bitter than the fight for independence. Internment without trial was introduced and 11,000 suspect republicans were detained. The civil war was brief but bloody, ending in 1923 without the republicans' achieving their objectives.

There was still the question of the border between the Irish Free State and Ulster. A boundary commission was set up to settle the matter. However, when the Free State learned that the commission was comtemplating transfer of southern areas to the north, it entered into an agreement which confirmed the existing boundary. One result of this was that one-third of the population of Northern Ireland was, and has remained, Catholic. Herein lies, of course, the root of the present-day problems for the province.

Northern Ireland and the Free State have since pursued divergent paths. In 1936 the Dail Eirean (the Dublin Parliament) passed an act by which the British king ceased to be the head of the Irish Free State. In 1937 a new constitution was adopted which declared Ireland to be a sovereign, independent, democratic state. Finally, in 1948, the Irish Free State became the Republic of Ireland and was excluded from the British Commonwealth. In 1949, the British Parliament gave a firm guarantee of Northern Ireland's position:

> It is hereby declared that Northern Ireland remains part of His Majesty's dominions and of the United Kingdom and it is hereby affirmed that in no event will Northern Ireland or any part thereof cease to be part of his Majesty's dominions and of the United Kingdom without the consent of the Parliament in Northern Ireland.[11]

The years between the division of Ireland in 1921 and the 1960s were marked by periods of comparative peace interspersed with periods of violence. In Northern Ireland, where Catholics suffered from discriminatory measures ranging from gerrymandering of electoral districts to injustices over housing allocations, the majority of Catholics hoped for a gradual and peaceful improvement of their situation. The more extremist Catholics, however, who were convinced that reunification with the south could be achieved through force, supplied successive generations of volunteers to the IRA.

On the Protestant side there was the fear of being a minority in a united Ireland and an overwhelming desire to retain union with the rest of Britain and maintain numerical superiority in Ulster. In contrast to the moderates, who have desired to improve the conditions of the Catholics gradually and to build good relations between the communities, the extreme Protestants saw any concession to the Catholics as the first step toward subjugation to Rome and hid behind the shadowy and well-armed Ulster Volunteer Force.

In all this the British government walked a difficult path. Even though its actions suggested that in many ways it preferred an independent Ireland, it was not free to force this on the north, where the majority of the population wanted to remain part of the United Kingdom. Furthermore, although Britain clearly supported reform in Northern Ireland, it was not in a position to force it upon Ulster, which was independent in internal matters. Westminster's attitude during this period seemed to be mainly one of hope that the problem might somehow just go away. It did not.

It should be noted that the IRA has generally been as unwelcome to the government in Dublin as to that in London.[12] The "old" IRA (those who fought for the independence of the south from Britain) are heroes to the Eire administration, but the "new" IRA (those who fought against the government in the civil war, and their successors who continue to fight for armed overthrow of the government in the north) is considered an illegal organization. The IRA, therefore, is not an officially sponsored southern Irish organization—it is proscribed in the south as well as the north.

During the period 1956–62 the IRA conducted the so-called border campaign to, once more, bring about the long-denied union with the republic. Despite a fairly extensive effort the campaign was unsuccessful because the Catholic populace in the north did not give it moral or material support. Yet just two years after 1962, when the IRA admitted defeat, the Catholic community began to demonstrate its displeasure with the state of affairs in the north. By 1968 the sickness had permeated the entire province of Ulster and the IRA received its new lease on life.

### Ulster: 1968 to 1978

The explosion in 1968 was somewhat perplexing because during the early 1960s there had been real hope that the hatred was diminishing and that the problems of Northern Ireland might be solved. Captain Terence O'Neill, who became prime minister of Northern Ireland in 1963, was a moderate man, anxious to improve the conditions of the Catholics and to promote rapprochement between the communities. At times the middle-class Protestants and Catholics displayed a recognition that they had much in common. In November 1967 a public opinion poll showed that 70 percent of the Catholics and 50 percent of the Protestants believed that interfaith relations were improving.[13] Nevertheless, within a few years the groups in Northern Ireland had been polarized, violence had become rampant, the IRA was back on the streets again (this time with the support of most of the Catholic population), the British army had been called in to prevent civil war, and Westminster had imposed Direct Rule on the province to try to bring order out of chaos. What went wrong?

The answer brings us back to the slightly more than one-third of Northern Ireland that is Catholic. The Catholics had genuine grievances, stemming from voting inequities, discrimination in housing and employment, gerrymandering, and the "emergency powers." Franchise inequities gave businessmen, mostly Protestants, additional votes; certain companies, for instance, had up to six extra votes, while the exclusion from the franchise of lodgers, subtenants, and adult children living at home led to a quarter million people's being disenfranchised – most of them Catholics.

Housing and employment discrimination abounded. Protestant councils discriminated against Catholics in several ways. For example, they would give Protestants better houses than Catholics for the same rent. "In Dungannon, for an identical rent, you got forty-two square feet of space less on the mainly Catholic Ballygawley Road estate than you got on the exclusively Protestant Cunningham's Lane estate."[14] In addition more Protestants were allocated houses than Catholics. In employment Catholics were also at a disadvantage – in the mid 1960s they numbered only 12 percent of local government and 6 percent of central government employees. Unemployment throughout Northern Ireland ran 5-8 percent but the unemployment rate among Catholics was 12-25 percent.

The manipulation of electoral boundaries (gerrymandering) to give the best results for the unionists was perhaps the most blatant injustice. This was most obviously seen in Londonderry. In 1966 Londonderry had 14,000 or so Catholic voters compared to 9,000 Protestants. However, by manipulating the electoral boundaries the unionists were able to elect sixteen councilmen and the Catholics only eight.

Probably the most objectionable issue was that of law and order. Catholics feared the Special Powers Act of 1922 that granted, among other things, indefinite internment without trial. Inequities in law enforcement were also a problem. Despite an effort to recruit one-third of the police force from the Catholic population, the Royal Ulster Constabulary (RUC) was largely Protestant, while the Ulster Special Constabulary (the B Specials) was completely Protestant. The B Specials were a police reserve especially intended for riot control situations, and viewed by Catholics as extremely sectarian.

Ironically, it was the attempt of O'Neill's government to remedy these grievances that led to the current problem. The smell of reform in the air encouraged the Catholics to demand it more quickly and more extensively, and caused Protestant extremists to take a stand against any change. Obsessed with the fear that they would become a minority in an overall Catholic Ireland, Protestant extremists moved to insure maintenance of the status quo. Many genuinely feared that any concession to the Catholics would open the flood gates to Catholic domination of all Ireland.

The Reverend Ian Paisley emerged in the mid–1960s as the leader of the extreme Protestants. The founder and moderator of the Free Presbyterian Church in Northern Ireland and a rabid antipapist, he sensed that successful reform by the O'Neill administration might lead to an ending of the Protestant control of Ulster and of the union with Britain. In 1965 Paisley began to preach vehemently against the liberal reforms of the unionist government. The challenge was taken up not by the IRA – still licking its wounds after the border campaign – but by the Civil Rights Association.[15]

The Civil Rights Association began as an attempt by moderates (both Catholic and Protestant) to encourage the unionist government to grant further reform. Modeled upon similar movements in the United States and elsewhere, its intention was to demonstrate peacefully and to make its demands known by civil protest. Its aims were six-fold:

1. One-man-one-vote in local elections
2. The removal of gerrymandered boundaries
3. Laws against discriminations by local government and the provision of machinery to deal with complaints
4. Allocation of public housing on a points system
5. Repeal of the Special Powers Act
6. Disbanding of the B Specials[16]

Prime Minister O'Neill was conscious of the validity of most of these aims, and, encouraged by the British government, he made public in November 1968 a package of five reforms meeting many of the Civil Rights Association's demands. But positions were already beginning to be polarized because of the earlier clashes between extreme Protestants, civil rights demonstrators, and the police. The worst of these – at Londonderry on 5 October 1968 – received worldwide attention.

Increasingly, moderates were forced out and extremists began to take over. The civil rights movement began to look more and more ominous to the authorities as IRA men appeared in its ranks and as the People's Democracy (PD), led by Bernadette Devlin, came on the scene. Although PD was not a violent movement, its Marxist aims were alarming to the civil power. Meanwhile Paisley's prophecies of the danger to Protestants seemed to be being fulfilled and the ranks of his supporters swelled. In the midst of all this, Prime Minister O'Neill struggled to find a balance between making reforms for the Catholics and keeping the confidence of the Protestants.

The year 1969 opened with the provocative "long march" from Belfast to Londonderry on New Year's Day by the PD and others. On the way they were ambushed by Protestant extremists. Once again the Catholics saw the police as less than neutral. The reaction in the Catholic Bogside in Londonderry was to set up barricades in the streets to protect themselves from both Protestants and the police. This threat to law and order, as the extreme Protestants saw it, led to a backlash on their side. O'Neill, finally forced out of office in May 1969, was succeeded by Major James Chichester-Clark—who arrived just in time for the parade season.

As noted previously, the Catholics march first, during Easter week, to celebrate the 1916 Rising, and then the Protestants march from late June to mid-August to celebrate the victories of 1689–90. Inevitably these parades lead to violence. This was particularly true of the apprentice boys' parade in Londonderry in August 1969. The Bogside was once more barricaded and the police were kept out of the area, despite repeated charges. The Bogside riots sparked off much more serious rioting in Belfast. In desperation, Prime Minister Chichester-Clark ordered the mobilization of the B Specials. For the first time British troops garrisoned in Northern Ireland were called into Londonderry and Belfast. Initially, the troops were welcomed by the Catholics as protectors against the Protestants. In a matter of days, however, they came to be seen as upholders of unionist power and consequently enemies of the Catholic minority.

Continued attempts were made by the Chichester-Clark government to ease the situation. Further measures of reform on housing and discrimination were announced. During October 1969 the B Specials were disbanded and the Royal Ulster Constabulary was deprived of its guns except when in actual pursuit of armed criminals. In addition, an Englishman was placed in charge of the RUC.

Despite these reform measures, riots and gun battles between snipers and the police continued in Belfast. During this period the IRA was able to reinforce its position as the defender of the Catholics and to control activities in the barricaded ("no-go") areas. It was also at this time that the IRA split into two factions.

Public opinion in Britain, initially in sympathy with the Catholic demands, now turned against them as IRA gunmen took control. The British became increasingly weary of the whole affair as the situation worsened and more and more troops were committed to the province.

Chichester-Clark was forced out of office by unionist hard-liners in March 1971, and Brian Faulkner became prime minister. Faulkner offered the chairmanship of two of the key committees in Stormont to Catholic members of parliament, but shortly thereafter the opposition party in Stormont, the Social-Democratic and Labour party (SDLP), withdrew from Stormont in protest against the shooting of two men by the troops in riots in Londonderry. In August 1971 the unionist-dominated Stormont was able to persuade the Westminster government to agree to the internment of IRA suspects under the Special Powers Act. Internment, whatever its success in curbing the IRA leadership (and initially this was not very great), polarized the communities even further. Reports of harsh army interrogation methods added to the Catholic population's hatred of the British troops.

"Bloody Sunday," on 30 January 1972, brought matters to a head. It is not clear who fired first, but thirteen people were killed in Londonderry when British troops opened fire. In Catholic eyes the British army was now comparable to the SS of Nazi Germany. The IRA retaliated by carrying its attacks over into England. The IRA also became less selective in its bomb attacks, injuring innocent bystanders as well as British troops.

It was obvious by this time that the Northern Ireland administration had lost control of the situation. The British government was faced with the specter that had haunted Westminster for years – that of having to take direct control of Northern Ireland to restore order and find a political solution. The decision was finally taken in March 1972. Faulkner was stripped of his power and Stormont was adjourned. William Whitelaw was made secretary of state for Northern Ireland with direct responsibility for the government of the province and, as a gesture of goodwill to the Catholics, 600 internees were released.

The first nine months of Direct Rule from Westminster were not particularly auspicious. Although many Protestants and Catholics were obviously weary of the bloodshed, sectarian violence increased. In fact, 1972 has been the worst year of violence to date. Execution squads on both sides (the IRA on the one hand and the Ulster Defense Association and other groups on the other) carried out their gangland killings, and bombings continued. A brief two-week truce during June 1972 was broken by more ferocious bombings and snipings, and in July more trouble broke out over housing in Belfast. "Bloody Friday," on 21 July 1972, which produced twenty-two bomb explosions in the middle of Belfast, with nine dead and 130 wounded, led to the decision to move troops into the "no-go" areas and remove the barricades.

The year 1973 was more hopeful. It was clear that the British army was winning the struggle against the IRA. During the summer about 100 IRA men a month were arrested. There was a decline in shooting incidents, a reduction in the deaths of soldiers, and increasing information coming in about both Catholic and Protestant extremists. The average age of the terrorists was younger, with fifteen-year-olds now being seriously involved – a sure sign that the army was getting a grip on the IRA. The terror bomb attacks in London at the end of the year were probably a further manifestation of weakness. The replacing of internment by "detention" (individuals could be held only if an independent judge on a tribunal decided they were public dangers)[17] in 1973 mitigated much of the bitterness of the Catholics toward the British.

However, it was on the political front that the most hopeful steps were made in 1973. In March, the British Parliament passed a Constitution Act which provided for the return of self-government to the province. Under the plan set forth in this act, certain legislative functions would be transferred to a Northern Ireland assembly, and certain executive functions to a Northern Ireland executive. A novel feature, intended to secure Catholic influence and allegiance, was "power-sharing." After months of negotiation, Catholic and Protestant moderates in the assembly were able to agree on the forming of a power-sharing executive, which was sworn in during December. It was the most promising development in years.

December 1973 saw the dramatic meeting at Sunningdale between the British and Irish Republic governments and members of the new Northern Ireland executive. A two-tier Council of Ireland, with representation from both north and south, was agreed upon. Following the Sunningdale agreement, the British Parliament approved the ending of Direct Rule and the return to the Northern Ireland Assembly of most of the constitutional power previously held by the Stormont Assembly.

Unfortunately, four months after it had been created, the power-sharing executive fell, following a fourteen-day general strike organized by trade union Protestants who believed that power-sharing was a first step toward Irish unification. Acting promptly, Britain once again established Direct Rule.[18]

Although the general strike by Protestants was directly responsible for the collapse of the coalition, some observers have suggested that Protestant actions were merely a reaction to the IRA campaign to destroy the Sunningdale agreements. If Sunningdale had brought peace, it is possible that Protestants would have accepted the accords. But expanded terrorism—including bombings in London, and bombings and destruction of public transportation in Northern Ireland—demonstrated the IRA's determination to wreck the Anglo-Irish accord and prompted the Protestant backlash.[19]

Recent polls have shown that both Catholics and Protestants in Northern Ireland now accept Direct Rule, at least as a second-best solution. In spite of growing impatience in Britain, it seems likely that the government in London will be in charge for a long time. Moderates on all sides believe that a restoration of the provincial parliament would quickly revive republican violence on a large scale.[20]

During recent years, IRA activities have shown signs of leveling off in spite of random incidents of violence. The British army is firmly in control. However, it is only in the political arena that the Northern Ireland problem will be settled, and such a solution is not on the horizon. The total failure of the power-sharing executive has forced many British politicians to doubt their own ability to ensure government in the province—with or without a desirable degree of consensus. The need to suspend an Ulster government twice over a two-year period produced a political vacuum that has yet to be filled.[21]

## Political-Military Analysis

> Although they are members of the world's oldest secret army, they are, by and large, a motley lot—a seemingly random assortment of bricklayers, house painters, plumbers and clerks. And for all their blarney about waging a holy war against a repressive foreign enemy, they spend as much time squabbling among themselves as they do fighting the "hated oppressor." In short, they are odd and somewhat inefficient killers, the men of the Irish Republican Army.[22]

The specific struggle for an Irish Republic has a history of nearly two centuries and even the organizational structure of the Irish Republican Army is over fifty years old. A long revolutionary tradition is not unique; but what is peculiar to the IRA, by contrast with most revolutionary groups, is persistence in the face of failure. "Generally revolutionary movements succeed or fail within a relatively brief space of time; they are transformed by power or wither away in isolation, evolve into new forms or are swallowed by old ones."[23] The militant Irish republican movement, however, has continued almost unchanged; the goal is the same—an Ireland, both free and Gaelic—and the means are the same—physical force. Time after time, as the means of the movement have proven inadequate and the strength of the opponent too great, the IRA has failed. Yet the IRA has nevertheless persisted and endured. As Bell notes in his study on the Secret Army, "The repeated failures of the IRA are hardly surprising; but the refusal to resign and flee as wild geese to Liverpool or Detroit or to withdraw into the Sunday papers and the race results and instead to persist is passing strange."

As the Irish Republic gained its independence, the raison d'etre of the IRA was put into question. The pure nationalists in the movement were left with Ulster as their last card. The modus operandi of the IRA has also been a source of dispute. Indeed, the years after 1962 have shown a new drift to the left and the search for a new approach. Still, despite the private doubts and the uneasy sense of marching along the wrong road back into the past, the IRA has not disbanded, has not turned to parliamentary politics, has not withered away. "What is special about the IRA is not the errors and defeats, which are legion, or the old successes, which are splendid; but the continuity, however futile such persistence may seem to the rational. Scorned or discounted, the IRA continues."[24]

In the late 1960s the potential for insurrection had existed in Northern Ireland for at least fifty years, yet there had been no serious challenge to authority. However, even though all the IRA efforts had proved abortive, it was evident that any future rebels could pick up the republican legacy. Thus the rebels against the crown would have, in the words of one observer, three readymade assets: "An inspiring revolutionary tradition that granted legitimacy, authorized an army without banners; a demonstrably viable alternative to the institutionalized sectarian injustice of the Northern Ireland establishment in [the Irish] Republic; and an organizational core of trained and zealous men to direct the rebellion."[25] This tradition, the republican alternative, and the band of IRA zealots had existed for fifty years without serious effect until the peculiar combination of circumstances arose in the late 1960s. At last the objective conditions seemed to favor the rebels.

## Unity and Organization of the Movement

As pointed out, the IRA grew out of the Irish volunteers who rebelled against British rule in 1916. During the war of independence of 1919–21, the IRA was recognized as the legitimate army of those fighting for freedom from Britain. After independence in 1921, the republican movement split. One faction accepted a treaty with Britain; the other refused it and was defeated a year later after a bloody civil war.

On the urging of de Valera, the dissidents laid down their arms. From the late 1920s on all political parties in Ireland shunned the IRA and it became an increasingly secretive underground movement, often with no more than a few hundred activists. In 1939, the IRA launched an ineffective bombing campaign in Britain. This led to wide-scale internment without trial, and the occasional execution of IRA men in the Irish Republic.

Although greatly weakened by the de Valera government, the outlawed IRA was not completely destroyed at the end of the 1940s. It nursed its strength, reorganized, and began preparations in the early 1950s for the initiation of a full-scale attack on the Northern Irish regime. In 1954 the IRA began conducting raids for the purpose of capturing arms and ammunition. During December 1956, the IRA initiated the most widespread series of attacks against the Protestant-dominated regime in Northern Ireland since the 1920s. However, despite some initial success, the northern campaign dwindled to a close in 1962, leaving the IRA in serious disarray. During February of that year, the "Irish Republic Publicity Bureau" announced the termination of the campaign as a result of the defeat of the militantly antipartition Sinn Fein party candidates in the Irish elections of October 1961 and the imposition of tough measures to prevent IRA terrorism by the Irish government. But there was another, and more important, reason for the campaign's failure: the IRA had failed to rally popular support on either side of the border.

Even before the 1956 campaign there had been feuding within the IRA roughly along northern versus southern factional lines – the northerners being the more militant. Now the movement was demoralized not merely by ignominious defeat, but by the popular rejection that, more accurately than the unionists, some of them discerned as its cause. But the IRA leadership drew conflicting conclusions from this. Some thought merely that the population had deserted a losing cause; next time, they said, a better organized campaign would succeed.

After the campaign, the IRA entered one of the periods of internal schism and decay that seems to have followed each of its defeats. According to Robert Moss, the IRA, "like most clandestine organizations, has had a labyrinthine history of internal feuds and betrayals and policy reversals."[26] The republican movement Sinn Fein (of which the IRA is the military army) became deeply engaged in a process of self-criticism. IRA councils met frequently during 1963–65 and it was widely accepted that new tactics were necessary. In 1965 a special conference of the IRA army council produced a nine-point program endorsing social revolution as well as political revolution. The council also endorsed the abandonment of abstention from parliament, so that "guerrilla activities" could be undertaken in the three parliaments then claiming some authority in parts of the thirty-two counties of Ireland. In social terms, the recommendations meant a turn to the left, resurrecting the socialistic ideals of James Connolly[27] and the language of Marxists. But the political implications were in the opposite direction – recognition of the Dublin and Stormont regimes, even if only tactically and temporarily. The Sinn Fein annual conference, however, showed little sympathy for the council's proposals and refused to accept so drastic a change in policy. Republicans then apparently deadlocked on the issue of maintaining or abandoning their traditional abstentionist policy.[28]

Despite the deadlock, Cathal Goulding, the new leader of the IRA, announced a basic shift in strategy in a speech delivered in the south during June 1967, in which he decried the movement's concentration on violence and declared that the IRA should now lay greater stress on social and economic goals. The Goulding strategy "was Marxism, of a modish kind."[29]

Throughout this period the Sinn Fein newspaper, *United Irishman*, struck up a medley of Marxist aims. Early in 1969 the Marxist influence began to make itself evident in some IRA policy documents. In a report called "Ireland Today" it was suggested that a national liberation front should be created and that the IRA movement should join forces with the Eire Communist party.[30]

The analysis of Ulster that the new IRA began to produce was straightforward Leninism: the root of the problem was the colonial relationship of Ulster to Britain. The economic links between the ruling unionists and the imperial power were central. The religious issue was a device which – by dividing the Protestant man from his natural ally, the Catholic worker – operated to the benefit of the ruling elite. The remedy was to bring this vision home to the Ulster masses by nonsectarian, nonviolent means. What it boiled down to, as one historian of the movement points out, was that the "physical force" party inside the IRA had lost.[31]

The militant leaders of the old IRA had to give way to men who were essentially political revolutionaries, committed to a peculiar, Irish brand of Marxism, that they called "socialist republicanism." These new leaders said that they were going to inspire a peaceful, parliamentary revolution of the proletariat, Catholic and Protestant, north and south. They resolved an end to military tactics and decided to sell what rifles they did have to Welsh nationalists to raise enough money to keep the newspaper, *United Irishman*, afloat.[32] "The surprising thing," according to a London *Sunday Times* Insight Team, "is that so many old IRA men . . . were willing to follow Dublin on its optimistically non-violent path towards a hazy Socialist revolution."[33]

But not all the "old" IRA men were willing to follow the new leadership; many "traditionalists" were bewildered by the changes in the organization, and in Belfast the bewilderment was most acute. The IRA in that city was unique in that, because of the long isolation of the Catholic population in ghettos, it had come to think of itself largely as a force to provide self-defense of Catholic areas from incursions by Protestant militants. For this reason Belfast had been notably absent as a theater of operations in previous IRA activities; the Catholic community was too exposed to Protestant reprisals. "The ending of the partition in Ireland–however supreme it ranked in the IRA theology–has come second in Belfast."[34]

The civil rights agitation that started in Northern Ireland during 1968 strengthened those republicans who argued that the regimes in Ireland could be repudiated primarily by nonviolent means. But the Protestant reaction to the civil rights campaign in August 1969 strengthened those IRA men who argued that only force would resolve Ireland's difficulties. The use of private and police guns against Catholics in West Belfast caught the IRA completely unprepared; it had less than a dozen guns available for use. Several of the retired volunteers of the previous generation rushed to the Dublin IRA headquarters seeking arms and reinforcements only to find that there were none to be had. Before August 1969 the Catholics of Belfast had assumed that the IRA could defend them. But no such armed underground army existed except in the popular imagination. As a result "there was a certain amount of ill-feeling against the IRA for not having produced any (i.e., guns)."[35] Indeed, "I.R.A.–I Ran Away" was frequently seen whitewashed on building walls in the Catholic ghettos.

As far as it can reasonably be ascertained, only a handful of republicans took to the streets of Belfast during the August 1969 riots. Nevertheless, the IRA issued a statement claiming that units of the IRA were active in the north and ready to take any and every action in the defense of Catholics and liberation of the north. The statements did nothing except bolster the charges by hard-line unionists that the Civil Rights Association and the IRA were identical. Relations between Belfast and Dublin reached their nadir. Republicans congregated in farmhouses along the border waiting for arms from Dublin that never came and the northern IRA came to the conclusion that it would have to act on its own.

The absence of weapons when needed intensified recriminations within the

IRA. Many Irish republicans had grave doubts about the new shift to radical politics and finding the IRA to be an army without arms completed their alienation. Those republicans in the north who felt that the IRA leadership had let them down moved to create a nine-county northern command to deal with the situation. The northern command existed alongside the official IRA unit in Belfast for several months, but a break was almost inevitable.

Two crucial conferences followed the intervention of British troops in Northern Ireland during August 1969. The IRA met secretly, while Sinn Fein held an open conference. Each meeting had the same political debates on its agenda, but they were dominated by opposite factions. One group, representing the new IRA, carried the self-criticism of the mid–1960s to its logical conclusion. They favored a continuing alliance with the "new left" forces of the civil rights coalition; a firm commitment to the electoral politics of the People's Democracy; and a more or less Marxist, nonsectarian progam. Ironically, this constitutional approach gained a two-thirds majority at the underground meeting of the IRA, whereas at the aboveground Sinn Fein conference the situation was quite different. The dominant group showed no affection for the constitutional approach and, borrowing from Mao, insisted that political power grows out of the gun barrel. They argued that the movement's military unpreparedness in August 1969 was an unpardonable shortcoming. Given the occupation of Northern Ireland by British troops, they claimed that all politics would be tested in the crucible of armed struggle.[36]

In January 1970 the split came into the open at the Sinn Fein annual conference in Dublin. The point of view expressed by the Marxist leadership was that, "there is no point in fighting unless you are going to win," i.e., achieve a regime with "correct" social and economic policies, as well as jurisdiction in all thirty-two counties of Ireland. A Belfast opponent stated a contrary point of view: "We are traditional Republicans fighting to free our people. When they are free they will decide what kind of government they want. But the communists in Dublin want to shove a ready-made worker's republic down the people's throat."[37]

About a third of the delegates to the Sinn Fein conference were convinced that the Marxist leadership had purposely disarmed the IRA in order to expose the northern Catholics to a program it could then exploit. They walked out, on the pretext of opposing a plan to abandon the party's traditional policy of abstention from parliamentary politics, and promptly declared themselves the true voice of the republican movement. Their defection left Ireland with two Sinn Feins – their own new, "true" Sinn Fein, which is called the Provisional Sinn Fein, and the original, so-called Official one – and, in effect, with two secret armies.

Thus, in an atmosphere of bitterness and emotion, the "Provisionals" were born. The executive of the Provisional Sinn Fein released the specific reasons

for the break other than the resolution on abstentionism: the leadership's support of extreme socialism leading to totalitarian dictatorship; the failure to
protect the people of the north; the suggestion that Stormont should be
abolished and the north should come under direct Westminster rule; and
finally the internal methods of operation within the movement since the
mid–1960s, methods that lead to the expulsion of the faithful and replaced
them with people interested "in a more radical form of movement."[38] But in
many respects the Provisionals' break with those who favored a policy of
social involvement "had more to do with the historical stance of the IRA – its
heroes and martyrs – than with political motives. Direct action is what they
knew and understood and the decision to break meant a return to violence."[39]

How badly the split affected the IRA can be judged from the fact that
before it happened the eleven members of the Belfast battalion staff had comprised four hard-liners, four soft-liners ("Marxists") and three fence-sitters,
who went with the latter when the split came. At the time of the split the
total IRA strength in Belfast was about 150 – of whom no more than thirty
joined the Provisionals. But while the majority of the battalion staff stayed
with the Officials, the split at the grass-roots level looked more promising for
the Provisionals. Of the eleven companies in the Belfast battalion at the time,
the officers of nine declared for the Provisionals.[40]

The lack of numbers did not worry the embryonic Provisionals. They
believed that, if necessary, they could mount effective urban warfare with
fifty people. At the beginning of 1970, there were still not more than a few
hundred Provisionals, but they soon enlarged their numbers by recruiting in
the northern ghettos. They set up training camps near the old Official camps
in Ulster and in counties just across the border in the Irish Republic. As soon
as the first Provisional recruits were ready, they spread across Ulster con-
testing the Officials for control of the Catholic towns and neighborhoods.[41]

The ranks of the Provisionals swelled greatly in the second half of 1970,
and by the end of the year they claimed to control some 90 percent of the
members of the movement in Belfast, although the Officials were stronger in
some smaller towns. During this period the Officials and the Provisionals
began to war with each other and, for a time, IRA units in Belfast "spent as
much time fighting each other as they did the British."[42] The terrorists were
clearly weakened by their internal rifts. Although occasionally they joined
forces for some individual operations in Ulster, their bloody gang war for
supremacy in the province from early 1970 may have cost them as many
casualties as those that died in skirmishes with the security forces. For example, early in March 1971 the Provisionals raided the Officials' headquarters in the Falls Road area of Belfast. This was intended to avenge an
earlier incident in which a Provisional had had his knuckles ground into
fragments of bone by a group of Officials using their revolver butts. The Of-

ficials, in turn, decided to pursue the vendetta and planned the assassination of eleven Provisional leaders. Although a tenuous truce between the two terrorist groups was worked out at the last moment, the Provisionals' chief of staff, Joe Cahill, was badly wounded by a gunman who was not called off in time.

The March 1971 truce lasted only a short time, but shortly after Prime Minister Brian Faulkner invoked Northern Ireland's 1922 Special Powers Act on 9 August 1971, and imposed a policy of internment, the two rival factions declared another truce in an effort to regroup their forces. This truce lasted exactly one day, because the two factions could not agree on common tactics. The Provisionals expressed their desire to launch a bombing campaign in major British cities against government installations and big business companies. The Officials indicated that they would not support reprisals in Britain. They called for an end to confrontation with British troops and urged a campaign of civil disobedience instead.[43]

The conflict between the two factions of the IRA has undoubtedly sapped the movement's strength. The competing centers of loyalty gave rise to command and control problems that, in addition to giving the appearance of a state of confusion, do indeed undercut military operations and initiative. Popular support was affected because potential supporters were bewildered by the spectacle of the two organizations fighting with each other.

For obvious reasons, the IRA leaders will say little about the size of the two armies. British intelligence reports place IRA strength, both Provisional and Official, at between 4,000 and 7,000 in the six counties.[44] The Officials have less than half as many members as the Provisionals, but they have the advantage of being better established in the neighborhoods and they are much more adept at local organization. They tend to think of themselves as part of a larger operation, directed from their Sinn Fein office in Dublin, and this gives them a discipline and cohesion that the Provisionals lack.

The Provisionals, on the other hand, "rarely agree on anything except fighting. They work in small, independent units, responsible to no one – certainly not to Dublin – and they are terrible at the sort of action that would involve efficient cooperation with the unit across the road."[45] Still, during the early 1970s the Provisionals did not lack manpower and they were able to recruit new members just as fast as the British arrested their old ones and drove them off to interrogation centers and internment camps.

The two factions of the IRA are organized similarly, but it appears that the various organizations are more elaborate on paper than in fact. The supreme authority is the army convention in session, which selects an executive that has the responsibility of defining policy for the army. The executive appoints an army council of seven, as well as a chief of staff who represents the general headquarters (GHQ). Below the GHQ are the brigades, which are organized into battalions representing the chief towns. Each battalion is divided into a number of companies that in turn are divided into sections, the smallest unit in the IRA. Battalions, companies, and sections are of unequal sizes and strengths. One company might have ten members, while another might have over 100. The organization is elastic, based on factors of population and terrain, and no attempt is made to form units on an established basis as in regular armies. This is important, because it allows the organizational structure, to the degree that it actually functions, to adapt to changing conditions.[46]

But it would be a mistake to credit either branch of the IRA with a closely knit organization or a coherent policy. The terrorists often refer to their military chain of command but it is doubtful that this guerrilla hierarchy really functions except in fond imaginings.

*Popular Support*

The IRA's border campaign, which began in December 1956, depended upon the fact that although Ulster's population is two-thirds Protestant, the province's 500,000 Catholics are not evenly distributed. Two of Ulster's six counties, Tyrone and Fermanagh, have Catholic majorities, while a third, Armagh, is almost evenly divided. Londonderry is two-thirds Catholic, and Newry and the cathedral city of Armagh are also Catholic-dominated. These areas, the IRA had planned, would be their strongholds. About twenty IRA "organizers" had come up from the south to set up local groups in Catholic areas for sabotage and ambushes, and then to be conduits for plans and supplies from the south. "The assumption, which the IRA never doubted, was that the local population would welcome them. They were mistaken."[47]

Internment (both in the north and south) was a key factor, but the real reason the campaign failed was the lack of nationalist unrest. Contrary to the IRA's expectations, the northern Catholic population did not support the campaign. Whatever their views about the legitimacy of the Protestant government and the injustices it visited upon them, the Catholics were not then ready to support its overthrow by violence. The IRA statement admitting defeat in 1962 acknowledged that: "Foremost among the factors motivating this course of action has been the attitude of the general public whose minds have deliberately been distracted from the supreme issue facing the Irish people—the unity and freedom of Ireland."[48] The Protestant government, in other words, enjoyed at least the passive support of the Catholic minority.

The IRA, in fact, failed to rally support on either side of the border. In the 1957 elections in the south their political arm, Sinn Fein, polled a trifling 66,000 votes. In the north, the IRA was frequently forced to use intimidation just to obtain shelter from the Catholic population. As a result, according to Robert Moss, the IRA members "were quickly seen as what they had become: military adventurers estranged from the Irish people. . . . Above all, their efforts to 'liberate' the North failed to strike any answering chord among the Catholics of Belfast and Derry. The gunmen from the South were fish out of water, and they quickly expired."[49]

The IRA offensive which began in mid–1970 in Northern Ireland was different in kind from the border campaign. The terrorists in Ulster no longer appeared as an isolated military force imported from Dublin. They managed to exploit genuine political sympathy among the Catholics of Northern Ireland. This, rather than their military proficiency, was their source of strength. By August 1971 British army spokesmen were ready to concede that as many as a quarter of the Catholics of Belfast and Londonderry were helping the IRA, and that as many as half were broadly in sympathy. "For the first time in the history of the IRA, Belfast had become the true hub of a terrorist campaign, and a terrorist organization had emerged, in the shape of the IRA Provisionals, that was basically composed of Northern Catholics and not merely another vehicle for Southern gunmen."[50]

When the civil rights movement began in the late 1960s, the Catholic community of Northern Ireland was no more disposed to resort to violence in vindication of its rights than it had been in 1956–62. It still believed in the possibility of effecting change through nonviolent means. But as the movement gained momentum there was growing disillusionment with the possibility of peaceful reformation. In qualitative terms the civil rights campaign gradually lowered the minority's capacity to tolerate further oppression; the question of a united Ireland aside, the minority wanted fair play. Many thus risked more by taking to the streets, and support for them grew among those who stayed home. For the first time the Ulster security forces could not maintain order. The riots that began in August 1969 created a need for a minority defense that the British army for various reasons could not fill. In filling the vacuum as Catholic defenders, the Provisional IRA had as a goal not simply the safety of Catholics but a united Irish Republic that in the long run was the only way to guarantee peace with justice.[51]

When the first British troops drove into Londonderry during August 1969, they were greeted by cheering Catholic crowds. Indeed, Protestant extremists looked upon British armed intervention as a Catholic victory and a defeat for the Royal Ulster Constabulary. For almost a year after the intervention there was a period of calm during which it was not uncommon to see Catholic housewives serving a cup of tea to British Tommies on duty in their neighborhood. But the "honeymoon" period ended during July 1970. The fundamental reason was "the growing perception by Catholics that when the Labour government sent troops to 'aid the civil power' in Ulster, they sent them to support the Orange supremacy."[52] This impression gradually sapped Catholic sympathy. The day of the friendly cup of tea ended. The

British army tried very hard to be evenhanded, but increasingly one hand lay more heavily on the minority. "Given the clash of historic loyalties, the use of British symbols for majority purposes and the existence of a legitimate provincial government, the erosion of British Army neutrality was probably inevitable."[53] After a battle between Catholics and British troops in July 1970, which left 10 people dead and 276 injured, the British army was transformed in the popular mind into Enemy Number One.

Once the events of the summer of 1970 transformed the British army into a threat, the Catholic minority increasingly had to depend on the IRA for defense; in fact, the Provisionals' growth was almost exactly proportional to the decay of British army neutrality as perceived by the Catholics. This came as no surprise to the two factions in the IRA. The border campaign had been successfully met by the security forces of Northern Ireland, without assistance from British troops. In retrospect, the IRA sees this as a central political factor in its defeat; without the physical presence of British troops, it was impossible to demonstrate to the local population that its campaign was directed at British imperialism.[54]

By 1971 the Catholic community could not repudiate the IRA without losing its only sure defense. This made possible an increase in offensive operations that, of course, provoked further British army retaliation. As the strength of the Provisionals increased—and with it effective control of the Catholic districts—the more ambitious began to recognize the advantages in fomenting a sufficient level of violence so that the British army response would solidify support for the Provisionals.

Then Faulkner invoked the Special Powers Act, which suspended habeas corpus and allowed indefinite internment without trial of suspected subversives. Faulkner, stressing that the measures were not aimed at "responsible and law-abiding" Catholic citizens, urged the moderate Catholic community to cooperate.[55]

As a security measure internment initially was less than a complete success—few active IRA men were immediately picked up. The policy failed to reduce terrorist activities in Northern Ireland and even seemed to spur the IRA to greater efforts to end the British occupation. Although a symbolic victory for the majority, it also had negative results. Instead of being humiliated, the minority had all but risen in arms. Internment was intended only to quash the gunmen; instead it swiftly radicalized thousands of Ulster Catholics, whose support enabled the IRA to expand and intensify its campaign of selective terror.

The misuse of internment powers became one of the most potent forces driving moderate Catholics away from the middle ground and, in many cases, into the arms of the IRA. The army's ham-handedness was the IRA's opportunity. The Provisionals were able to extend their influence to communities where they had not exerted it before, and to recover it where they felt in danger of losing it. Indeed, they positively used the army for that purpose. For example, the IRA would actually call the army into an area in an attempt to turn the population against it.

"Because of internment," an opposition M.P. in the Stormont Parliament stated, "there is more support for the violent men than ever before in my experience."[56] Not until the use of internment could the Provisionals be certain that the people would support a campaign as much out of conviction as from fear. After August 1971, the terrorists could count on otherwise peaceable men to open their doors to them in the night, and on the occasional priest to stow their stockpiles of arms away in a country church. By then the Provisionals were at the crest of the tide in Irish affairs, for which they were only marginally responsible.

Why did the Catholic community support such violent activities? The answer lies in the loss of hope of the Catholic community's obtaining justice through nonviolent measures. The support it gave the IRA was born out of despair. Those who condemned the violence had no viable alternatives to offer. Reasoned discussion, appeals to civic conscience, and nonviolent mass demonstrations might have been considered possible alternatives. But in the view of the Catholics of Northern Ireland these were all ruled out and they were left with the feeling that they had no alternative but to support the violence. As a priest of Falls Road commented at the time: "As long as this is how they feel (and it is a question of feeling, not reasoning), they will continue to support the IRA, even though it means in the end that they will 'go down fighting.'"[57]

Terrorism as practiced by the IRA has been described as an "entering wedge"—a technique that can be used by a minority to build a popular movement. It is the type of action that, according to one IRA leader, would "force the people to take sides either with us or against us."[58] By placing the government on the offensive, the terrorists hope to cause the government troops to overreact and, in so doing, alienate the people. Initially it appeared that, however brutal its methods, the IRA would continue to receive Catholic support. Indeed, the ongoing rush to join its forces was so great that both factions (but primarily the Provisionals) had to turn away would-be recruits. At times there seemed to be an almost inexhaustible supply of youngsters who had been nourished on hatred of the British and were ready to offer themselves as recruits.

Catholic support for the campaign of terrorism was short-lived however. When the Provisionals began to bomb indiscriminately during 1972–73, they began to lose the unified allegiance of the Catholic people that they had previously enjoyed. The reaction of a nurse to the events of Bloody Friday in July 1972, in which a series of IRA bombings took 9 lives and injured 130 people, was not atypical: "I'm a Catholic and I live in Falls Road, but this kind of bombing is senseless."[59] In December 1972, a Labour party official in Dublin stated that the "people could stomach the IRA as long as they remembered them as romantic figures from the history books. But the bombing has come too close to home now and they are in a quite different mood."[60]

Soon the British army began to receive a greatly increased flow of information about IRA activities from disenchanted Catholics, and there was a notable upswing when internment was replaced by a less harsh system of "detention." By 1974–75 it was clear that the Catholics were wearying of the Provisionals. As of this writing the vast majority of Ulster's Catholics do not want to bomb their way into unity with the Irish Republic and do not support IRA terrorist activities. But their resentment over their plight, their fear and suspicion of British soldiers, and the existence of a largely Protestant police force will still provide an uneasy sea for the IRA terrorist-guerrillas.

As time went by, it became obvious that strategy and tactics had an important impact on popular support. In discussing IRA strategy during the border campaign, an IRA spokesman in 1959 declared that the border would be abolished in the course of "a successful military campaign against the British forces of occupation." But no rational leader today believes in the possibility of a military victory against the British army. The IRA hopes for political victory, as in 1921. To the extent that it has had a long-range strategy, that strategy is to spark off a political crisis in Ulster in order to provoke direct intervention from Westminster. The objective is one of tiring the British government and public of a contest in which they are the third party and for which there seems no solution except that of withdrawal. The hope is that the British will simply give up and go home, much as they did in 1921 in Ireland itself, in Palestine in 1948, and in Cyprus in 1959.

In their campaign of political and psychological attrition, the leaders of the IRA are well aware that they stand an immeasurably greater chance of success if they can widen the struggle by dragging in the Irish Republic. That way, not only will Britain's embarrassment be increased, but one of the essential preconditions for any successful insurgency will be obtained, namely that the movement will be able to enjoy the potential support of a majority of the population, which can never be the case while the conflict is confined to the north.

The IRA has obviously been successful in its objective of provoking direct British intervention to halt terrorist violence in Ulster. The British army has served as a security force in Northern Ireland since 1969 and, except for a four-month period in 1974, the province has been under direct British political control since 1972.

The IRA has been less successful in its attempt to drag the Dublin government into the crisis between Britain and the republic. Far from feeling compelled to intervene in the conflict, the Irish government and the people of the republic as a whole strongly oppose the IRA, and the government would like to cooperate fully with the British in defeating the terrorist organization. However, Dublin has criticized Britain for using "torture and inhuman and degrading treatment against suspected terrorists in Northern Ireland."[61]

The IRA has used a variety of methods to achieve its basic objectives and to demonstrate that the security situation in the north is insoluble. In the initial phase of its present offensive, from June to October 1970, the IRA emphasized the tactic of "stiffening riots and strikes." Hostile mobs were orchestrated and incited by the IRA to attack British troops. Street violence was drawn out in Belfast and Londonderry for five or six nights on end. The riots became associated with methodical arson and the destruction of property. Pitched gun battles between IRA snipers and British troops became common, and it was not uncommon for the snipers to use crowds as a human shield. In sum, during the summer of 1970, the rioting of the Catholic minority had been converted into a military weapon by the IRA Provisionals.

From October 1970 to August 1971 the IRA relied increasingly on systematic bombing and selective terrorism. Assassinations of British soldiers were timed to have instant political repercussions. The most notorious attack during this period was the murder of three soldiers in Belfast on the night of 10 March 1971. Although both wings of the IRA immediately denied responsibility for the murders, the method of assassination—a bullet in the back of the neck—was a traditional form of IRA "execution." The March killings stirred up a furious uproar in Stormont, and Prime Minister Chichester-Clark resigned after the Protestant right wing accused him of being too "soft." His resignation was regarded by the IRA as a major victory. It seemed to convince the IRA that selective terrorism could bring down unionist government. The bombing campaign continued, and IRA saboteurs concentrated on targets similar to those that were chosen during the border campaign: police stations, customs posts, railway lines, and the like.[62]

IRA tactics changed again with the introduction of internment without trial in August 1971. Initial IRA reaction to internment was to engage British and RUC patrols in standup gun battles. During this period the IRA seemed to forget the most elementary principle of urban warfare: to hit and run, to stay on the move. Army spokesmen claimed that between 15 and 30 terrorists died in the gun battles that took place in the week following internment. After a week or so of this emergent urban warfare, the IRA switched tactics and murder squads adopted a policy of "an eye for an eye," picking off a British soldier each time an IRA man fell in battle. Then, in anticipation of its failure to bring about a "climate of collapse" or in consequence of the elimination of many of its more experienced members, the IRA changed its tactics again. In place of selective assault upon soldiers and policemen, it em-

barked upon a campaign of indiscriminate terror, aimed at civilians. The intent was to bring the Protestants out on the streets and precipitate civil conflict in which the British army would find it difficult to maintain order
without killing Protestants.

During the early 1970s both wings of the IRA were engaged in terrorist activities. Despite their advocacy of civil disobedience rather than violence, the
Officials were concerned with the support of the Provisionals were receiving
from Catholics in Ulster. Even some of their own members were beginning to
drift over to the Provisional camp. During late 1970, there were signs that the
Officials had decided to play a more vigorous part in the terrorist campaign in
Ulster. There were reports during the spring of 1971 that the Officials had
revived their training camps all over Ireland and had begun recruiting for
their own campaign. In July 1971 a leader of the Officials made a ferocious
speech in which he declared that "the bullet and the bomb" would provide
the final solution both for Ulster and the republic. A spokesman for the
Belfast wing of the Officials told an Irish journalist at about the same time
that his movement had never renounced armed struggle and prophesied intensified urban guerrilla warfare: "You can defeat any Army no matter how
big by guerrilla warfare with the support of the people."[63]

However, the Official terrorist campaign never fully materialized, and in
May 1972 the Official IRA, pressured by a peace movement in minority
neighborhoods, called a cease-fire. When the Official wing dropped its terrorist campaign, the Provisionals reacted with undisguised contempt. Yet the
Provisionals, under intense pressure from the Roman Catholic community to
end their campaign of terror, also announced a conditional cease-fire. An IRA
statement from Dublin said that the group would suspend "offensive operations," provided there was a "public reciprocal response" from the British
army. The truce was in effect for only a matter of days and ended when the
IRA, attempting to move Catholics into a mixed area of Belfast, clashed with
British troops. Shortly thereafter, on 31 July 1972, British troops entered the
"no-go" areas in Catholic districts in Londonderry and Belfast. The army
move, which deprived terrorists of haven within these areas, greatly weakened the IRA.[64]

By calling off the truce, the Provisional IRA bewildered and angered large
sections of the Catholic community. The feeling is that the IRA blundered by
breaking a truce they had arranged themselves. As one Bogside Catholic put
it: "The Provos bombed themselves to the conference table, and then they
bombed themselves away again." Since 1972 the Provisionals have increased
their tactical reliance upon bombing. The bombing campaign or, in Provisional
terms, "The War," was exported to the U.K. mainland in 1973. The Provisionals had threatened to mount such a campaign since 1971. From March
1973 to March 1974 alone there were 130 bomb incidents on the mainland.

The rationale for their campaign of random terror is, as in 1938, the wish to renegotiate Irish sovereignty and weary the British of Northern Ireland.

Though bombing is the principal weapon of the current Provisional campaign, small arms are used mainly against the security forces on the streets of Belfast and in assassinations, sectarian or otherwise. Indeed, events during the last few years in the north and on the mainland have indicated that the Provisionals have seen increasing utility in political assassination. Soldiers, policemen, judges, politicians, and other public figures have been IRA targets and victims.

The Provisional IRA has consistently refused to accommodate other groups—even the other wing of the republican movement—or accept strategy, tactics, and solutions other than its own. It is prepared to keep bombing and shooting until its solution is applied. There are few, if any, rules governing Provisional operations. Its mode of warfare is unconventional and ruthless—because for the Provisionals a war situation exists and, as their leaders have stated numerous times from public platforms, "in war people get hurt."[65]

## External Support

With respect to material aid, the IRA has never been short of weapons. The Provisionals have shown repeatedly that they are able to turn up new sources of arms and explosives, no matter how often the old sources are blocked. Since it is no longer easy for them to get their rifles, pistols, and submachine guns in the time-honored way—by raiding armories in England and Ireland—they now increasingly equip the new recruits coming into the movement simply by turning to foreign arms dealers.

Most of the money for IRA arms and explosives has come from the United States. After the north exploded in 1969, Irish relief committees sprang up across the United States. In traditionally Irish communities of Boston, New York, Chicago, and Philadelphia, old machinery was set up again and started pumping money across the Atlantic. Ostensibly, this money has been for "relief." However, much of it has been diverted for weapons, according to intelligence sources. It has been estimated that as much as 90 percent of the money for IRA weapons is donated by Irish-American sympathizers.[66]

During the early 1970s, IRA arms purchasers toured Europe with the U.S. dollars, seeking out weapons wherever they could be bought. Most of the weapons at that time came from European sources. During recent years, however, most of the IRA weapons have come from the United States. This would be difficult to prove, of course, but an official of the U.S. Treasury Department admitted during 1976 that most of the semiautomatic rifles used by the IRA are American-made.[67]

European police have been working closely with British intelligence in an effort to cut off the arms trade. But it will not be easy to stop. "The police are watching us all right," remarks one European arms merchant, "but as long as the IRA can come up with the dollars, I imagine we will be able to find them some guns."[68]

A crucial factor in what success the IRA has achieved thus far has been the existence of a sanctuary in a contiguous country. The border between the six counties of Northern Ireland and the republic meanders for 302 miles across unguarded fields and hedges, sometimes halving villages and occasionally even passing through houses. There are more than 250 roads and tracks across the border and it has been estimated that there are some 100,000 border crossings daily, including 50,000 vehicles and twelve trains.

Thus, the terrorists in Northern Ireland are able to operate across an open frontier over which movement is for all practical purposes unrestricted. IRA gunmen and bombers are trained in the republic, and can cross, kill, and return in a few hours. Republic border towns, particularly Dundalk, provide the IRA with convenient safe areas from which to mount raids into the north. There is a constant flow of arms, ammunition, and explosives across the border. Smuggling is a long-established occupation along the border and the IRA do not find it difficult to obtain expert assistance when they need to cross.

The ability, or lack of it, of the Irish Republic to control its side of the frontier is a key factor. Whereas road blocks can check free movement of vehicles, that of individuals across country is exceedingly difficult to control. The situation is complicated by the close affinity that binds most Irishmen. "A man crossing from South to North is an Irishman, looks, dresses and speaks the same language and without identification cards is indistinguishable from his Northern neighbor." Road blocks and mining have the inherent disadvantage that they bring inconvenience to farmers and other harmless people whose property spans the border.[69]

The degree of moral and political support in the Republic of Ireland for the IRA is difficult to determine. No doubt Jack Lynch, prime minister of Ireland until 1973, was correct in asserting that the majority of the citizens in the republic do not actively support the IRA's campaign of terror in the north. He admitted, however, that, "The vast majority aspire to what the IRA wants, a unified Ireland. Therefore, there is some sympathy for the ideas of the IRA, not their methods."[70] Indeed it is likely that the majority in the south has still not been able to bring itself to repudiate the IRA completely, or to welcome with enthusiasm the prospect of jailing IRA men in the republic. A major reason for this is that many of the Irish see the IRA as the inheritor of the nation's patriotic heritage.

The outbreak of killing in 1969 immediately brought to life the republic's dormant commitment to a united Ireland. Catholics in the south sympathized with their coreligionists in Northern Ireland. Moreover, Ulster Catholics looked to the republic for many things: a haven for families who had lost their homes; political influence in London, Washington, and the United Nations; and, at times, arms and assistance for "self-defense" measures. There is also reason to believe that officials of the Dublin government began assisting Northern Catholic groups to receive arms training in the south and to buy arms on the continent with government funds.[71]

While the Dublin government had openly condemned IRA activities in the north, until the fall of 1972 it had cautiously refrained from stripping the IRA of its sanctuary in the south. Attempts to eradicate the IRA were less than halfhearted and one Dublin weekly was moved to describe the lethargy of Dublin's Special Branch police in moving against known IRA men as "the politics of 'underkill.'"[72] In fact, IRA leaders campaigned from the public platform and even recruited openly.

But during the last months of 1972, the Irish government started a crackdown on IRA gunmen who had been making raids across the border. When the Dail passed an arrest and detention ("anti-IRA") bill, which allows for the detention of any suspected IRA member on no more evidence than the word of a senior police officer, the IRA had to go underground much more than ever before.

As a result of this new era of goodwill, the police in Britain, Ulster, and Eire were, for the first time, exchanging mugshots and updated lists of IRA leaders. Armed with this information, Scotland Yard has been able to keep a close watch over Catholic ghettos in England to nab any IRA gunmen attempting to slip out of the Irish net. In Dublin, the Special Branch police have opened an old detention center to be used for the "detainees."[73] Since the crackdown on the IRA, there have been hundreds of trials for "political offenses," with a high rate of conviction.

The close links between Moscow and the IRA and its Sinn Fein political front are well known. The IRA has had links with Arab terrorist groups, including the now defunct Black September movement. The Provisionals have been trained by Palestinians. Libya is a source of arms and money. In July 1973 there were IRA representatives at a meeting in Tripoli, Libya, of terrorist organizations that included the German Baader-Meinhof, the Japanese United Revolutionary Army, the Liberation Front of Iran, the Turkish People's Liberation Army, and the Uruguayan Tupamaros. It was reported that Palestinian and IRA representatives agreed on joint military operations on British territory against Zionist organizations.

In France and Spain, the IRA has its contacts with Breton and Basque separatists. It has also received some support from the Portuguese Left.

In short, Ulster has been and likely will continue to be, as one political commentator has put it, "a magnet for subversives of every hue."

*Government Response*

The British government has shown great determination in the pursuit of political and military solutions to the conflict in Ulster. Westminster is not prepared to let an integral part of the United Kingdom fall into civil war by default and is similarly determined to try to find a solution acceptable to all concerned.

Politically, from 1968 to 1972 Westminster depended on the Stormont regime to accelerate its reform toward the Catholics. It was, for instance, the British-initiated Hunt Report which led to the disbanding of the B Specials (a paramilitary police force regarded by the Catholic community as a hostile sectarian force), the disarming of the Royal Ulster Constabulary police force, and the placement of an Englishman as head of the RUC.

Furthermore, when it was obvious that the Northern Ireland government had lost control of the province and would not be able to effect a reconciliation with the Catholics, the British government took the bold step of instituting Direct Rule. Since then Westminster has labored ceaselessly for a political solution, with the power-sharing arrangements between Catholics and Protestants attempted in 1973 the most noteworthy example.

A primary objective of the British government is to restore civil government in Northern Ireland. In pursuit of this aim, Westminster was prepared to negotiate with the IRA in 1972 and again in 1974–75. It has not been anxious to negotiate with Protestant paramilitary forces, but does so from time to time. In effect, it has left control of these forces to the RUC, thus avoiding the prospect of a British army–Protestant paramilitary confrontation that would result in a "two-front" war.[74] So far the British public has accepted Westminster's approach to the problem, despite a growing uneasiness with the whole business.

Militarily, the British government has shown great strength of will. It has been prepared to put the number of soldiers into Ulster necessary to "hold the ring" while a political solution is being worked out. As has been pointed out, the British army has succeeded in gaining time for the politicians, albeit not without strain. In order to maintain around 15,000 men in Northern Ireland, the strategic reserve has been almost completely absorbed and there is a standing requirement for five major units to be detached from Germany. This not only reduces the British contribution to NATO but has an adverse effect on the training of the formations remaining in Germany. Family separation has had an adverse effect on troop morale. Primarily for these reasons tours in the "emergency area" have been restricted to a few months. Such short tours of course do not allow for continuity of operations in Ulster.

Four security forces are operating in Northern Ireland under the authority of the British government. The army is manned by British personnel recruited primarily in Great Britain and rotated in and out of the province as needed, in numbers ranging from 10,000 to 22,000. The great bulk of the army is not deployed on the border, but rather in the province, patrolling and policing within neighborhoods. The more contact the army has with Ulstermen, the more effective it can be in arresting terrorists and seizing arms and ammunition. Such close contact, however, increases the potential friction between the army and the Catholics and Protestants it is policing and increases the possibilities of the army itself being attacked. Between 1969 and 1976, 246 British soldiers were killed in Ulster, almost all by republican gunmen or bombs.[75]

The British army is relieved of some patrol duties by the part-time Ulster Defence Regiment (UDR), a fully armed, locally raised force of approximately 8,000 men. The UDR's functions resemble those of the old B Specials; however, it is under British army command rather than under the command of Stormont politicians. Despite an effort to recruit Catholics, only a few have joined the force.

The RUC has grown in numerical strength since 1969, but its peacekeeping role has declined. First, the British army has taken over responsibility for maintaining order in the streets. Second, the army seeks out and apprehends individuals suspected of rebellious activities. Furthermore, given the level of activities, the 5,000-man RUC (1,700 below authorized strength) is inadequate to contain the violence.

Fourth among security forces is an RUC Reserve of about 5,000 part-time policemen. This force is not concerned with serious security work and is 2,000 below its authorized strength.

The RUC and RUC Reserve are overwhelmingly Protestant. Before 1969, Catholics constituted about 10 percent of the force, but the IRA campaign of assassination aimed at the police has discouraged Catholics from joining the RUC.

The inclination of security forces directed by professional soldiers was to identify actual or potential rebellious individuals and imprison them, and the powers of internment and detention that they were granted have placed few legal obstacles in their way. In pursuit of order, British-led security forces have dispensed with various conventional rules of law recognized in English and American courts: the right of habeas corpus, the calling and cross-examination of witnesses, and the explicit delineation of charge and sentence.[76]

Until mid-1970, the army's response to the situation in the province was largely reactive because of the nature of the threat. This threat was the ability of Catholics to create a large crowd at short notice that would threaten to overrun a small detachment of soldiers. After IRA gunmen increased their activities in mid-1970, the situation became much more dangerous for the troops, who were constantly at risk from the concealed gunmen. Although relatively few in number, the snipers posed a serious threat. It was not uncommon for a sniper to ambush and kill several British soldiers on patrol and then successfully disappear from the scene. The army's reaction to this type of warfare was to take the IRA on in a firefight and it was generally successful in this approach.

Unable to stand up to British forces in a firefight, the IRA switched to its campaign of selective terrorism. Bombing activities also increased at this time.

Following the introduction of internment in 1971 and the destruction of the "no-go" areas in July 1972, the IRA began to look somewhat desperate. During 1973 and 1974, it resorted to even more indiscriminate bombing and attempted assassination, including attacks on targets in England. The major reason for this was the success of the military in picking up the IRA leadership.

There is no doubt that the army has developed effective tactics to deal with the many situations it has had to face. Its bomb disposal procedures are good. Its patrols are carried out on foot or in armored vehicles and frequently one patrol shadows another. In carrying out sweeps for suspects, blanket searches of whole areas are avoided; selective searching of occupied houses takes place immediately following an incident or when grounds exist for suspecting a particular dwelling. These house searches are also used as cover-ups to get information from friendly inhabitants – while the houseowner curses and swears at the soldiers for the benefit of his neighbors, he is able to pass on information in the privacy of his home. Observation posts are established in unoccupied private houses at this time, with men left behind to observe from the attic of the house. The observers later leave during another house search.[77]

The attempt to win the support of the Catholic population for government policies has had mixed results. It is true that much moderate Catholic opinion has moved away from the IRA since 1972 to the Social-Democratic and Labour party, which advocates a political solution. The army's successes in forcing the IRA onto its indiscriminate terror path has been a large factor in alienating many Catholics from the IRA. Likewise, the destruction of the "no-go" areas has helped prevent IRA intimidation of moderates. However, viewed as a defender of Protestant supremacy, the British army has had great difficulty in gaining Catholic support. Traditionally connected with the Black and Tans and other "units of repression" in the south's war for independence, the army had much to overcome to begin with.

The difficulties encountered by individual soldiers on patrol in the communal ghettos illustrates the delicate position in which the British army has been placed. Patrolling among the civilian population requires strict discipline and self-control by individual soldiers. They must always retain their "cool," even when grossly insulted.[78] Overall it can be said that the British army has shown admirable restraint in the face of great provocation. Each soldier is issued a card that outlines in simple terms the circumstances and the methods under which he can open fire. This, and excellent discipline, have helped to keep incidents such as Bloody Sunday to a minimum.

Bloody Sunday, which occurred on 30 January 1972, began as an illegal civil rights demonstration and ended with an exchange of shots between British troops and demonstrators. The result was the death of thirteen demonstrators (including six teenagers). Catholic emotions blazed, despite the claim by the troops that they only opened fire after they had been shot at and that they only fired at snipers. The British government conducted an independent inquiry into the affair but this did little to assuage feelings. The board of inquiry's findings did not fully substantiate the position of either side, but it was no help to the army's case when the board reported that only two of the thirteen dead were "probably armed" and that the army's shooting "bordered on the reckless." The shooting of a man in the Springfield Road area when a car backfired was a further encouragement for hatred toward the British army.

An example of the steps taken by British authorities to stop such incidents was the sentencing of a young soldier to three years in jail for the manslaughter of a twelve-year-old boy whom he shot while on patrol. The sentencing clearly showed a concern for due process to be followed in cases of abuse by the army. However, the judge's comments to the soldier are illuminating.

> You have been subjected to the daily threat of death or serious injury. You have been subject to almost daily stone-throwing, bottle-throwing, catcalling or vulgar abuse. At the best you have been treated with much hostility, but like your colleagues you have accepted this with cheerfulness, dignity and restraint. I believe that your conduct was a momentary lapse in your normally high standard of discipline and restraint.[79]

The British army has also been severely criticized for its riot control techniques. Particularly during the early years of the emergency, the IRA found it easy to turn a civil rights protest march into a riot, forcing deployment of riot squads. Street battles ensued and the army replied with the use of water cannons, tear gas, and then rubber bullets, which cause some pain but are not lethal.[80] Typical of the critical response to these techniques was the call by the British Society for Social Responsibility in Science for a halt to "technological escalation."[81]

Internment, in particular, produced a revulsion against the army by the Catholic population. The initial sweeping for suspects was too wide and some innocent men were undoubtedly locked away (many of these were probably framed by the IRA to make sure that the innocent as well as the guilty were detained). Overall, it is doubtful that a large number of individuals were wrongfully held. Nevertheless the damage had been done. The British move to replace internment with detention (a man can be held only if an independent judge agrees that he is a public danger) in 1973, and then to terminate that policy in 1975, helped to reduce some of the violent emotions aroused by the programs.

The reports of the use of brutal methods of interrogation by the British army have also provoked strong emotions. The army admitted during the early 1970s that it was utilizing "sophisticated disorientation techniques" in interrogation. The British government also acknowledged that following an August 1971 dawn swoop in which 337 Catholics were arrested, the detained men were subjected to a five-point program of: extreme noise; hooding; isolation; sensory disorientation; and deprivation of sleep and/or food. These methods were stopped after a British board of inquiry looked into the matter and, thereafter, very stringent regulations were applied to methods of interrogation. Furthermore, the British government paid out large sums in compensation to many of those experiencing this treatment.

These interrogation techniques led the Irish government to charge Britain before the European Commission on Human Rights with the use of torture and "inhuman and degrading treatment" against suspected terrorists. According to a report published by the commission in September 1976, British troops and police tortured and mistreated suspected IRA members during the last five months of 1971. The British government did not deny the charges, but said its forces no longer used such tactics. A British government official stated: "We do not deny that unpleasant things happened. But it's a thing of the past. We no longer use the interrogation techniques described in the report." The torture "techniques" reported by the commission were designed to deprive victims of their sources of sight, touch, and hearing and restrict their movement. In addition to hooding, sleep deprivation, and depriving detainees of food and water, the commission accused the British of subjecting detainees for long periods to "white noise" (continuous high-pitched hissing) and forcing them to stand spread-eagled against a wall, supported by their outstretched fingers, for long periods.[82]

Although it feels compelled to use severe techniques against the terrorists, the army has continuously sought to improve relations with the inhabitants of the province. The army has worked to establish and maintain good community relations by encouraging and running youth clubs, building community centers and playgrounds, and sponsoring many other forms of activity at which youth can meet and be diverted from the streets. Army activities have ranged from entertaining very small children to taking part in university debates.

British forces have also repaired roofs, floors, and windows in damaged houses occupied by the elderly and infirm; visited and helped old people's homes; traced lost children; pulled cows out of bogs and built bridges; and, "capitalizing on the genuine friendliness of the British Soldier, . . . tried, with permanent smiles on their faces, to win the confidence of the mothers and fathers and children alike."[83]

This approach has not been entirely without success. The troops have received numerous messages of goodwill from the people of the province. Typical of these is a Christmastime 1973 message that read: "A special thanks to all the boys who have manned the barriers in our segment for their unfailing courtesy and cheerfulness – if more of the 'natives' would follow their example, this would be a much better place to live in."[84]

British army intelligence in Northern Ireland has generally been good. There has been effective coordination between the army and the police Special Branch and the move from the reactive stage to the offensive in 1971 brought great improvements in the amount of information received. Internment and interrogation especially brought good information on IRA men. Rumors of British atrocities may have fed the fires of hatred toward the British but they also put fear into many who were captured. The Parachute Regiment (the Paras) especially found that the "airborne" image from previous wars such as Algeria made those they picked up inclined to talk.

Other information has been gained through observation posts in Catholic areas and "chatting-up" patrols, where the soldiers just talk to local people.

British troops assigned to a particular area are responsible for getting to know every inch of their allotted "parish," not only the terrain, roads, streets, and alleyways, but also the local inhabitants. By constant patrolling on foot, by helicopter, in vehicles, and from protected observation posts, they must recognize instantly any change in the usage of buildings and in the general pattern of life. The gathering of information is carried out in close collaboration with the police, the UDF, and, where possible, by contact with responsible local citizens – schoolmasters, the clergy, and community leaders.[85]

The best method of obtaining information is by the use of constant patrols. This ensures that a military presence is maintained, knowledge of the area is increased, and the movement of terrorists is hampered. In a large area, much of this is done in wheeled armored cars known throughout the province as "pigs." Foot patrols allow more actual contact with the local people, but they must be carried out with care. In urban areas, a small patrol can easily become embroiled in a framed "riot," stoned or attacked by IRA sympathizers, or become the target for a sniper.[86]

One of the thorniest problems for the British army has been IRA use of the Republic of Ireland as a sanctuary. As discussed earlier, the border is open, with infrequent customs posts and no passport formalities. Although the Irish government has proscribed the IRA, it does not allow British forces to pursue the terrorists across the border onto republic territory.

In an attempt to control border crossings, the army employs foot patrols, helicopter flights, and radar surveillance techniques. It also craters roads and erects substantial concrete and steel barriers. These actions have had only limited success in restricting IRA movement and, unfortunately, they have created considerable ill will with the local populace because of the restrictions they place on normal contact between the two sides of the frontier.

Efforts by the Irish Republic to control its side of the border and clamp down on IRA raids from the south into Ulster have helped. Increased consultation between north and south has enabled both sides to implement more effective border control measures.

## Conclusion

If the IRA were to win in Northern Ireland it would be the first major victory for the urban terrorist. Despite the attention urban insurgency has attracted, it has yet to be completely successful. Experience has shown that most modern governments can contain urban terrorism and it is unlikely that Northern Ireland will prove to be an exception. The failure to mobilize popular support is the weakness of most contemporary urban guerrilla movements. "Where they find this support they have a chance of success; where they can't, they fail."[87]

At times during the early 1970s it appeared that the IRA was receiving the support that was necessary for victory. The Catholic community of Northern Ireland appeared to support the IRA's terrorist campaign as much out of conviction as from fear. By forcing the government to take the offensive, the terrorists caused the British army to overreact and in so doing the alienation of the people was completed. In this sense, IRA terrorism succeeded.

However, the IRA's switch to indiscriminate bombings during 1972–73 cost them the unified allegiance of the Catholic people that they had previously enjoyed. Since the peak of its activities during that period, the fortunes of the IRA have declined dramatically. The British army has benefited from a greatly increased flow of information about IRA activities from disenchanted Catholics. Tips on hideouts and arms caches are frequent. There has been a decline in shooting incidents and a reduction in the deaths of soldiers. British troops now control most of the former IRA strongholds. The crackdown on IRA gunmen by the Irish Republic and the exchange of information concerning the IRA and its supporters among the police in Britain, Ulster, and Eire has clearly had an impact. Indeed, as shown by the recruitment of teenagers, both IRA wings are apparently desperately short of experienced men.

With relaxation evident almost everywhere, the British troops have been handing over security duties, including riot control, to the police. Soldiers are a rare sight in much of the province except in a few problem spots such as the border. Even Belfast, where many buildings are burned shells, is bustling.

This state of affairs has led to some very optimistic statements regarding the condition and future of the IRA terrorists. Early in 1973 a Belfast politician announced that: "People are putting the finger on the Provos, there aren't any demonstrations against the Provos, but people show their resistance. The curtain has begun to come down."[88] When Roy Mason became secretary of state for Northern Ireland in September 1976, he declared that the Provisional IRA "was on the run; the security forces were winning the battle against terrorism; ordinary people were rejecting the bombers and gunmen."[89] During December 1977 Mason boasted: "There can be no doubt that the tide has turned against the terrorists." He looked back with satisfaction on the year: bombings down, killings down, injuries down, security shifting from soldiers to police.[90]

But as this is being written there is an absence of boasts by British authorities that the British army has won the struggle against the IRA. It is now painfully evident that, despite those optimistic statements, the Provisional IRA never died and is back in business and once again demonstrating its capacity to make headlines. The Provisionals have again launched a well-advertised bombing campaign in London and five provincial cities. Moreover, for the last three months of 1978 an average of more than two bombs a day exploded in Ulster. During this period the Provisionals burned and bombed more than $50 million worth of property. In the face of continued military pressure and declining support in war-weary Catholic communities, the IRA has shown again that it can strike almost at will.[91]

After nine years of killing and the maturing of an entire generation, the IRA has persisted and endured. It seems to have become a permanent terrorist force. "The violence goes on," asserts Bernard D. Rossiter, "quite simply because its practitioners have now developed a vested social, psychological and pecuniary interest in it."[92] The IRA has shown repeatedly that it has the imagination and skill, despite repeated defeats, to return to the fray. Its pace may slacken from time to time as it did in 1977, but in all probability it can and will continue. "Defeat of the IRA is wishful thinking," a middle-aged Catholic priest recently said, "I don't believe a body of armed citizens can be defeated in these circumstances."[93]

But if it is unlikely that the IRA can be totally defeated by the British army, it is just as improbable that the Irish Republican Army will register the first military success for the urban terrorist. The key to resolving the conflict in Northern Ireland is not military but political. Just as the IRA received its opportunity in the current troubles because of a political vacuum, so its future depends on whether or not there is a political solution. But, again, there is no reason for optimism. As one expert states: "The problem is that there is no solution."[94] This is because the minimum Catholic demand exceeds the max-imum that Protestants will yield.

## Postscript

The IRA returned dramatically to public attention with the killing of Lord Mountbatten and 17 British soldiers in August 1979. The killings were part of an escalation of violence that has occurred in the late 1970s. A secret analysis prepared within the British army concluded that the Provisionals had the dedication and the ability to raise violence intermittently for the foreseeable future and that violence would continue while the British remain in Northern Ireland. Informed reports indicated that the "Provos" have pared down to a smaller, yet more professional, organization composed of 40 or 50 independent cells of 4 or 5 fighters each. They continue to receive financial support from sympathizers in the United States and to acquire weapons from a variety of sources, particularly the Middle East. Some authorities believe there is a strong connection between the IRA and the PLO.

Meetings between the leaders of Britain and Ireland have sought ways to combat the IRA; however, popular support along the 300-mile border be-tween Ireland and Northern Ireland continues to be a vital factor. The over 1,000 IRA members who remain in jail, for example, continue to receive the passive support of a substantial portion of the Catholic community and their families receive both cash and sympathy from IRA supporters. These recent developments confirm the analysis in the foregoing chapter. After ten years of active counterinsurgency by the British army the IRA has failed in meeting its original objectives, but continues and may even expand its terrorist cam-paign.

## Notes

1. W. C. Sellar and R. J. Yeatman, *1066 and All That* (London: Methuen and Co., 1930), p. 5.

2. Richard Rose, *Northern Ireland: Time of Choice* (Washington, D.C.: American Enterprise Institute for Public Policy Research, 1976), p. 9.

3. Roger H. Hull, *The Irish Triangle: Conflict in Northern Ireland* (Princeton, N.J.: Princeton University Press, 1976), p. 4.

4. "The Irish Question," *World Survey* (April 1972):1.

5. The name of this city is an irritant in itself to the Catholics, since its original name was "Derry"—the "London" was added later.

6. "The Irish Question," p. 3.

7. Hull, *Irish Triangle,* p. 29.

8. Ibid., p. 33.

9. Ibid., p. 34.

10. "The Act contemplates and affords every facility for union between North and South, and empowers the two Parliaments by mutual agreement and joint action to terminate partition and to set up one Parliament and one Government for the whole of Ireland." *Government of Ireland Act,* December, 1920.

11. *The Ireland Act,* 1949, Section 1(2).

12. A. J. Barker, *Bloody Ulster* (New York: Ballantine Books, 1973), p. 81.

13. National Opinion Poll Market Research, "Opinion Survey in Ulster," *Belfast Telegraph,* November, 1967.

14. The London *Sunday Times* Insight Team, *Northern Ireland: A Report on the Conflict* (New York: Random House, 1972), p. 36.

15. Ian Hamilton and Robert Moss, *The Spreading Irish Conflict* (Conflict Studies No. 17, The Institute for the Study of Conflict, 1971), p. 8.

16. The London *Sunday Times* Insight Team, p. 49.

17. The procedure was as follows: a suspect could be held for up to 72 hours, after which he would have to be released, charged, or become the subject of a custody order. The order was current for 28 days, during which time the case had to be referred to one of the 16 commissioners drawn from the judiciary or from barristers or solicitors within the United Kingdom (none of the commissions were from Ulster). A commissioner decided on each case, ordering either the release of the suspect or indefinite detention, against which appeal could be made.

18. Rose, *Northern Ireland,* p. 31.

19. "The Failure of Power Sharing in Northern Ireland," *Orbis* XVIII, no. 2 (Summer 1974):371.

20. *New York Times (NYT),* November 18, 1978, p. A12.

21. Rose, *Northern Ireland,* p. 31.

22. *Newsweek,* October 18, 1971, p. 56.

23. J. Bowyer Bell, *The Secret Army* (New York: John Day, 1971), pp. 373, 376.

24. Ibid., p. 378.

25. J. Bowyer Bell, "The Escalation of Insurgency: The Provisional Irish Republican Army's Experience, 1969–1971," *Review of Politics,* 35 (July 1973):409.

26. Robert Moss, *Urban Guerrillas* (London: Temple Smith, 1972), pp. 98–99.

27. James Connolly was a leading trade unionist who advocated an Irish workers' republic. His philosophy was basically a mix of Irish republicanism and socialism. He was executed by the British in 1916 for taking part in the Easter Rising.

28. Richard Rose, *Governing Without Consensus* (Boston: Beacon Press, 1971), p. 164.

29. The London *Sunday Times* Insight Team, pp. 23–24.

30. Barker, *Bloody Ulster,* p. 84.

31. The London *Sunday Times* Insight Team, p. 24.

32. Hearings Before the Subcommittee on Europe of the Committee on Foreign Affairs, House of Representatives, 92nd Congress, 2nd Session (February 28–29; March

1, 1972), p. 488. The IRA Officials claim now that the guns were never sold.

33. The London *Sunday Times* Insight Team, p. 25.

34. Ibid.

35. Rose, *Governing Without Consensus*, p. 164.

36. Russell Stetler, "IRA: Beyond the Barricades," *Ramparts,* 10 (March 1972):12.

37. Rose, *Governing Without Consensus*, p. 165.

38. Bell, *The Secret Army,* p. 368.

39. Barker, *Bloody Ulster*, p. 84.

40. The London *Sunday Times* Insight Team, p. 194.

41. Hearings Before the Subcommittee on Europe, p. 489.

42. *Time,* January 10, 1972, p. 33.

43. Richard W. Mansbach, ed., *Northern Ireland: Half a Century of Partition* (New York: Facts on File, 1973), p. 127.

44. W. R. Corson, "My Dispatch from the IRA," *Penthouse* (May 1972):47.

45. Hearings Before the Subcommittee on Europe, p. 489.

46. Tim Pat Coogan, *The I.R.A.* (New York: Praeger Publishers, 1970), pp. 43–44; Colin Beer, "Impressions From Ulster," *The Army Quarterly* 102, no. 3 (April 1972):367; Tom Barry, *Guerrilla Days in Ireland* (Tralee, Ireland: Anvil Books, 1962), p. 13.

47. The London *Sunday Times* Insight Team, p. 16.

48. Ibid., p. 51.

49. Moss, *Urban Guerrillas*, p. 93.

50. Ibid., p. 94.

51. Bell, "The Escalation of Insurgency," p. 409.

52. The London *Sunday Times* Insight Team, p. 2.

53. Bell, "The Escalation of Insurgency," p. 404.

54. Stetler, "Beyond the Barricades," p. 12.

55. Mansbach, *Partition,* p. 105.

56. *Time,* January 10, 1973, p. 34.

57. George H. Dunne, "The Irish Sea of Troubles," *America* 126 (March 4, 1972):227–229.

58. Corson, p. 50.

59. *Time Education Program,* "Northern Ireland," pp. 6–7, 13.

60. *Newsweek,* December 11, 1972, p. 46.

61. *Washington Post (WP),* January 25, 1976.

62. Moss, *Urban Guerrillas*, p. 104.

63. Ibid., p. 100.

64. *NYT*, November 30, 1972.

65. Tom Bowden, "The IRA and the Changing Tactics of Terrorism," *Political Quarterly* 91 (October–December 1976):428–436.

66. *Newsweek,* March 6, 1972, p. 49.

67. *Milwaukee Journal,* September 15, 1974; *NYT*, March 18, 1976.

68. *Newsweek,* March 18, 1972, p. 49.

69. General Sir Richard Gale, "Old Problem: New Setting," *Journal of the Royal United Services Institute for Defence Studies* 117, no. 665 (March 1972):46.

70. Hearings Before the Subcommittee on Europe, p. 625.

71. Rose, *Northern Ireland*, p. 66.

72. Rose, *Governing Without Consensus*, p. 167.

73. *Newsweek*, December 18, 1972, p. 47.

74. Rose, *Northern Ireland*, p. 64.

75. Ibid., p. 62.

76. Ibid., pp. 62–63.

77. Michael Banks, "The Army in Northern Ireland," *Brassey's Annual*, 1972. Reprinted with additions in Frank B. Horton III, Anthony Rogerson, and Edward L. Warner III, eds., *Comparative Defense Policy* (Baltimore: The Johns Hopkins University Press, 1974), pp. 530–537.

78. Colonel Norman L. Dodd, "The Corporal's War: Internal Security Operations," *Military Review* LVI, no. 7 (July 1976):63.

79. *London Daily Telegraph*, March 16, 1973, p. 1.

80. Dodd, "The Corporals War," p. 64.

81. Jonathan Rosenhead and Dr. Peter J. Smith, "Ulster Riot Control: A Warning," *New Scientist and Science Journal* (August 12, 1971), p. 374.

82. WP, September 2, 1976; WP, September 3, 1976.

83. Brigadier P. Hudson, "Internal Security Operations in Northern Ireland," *The Infantryman* (1970):9.

84. *London Daily Telegraph*, December 22, 1973.

85. Dodd, "The Corporal's War," p. 62.

86. Ibid., p. 63.

87. Robert Moss, "Urban Guerrilla Warfare," *Adelphi Papers* 79 (1971):13.

88. *Time*, January 29, 1973, p. 34.

89. *NYT*, January 16, 1977.

90. WP, December 22, 1978.

91. *NYT*, December 2, 1978.

92. Bernard D. Rossiter, *Britain—A Future That Works* (Boston: Houghton, Mifflin Co., 1978), p. 186.

93. *NYT*, December 2, 1978.

94. Rose, *Governing Without Consensus*, p. 21.

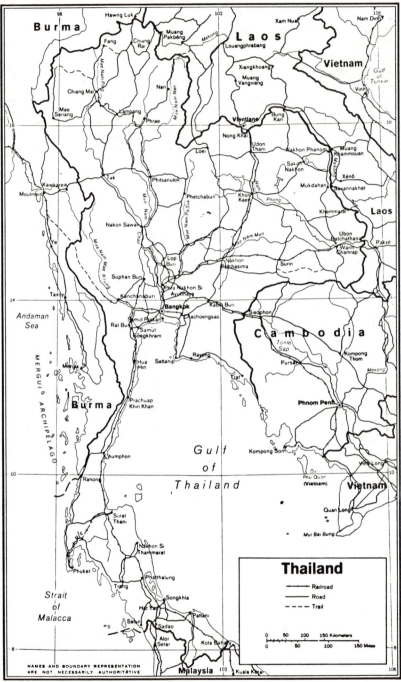

**Thailand**

⊢—⊣—⊢ Railroad

——— Road

- - - - Trail

| 0 | 50 | 100 | 150 Kilometers |
| 0 | | 50 | 100 | 150 Miles |

NAMES AND BOUNDARY REPRESENTATION
ARE NOT NECESSARILY AUTHORITATIVE

Base 502265 6-74

# 3
# People's War in Thailand

*William R. Heaton*
*Richard MacLeod*

For several years the Communist Party of Thailand (CPT) has confidently predicted victory in its armed struggle against the Thai government. In spite of these predictions the insurgency itself has been undergoing rapid transformation stimulated by changes in the international situation and the domestic political environment. A recent broadcast by the clandestine Voice of People's Thailand (VOPT), noting the changes which were occurring, broadcast its hope and prospectus for the future as follows:

> We—the people—must closely unite, expand the patriotic and democracy-loving forces, consolidate our forces to attack the enemy, scientifically study and analyze the fast-developing situation with the interest of the people at heart, expose all tricks concocted by the reactionary ruling class, continue to wage a resolute struggle for legitimate rights and interests and for national independence and democracy, energetically score new achievements for the revolution, diversify the struggle, grasp greater victories, advance the struggle a big step forward and hasten the day for the liberation of the Thai people. Let us try harder![1]

The Thai insurgency is a revolutionary movement committed to armed struggle. It is based on the Maoist "people's war" concept and envisions fundamental alteration in the political structures and values of Thailand. It is precisely this vision of revolutionary change that offers both prospects and problems for the future. On the one hand, the insurgents have been able to escalate the level of violence in the Thai countryside and to increase harassment and embarassment of the central government. On the other hand, the changed situation between Vietnam and China has altered the amount of external support the insurgents receive. Furthermore, the present government of Thailand appears to be making a somewhat more realistic appraisal of the insurgency.

The continuation of the Thai insurgency over a long period of time and the inability of the government to defeat it, in spite of a host of counterinsurgency efforts, entitle it to further examination. A complete and thorough assessment of the Thai insurgency can be made by utilizing the variables presented in Chapter 1.

## Environment

Four separate areas of insurgency exist in Thailand: North, Northeast, Central and South. While there has been an effort to link these by the CPT, each enjoys considerable autonomy, according to reliable observers.

The insurgency has its greatest stronghold in the Northeast, where a near classic insurgency environment prevails. There, about 11 million people, roughly 25 percent of Thailand's 44 million, live in fifteen provinces comprising the Korat Plateau which extends to the borders of Laos and Cambodia. The great majority of these people are ethnically akin to the Lao and speak a distinct dialect of Thai known as Isan. The area is poor economically, having few natural resources, poor soil, inadequate moisture, and a poor drainage system. More than 90 percent of the people are engaged in subsistence farming; in the early 1970s the average per capita annual income was about $42 compared with the national average of about $100. Moreover, the income of more than 75 percent of the people of the Northeast was only about $15–$30 annually, indicating broad disparity between the more wealthy landholders and the peasant farmers. The birthrate has been very high – about 3.5 percent annually – but the population is slightly less dense than the national average. Most people live in relatively isolated hamlets and villages dispersed throughout the countryside. Laos and Cambodia from time to time have both claimed portions of Northeast Thailand. The relative poverty, geographic isolation from Bangkok, proximity to Laos, Cambodia, and Vietnam (countries from which the insurgents derive support), and ethnic and social diversity from the remainder of Thailand have contributed to the development of insurgency in the Northeast.[2]

North Thailand is also an ideal area for insurgency. Bordering on Northern Laos and on Burma, the North is inhabited by several hundred thousand tribesmen (primarily Meo and Yao) who have little allegiance to the government in Bangkok. The provinces of Chiangrai, Nan, and Uttaradit are mountainous with heavy jungle. There are few roads and only limited communications in many areas. The Meo are slash-and-burn agriculturalists and many grow opium as a cash crop. The antiinsurgent campaign in the North has a distinctively anti-Meo flavor owing to traditional Thai-Meo animosity. For example, a 1969 survey in Bangkok asking how to deal with the "red Meo" drew responses ranging from "kill them all" to "use napalm . . . but don't set the forest afire, it is bad for the economy."[3] Indiscriminate bombing of Meo villages by the Thai military has sometimes contributed to the expansion of the insurgency in this region.[4]

The insurgency in Central Thailand has also drawn support from Meo tribesmen. The three provinces of Pitsanulok, Loei, and Petchabun, which are affected by the insurgency, are not as remote from Bangkok as the North and the Northeast regions; however, they are plagued by similar problems. The area lacks sufficient water and has poor soil, with the attendant serious agricultural problems. As in other areas, the Thai government, in spite of a host of land reform programs, has done little to solve problems of tenancy, taxes, and other matters close to the needs of the villagers. Many people in this area feel that the government has neglected education and other services. Also, previous government counterinsurgency programs have been regarded by the populace as little more than official banditry.[5]

Perhaps the most complicated and intense area of insurgency is in the provinces bordering Malaysia in the South, where some 85 percent of Thailand's nearly 2 million Malay-Muslims live. The terrain, social and economic diversity, and other cleavages characteristic of this region also favor insurgency. Yet is it difficult to discern which of the many groups offering resistance to the government are true insurgents and which are merely bandit gangs. There are Muslim separatist groups, groups linked with the Malaysian Communist party, Thai communists, and bandits, to mention a few. The situation is not helped by the tendency of Thai authorities to lump them all as "communist terrorists." While the Thai Communist party often claims credit for the activities of these various groups, there is some question as to how many actually operate under communist auspices.

All of the insurgent areas are geographically separate and fairly remote from the Bangkok area, the heartland of Thai society. Social cleavages stemming from diverse ethnicity, religion, customs, and language dialects have prevented full integration of the Thai polity. The insurgent areas generally are characterized by a lower standard of living and occasionally a different means of livelihood than that of most Thais. The areas tend to be poorly penetrated by roads or other forms of transportation and communications are sparse. They are frequently characterized by jungle or mountainous terrain. Furthermore, particularly in the North and the Northeast, they border on countries from which external support for insurgency is derived.

At the same time, there are some environmental characteristics that pose serious problems for the Thai insurgents. The Thai people, apart from the small minority of Meos and other tribal peoples, have a fairly strong sense of national identity, reinforced by loyalty to the monarchy and the Buddhist religion. The Thai people generally take great pride in their history, particularly in the fact that they were never colonized by a Western colonial power. The concept of independence from foreign influence is emphasized in the education system, which is extensive, even in remote rural areas. The Thai monarchy reinforces the feeling of nationhood by frequent visits into the rural areas by members of the royal family. Buddhist monks are usually the leaders in the villages; many are educated and have a strong distaste for the insurgency.

Consequently, most of the Thai people view the insurgency as a threat to their values and way of life. Insurgents are felt to have abandoned their country and religion. Insurgents are also viewed as being foreigners or outsiders, people who are not really Thais, who affect only the remote areas. In essence, the insurgents have a serious image problem with the vast majority of the Thai people. The environment has been an asset to the insurgency in terms of its remoteness from the central government, yet it has been a liability in terms of the ability of the insurgents to appeal to the overwhelming majority of the Thai people.

## Organization

The *scope* of the insurgency has remained small. Perhaps only 100,000 of Thailand's nearly 45 million people are controlled by the insurgency and only about 10,000 are "hard-core" guerrillas. It has been reported that fewer people are killed by insurgents annually than are murdered in the course of ordinary criminal activity. Nevertheless, the insurgency has grown steadily. The number of armed insurgents climbed from an estimated total of about 1,200 in 1965, to about 5,000 in 1973, to nearly 10,000 in 1980.[6] Initially, the guerrilla units numbered about 20 persons, but in recent years the size has been expanded. A unit usually numbers 40–50 but may include as many as 300 guerrillas. Military operations have escalated from terrorist attacks on isolated police stations and rural defense units to assaults on regular army units and border police, village raids, and even a train robbery in 1978.

The insurgency has become more complex as it has progressed. The CPT was formed by a handful of intellectuals in 1935. It was not a significant voice in Thai politics because it was persistently suppressed by the government, numbering only about 200 in 1950 and not many more than that in the late 1950s and early 1960s, when most of the leaders were in jail or underground.

In 1962 the Thai Communist party received ideological direction and considerable support from China. In March 1962 the clandestine VOPT, broadcasting from South China, began proclaiming the organization of a rurally based "people's war." In that same month Thai Foreign Minister Thanat Khoman and U.S. Secretary of State Dean Rusk issued a joint statement in which the United States pledged to assist Thailand in defending against communist subversion and aggression. In May, because of the political situation in Laos, President Kennedy dispatched 5,000 U.S. troops to Thailand. Over a period of years, owing to the Vietnam conflict, the number of U.S. forces in Thailand was gradually increased.

Prior to U.S. involvement, anticolonialism had not been a major force in Thai nationalism, because an outside power had never been able to dominate Thailand the way other Southeast Asian countries had been dominated. The highly visible U.S. military presence, continuing until 1973, provided ample grist for the mill of insurgent propaganda. Anti-U.S. propaganda by the insurgents, in turn, induced U.S. support for the Thai counterinsurgency.

During the U.S. buildup in Thailand, China became increasingly committed to the diplomacy of encouraging and supporting "people's wars of liberation" in areas where the circumstances seemed appropriate and where it might serve China's national interests. Since Thailand was cooperating with the United States in the escalation of the Vietnam War, China's support for the Thai insurgency was in part a response to this escalation.[7] By 1964, with Chinese support, the insurgency had grown sufficiently strong to launch attacks along the American-built friendship highway linking Bangkok with the Northeast.

On 1 October 1964, China's national day, the New China News Agency published a message of greeting from the CPT calling for the formation of a "united front" in Thailand against "U.S. imperialism and its lackeys."[8] A month later Beijing announced the formation of a Thailand Independence Movement (TIM). On 1 January 1965 China further announced the formation of the Thai Patriotic Front (TPF), coinciding with a reported remark by Chinese Foreign Minister Chen Yi that he looked forward to the development of a "people's war" in Thailand later that year. Indeed, after a skirmish with government forces in August, the insurgents announced through VOPT that the era of armed struggle had begun. In November the TIM merged into the TPF to formally consolidate the United Front.[9]

Upon its inaugural the TPF published a six-point program calling for overthrowing the Thai government and getting rid of U.S. imperialism, cooperating with "international peace forces," developing the national economy, improving the standard of living, land reform, eliminating corruption, and developing health, education, and social welfare. These elements have continued to be a central theme of insurgent propaganda up to the present.

As far as complexity was concerned, the Thai Patriotic Front was similar to the National Liberation Front of South Vietnam. At inception it was a coalition of various groups united on the basis of the six-point program. Among groups said to be attached to the front were the Thai Patriotic Workers, the Thai Patriotic Teachers and Professors, the Thai Lawyers, Thai Patriotic Youth Organization, Self-Liberated Farmers and Planters Association, Poor People's Group, Southern Rubber Plantation Workers, and the Thai Monk's

Group. These organizations received much attention in initial propaganda, but they were hardly more than paper organizations for the most part. In recent years they have not been mentioned.

The CPT evolved from a position as a theoretical coequal member of the front in 1965 to its leader and primary element in 1968. Between 1968 and 1977 the CPT claimed to be the leading force; the TPF has not been mentioned since the early 1970s. During this decade, the CPT and its military arm, the Thai People's Liberation Armed Forces, received nearly all the attention of insurgent propaganda. In 1977, because of the change in Thailand's internal situation, there was a renewed emphasis on the United Front.

In 1973 the military rulers of Thailand were forced out after a series of student demonstrations. Between 1973 and 1976 a series of shaky civilian coalitions tried to rule Thailand. Civilian rule was ended after a series of bloody confrontations in October 1976 and the military again seized control. A subsequent military coup, led by Kriangsak Chamanan in October 1977, brought the present government to power. During the "October 6" incident of 1976 about 2,000 university students defected to the insurgency after the government suppressed demonstrations at several universities, most notably Thammasat University. The insurgency subsequently announced the formation of a new united front, called the Committee for Coordinating Patriotic and Democracy Loving Forces, in September 1977.[10] The committee consists of elements of such government suppressed organizations as the National Student Center of Thailand, the Socialist party of Thailand, the Socialist Front party and the CPT. Various other groups have been identified as participants in the committee. In an important departure from past practice, leaders of the movement are identified in insurgent propaganda. The leader of the CPT is identified as Mit Samanan and the leader of the committee is identified as Bunyen Wothong. Little is known about these two leaders; however, other important figures have had their backgrounds detailed in insurgency propaganda. According to David Morell and Chai-anan Samudavanija, the insurgency gained several experienced and influential Thai leaders after the 1976 coup. While some of these have subsequently defected back to the government, they have unquestionably improved insurgent leadership.[11]

Since the formation of the committee, the CPT theoretically has once again opted for coequal membership, and other groups are also propagandized in the insurgent media. Probably because of the influence of the students, more emphasis has been placed on circulating publications, promoting culture and drama, and assisting the farmers. While armed struggle continues to receive primary emphasis, the other organizational activities have received more attention than in the past.

Between 1964 and 1965 training camps for political and military cadres were established in North Vietnam and Laos. Some cadres received additional training in China, notably the members of the CPT Politburo, who are ethnic Chinese. People recruited for the insurgency were brought to the camps for training, then infiltrated back into Thailand. Gradually, the insurgency was able to expand base areas, develop political infrastructure, and recruit more insurgents, particularly in the Northeast.

The insurgents initially sought assimilation into village life by assisting with the rice harvest, road and dike repair, and other village work as evidence of friendship. They provided or brought their own food, in sharp contrast to the government officials, who, on their occasional visits to the village, often expected the villagers to feed them. In some areas the insurgents took a census, sometimes displaying their weapons in a kind of subtle coercion, and determined the location of residences of village chiefs, teachers, and other government officials.

Another tactic now frequently employed by the insurgents is to enter a contested area at night and propagandize the villagers about the evils of the "corrupt warlords" in Bangkok who are manipulated by U.S. imperialism. Villagers are told that the insurgents will remove the yoke of government oppression and corruption and will improve the people's livelihood. At times, the insurgents have executed government officials; more often, they attack a police or militia station. By 1974, some schools constructed under auspices of the government in border areas were attacked with such frequency that log and earth revetments were built nearby to afford protection to the students and teachers. Such demonstrations of potency by the insurgents were designed to pressure villagers to identify with the revolutionaries.

When the insurgency has achieved control in an area, the party and other front organizations seek to consolidate political control by linking the newly "liberated" area with other base areas. New cadres are then recruited and trained to provide administration. At one time or another the government has declared that nearly half of Thailand's provinces have been "communist infested," but the insurgency has not been able to expand the areas under its control significantly in the past several years; in some areas it has even lost ground. Nevertheless, in the long-held base areas it has become organizationally more complex and has solidified its position.[12]

Unified direction of insurgent military activity was sought with the establishment of the Supreme Command of the Thai People's Liberation Armed Forces in 1969. The doctrine of the insurgent military forces borrows heavily from Mao Zedong's military writings; the armed forces have even adopted the "three rules" and the "eight points" of the Chinese People's Liberation Army.

The insurgency has experienced factionalism. In spite of the establishment of overarching organs such as the "committee" or the supreme command, there is persuasive evidence that local insurgent bases have considerable flexibility in their operations and some authorities suspect that many insurgent units operate completely independently. The difficulty of coordinating a geographically diverse situation has been a limiting factor on organizational cohesiveness. Also, there have been ideological deviations. A history of the revolutionary struggle broadcast over VOPT in 1977 revealed considerable conflict within the insurgent leadership over strategy and tactics. The defection of large numbers of students to the insurgency in 1976 also produced organization pressures; some of these students have subsequently defected back to the government, bringing stories of intrigue and disunity in the insurgent movement. The conflict among Vietnam, Cambodia, and China resulted in a sharp slowdown of insurgent activity, indicating that a factional conflict over external support was affecting the organization.

In spite of these difficulties, the insurgency has developed an infrastructure in the base areas. Leaders and cadres have gained experience in military affairs and political administration. The continuing ability of the insurgency to survive, in spite of government counterinsurgency and the factors noted above, testifies to its organizational competence.

## Popular Support

The framework identifies two general categories of support for an insurgency: active and passive. Active support comes from the central core of political and military cadres, many of whom have received training outside Thailand. The active supporters of the Thai insurgency constitute part of a heritage rooted in the Chinese communist revolution and continuing with other communist-inspired insurgencies in Southeast Asia. Basically, this strategy emphasizes the development of a highly motivated leadership elite linked to the peasantry by means of an elaborate political infrastructure. Mass organizations, led by the revolutionary party, are used to mobilize peasant support. This strategy requires at least initial passive support among the people until they can be mobilized to become more actively involved through positive identification with the esoteric or ideological precepts of the leaders. The "fish-ocean" metaphor of Mao (an insurgent is like a fish swimming in the ocean of the people) is highly relevant to the Thai situation; the entire strategy hinges on a highly motivated, dedicated, and persistent elite.

Charismatic leadership plays little, if any, role in the insurgency. Little is known about most of the leaders of the insurgency and personalities are not played up in insurgent propaganda. Rather, mobilization is based on strong organizational linkages within the infrastructure in the base areas. At the center of the network, as discussed in the section on organization, is the communist party, which provides leadership, recruitment, and training for those who join the insurgents.

Villager support for the insurgency is mostly passive. The insurgents use a mixture of persuasion and coercion in their approach to the peasants; the response is usually indifference or fear. When insurgents enter a village peasants usually give aid because they are afraid; in some instances there are economic benefits in selling rice and supplies to the insurgents.[13] In areas where the insurgency has been established longer and there has been a greater degree of mobilization among the peasants, the level of active support is higher. In areas contested by the insurgents and the government there is constant battle by the insurgents to increase support, usually through the mixture of propaganda and terror noted above.

Insurgent propaganda in the villages is simple and largely exoteric. It stresses concrete grievances such as government corruption. For example, a recent insurgent broadcast entitled "Rural Development Infiltrated by Imperialists" stated that the money committed by the government for agricultural development in rural areas was really being used to enrich government officials and to fatten large U.S. and Thai corporations.[14] Another common theme is the claim that the authorities in Bangkok are really creatures of U.S. imperialism.

Typical of insurgent propaganda is the ten-point statement of policy issued by the CPT in 1969 and modified slightly by the "committee" in 1978 as enunciated in a series of broadcasts over VOPT in 1978–79. In abbreviated form these points are:

1. Establish a "democratic" government representative of the people and rid of the influence of the United States
2. Abolish corruption and all laws detrimental to the people; establish freedom of speech, assembly, publication, religion, and other basic human rights
3. Conduct land reform and punish counterrevolutionaries and traitors
4. Abolish all unjust treaties; unite with all countries that support the Thai revolution; maintain friendly foreign relations with various countries on the basis of sovereignty and equality
5. Grant autonomy to minority nationalities; outlaw discrimination and improve health, education, and welfare
6. Carry out an agrarian revolution and raise the standard of living for peasants
7. Promote and develop state and private industry and commerce
8. Establish equal rights for women and promote loyalty and democracy in the collective unit
9. Improve wages for industrial workers, workers security, and other benefits
10. Rid the country of harmful cultural influences; promote culture, art, and science

Another common theme of insurgent propaganda is the inevitability of revolution. The government, captured by corruption, warlordism, and U.S.

imperialism, is doomed to collapse. According to one editorial:

> The Kriangsak government—representing big landlords, big capitalists and
> lackeys of US imperialism—became increasingly confused, isolated, divided and
> unstable. It followed a two-faced counterrevolutionary policy, that is, it
> simultaneously carried out suppression and deception activities with the hope of
> containing and destroying the revolutionary forces. However, it did not suc-
> ceed; it only suffered more shameful defeats.[15]

Insurgent propaganda seeks to present the image of increasing potency. The
insurgents are said to be gradually expanding the people's war, creating new
base areas and guerrilla zones, killing more of the enemy, and inflicting greater
defeats on the government. The insurgents claimed to have inflicted 2,600
government casualties in 1976, 3,400 in 1977, and 3,900 in 1978. They also
claim increased damage to government installations and equipment. In 1973
the insurgents claimed there were 80 armed clashes between the government
and the insurgents; in 1978 they claimed there were 930.[16]

Insurgent exoteric appeals are linked with concrete grievances. If production is bad it is the fault of the government and the U.S. imperialists. If there
are shortages of educational opportunity, the reasons are similar. Exoteric appeals seek to produce hostility to the government while demonstrating that
the insurgents are capable of solving problems and eliminating grievances.
While this propaganda may not create immediate support for the insurgents,
it can frustrate government activities. For example, in one rural area in the
Northeast the pump for a U.S.–designed irrigation system that had greatly
improved rice yields failed. Government officials—bogged down in bureaucracy—failed to help repair or replace the pump, leading to the failure of the
new rice crop. Shortly thereafter, insurgents entered the area and propagandized the villagers; the villagers did not report the presence of the insurgents
to the government until well after the insurgents had already departed.

Government corruption often plays into the hands of the insurgents. Petty
corruption at the local level, as well as at higher levels, is common in Thailand. The secretary general of the anti-corruption committee, Suthi Akatroek,
estimated that about one-third of the national budget found its way into the
pockets of unscrupulous government officials each year.[17] At the local level
district officials often require payment of a few *baht* (1 *baht* = $.05) for routine
services such as supplying forms to a villager who is applying to cut trees on
his own property, then turn around and charge more for a favorable decision
once the forms have been completed.

In an unusual development in early 1978, insurgent propaganda attacked
the Thai royal family for the first time. The queen was described as a
"feudalist" and the king as an "archfeudalist."[18] Given the overwhelming
popularity of the royal family with the Thai people, this was probably a

mistake. Indeed, in tacit recognition of this reality, the king and queen were not subsequently mentioned in insurgent propaganda. The insurgency has also avoided direct criticism of Buddhism. While Buddhism is antithetical to the insurgent program, the insurgents limit their condemnation to the corruption of religion by the monks, who allegedly manipulate religion for social position and economic and political power. One insurgent broadcast, for example, observed that the slogan "nation, religion, monarchy," long used as the basis of antiinsurgent propaganda by village monks, "could no longer disguise" the inherent corruptness of the clergy.[19]

In addition to exoteric appeals, coercion and terrorism are utilized in an effort to undermine confidence in the government and to demonstrate insurgent potency. As noted earlier, the insurgents attack isolated outposts, kidnap and execute officials, and stage robberies. The attacks on outmanned outposts are proclaimed victories and held as evidence that the insurgency has momentum. Some peasants are induced to give passive support to the insurgency through fear of reprisals. Typical is the statement of one Northeast villager: "We are afraid to go to our fields far from the village. The jungle soldiers come and talk to us. They say they are good, not to be afraid. But we are afraid they will kill us."[20]

Some recent examples of how the insurgents operate may be seen in two assaults on government outposts in June 1978, one in the North and the other in the South. In both instances, insurgent forces numbering about 300 attacked during the predawn hours. In the South, the insurgents attacked the outpost at Ban Thayung village in Phatthalung Province. Of 80 border patrol police the insurgents killed 14 and wounded 28. The army was called in to recapture the village, but government forces were repeatedly forced to retreat until they launched heavy air strikes. During the period the insurgents held the village they levied a tax of 30 *baht* per person, payable in cash, rice, or rubber.[21] In the North, in Chiang Rai Province, the insurgents killed five officials and wounded 12. The insurgents were repelled only after helicopter gunships inflicted heavy damage on the village.

Another incident that occurred in the South in late 1978 was a train robbery by the insurgents. Guerrillas held up the Bangkok–Nakhon Si Thammarat rapid train at the Phruphi station in Surat Thani Province, killing the senior police guard and making off with a 1.2 million *baht* government payroll. While some of the 300 insurgents were making off with the loot, the remainder delivered political lectures to the passengers for about half an hour before allowing the train to continue. The insurgents were able to get away before government forces could respond.[22]

While government efforts to use military force to dislodge the insurgents are usually well intentioned, sometimes the government blunders. One of the best examples occurred in the village of Ban Na Sai in Nong Khai Province in the Northeast. In January 1974, 59 insurgents attacked the village defense post and burned it, killing one of the 30 defenders; the remainder fled. For the next few days, as best as can be determined, the insurgents engaged the villagers in political discussions and asked for food and supplies. After several days about 190 government troops surrounded the village. What happened next is uncertain. The government forces claimed that they received hostile fire from the village, whereupon they took countermeasures. Villagers, however, claimed that government forces opened fire without provocation. In the ensuing action, the government forces burned 130 huts and killed four villagers (authorities asserted they were guerrillas, villagers claim otherwise). The villagers claimed before a special investigatory commission that the soldiers entered the huts, stole everything of value, and then burned them. The soldiers said they were burning the village because the people were "communist sympathizers."[23]

Such indiscriminate use of force by the government, including the use of napalm on Meo villages and the use of bombing, airstrikes, and helicopter gunships, does little to destroy the insurgents and indeed most often has the opposite effect. The successful provocation of government counterterror lends credibility to propaganda regarding the hostile and violent nature of the reactionary authorities. Moreover, the uncertainties created for peasants in contested areas helps to undermine government control.

Through the mixture of exoteric appeals and demonstrations of potency by terror the insurgency has been able to increase its size only modestly, approximately 6–8 percent annually. This gradual increase suggests that insurgent tactics are partially effective, although given the lackadaisical approach to counterinsurgency by the government (covered in greater detail in the section on government response), they might even be more effective if they could overcome some traditional barriers. As noted in the section on environment, there are major impediments in the ability of the insurgents to garner popular support because of the stability and resilience of traditional Thai culture, and the strong sense of Thai nationalism. The insurgents have yet to effectively combat the image that they are interlopers – intruders who have abandoned their heritage. Unless they can overcome this image, the insurgents will not be able to make major advances in increasing popular support.

### External Support

The North and Northeast insurgent areas border on territories in which support for the insurgency can be obtained. Since the creation of communist governments in Cambodia and Laos in 1975 it has been somewhat easier for the insurgents to receive material support. With North Vietnam in control of Cambodia such support is certainly facilitated. The insurgents have received sanctuaries and training bases in North Vietnam, Laos, and Cambodia and have received a variety of weapons from these countries and China. Prior to the Vietnamese invasion of Cambodia in 1978–79, Cambodian forces frequently joined with Thai insurgents to make cross-border raids on Thai villages. After the defeat of the Pol Pot regime these raids subsided, at least temporarily.[24]

Of key significance is China's role. A number of scholars have demonstrated that the escalation of insurgency in Thailand was directly related to Chinese foreign policy considerations.[25] For a time the leadership of the insurgency was headquartered in Beijing and the Chinese gave both moral and material support to the insurgent cause. Through VOPT, which broadcasts from South China, the CPT supported China's ideological position in the Sino-Soviet dispute and acknowledged its reliance on Mao's thought.

Strong Chinese support continued during the Cultural Revolution of 1966–69, but by 1973 the Chinese were beginning to dampen their support. Zhou Enlai expressed a desire to normalize relations with Thailand on the basis of the Five Principles of Peaceful Coexistence and shortly thereafter China and Thailand normalized diplomatic relations. State-to-state relations between China and Thailand have gradually improved since then.

China now takes the position that it wants to have good relations with Thailand – yet without renouncing support for the insurgency. The Chinese consider government relations to be one thing, and communist party relations quite another. Just prior to a goodwill visit to Thailand in November 1978, Deng Xiaoping stated that China would not renounce the Thai insurgency even though it sought better relations with Thailand.[26] The Kriangsak government declared that the insurgency was an internal Thai problem which would not affect Thailand's relations with China. Kriangsak took the view that if Thailand could solve the root environmental problems that have led to the development of the insurgency there would be nothing for China to support.

The situation is made more complicated by the role of Vietnam. After the unification of Vietnam, the Vietnamese government continued to provide political and material support to the Thai insurgency. Thailand and Vietnam announced the establishment of diplomatic relations on 6 August 1976 on the basis of four principles including "respect for each other's independence, sovereignty and territorial integrity, nonaggression, noninterference in each other's internal affairs, equality, mutual benefit and peaceful coexistence."[27] When the Thai foreign minister raised the issue of Vietnamese support for the insurgency he was reassured that Vietnam did not intend to interfere in Thailand's internal affairs.[28] Yet, in an editorial hailing the establishment of diplomatic relations with Thailand, *Nhan Dhan* (the official Vietnamese news agency) stated that "the Vietnamese people fully support the Thai people's just struggle and are resolved to contribute to the common revolutionary cause of the peoples of Southeast Asia."[29]

Vietnamese Prime Minister Pham Van Dong made a goodwill visit to Thailand in October 1978 and told Thai officials that Vietnam would not support the insurgents. Deng Xiaoping warned Thai reporters to be wary of Dong's promise since it amounted to no more than clever semantic duplicity.[30] Communist parties do not refer to legitimate struggles for liberation as "insurgencies." Since the invasion of Cambodia by Vietnam, Thai authorities are increasingly concerned about Vietnamese support for the Thai communists.[31] Thailand is now in the somewhat paradoxical situation of enjoying good diplomatic relations with a country that has refused to renounce the insurgency (China) but poor diplomatic relations with one that has (Vietnam).

The falling out between Vietnam and China has affected the unity of the insurgency. In the past China was the primary supporter of the insurgents with other countries such as Vietnam providing sanctuaries. After the split between China and Vietnam, the Laotian government, which supports Vietnam, concluded an agreement with the Thai government to allow hot pursuit of Chinese-supported insurgents. Laos has also tried to deprive the Thai insurgents of sanctuaries. Cambodia has also largely come under Vietnamese control. An army that supports the former regime of Pol Pot is conducting a limited civil war in Cambodia, sometimes using Thai border areas as sanctuaries. The Thais do not particularly approve of the Pol Pot insurgents, since they earlier collaborated with the Thai insurgents; however, Thailand is more concerned with the North Vietnamese presence near the Thai-Cambodian border. Thus, the Thais are placed in the paradoxical situation of granting some limited support to an insurgency that in the past has abetted the Thai insurgency. For a time VOPT avoided denunciations of North Vietnam and Laos, but by mid-1979 it began wholesale denunciations of both countries. Then, VOPT suddenly stopped broadcasting in the late summer of 1979, probably an indication of improved relations between China and Thailand. The complicated international situation combined with the defection of students to the insurgency in 1976 bringing new blood into the insurgent movement has apparently resulted in a split in the insurgency. Some analysts believe that the insurgency is now divided into pro-Chinese and pro-Vietnamese factions.[32]

In recent years there has been a resurgence of the Southern insurgents near the Malaysian border. While the situation in the South is unclear, given the diversity of the various antigovernment movements, some insurgents claim to be linked with the communists. These insurgents have received support from the Malaysian Communist party and operate back and forth across the borders of Thailand and Malaysia. The Thai and Malaysian authorities have a variety of cooperative agreements concerning hot pursuit for coping with the insurgents, but these have been relatively ineffective.

External support has been a vital factor in starting and maintaining the in-surgency, but it is now a mixed blessing. The proximity of other communist movements has facilitated moral and material support in the past. However, division among these countries is now affecting the unity of the Thai in-surgents. Resolving the demands brought about by the need for external sup-port while maintaining unity will be a most serious challenge for the Thai in-surgents in the future.

## Government Response[33]

On the surface it would appear that the Thai political situation presents an ideal climate for revolution. The government has been unstable (there have been six governments since 1973), there are serious problems with balance of trade deficits and inflation, and there has been a serious drought combined with a decrease in rice production and an increase in peasant indebtedness. Added to these problems have been strikes, demonstrations, and student unrest. In spite of these difficulties for the government, the insurgency has grown only modestly, and with the exception of a small area of central Thailand, growth has only occurred in areas immediately adjacent to sources of external support.

The failure of the insurgency can be attributed, in large part, to the political culture of the Thai people. In spite of frequent changes in government, the Thais have maintained their strong sense of national and cultural identity. As previously noted in the section on environment, they are proud that Thailand never became a colony of a foreign power and have demonstrated strong loyalty to the monarchy and to Buddhism. Village life centers around the *Wat* (Buddhist temple) and the monks exert a powerful influence on the daily lives of the villagers. The monks are usually the best educated people in the rural areas and their strong opposition to communism has broad accep-tance among the people.

The royal family has greatly aided the counterinsurgency effort. The king and queen frequently visit the rural areas to participate in ceremonies and festivals which enhance support for the monarchy. The queen mother (mother of the king) is widely revered as the sponsor of rural development projects. Not only does she travel in the border areas frequently to dedicate schools, government-sponsored development projects, and so on, she also publicly recognizes government officials and private businessmen who sup-port rural development. She personally distributes booklets on Buddhism which are highly prized by villagers. Gold and silver medallions depicting the king are also treasured. Her efforts have stimulated religious growth, rural education, and public health—particularly in the border areas—and she is highly popular.

In addition to cultural and religious objections to the insurgency, most Thais feel that the insurgents are geographically isolated and ethnically distinct. Many Thais feel that the insurgents are not really Thais, but people who are ethnically and culturally akin to the Meo, Lao, or Vietnamese. Many students who went over to the insurgency in 1976 subsequently defected back to the government because they found conditions oppressive in the jungle as compared to the relative ease and quality of life in Bangkok and other urban centers.[34] In short, once the original thrill of revolutionary fervor waned, the students were anxious to get back to civilization.

Thus, "nation, religion, monarchy" are the primary forces impeding the development of the insurgency. Beyond this, the government response has been a host of slogans and programs, with mixed results. The counterinsurgency programs have tended to emphasize a military response rather than a well-coordinated program of civic action designed to address the root problems in the areas where the insurgency has gained ground.

Prior to 1965 the Thai government had a variety of rural programs such as "happiness to the rural population" or "village self-help" that consisted more often than not of halfhearted and disorganized measures to improve the quality of village life. After the insurgency launched its "people's war" phase in 1965 the Thai government announced the formation of the Communist Suppression Operations Command, later renamed the Internal Security Operations Command (ISOC), to coordinate military and civic action against the insurgency.

Nearly all critics of Thailand's counterinsurgency effort agree that lack of cooperation among agencies and failure to coordinate programs is a major problem. The ISOC, though it has a broad grant of authority, has not been able to overcome the rivalry of the Interior Ministry, the Defense Ministry, and the other government agencies involved. The border patrol police, the army, and the militia each have a vertical chain of command originating in Bangkok and often fail to cooperate at the lowest levels. The central government wants to prevent the establishment of a geographic power base for any one official so it encourages separation and diversity; at the same time this segregation of authority and responsibility denigrates effective coordination of counterinsurgency and development programs. The village security and development units and the volunteer defense corps, under control of the provincial governors, are supposed to provide security in the villages, but they are usually poorly trained, ill-equipped, and ineffectual against the insurgents.

The government has repeatedly called for a reorganization and renewal of counterinsurgency, most recently when Kriangsak pledged to "exterminate" the insurgents in 1978. The Kriangsak government has proposed a variety of rural aid and development programs, but whether these will be any more effective than their predecessors remains an open question. One positive step taken by the Kriangsak government to enhance its political support was to

release students imprisoned after the October 1976 disturbances. This sig-
naled the intention of the government to alleviate conditions that resulted in
the defection of students, intellectuals, and even some members of parliament
to the insurgency.[35]

There have been two major problems facing the government. First has been
instability at the highest levels. In 1973 the Thanom-Praphet military government collapsed in the wake of student riots. During a three-year interlude
several civilian governments were formed and there were two elections. The
large number of political parties and constantly changing coalitions precluded
firm direction at the top. Military rule was restored in October 1976, but
another coup in 1977 again changed the leadership. Although the current
government of Kraingsak gives indications of being more stable than its
predecessors, the years of bickering and infighting at the highest levels have
prevented the establishment of a coherent counterinsurgency program.

The second problem, noted previously, has been corruption, which has
been just as pervasive in the various counterinsurgency programs as in other
government functions. Much of the money designed for rural development
has found its way into the pockets of officials. What Western civilization calls
"graft" is accepted to some degree in Thai society; nevertheless, the public
complaints of various directors of the ISOC that dishonesty, corruption, and
bad behavior on the part of officials have undermined these programs indicates that loose fund accounting plus loose supervision of widely scattered
counterinsurgency officials fosters blatant dishonesty.

Another detrimental factor has been the stress placed on military action
rather than socioeconomic development and political reform. The military
response has frequently been erratic as well, cases of military overreaction
having been noted earlier. If the military overreacts in some cases, it seems to
underreact in others. Villagers along the Cambodian border have complained
of military inaction after incursions of Khmer and Thai insurgents. Certainly,
the Thai military seems to continue to place more faith in bombs and napalm
than it does in civic action.[36] That the present government acquiesces in this
approach was dramatically emphasized by the type of military requests
Kriangsak made to President Carter in his visit to Washington in 1979.

Prior to the pullout of U.S. forces in 1976, the United States provided most
of the advice and much of the funding for Thailand's counterinsurgency effort. Between 1950 and 1969 the United States gave about $1 billion in aid to
Thailand—about 60 percent in military aid and 40 percent in economic aid.
The quantity of aid greatly increased during the early 1970s but then tapered
off after the withdrawal of U.S. forces from Indochina. In 1979 the United
States planned to extend Thailand $24 million in foreign military sales credits;
this was increased by $6 million after the Vietnamese invasion of Cambodia.
Some observers anticipated that the United States might increase aid beyond
this figure.[37] Thailand has also sought bank loans to support economic

development programs, some of which have a counterinsurgency application, in recent years.[38]

Besides aid, U.S. advice also provided much of the incentive for Thai counterinsurgency during the 1960s and into the 1970s and 1980s. The Thai counterinsurgency has been heavily influenced by the U.S. experience in Vietnam, but since the withdrawal of U.S. forces the Thais have apparently recognized that they must become more self-reliant if they are to defeat the insurgents. Perhaps it is this awareness that bodes best for the future of Thai counterinsurgency.

Also not to be underestimated is the gradual change that is occurring with the return to Thailand of large numbers of foreign-educated specialists in engineering, medicine, public health, and public administration. An extensive program with the United States and other countries such as the Philippines has produced thousands of new civil servants. Many of these have shown genuine altruistic and energetic qualities as they are spread throughout the bureaucracy. They face great challenges in coping with the inadequacies of the long-established bureaucratic system (often characterized by indolence as well as corruption), with the lack of coherent planning and coordination, and with underfunding, but there are numerous examples of honest and innovative effort. A district education officer in one area, a public health officer in another—each displaying determined and innovative leadership—stimulate many others to greater effort. For example, one official responsible for an artificial insemination program for cattle in the Northeast achieved great respect from the villagers for his dedication in assisting farmers.

There are also more frequent examples of Western-style service organizations such as Rotary International, Lions clubs, and so on becoming active on a modest scale in communities near insurgent areas. For example, the Rotary Club of Ubon in Northeast Thailand sponsors rural health care visits to villages twice weekly by district health officials and medical teams from the Ubon hospital. Club members accompany the teams to provide supplies and to assist. This type of activity is not yet widespread, but is evidence of increased local concern with the problems upon which the insurgency gains support. The personal and civic pride of such local groups helps to reinforce the sense of cultural solidarity that characterizes the Thai people.

Should the Bangkok authorities successfully implement a reasonably well-funded program of small, low-scale rural assistance projects aimed at gradual improvement of village life without radical social change, and should they somehow achieve a cadre of local military and police officials who can aggressively and honestly carry out government policy to improve the economy, health, education, and welfare of the villages over the next few years, then Thailand could become a model of successful counterinsurgency. This, of course, is a tall order considering present realities.

## Summary and Conclusions

The insurgency in Thailand feeds on environmental and social conditions, of which geographic proximity to areas from which support can be obtained, terrain and climate, isolation from Bangkok, ethnic cleavages, and economic disparity are especially important. The insurgency received its initial stimulus from China, but Vietnam is now apparently becoming a principal supporter. The falling out between China and Vietnam has created problems of unity for the insurgents, though they need outside support for weapons and training.

The insurgency is headed by the Communist Party of Thailand (CPT), which seeks a radical reorganization of Thai society. Since 1965 it has sought to achieve its goals through armed struggle or "people's war." Its strategy is to form a united front with groups disaffected from the government to build a broad base of popular support. It has grown to about 10,000 armed insurgents and a militia of perhaps 12,000, and controls nearly 100,000 of Thailand's 44 million people. Because of the geographic diversity of the insurgent bases, the insurgency does not enjoy complete unity. The CPT does not enjoy strict control since many operations are apparently conducted by self-reliant and self-sustaining bands with divergent goals and methods.

The insurgency has not been able to expand as rapidly as it might because the Thai people feel a strong affinity to "nation, religion, monarchy." Though government counterinsurgency programs have not been particularly effective, the strong bonds of patron-client relationships in the villages and traditional religious and cultural values have hampered the development of the insurgency.

It would be premature to make a final pronouncement on the Thai insurgency. At present it is a revolutionary movement in an apparently nonrevolutionary society. An examination of the variables discussed in the framework does reveal the strengths and weaknesses of the Thai insurgency. Because it has been able to maintain itself, and even expand modestly, it will likely continue to be a factor in Thai politics. The level of support Vietnam or other outside countries choose to provide will be a vital determinant of its future role. The insurgency does not now pose a major threat to the survival of the regime, but if it does continue to expand it will have demonstrated its potency and will likely constitute a gradually increasing challenge to the Thai political system.

## Notes

1. Voice of People's Thailand (VOPT), Jan. 1, 1979; Foreign Broadcast Information

Service, *Daily Reports* (Asia and Pacific), Jan. 5, 1979. The latter source is hereafter re-ferred to as FBIS.

2. For a background on the Thai insurgency see the following sources: Daniel Lovelace, *China and "People's War" in Thailand 1964–1969,* No. 8, China Research Monographs (Berkeley, CA: Center for Chinese Studies, 1971); Donald E. Weatherbee, *The United Front in Thailand: A Documentary Analysis,* Studies in Inter-national Affairs No. 8 (Columbia, SC: Institute for International Studies, 1970); Assandro Casella, "Communism and Insurrection in Thailand," *World Today*/May 1970/, pp. 197–208; Robert F. Zimmerman, "Insurgency in Thailand," *Problems of Communism*/May–June 1976/, pp. 18–39; Justus M. van der Kroef, "Guerrilla Com-munism and Counterinsurgency in Thailand," *Orbis*/Spring 1974/, pp. 106–39. The authors also recommend a review of the annual survey on Thailand in *Asian Survey* and periodic articles in the *Far Eastern Economic Review.*

3. Casella, "Communism and Insurrection," p. 205.

4. See Robert McColl, "A Political Geography of Revolution: China, Vietnam and Thailand, *Journal of Conflict Resolution* /June 1967/, pp. 153–67. In recent years Thai-Meo relations have been complicated by the tens of thousands of Meo refugees pour-ing into Thailand from Laos escaping communist repression. While these refugees do not support the insurgency they are a source of political embarrassment to and an economic strain on the Thai government.

5. Arnold Abrams, "Back to the Plain," *Far Eastern Economic Review (FEER)* /September 18, 1971/, pp. 21–4.

6. For an estimate on insurgent strength in 1979 see the *Washington Post* (WP), Jan. 20, 1979.

7. This is one of the primary points made by Lovelace in *China and "People's War."* Also see Peter Van Ness, *Revolution and Chinese Foreign Policy* (Berkeley, CA: University of California Press, 1970).

8. The concept of the "united front" is based on the experience of the Chinese Com-munist party, which formed several united fronts during its history. Essentially, it is a policy whereby the revolutionary party unites with other groups and organizations in a common struggle, usually on an expedient and temporary basis. For the Chinese ap-plication of the united front concept in foreign policy see J. D. Armstrong, *Revolu-tionary Diplomacy: Chinese Foreign Policy and the United Front Doctrine* (Berkeley: University of California Press, 1977).

9. Lovelace, *China and "People's War,"* pp. 44–5; Weatherbee, *The United Front,* pp. 25–8.

10. "Brief History of the Struggle of the Communist Party of Thailand from 1942 to 1977," VOPT, Dec. 9, 1977; FBIS, Dec. 15, 1977.

11. David Morell and Chai-anan Samudavanija, "Thailand's Revolutionary In-surgency: Changes in Leadership Potential," *Asian Survey* 19, no. 4/April 1979/, pp. 315–332. This article contains excellent background information on some of the in-surgent leaders. For additional background about a former member of the parliament and an advisor to the prime minister who defected to the insurgency see VOPT, Dec. 31, 1978; FBIS, Jan. 3, 1979.

12. Jeffrey Race, "Thailand," *Asian Survey* /February 1974/, pp. 200–201; Also see *New York Times* (NYT), Dec. 28, 1973.

13. Abrams, pp. 22–4.

14. VOPT, Mar. 19, 1979; FBIS, Mar. 22, 1979.

15. VOPT, Jan. 1, 1979; FBIS, Jan. 5, 1979.

16. VOPT, Dec. 27, 1978; FBIS, Jan. 3, 1979.

17. *Nation Review* (Bangkok), May 27, 1978; FBIS, June 1, 1978.

18. "Conflicts and Rifts Amid Cries for Unity," VOPT, Jan. 9, 1978; FBIS, Jan. 13, 1978.

19. VOPT, Sept. 3, 1978; FBIS, Sept. 14, 1978.

20. *NYT*, Dec. 28, 1973.

21. See the reports in the *Bangkok Post*, June 8, 9, 1978; FBIS, June 8, 9, 1978.

22. *Bangkok Post*, Dec. 27, 1978; FBIS, Dec. 28, 1978.

23. Extensive coverage was given this incident in the Thai press. For example see translations of various Thai newspapers and broadcasts in FBIS, Feb. 11, 12, 21, 27 and Mar. 11, 14, 1974; also see the *WP*, Feb. 2 and Mar. 31, 1974.

24. *NYT*, Jan. 23, 1979.

25. See Peter Van Ness, "Is China An Expansionist Power?" *Problems of Communism* /January–April 1971/, pp. 68–74; Also see Lovelace, *China and "People's War,"* pp. 73–4, 199–201, 215–18.

26. *Nation Review,* Oct. 13, 1978; FBIS, Oct. 13, 1978.

27. Radio Hanoi, Aug. 6, 1976; FBIS, Aug. 9, 1976.

28. Radio Bangkok, Aug. 6, 1976; FBIS, Aug. 9, 1976.

29. Radio Hanoi, Aug. 8, 1976; FBIS, Aug. 9, 1976. For a good summary of Thailand's relations with Vietnam, Cambodia, and Laos refer to the annual *Asia Yearbook* published by the *Far Eastern Economic Review*. Also see William R. Kintner, "Thailand Faces the Future," *Orbis*/Fall 1975/, pp. 126–40.

30. *Nation Review,* Oct. 14, 1978; FBIS, Oct. 16, 1978.

31. *WP*, Jan. 20, 1979.

32. *NYT*, Jan. 23, 1979. According to *Nation Review,* Thai intelligence officials believe the CPT has split into pro-Chinese and pro-Vietnamese factions. The latter faction is setting up its own radio station to compete with VOPT. It consists primarily of post–1976 adherents to the insurgency. (FBIS, June 14, 1979.) In July VOPT announced it would cease broadcasting temporarily. For reasons see *Nation Review,* July 1979; FBIS, July 19, 1979.

33. See the chapter on Thailand in Douglas S. Blaufarb, *The Counterinsurgency Era: U.S. Doctrine and Performance* (New York: The Free Press, 1977), pp. 169–204. Also see William Heaton, "Counterinsurgency: The Thai Case," *American Defense Policy,* ed. John E. Endicott and Roy Stafford, 4th ed. (Baltimore: Johns Hopkins Press, 1977), pp. 177–83.

34. Several reports on the situation of the students who have become insurgents then defected back to the government have appeared in the Thai press. For figures on insurgent defections see Radio Bangkok, Sept. 21, 1978; FBIS, Sept. 25, 1978. The government publishes statistics on the insurgency on a monthly, quarterly, semiannual, and annual basis.

35. Radio Bangkok, Sept. 15, 1978; FBIS, Sept. 18, 1978.

36. *WP*, Jan. 21, 1979.

37. Ibid.

38. *WP*, Sept. 6, 1978.

# Guatemala

MEXICO

Chetumal
Corozal
Orange Walk
Belize City
Tikal
Lago Peten Itzá
Flores
Ceyo
Belmopan
Stann Creek
Belize (U.K.)
Comitán
San Antonio
Gulf of Honduras
Punta Gorda
Bahia de Amatique
Rio Sarstun
Puerto Barrios
Sebol
Lago de Izabal
Santo Tomás de Castilla
Morales
Cobán
Rio Motagua
Rio Cuilco
Huehuetenango
Rio Chixoy
Salamá
Santa Cruz del Quiché
Rio Hondo
Zacapa
San Marcos
Totonicapán
Chichicastenango
Rio Grande
Santa Rosa de Copán
Tapachula
Quezaltenango
Sololá
San Raimundo
El Progreso
Chiquimula
HONDURAS
Ciudad Tecún Umán
Lago de Atitlán
Chimaltenango
Jalapa
Retalhuleu
Mazatenango
Antigua Guatemala
Guatemala
La Aurora Airport
Anguia
Nueva Ocotepeque
Amatitlán
Champerico
Escuintla
Cuilapa
Jutiapa
Inter-American Highway
San José
Iztapa
Rio Paz
Santa Ana
EL SALVADOR
PACIFIC OCEAN
San Salvador
Zacatecoluca
San Miguel
Rio de la Pasión
Rio Usumacinta
Inter-American Highway
Rio Lempa
Rio Madre Vieja
Rio Samalá
Rio Suchiate
Rio T.?
Rio Nentón

0   25   50   100 Miles
0   25   50   100 Kilometers

—— Railroad
—— Road
✈ Airport

502473 1-76 (541403)
Lambert Conformal Projection
Standard parallels 9°20' and 14°40'
Scale 1:2,800,000

Boundary representation is
not necessarily authoritative

# The Guatemalan Insurrection

*Vincente Collazo-Davila*

## The Historical Context

For the greater part of the 1960s Guatemala was subjected to a revolutionary insurgency aimed at changing political values and structures and transforming the economic and social order. In fact, this was the first insurgency in Latin America to openly declare itself socialist.[1] In pursuing their strategy of protracted armed struggle, the Guatemalan revolutionaries stressed political, guerrilla, and terrorist actions that involved, inter alia, attacks on small army patrols and outposts in order to gain supplies and weapons, disruption of truck traffic on the major highways, distribution of propaganda material involving appeals to both the masses and the intellectuals, and the creation of an infrastructure to challenge the government's control over the countryside. Moreover, the insurgents were among the first in Latin America to make widespread use of urban terrorist tactics. These included the kidnappings of rich businessmen and diplomats which have become so prevalent in recent years, as evidenced by occurrences in Argentina and Uruguay.

Many observers, both within and outside of Guatemala, trace the origin of the insurgency to June of 1954 and the overthrow of the reformist regime of President Jacobo Arbenz by Colonel Castillo Armas.[2] Arbenz, and Juan José Arévalo before him, had been conducting a socialist reform movement that included the strengthening of labor unions, the extension of suffrage to illiterates, and widespread land reform.[3] This reform movement alienated the traditional elite, which included the Guatemalan *Latifundistas* and foreign firms, such as the United Fruit Company, that had had some of their idle lands expropriated. Unfortunately for Arbenz, he had allowed his regime to be infiltrated by communists, and this led to U.S. support of the Castillo Armas coup.[4] Colonel Castillo Armas angered the peasants by returning approximately one and a half million acres they had received under the two previous regimes to the rich, and also by disfranchising the illiterates. Castillo Armas also antagonized the working class by abolishing labor unions. The 1954 coup resulted in a political division that has plagued Guatemala to this day. On the right the traditional elite, composed of the rich and the army, refer to it as the "liberation." The left, composed of the insurgents and many of their peasant and intellectual supporters, see the coup as an abortion of the 1944 revolution that brought Arévalo to power and ended thirteen years of dictatorship under the hated General Jorge Ubico.

Whereas the 1954 coup can be called the ideological beginning of the insurgency, in more practical terms the birth of the insurgency can be traced to the coup staged on November 13, 1960, by a group of nationalist army officers against the regime of Miguel Ydígoras Fuentes, who had been elected president after the assassination of Castillo Armas in 1957. Several observers have stated the following to be the goals of the forty-five officers who led the coup: to end corruption in the army, to end corruption in the government, and to terminate the presence of Cuban exiles who were then being trained in Guatemala for the Bay of Pigs invasion. (The officers saw this as a stain on their national honor since it implied that their country was a puppet of the United States.)[5]

The coup met with initial success as the rebels found themselves in control of a military zone and its huge arsenal. Furthermore, some 800 peasants came to them requesting arms and the opportunity to join the revolt. However, when the government did not capitulate immediately, the rebels found themselves without a plan and the movement collapsed.[6] The officers fled the country. In the course of their escape, many of the plotters were hidden and fed by peasants, even though it involved sacrifice and great personal risk for the peasants.

Several of the veterans of the coup eventually became leaders of the insurgency. Of these, two in particular deserve special attention, as they became the primary leaders of the insurgency during its years of greatest success. The first was Lieutenant Marco Antonio Yon Sosa, who came from a middle-class background and who had studied counterinsurgency under U.S. auspices at Fort Gulick in the Panama Canal Zone. The second officer was Second Lieutenant Luis Turcios Lima. Turcios Lima also came from a middle-class family and graduated second in his class at the Guatemalan military academy. Following his academy graduation, he attended Ranger school in Fort Benning, Georgia. These two individuals were without a doubt the most effective leaders of the insurgency.

## Development of the Insurgency

After several months of exile in Honduras and El Salvador, Yon Sosa, Turcios Lima, and others returned to Guatemala and began discussions and negotiations with various political groups in an effort to gain political support. They found the communist party, *Partido Guatemalteco de Trabajadores* (PGT), to be the only party sympathetic to their goals.[7] However, it appears that Yon Sosa and Turcios Lima never thought of themselves as communists but rather as nationalistic-socialist reformers who shared certain goals with the communists.

In late 1961, after giving up hope of another coup, frustrated in their contacts with the bourgeois parties, and after one of their group, Alejandro de León, had been killed by the *judiciales* (secret police), the officers left the cities to contact the peasants in the mountains of eastern Guatemala. They established a guerrilla group called *Movimiento Guerrillero Alejandro de León 13 de Noviembre* (MR-13) in commemoration of their coup in November 1960. The rebels were organized in three columns operating from the Sierra de las Minas mountain range in the department of Izabel. The first column was led by Zenon Riena, a second by Yon Sosa and Turcios Lima, and a third by Lois Trejos Esquivel and Rodolfo Chacón. In February 1962 the insurgents began operations against the United Fruit Company and small military garrisons. As one insurgent leader put it: "The 6th of February, 1962, marks the conscious beginning of guerrilla warfare in our country, in the sense of an armed struggle taking place in the countryside, with the political and social support of the peasantry, initially carried out by a small, unsophisticated, irregular military force."[8]

The insurgents called upon their countrymen to rise and overthrow the Ydígoras regime and, "set up a government which respects human rights, seeks ways and means to save our country from its hardships and pursues a serious self-respecting foreign policy."[9] The first and third columns, under Zenon Reina and Trejos Esquivel, were quickly destroyed by the army and *comisionados* (militia). The insurgents' plea to their countrymen resulted in student demonstrations during March and April, but these too were finally put down. The remaining rebels returned to Guatemala City to hide, an act that was to be repeated again in 1967 after another serious setback.

In November 1962 a separate group of insurgents attempted to establish a guerrilla front in the department of Huehuetenango in western Guatemala. Since the leaders were unfamiliar with the terrain and had failed to gain the support of the local peasants, the latter informed the authorities of the insurgent presence, with the result that all of the members of the group were captured and shot.[10]

Despite their failures, the insurgents learned some valuable lessons. For one thing they concluded that their hopes for a quick victory were both impractical and costly and therefore resigned themselves to a long, drawn-out struggle. These early failures also taught them the importance of carefully setting up a viable infrastructure before commencing military operations.

In September 1962 Yon Sosa, Turcios Lima, and Trejos Esquivel went to Cuba, where they met with Jacobo Arbenz and Che Guevara, and in December of the same year they returned to Guatemala determined to create a strong insurgency.[11] In 1963 the rebels resumed operations in the Sierra de las Minas. However, during most of 1963 and 1964 they generally avoided military action and concentrated their efforts on organizing and politicizing the peasants. During these years the two operational guerrilla fronts were Turcios Lima's Edgar Ibarra front in the department of Zacapa and Yon Sosa's Alejandro de Léon front in Izabal. Throughout 1965 the guerrillas conducted small-scale attacks and ambushes on military outposts and patrols. The guerrillas were generally satisfied with killing three or four soldiers and then breaking the contact. In early 1965 Yon Sosa said that results of the first two and one-half years of struggle were 142 soldiers and policemen killed in contrast to 12 *guerilleros*. By early 1966 they were staging larger raids, some of which resulted in the deaths of as many as a dozen government troops. It was in 1965 that the guerrillas initiated a series of spectacular political kidnappings. At one time in 1965 they held hostage the president of the congress, the president of the supreme court, and the propaganda minister.[12] It was in 1965 also that the chief of the U.S. military mission was shot and the deputy minister of defense, Colonel Ernesto Molino Arreaga, was assassinated. The increasing success of the guerrillas in their military and organizational efforts made them a major issue in the March 1966 elections, which were won by Julio Cesar Méndez Montenegro, a moderate civilian.

On November 7, 1966, the army began a large-scale counterinsurgency operation in Zacapa against the Edgar Ibarra front. A tough military officer, Colonel Carlos Araña, was in charge of the operation conducted by five rifle companies and several paramilitary groups. Araña had been putting his troops through intensive training since July 1966, with the aid of a detachment of Green Berets, and he had also initiated a civic action program in the contested region.[13] Araña pursued the insurgents relentlessly throughout the rest of 1966 and most of 1967. By the end of the year he had broken the back of the insurgent movement in the Sierra de Las Minas region. It was obvious that the rebels had been seriously hurt by the death of Turcios Lima in an automobile accident in 1966. His successor, Cesar Macias Mayora (better known by his alias, César Montes), was not as effective a leader. César Montes was a former student leader and a member of the central committee of the PGT, but he lacked the charisma and military skill of Turcios Lima.[14] The Latin American characteristic of *personalismo* (the tendency to give allegiance to the individual rather than to his principles) was probably at work here, and FAR (*Fuerzas Armadas Rebeldes*) lost much popular support.[15] As a consequence, the army's intelligence effort was more successful. By the end of 1967 the Edgar Ibarra front had been destroyed and those guerrillas that survived fled to Guatemala City, where it was easier to avoid detection and capture.

Yon Sosa's Alejandro de León front did not fare much better, and in late 1966 Yon Sosa escaped to Mexico badly wounded. The remnants of his force fled further into the hinterland. Yon Sosa later returned but his group never regained its former effectiveness.

The insurgents, however, reorganized themselves in their new urban environment, and from 1967 to 1970 staged a very active campaign of urban terrorism. The guerrillas perfected their techniques in both political assassination and kidnapping to the point that for several years it appeared that the government was incapable of interfering with their operations. While many of the kidnappings were strictly for political goals, the majority appeared to be aimed at securing funds. For example, in 1970 alone they managed to collect over $1 million in known ransoms.[16] The government was so incapable of putting an end to this that many of the well-to-do families began to make regular extortion payments to the insurgents as insurance against kidnapping. The political kidnappings were perhaps a different story, as the insurgents could be quite bloody if their demands were resisted. For example, in 1967 U.S. Ambassador Gordon Mein was to be kidnapped and then exchanged for FAR leader Camilo Sanchez, who was in police custody. Mein attempted to run when his car was stopped and the rebels machine-gunned him to death.[17] In April 1970 the FAR kidnapped West German Ambassador Count Karl von Spretti and demanded the release of 22 political prisoners and a $700,000 ransom. Even though West Germany was willing to pay the money, the Guatemalan government refused to negotiate, and the insurgents killed the ambassador. During this same period (1967–70) there were also a number of political assassinations carried out by the rebels. Generally the victims were army officers or police officials, but in January 1968 the rebels assassinated two U.S. military attaches and wounded their aides. The rebels claimed that the assassinations were in retaliation for the U.S. intervention that had cost them so dearly since 1966.

The terrorism and assassinations, however, were not solely a tool of the guerrillas. It was also during this time period that the actions of right-wing terrorist groups such as *Mano Blanca* (MANO), *Consejo Anti-Comunista de Guatemala* (CADEG), and *Nueva Organización Anti-Comunista* (NOA) were at their peak. These groups assassinated many times more individuals than did the insurgents.

Events in 1970 once again went against the guerrillas. Perhaps the greatest loss of all was the death of Marco Antonio Yon Sosa, who was killed by a Mexican army patrol in August 1970 after he had been chased out of Guatemala by pursuing army forces. The other significant event that boded ill for the guerrillas was the election of Colonel Carlos Araña Osorio as president in March 1970. Araña ran on a law and order platform and on his record as a successful antiguerrilla fighter. Araña had stated during the election campaign that he intended to pacify the country even if it meant turning it into a vast cemetery.

For two months after Araña's inauguration, in July 1970, things were fairly quiet. Many Guatemalans had been surprised by Araña's conciliatory attitude and his mildly reformist plans in taxation, land reform, and banking. In mid-September the left moved to test him with a series of attacks on banks and police posts as well as the kidnappings of several wealthy businessmen. By mid-November, when four policemen had been killed in a forty-eight hour period, demands for strong action from his party, the National Liberation Movement (MLN), were so strong that Araña declared a state of siege that gave the army the right to arrest and search without warrant. In March 1971 the army discovered a major guerrilla stronghold and seized a large quantity of weapons, money, and documents covering rebel plans for the future. In April they discovered another hideout and reported killing three guerrilla leaders, one of whom had been sought for the murder of Ambassador Mein in 1967.[18] It has been reported that in the first three months of the state of siege some 1,600 persons were arrested without warrant and that some 700–1,000 individuals were assassinated by right-wing vigilante groups or police. During the same period, the guerrillas were reported to have killed 25 or 30 individuals, most of whom were army or police officers and suspected government informers. During 1972 and 1973 there were only a few sporadic actions that were attributable to the guerrillas. It seems that by the end of 1972 Araña's repressive policies had been effective in breaking the back of the insurgency. In September 1972 the entire central committee of the PGT disappeared, and it is generally believed that the government police killed them.[19]

At the time of this writing, it can be fairly said that, though there are still some remnants of the movement, it is leaderless, broken, and so concerned with mere survival that it cannot carry out effective operations. Viewed in the context of the Maoist strategy discussed in Chapter 1, the insurgency was never able to advance beyond the early stage of phase two (guerrilla warfare) and it was forced to revert to the very rudimentaries of phase one (political organization and terrorism). Analysis of the insurrection in terms of the framework for analysis suggests why this was so.

## Political-Military Assessment

### Effectiveness of the Government

As indicated in Chapter 1, government effectiveness is perhaps the cardinal strategic variable. As we will see, the Guatemalan government's performance varied from time to time, but on the whole it was strong and positive.

During the initial period of the insurgency from 1962 until mid–1966, the government was very ineffective. The reader will recall that the army did destroy the insurgent forces in 1962, but this was as much due to insurgent ineptitude and impatience as it was to government effectiveness. From 1963 to mid–1966 the insurgents in the countryside enjoyed their greatest successes as the army and the police appeared incapable of countering them. Speaking in January 1967, Minister of Defense Colonel Rafael Arriaga Bosque said that instead of taking the initiative, the Peralta Azurdia regime (March 1963–July 1966) would only *react* to guerrilla strikes and then only with isolated operations.[20] It seems that the Peralta regime thought of the insurgent problem as one of isolated banditry rather than as a threat to the central authorities.

However, 1966 was a turning point in the fortunes of the insurgents, and much of this can be attributed to a significant change in the government's attitude toward the insurgents, in its capabilities, and finally in its strategy and tactics.

The guerrillas were one of the major issues in the elections in March of 1966. After taking office, President Méndez Montenegro offered amnesty to the insurgents, but right-wingers in the army and other conservative elites put so many qualifications on the offer that even the PGT, which had originally supported acceptance, later withdrew its support. As a moderate reformist—and knowing that the army and other powerful groups distrusted him—Méndez Montenegro had to give the army a free hand with the insurgents once the offer of amnesty was rejected. He even allowed a contingent of Green Berets to enter the country to assist the army. This was something that Peralta had been against even though he was an army man himself. Having been given a free hand by Méndez Montenegro, the army was determined to destroy the insurgents by any means possible.

Not only had government determination increased but so had government capabilities. At the beginning of 1966 the army was a largely ineffective force numbering some 12,000 men. By the end of the year the army was much improved, due to more intensive training and a good deal of U.S. military aid, including both advisors and equipment. The government also began a concerted effort to arm and train irregular forces for local defense purposes. The police numbered only about 4,000 and had little, if any, counterinsurgency training, but it should be remembered that the insurgents were still operating in the rural environment during this time so the police did not yet face a serious challenge.

The government strategy through the latter half of 1966 and most of 1967 appeared to be threefold. First, the regular army units would attempt to

destroy the main force guerrilla units; second, the militia forces would provide local security and attempt to destroy the guerrilla infrastructure; and
third, the government would initiate a serious civic action program.

The regular army effort commenced on November 7, 1966, under the command of Colonel Araña. His five rifle companies, with support from the
Guatemalan air force, relentlessly pursued the insurgents from hideout to
hideout. This regular force worked closely with the irregular one on both
military operations and in the acquisition of intelligence. The irregular forces
were armed and supplied by the government, and were mainly composed of
small landowners. These forces were indiscriminate in their operations and it
has been reported that thousands of peasants died or were tortured.[21] By
mid-January 1967, the government claimed to have killed 200 guerrillas,
though independent sources reported only about 90. In any case, these were
serious losses since the hard-core rebel forces probably never exceeded more
than two or three hundred men. How much the irregular forces contributed
to this success is difficult to ascertain. Many of the individuals, if not most,
who were killed or tortured by the irregulars were innocent peasants. Many
of the victims were supporters of the president's party, but the government
seemed to be unable or unwilling to intervene. In addition to these overt irregular forces, the army apparently set up (or at least supported) several extreme right-wing terrorist organizations—*Mano Blanca* (MANO), *Nueva
Organización Anti-Comunista* (NOA), and *Consejo Anti-Comunista de
Guatemala* (CADEG). The first two of these organizations seemed to operate
primarily in the urban areas, while CADEG was created by rich landowners
to take care of troublemakers in the countryside. One view of the effectiveness of CADEG and other rural right-wing terrorist groups during the
1966–67 campaign in Zacapa is illustrated by Richard Gott's comments.

> Whoever authorized the use of these para-military vigilante groups, they proved
> to be remarkably successful in slowly eroding the guerrillas' peasant base. This
> was an area, after all, in which the guerrillas had been active for five years or
> more. Yet, faced by a systematic military push, and the use of informers, civic
> action programs, and the indiscriminate methods of attack which led to huge
> casualties among innocent peasants, the guerrillas soon found themselves very
> much on the defensive, and forced to adopt a strategy of mobility.[22]

The civic action program set up by Colonel Araña was also instrumental in
eroding support for the insurgents and gaining support for the army. The
army set up an office called *Acción Cívica Militar* to organize and coordinate
the program. This program eventually included such activities as providing
school lunches, building schools and hospitals, drilling wells, building roads,
developing a literacy program (from 1945 to 1959 the army had the only
organized literacy program in the country), and providing medical care and

vaccination, and vitamins and nutrients.[23] Electrification, water supply, housing, and improved agricultural techniques in the Sierra de las Minas region of
Zacapa also received added attention from various government ministries.
This overall government effort was called the *Plan Piloto* for the social and
economic development of the Northeast. This pilot program for the Zacapa
region was financed in part by increased taxes and in part by a U.S. loan for
$500,000. In addition to the civic action program, Minister of Defense Col-
onel Arriaga Bosque said that the regular army forces had begun to use more
discrimination and courtesy in dealing with the peasants so as to improve the
poor image that the army had had when Colonel Araña first arrived in Zacapa
in July 1966.

The insurgents' decision in 1967 to shift most of their operations to the urban environment called for some modifications in the government's strategy
and tactics. Although in this new environment the police force was of crucial
importance, it was inadequate for the task with which it was suddenly confronted in 1967. The insurgents had been operating in the cities for several
years, albeit on a small scale. The kidnappings to obtain funds had begun in
1963 and the political kidnappings in 1965, but it was not until 1967 that the
insurgency took on major proportions in the urban areas. Initially the insurgents fled to the cities in a desperate bid for survival, but soon they had
adjusted to their environment and put the government on the defensive once
again. In July 1967 the police force numbered 4,000 men and had little or no
training in combatting urban guerrillas. Plans were soon developed to increase this number to 6,000 and to provide them with better training. By
1968 the national police force had reached a 5,000–man level and was much
improved, as a result of U.S. aid and training. Two-thirds of that force was in
Guatemala City where the urban terrorist threat was the greatest. At this
time the judicial police (*judiciales*), who did most of the investigative and intelligence work, numbered approximately 450 personnel. This group was the
elite of the police and was entirely committed to the protection of the capital
city. By 1970 the national police was at the 6,000-man level and was a highly
effective force. This was in large part due to heavy U.S. aid. In that year
roughly half of the United States Agency for International Development
(AID) budget for Guatemala, or about $1.5 million, went to support a training
school for the police. It also appears that some of the police personnel received
training at schools in the United States.

The right-wing terrorist organizations were also very active from 1967
through 1970. There is a good deal of evidence that MANO and NOA were
controlled by the army and that many of the actual gunmen were off-duty
policemen and army officers. (There exists a strong parallel between these
gunmen and the "death squads" that have operated in Brazil. Both regularly
put out death lists with the names of those who were marked for execution.)

During these years it was a daily occurrence to find bullet-riddled and mutilated bodies next to roads on the outskirts of Guatemala City. The author worked at the Guatemalan desk at the State Department in the summer of 1967 and remembers the daily dispatches with the names of the dead (those who could be identified). Many times it was impossible to determine who was responsible for a particular assassination, since the same individual's name often appeared on both the left's and the right's death lists. During these years the country was permeated by an all-encompassing trepidation. Anyone who had ever had any association with the left lived in fear, and often all that was required to bring about an assassination was that an individual be fingered by an informer who might be acting out of personal animosity. Among the victims of MANO were Rogelia Cruz Martinez, a former Miss Guatemala who was known for her leftist contacts, and Yon Sosa's sister, who was killed simply because of her kinship. Thousands of Guatemalans died as a result of this right-wing terrorism, and the police looked the other way. For example, in 1970 Julio Camez Herrera, a one-time private secretary to Arbenz, was killed at one of the city's main intersections while a police cruiser was on the scene and its occupants stood idly by.[24]

The right-wing violence actually hit a peak in March 1968 when MANO kidnapped the archbishop of Guatemala and held him for several days. This action proved very embarrassing for the government. Méndez Montenegro, in an attempt to show that he was not a puppet of the military, dismissed three key military officers who were thought to be connected with the right-wing terror. The three who were sent into diplomatic exile as ambassadors included the chief of police, Minister of Defense Arriaga Bosque, and the commander of the Zacapa region, Colonel Araña. That there was no military coup as a result is probably due to strong pressure from the United States, which was determined to see Méndez Montenegro end his term peacefully. After this there was a decrease in the level of violence, though it did not end completely. On June 20, 1968, the government lifted a state of siege that had been in effect since March 18.

The army's role during the urban phase was very important, but it was a different role from the one it played in the countryside. The army provided the hierarchy of the national police and thus was able to coordinate the actions of the police with its own. The primary army responsibility remained in the rural area, but it did provide personnel and equipment to bolster the effectiveness of the police.

The tactics used in combatting the urban guerrillas were rather straight forward. Soldiers and policemen enforced tight security measures that included guarding all government buildings, key intersections, banks, embassies, and overpasses. Well-armed patrols constantly cruised the streets. At times whole neighborhoods would be cordoned off and then methodically searched by the army and police. The police would make lightning raids at night to arrest individuals and search for arms. The right-wing counterterrorists, with their indiscriminate killings, made it more difficult for the rebels to get support. It was as if the right was out to eliminate anyone who might have any possible reason to even sympathize with the insurgents. Although such methods met with some success, the guerrillas were still strong enough in March 1970 to engage in terrorist operations. In that month, the insurgents kidnapped Foreign Minister Alberto Fuentes Mohr in an effort to embarrass the government prior to the upcoming elections. A week later they kidnapped a political secretary of the U.S. embassy, holding him in exchange for the granting of political asylum (in the Mexican embassy) to four incarcerated insurgents.

These elections resulted in Colonel Carlos Araña Osorio's coming to power as president. Araña had run on an antiguerrilla and antiterrorism platform, and he was to prove true to his word on this matter. During his four years in office Araña continued improving and maintaining the quality of the army and the police.

As mentioned in the introductory section, there was brief relaxation of subversive activities after Araña's election, but this was followed by an outbreak of hostilities on an intensive basis. The government countered with security measures to include the implementation of an 11:00 P.M. to 5:00 A.M. curfew. There were assassinations by both the right- and left-wing terrorist groups, and the police took advantage of the situation to eliminate criminals with long records. During the first 12 weeks of the state of siege (declared on November 12, 1970), approximately 1,600 individuals were arrested without formal charges and 700 to 1,000 were killed by the vigilante groups. The guerrillas accounted for 25 or 30 deaths including that of Arnaldo Otten Prado, a federal deputy and leader of the National Liberation Movement (MLN), which was Araña's political party.[25] During 1971 the government's intelligence apparatus in Guatemala City seemed to operate more efficiently than in the past, and the insurgents suffered severe reverses. In November 1971 the government lifted the state of siege that had been declared one year earlier.

After this, left-wing terrorism was practically nonexistent, but in late June 1972 Olivero Castaneda Paiz was gunned down in a restaurant as he was celebrating his daughter's birthday. He was first vice-president of the Congress and a member of MLN, and was reputed to be the head of MANO. He had participated in Araña's Zacapa campaign in 1966–67 as a leader of irregular forces and had come to Guatemala City when the guerrillas moved there. At first it was assumed that the left had killed him, but later evidence indicates that the army was behind the assassination. Apparently the army felt that MANO and NOA had served their purpose and that they had become a nuisance and danger to economic prosperity.[26] The country had been undergoing an economic boom since 1970 and the government wanted it to continue. This boom was in part due to increased foreign investment reflecting confidence in Araña's ability to pacify the country, and it was also due to Araña's implementation of a five-year development plan that included a $150 million rural development program. By 1973 Guatemala was exporting manufactured goods throughout the rest of Latin America and the gross worth of exports was $300 million. Araña also spent two years touring various parts of the country, talking to peasants and doling out development funds to take care of specific problems (lack of potable water, schools, hospitals, etc.).

In summation, it must be said that the Guatemalan government took strong, decisive action beginning in mid-1966 and that it adjusted its strategy as the insurgents varied theirs. The government successfully differentiated among the various types of threats and replied with various countermeasures based on a coordinated political, administrative, military, police, and intelligence effort. The organizational and propaganda threat was countered by civic action, right-wing counterterror, a low-level police effort, and a concerted intelligence effort. Terrorism was countered mainly by a combination of intensive police action, tight security measures, and a continuous intelligence effort. Guerrilla warfare was met by defense of vital targets, mobile operations by company-sized units, and—once again—by a good intelligence effort. Furthermore, the government launched a national program aimed at eliminating many of the economic grievances used by the insurgents to gain support. As government success increased, it became easier to bring about desertion and defection among the insurgent forces. The government interrogators used techniques ranging from torture to bribes to get information from prisoners. It appears that near the end, the guerrillas lived in fear of the collaborators and government agents among their ranks. While the contribution of U.S. aid to the counterinsurgent effort should not be underestimated, it would not have been decisive without a Guatemalan government totally dedicated to the task at hand. The government made good use of current counterinsurgency doctrine and in fact added a new twist with the widespread use of the covert terror groups.

## The Environment

In the Guatemalan case the environment was generally a neutral factor. It held some advantages for the insurgents but, at the same time, it placed certain obstacles in their path and provided some advantages to the government forces.

The size of the country was certainly adequate to give the insurgents room in which to operate. In fact most of the 42,000 square miles of national territory is jungle and/or mountainous terrain, which many claim to be the ideal for insurgent operations. The road and communications network would also seem to favor insurgents since it is rather limited. There are only three major all-weather highways in the nation: the Pan American Highway; the Pacific Coast Highway (which parallels the Pan American but runs along the coastal lowlands); and the Inter-ocean Highway (which runs east and west along southern Guatemala). There are few, if any, roads in the northeastern region, but there are not many people living there either. Aurora Airport in Guatemala City is the best in Central America and there are 46 smaller airports, half of them unusable during the rainy season. There is one major railroad that parallels the Inter-ocean Highway. The quantity and distribution of the people is another factor that should have favored the insurgents. Some 70 percent of the almost 5 million population live in the rural areas, removed from the urban centers of government power. On the whole, these factors would tend to favor the insurgents; however, they were offset by other key environmental factors.

The environmental consideration that hurt the insurgent cause most was the cultural and ethnic composition of the rural population. The majority of these people are Indians, which posed serious obstacles to politicization by the insurgents. The first barrier was one of language. Even though Spanish is the official language, the majority of the Indians speak no Spanish, but rather one of some twenty different Indian languages. This not only hampered the insurgents' efforts to communicate with the Indians, but it also made them seem foreign to the Indians. The second problem was the political attitudes of the Indians. Simply put, they had none. Many of the Indians felt no loyalty to any social organization beyond their villages and saw the insurgents only as a threat to their isolation.

Local economic conditions were a factor that both helped and hindered the insurgents. The rural population in Guatemala is extremely poor and this, at least on the surface, tended to favor the insurgents by providing them with a forum for exoteric appeals. On the other hand, many of the Indians are so poor that they are completely outside of the country's money economy and have time for nothing but subsistence farming. This, combined with the previously mentioned cultural factors, placed a stumbling block in the path of the insurgent propaganda and organizational efforts.

There is one unique environmental factor that deserves special attention in discussing the Guatemalan case. This has to do with the relationship between the Sierra de Las Minas mountain range and the Puerto Barrios–Guatemala City Highway (the eastern portion of the Inter-ocean Highway). Unfortunately for the guerrillas, the Sierra de Las Minas has this all-weather highway running along its base for its entire length, with numerous feeder roads going into the Sierra along the entire length of the highway. Initially this situation was an asset to the insurgents, since it allowed them to easily interdict the traffic between the capital and the country's major sea port. However, in 1966 and 1967 government troops took advantage of this situation to increase their mobility in the guerrillas' base of operations.

In conclusion, it must be said that the environment was not a decisive factor in determining the success or failure of the Guatemalan insurgency.

## Popular Support

The third strategic variable that we will discuss is that of popular support. That the insurgents were always aware of the importance of this variable was evidenced by statements made by their leaders at different times during the course of the insurgency. In 1967 Marco Antonio Yon Sosa said that weapons merely provided a base for contact with the peasants. He thought that propaganda and popular support would be the key weapons. As he put it, "The peasants are the guerrillas' eyes and ears. We always know what the enemy is doing, and the enemy never knows what we're doing."[27] Turcios Lima and César Montes also agreed on this point. They desired the support not only of the peasants but also that of the proletariat and the intellectuals.

The insurgents resorted to a variety of methods in their attempts to obtain this support. Among these were esoteric appeals, exoteric appeals, terror, provocation of government, counterterror, and demonstration of potency. More specifically, they used "armed propaganda"; interviews with foreign press correspondents and writers; a guerrilla newspaper titled *Revolucionario Socialista;* pamphlets; assassinations and kidnappings aimed at individuals identified as enemies of the people; public declarations and letters released through their newspaper, handbills, or Radio Havana; and finally, military actions. Of these, armed propaganda merits closer consideration.

Armed propaganda involved militarily securing a village, then holding a meeting and requiring the attendance of all the villagers. Various members of the rebel patrol talked to the villagers about such things as exploitation, the people's army, security measures, and so forth. The villagers were encouraged to take part in the discussion. Turcios Lima, César Montes, and Yon Sosa all considered armed propaganda to be the primary method of explaining their cause to the peasants and of securing their support.

The insurgent leaders were very much aware of the importance of esoteric appeals. Turcios Lima said, "Military training without political understanding is as useless as a gun with damp ammunition. With it, even a machete is enough."[28] The central themes of their esoteric appeals were the resurrection of the 1944 revolution, nationalism, antiimperialism, and socialism. The insurgents constantly made reference to the idea that the people's revolution of 1944 had been subverted and stolen from them by the Castillo Armas reactionaries. Theirs was a continuation of the 1944 revolution, but it would not fall prey to the errors that led to the downfall of the Arévalo-Arbenz revolution. As they saw it, the lesson of the Arbenz overthrow was that the revolution must "go all the way" in dispossessing the rich and giving the peasants and the poor a stake in the revolution: what Arbenz did was enough to upset the rich but not enough to create strong support among the peasants. Their appeals to nationalism and antiimperialism were complementary. The insurgents often blamed the "Yankee imperialists" and United Fruit Company for reversing the agrarian reform that had been initiated by Arbenz. César Montes said that the movement was very nationalistic and that both communists and fervent Catholics were fighting side by side. The first *Declaración de La Sierra de Las Minas* called for expropriation without compensation of foreign-owned companies, and the insurgents often called the government a puppet of the U.S. imperialists. The final theme of the esoteric appeals was socialism. During the 1962 to 1963 period, the insurgent leadership leaned more and more toward a Marxist philosophy and began to articulate their goal as socialism, with a government of peasants and workers as the final goal of the revolutionary struggle. Yon Sosa said, "Our struggle is not primarily military but social. . . . It's not our intention to destroy the government by military means; we intend to dissolve it through social action."[29] Furthermore, he said: "It is impossible to fight for very long side by side with peasants, and not become a Socialist. An armed revolution must become a Socialist revolution. . . . A backward country cannot advance along a capitalist path, and there is no third alternative."[30]

Though they appreciated the importance of the esoteric appeals, the guerrillas did not neglect the exoteric appeals. The major exoteric appeal used by the insurgents was land reform. The insurgent view of land reform was more than just the simple one of taking land from the rich and giving it to the poor. César Montes said that one of the most urgent changes needed was land reform, and he went on to add:

> But you cannot simply turn over great tracts of land to the people and say, "Go ahead, it's all yours." Nor can you collectivize land where there is a long tradition of small property owner. In fact when you talk about a program of national land reform you are actually talking about many different regional programs, each fitting the distinct needs and peculiarities of a particular region of the country.[31]

At that time in Guatemala, 2 percent of the landholders held 70 percent of the land; in a country where 70 percent of the population was employed in agriculture, 57 percent of the peasants owned no land. During the same interview Montes said that his group could not be defeated until the needs of the people were satisfied. Besides land reform, the guerrillas defined some of these needs as better health services, education, more equal distribution of income, and giving the people a greater voice in their government. All of these were valid grievances against the government, for Guatemala was actually two countries: the modern capital and the countryside where 70 percent of the people lived. As one observer put it: "This other Guatemala is a land of the forgotten and futureless. . . . It is a country pregnant with revolution."[32] In 1967, 80 percent of the adults in the Zacapa region were illiterate. In the nation as a whole the illiteracy rate was 70 percent, and the vast majority of illiterates were in the countryside. Public health services in the countryside were practically nonexistent in the mid–60s, though in the urban areas they were adequate. To this day the tax system is quite regressive. In 1967 Guatemala had the second smallest tax burden in Latin America, and 90 percent of the taxes came from business, which passed some 80 percent of the burden to the consumer. The rich paid little or no taxes and were adamantly opposed to progressive tax reform. In 1967 the average annual per capita income in the rural areas (where 70 percent of the population lives) was $300, while in the urban areas it was $2,200 (one of the highest in the world).[33] The final exoteric appeal mentioned was popular participation in the government. The need for change here was reflected in the fact that in 1970 Guatemala had the lowest percentage of voters in Latin America.

As the foregoing suggests, the insurgents had legitimate grounds on which to challenge the government for the people's loyalty, and they told the people that the only way to bring about the needed changes was armed force. One U.S. author writing in 1971 summarized the situation by writing that: "Politically the survival of the *Latifundias*, the dominance of large native and foreign *Latifundia* owners, the historical *status quo* position of the church, and the conservative orientation of the army have produced a hostility to socioeconomic change and enlargement of opportunities for the bulk of Guatemala's people."[34]

The author agrees, except for the comment about the Church. The Church is not as influential in Guatemala as in most Latin America countries; and, in any event, in a 1967 pastoral letter it came out in favor of land reform, an end to violence, increased literacy, increased social justice, etc.

Terrorism was used by the rebels in two different ways. During the early years—when the rebels were more successful—terrorism was considered primarily a way of striking at the enemies of the people. The rebels were quite discriminating and sophisticated in the manner in which they used terrorism (selective terrorism). Yon Sosa said that he was against terrorism that had no concrete political purpose. It had to be a part of wider political action or it would lead to the people's repudiation rather than their support.[35] One writer who had been with the guerrillas in 1967 reported that they avoided the wanton killing of individual soldiers and policemen. They went after chiefs or henchmen, since they felt that indiscriminate killing was counterproductive.

The attitude of the insurgents regarding terrorism in the post–1970 era seemed to be somewhat different. As Robert Moss argued: "The basic aims of the terrorist [were] to place the government on the defensive, to create a general sense of insecurity, and to isolate the regime from the people by forcing it to resort to counterproductive repression."[36] In other words, the insurgents were attempting to provoke government counterterror. The insurgents did succeed in provoking extensive government counterterror, but this failed to gain any active support for the insurgents.

The insurgents were aware of the need for a demonstration of potency. Their infrastructure did provide social and economic services in villages in which it operated. And many of their political kidnappings, such as that of Fuentes Mohr in 1970, were intended primarily to show that the government was unable to cope with the insurgents. The bombings that took place in the urban areas could also be said to have had this goal in mind. In the end, however, the government regained the military initiative, and when this happened many of the insurgents' lukewarm supporters abandoned them.

In summary, the insurgent leadership was always aware of the crucial importance of popular support. It developed a variety of means to obtain this support, and to some degree was successful. However, observers of the situation seem to disagree on the extent of the guerrilla success in this area. In his book, *Guerrillas in Latin America*, Luis Mercier Vega contends that the movement failed to take root among the peasants. On the other hand, Robert Moss writes that the rural guerrilla always had a stronger popular base in Guatemala than in most other Latin American countries.[37] It appears to this author that the truth is somewhere in between these interpretations. The rebels did garner a great deal of peasant support from 1962 to 1967, but their success was blunted by several adverse factors, such as the apathy of many Indians toward anything outside of their daily village routine; language problems; and, finally, strong resistance from the government beginning in 1966. During the urban period of the insurgency, the rebels did gain a number of adherents among the students and intellectuals, but once again this support proved inadequate to counter the strong government reaction. Terrorist acts brought about repressive action by right-wingers against both the far left and the moderates, but the moderates failed to give active support to the insurgents. If the society was in fact polarized by the repressive action from the right, this was not reflected by a strong wave of support for the insurgents. It appears that the great majority of the population had either become callous to all the violence or were too afraid to act. Perhaps they blamed the insurgents for bringing about the violence. Unfortunately the truth in this matter is not yet available to us.

## Organization

The scope of the insurgent organization in Guatemala was always limited.

In terms of the over four and one-half million population of the country, only a small proportion ever belonged to insurgent organizations. The strength of the hard-core guerrilla units was variously estimated at between 200 and 300 men. Some reports said that the insurgents had as many as 1,000 supporters in the urban areas, but even this would be a relatively small number. As for the membership in nonmilitary organizations in the countryside, there are few useful statistics. However, as can be seen from the material that follows, the insurgent organization, though short on scope, did not lack in complexity.

As a result of their initial failure in 1962, the insurgents realized that theirs was going to be a very long struggle that could drag on for decades, so from late 1962 to 1966 they concentrated many of their efforts on building a solid base of resistance. In December 1962 MR-13 joined the 12 April Revolutionary Movement (a student group) and the 20 October Column (a guerrilla group led by Carlos Paz Tejada and sponsored by the PGT) to form the *Fuerzas Armadas Rebeldes* (FAR).[38] FAR was to coordinate the actions of the surviving guerrilla groups. Initially there were three main guerrilla fronts under the leadership of Turcios Lima, Yon Sosa, and Chacón. In mid–1963 Chacón's group was destroyed and he was killed, leaving the Alejandro de León front in Izabal under Yon Sosa and the Edgar Ibarra front in Zacapa under Turcios Lima to carry on the struggle. Furthermore, FAR was integrated with the PGT and other dissident groups under a united front called *Frente Unido de Resistencia* (FUR). (More will be said on the evolution of FAR and FUR in the section dealing with unity.)

Their failure in 1962 also taught the insurgents the importance of establishing a solid infrastructure. As mentioned earlier MR-13 used armed propaganda, and after it split with MR-13 in 1965, Luis Turcios Lima's Edgar Ibarra front (also known as FAR) continued to use it, but with a modification. Both groups would occupy a village, explain the reasons for their struggle, and then leave behind them organized cells of resistance. As Eduardo Galeano noted:

> In the case of MR-13, the guerrilleros create, in addition, "peasant committees" which dispute the *real* authority in each village with the military commissioners and the auxiliary mayors, impart justice "outside the framework of bourgeois justice," coordinate efforts to repair the damage the army provokes in its excursions into the zone, and economically sustains the families of comrades incorporated into the guerrilla struggle or killed by the army. For some time, these committees have left in the hands of the clandestine cells the task of the distribution of propaganda materials. The committees have public existence, and are appointed in an assembly of all the inhabitants of the village.[39]

The FAR, however, considered that method too risky because it exposed

their supporters to repression. The FAR preferred to operate its infrastructure in a more clandestine manner so that it would not be destroyed as soon
as the guerrillas left and the army moved in. Both groups attempted to convince the local government representative to join their cause or at least be
neutral; if he actively opposed them, they executed him.

Even before 1967, the guerrilla infrastructure extended to the urban areas.
The city organization in these early years was primarily to secure weapons,
supplies, and funds; to spread propaganda; and sometimes to carry out attacks. After 1967 the city organization became the heart of the insurgency. It
was in these years that it was organized into small, relatively independent
cells of six to eight members in order to protect itself from the increasing
number of informers and turncoats. In the cities the guerrillas always seemed
to have a broad base of at least passive supporters, including students, blue
collar workers, and intellectuals. The right-wing terrorism, however, limited
the amount of active support that these segments of the population were willing to give the insurgents.

The military organization consisted of both full- and part-time guerrillas.
The full-time force in the countryside probably never numbered more than
two or three hundred men, and in part this limited number was a result of a
cautious attitude by the insurgents after their 1962 experiences. They initially concentrated on forming the peasants into groups, but they did not form
military units until they were certain of peasant support and were assured of
sources of supply and information. In 1965 Turcios Lima said that his group
was at the first stage of "survival," seeking to get support from the peasants
and to form cadres. At this time his forces were generally trying to avoid contact with the army, and he noted that the second stage might not come for
years. Accurate figures on the number of part-time guerrillas have remained
elusive.

In conclusion, the insurgent organization was adequate for the needs of the
insurgents at their stage of development. In terms of the total population of
the country, only a small proportion ever belonged to insurgent organizations.
This is congruent with the fact that the insurgency was halted as it was
emerging from its embryonic stage and that its operations were limited to a
relatively small geographic area. The organization had attained a modicum of
complexity, as the guerrillas had joined umbrella organizations such as FAR
and FUR, and they had both military and government organizations in operation. In short, as far as organization was concerned, the insurgents appear to
have been on the right track.

## Unity of the Movement

As noted in the framework for analysis, an insurgent movement needs
cohesion to maximize its effectiveness. On the whole the insurgent movement

in Guatemala effectively achieved and maintained unity on two levels: unity within each separate guerrilla front and unity among the separate fronts.

The unity within the fronts was excellent. The ex-officers realized the importance of the political role and did an effective job as both political and military leaders. The activities of the various patrols in the fronts were centrally coordinated, but the patrol leaders were given the tactical flexibility to carry out their missions in the most effective manner possible.

The unity among the various fronts was a different story, however. During most of 1963 and 1964 MR-13 and its two fronts generally avoided military action and concentrated on organizing and politicizing the peasants. During this time FAR was basically a tool of FUR, and MR-13 was not represented in the leadership of FUR, which was dominated by the PGT. This situation, along with other factors that we will discuss, led to friction between Yon Sosa's MR-13 and the PGT. The first of these was the overthrow of Ydígoras in March 1963 by his defense minister Colonel Enrique Peralta Azurdia. The coup took place because Ydígoras had allowed ex-president Arévalo to return from exile in order to participate in the upcoming elections, and many in the army feared that Arévalo would win any honest election. Peralta Azurdia suspended the constitution and dissolved congress. The coup of course gave weight to the arguments of those who, like Yon Sosa, saw military action as the only solution to the country's problems. Another factor was that the peasants were putting pressure on the rebel leadership to take a more active military role. Finally, FUR and the PGT viewed the rebels as merely a tool to put pressure on the government so as to open the electoral path to change.[40] In July of 1964 the issue was settled when Yon Sosa removed MR-13 from FAR and launched a more active military role. In December 1964 MR-13 issued the first *Declaración de la Sierra de las Minas*, explaining its withdrawal from FAR and attacking the PGT for subservience to Moscow.

Yon Sosa's removal of MR-13 from FAR, however, led to some friction between him and Turcios Lima; and in March 1965, Turcios Lima took his Edgar Ibarra front out of MR-13 and allied with the PGT, readopting the name of the by then defunct FAR. Turcios Lima charged that he did not like Yon Sosa's go-it-alone attitude, that he felt MR-13 and Yon Sosa were under the influence of the Trotskyites, and finally that Yon Sosa's idea of a socialist revolution not involving the bourgeoisie was a dream because the requisite social consciousness did not exist.[41] Yon Sosa, on the other hand, thought that Turcios Lima's idea of a democratic revolution in alliance with the progressive bourgeoisie was unworkable since Yon Sosa saw the bourgeoisie as a class enemy. In any event Turcios Lima reestablished FAR and coordinated his actions with the PGT, though he did not allow his force to become subservient to the PGT. By 1966 FAR, under Turcios Lima, had become the preeminent guerrilla group in the country. There are three possible reasons for this: the stature that Turcios Lima had gained by being invited to represent Guatemala at the Tricontinental Conference in Havana in 1966; the fact that FAR had been more active in both guerrilla activities and spectacular kidnappings; and finally Fidel Castro's vituperative attack on Yon Sosa, in which he said that MR-13 was nothing but a puppet of the Posadist wing of the Trotskyites. The split in 1965 was followed in October 1966 by the death of Turcios Lima in a fiery car crash. There is some evidence that the accident might have been engineered by the PGT, as Turcios Lima had become disenchanted with its gradualist approach and had initiated contact with MR-13 in an attempt to effect a reconciliation. (On May 15, 1966, Yon Sosa had, after investigating Castro's charges, expelled from his group four Trotskyite members of the Fourth International who had been diverting some of his funds to support Posadist action in Mexico.)

The effects of this split should not be overestimated. Other than giving the appearance of a divided effort, the ideological split did not harm the movement very much, since the insurgents never resorted to internecine warfare and continued to deal with each other in a respectful manner. In any event, the split was healed in late 1967 for various reasons: Turcios Lima had died, Yon Sosa had expelled the Trotskyites, César Montes and his FAR had become disillusioned with the PGT, and the army's strong offensive in Zacapa had forced FAR closer to MR-13 and away from PGT. In January of 1968 the FAR leadership released the following statement: "After four years of fighting, this is the balance sheet: 300 revolutionaries fallen in combat, 3,000 men of the people murdered by Julio Cesar Méndez Montenegro's regime. The PGT (its ruling clique) supplied the ideas and the FAR the dead."[42] In February 1968, FAR and MR-13 announced that they had reunited under the name of FAR with Yon Sosa in overall command. One year later the two movements split again; and of course a year after that, in 1970, Yon Sosa was killed and MR-13 practically disintegrated. FAR continued operations in the urban areas, but the repeated blows of the government seem to have gradually sapped it of its strength.

The overall assessment of the guerrillas' performance in terms of this strategic variable would have to be that unity was good but not excellent. It can be argued that the split between FAR and MR-13 did hurt to some extent, but the damage done was on a low order. It should be remembered that though the official reunion did not take place until 1968, Turcios Lima had already initiated action to bring it about shortly before his death in 1966, and César Montes continued these efforts. Also, the differences between them were less than the values they had in common.

*External Support*

In terms of material aid the Guatemalan insurgents received no external support. When Turcios Lima attended the Tricontinental Conference in

Havana in 1966, Fidel Castro is reported to have offered him arms and men, but Turcios Lima declined saying that he wanted his movement to remain strictly Guatemalan.[43] The guerrillas stole or seized from the army some 80 percent of their weapons and the rest they could buy with their plentiful sup-ply of funds obtained through kidnappings. As for personnel, the strong nationalistic feelings of the insurgent leaders ruled out the possibility of accepting that kind of external support.

The insurgents had some success in obtaining political and moral support, largely from the socialist countries (especially Cuba). However, political and moral support from the Soviet Union ceased after 1965, when the Soviets began to oppose the idea of supporting guerrilla movements in Latin America. The Communist Chinese, of course, were unable to provide anything but limited propaganda support. The Moscow-line communist parties in Latin America gave grudging support to guerrilla movements until after the Organization of Latin American Solidarity Conference held in 1967; then they became openly hostile to guerrillas.[44]

The insurgents received no external aid as far as adjacent sanctuaries are concerned. The antagonism of Guatemala's neighbors to the insurgents was il-lustrated on a number of occasions. For instance, in 1965 Honduran troops clashed with Guatemalan guerrillas fleeing Guatemalan territory, wounding several of them and capturing one. And in 1970 Yon Sosa was killed by a Mexican army patrol, while in 1972 Francisco Lopez, the number two man in FAR, was captured in the Mexican border state of Chiapas.

The Guatemalan insurgents received little external support. Although they were self-sufficient in terms of personnel, funds, and arms, it certainly would have helped to have a contiguous sanctuary, especially during the govern-ment's 1966–67 offensive. Such a sanctuary, particularly in Honduras, which bordered the departments of Zacapa and Izabal where the guerrillas operated, could have altered the course of subsequent events.

## Conclusions

At the time of this writing it appears that the Guatemalan government has succeeded in putting down the insurgency within its country. Almost all of the leaders of the movement have been killed, and its few remaining members seem to be so concerned with survival that they are unable to take action against the government. The insurgents were no factor in the March 1974 elections, which were won by General Eugenio Kjell Laugerud. Laugerud said during his campaign that the rebels had been neutralized and that most of the subsequent disturbances that had occurred could be attributed to common banditry.

Of the six strategic variables used in our framework, the guerrillas fared well in terms of four but poorly with respect to the other two: government effectiveness and external support.

As this analysis has pointed out, the authorities took strong and well-orchestrated action against the guerrillas. In 1966 the government began increasing its army strength from 10,000 men to an eventual strength of 15,000; furthermore, it provided these men with concentrated counterinsurgency training. At the end of 1966 Colonel Araña launched his successful operation aimed at surrounding and annihilating the guerrillas in the Sierra de Las Minas region. It is significant also that the government recognized the danger posed by the insurgents and struck before the insurgents felt that they really had a firm hold on the countryside. In 1966 the guerrillas were still avoiding large-scale confrontations with the army and were concentrating on establishing their infrastructure. It will be remembered that in 1965 Turcios Lima said that he still considered himself in stage one and did not expect to enter stage two for several years. When the insurgents moved to the city, the government reacted by launching a program to increase the size of its police force and to increase its training. The right-wing terrorist groups were a government innovation that seems to have been highly successful. The government civic action program, the reforms instituted by Araña's government, and the post–1970 economic boom were all part of the government's efforts to undercut the insurgents' appeal by removing some of the economic and social grievances of the people. Finally it must be said that large-scale U.S. aid ($130 million from 1967 to 1972) played a decisive role in increasing the effectiveness of the Guatemalan counterinsurgency effort.

Many writers on insurgency, including Bernard Fall, have said that an insurgency without a sanctuary is doomed to failure. While we have called attention to some exceptions to this proposition in Chapter 1, it seems to have held true for protracted insurgencies. The Guatemalan case supports this conclusion. Had Honduras or El Salvador been willing to provide a sanctuary, the insurgents might well be operating on a large scale today.

As far as the government response was concerned, the apparent effectiveness of MANO, NOA, and CADEG is a point that deserves special attention. The indiscriminate methods that they used risked a serious backlash against the right and the government. In a five-year period those groups were reported to have killed some 10,000 individuals. The FAR leadership certainly agreed with most contemporary writers on this issue: in 1970 one FAR leader is reported to have said that Araña was FAR's choice for president. Their bet, of course, was that the repression that would surely come with Araña's election would make compromise impossible. Robert Moss wrote that the guerrillas were attempting to move the moderates left by unleashing a civil war through a polarization of politics.[45] Another observer of the situation argued that the repression against the moderate sectors would force them to choose between complete apathy and revolutionary violence.[46] Writing in 1968, Father Thomas Melville, a Maryknoll priest exiled by the Guatemalan government, said: "During the past 18 months, these three groups together have assassinated more than 2800 intellectuals, students, labor leaders, and peasants who have in any way tried to organize and combat the ills of Guatemalan Society. The 'Mano Blanca' itself admits that not more than one in ten of these is probably a Communist."[47]

Yet the moderates did not revolt and there was no civil war. What happened? Are popular notions about the effects of such terrorism as used by the right wing wrong? Perhaps the moderates chose complete apathy. Did the government buy out the middle class through the reforms which in part lead to the latter's increased affluence? Were the moderates so shaken with fear that they were incapable of acting? There are other possible explanations that could be advanced, but it would be mere speculation. This characteristic of the Guatemalan situation will perhaps some day be the subject of a thorough sociological study. The point is that perhaps our ideas about the role of terror in a counterinsurgent strategy need to be revised.

The Guatemalan case is illustrative of the linkages among the various strategic variables. The strong government response undercut the popular support of the insurgents. For example, the guerrillas probably lost adherents because they were unable to protect their supporters from right-wing terrorism. The civic action and economic programs of the government detracted from the effectiveness of the insurgents' exoteric appeals. The government response resulted in a protracted struggle which made adjacent sanctuaries practically imperative for insurgent success. Without these sanctuaries the insurgents were unable to recover from the steady blows dealt them by the government and, as they lost their strength, they found themselves increasingly forfeiting demonstrations of potency and initiative to the government. These are only the most salient of the linkages involved, but they are indicative of the importance of the linkages.

What the future holds for Guatemala is difficult to tell. Many claim that Araña's reforms were merely window dressing to rob support from the insurgents and to appease the United States. The conservative elements are still very strong. In 1971 Senator Fulbright, in criticizing that year's foreign aid bill, pointed out that a Government Accounting Office report indicated that Guatemalan self-help was limited by political inability and resistance to fundamental change.[48] It was said that without the significant tax reform the wealthy right had opposed for years, there could not be any significant economic development in Guatemala. On the other hand, at least one writer felt that many of the officers who, as a result of the antiinsurgent campaign, had been exposed to the miserable living conditions of the peasants and the wealth of the landowners had begun to think along nationalist reformist lines similar to those espoused by the Peruvian military. That writer went on to say that these reformist officers believed peasant discontent was justified, and they no longer wished to act in the interest of the powerful land owning oligarchy that has dominated for so long. Until the government effectively addresses the fundamental grievances of the deprived sectors of society it will remain vulnerable to insurgent violence. But, in the next round, such activity might well come in the form of a conspiracy within the military rather than in the form of a protracted struggle in the countryside.

## Notes

1. Adolfo Gilly, "The Guerrilla Movement in Guatemala," *Monthly Review*, May 1965, p. 11.

2. "Interview With Guatemalan Guerrilla Fighter in Algeria," *L'Espresso* (Italy), February 21, 1971, p. 11; translated in Joint Publications Research Service (JPRS), *Translations on Latin America* no. 508, April 23, 1971, p. 57.

3. This supports Gurr's relative deprivation hypothesis noted in Chapter 1.

4. Richard Gott, *Guerrilla Movements in Latin America* (Garden City, NY: Doubleday, 1972), p. 42.

5. Allan Howard, *The New York Times Magazine,* June 26, 1966, p. 20.

6. Gilly, "Guerrilla Movement," p. 14.

7. Gott, *Guerrilla Movements,* p. 50.

8. Ibid., p. 52.

9. Ibid.

10. Ibid., p. 56.

11. Kenneth F. Johnson, "Guatemala: From Terrorism to Terror," *Conflict Studies* no. 23, p. 5.

12. *Wall Street Journal*, January 14, 1971.

13. Gott, *Guerrilla Movements*, p. 98.

14. Johnson, "Terrorism to Terror," p. 6.

15. The name *Fuerzas Armadas Rebeldes* was used by Turcios Lima's Edgar Ibarra front after its split with MR-13 in late 1964.

16. *New York Times (NYT)*, June 13, 1971.

17. "Leftist Looks at Guatemalan Revolutionary Movement," *Izquierda* (Montevideo), November 8, 1968, p. 16; translated in JPRS no. 124, December 23, 1968, p. 90.

18. *NYT*, May 8, 1971.

19. *Washington Post* (WP), July 22, 1973.

20. *NYT*, January 15, 1967.

21. Ibid.

22. Gott, *Guerrilla Movements,* p. 101.

23. John Dombrowski et al., *Area Handbook for Guatemala* (Washington, DC: Government Printing Office, 1970), p. 310.

24. *NYT*, December 27, 1970.

25. *NYT*, May 8, 1971.

26. "Guatemala: Winds of Change," *Latin America* vol. VII, January 19, 1973, p. 22.

27. Eduardo Galeano, *Guatemala: Occupied Country*, trans. Cedric Belfrage (New York: Monthly Review Press, 1969), p. 33.

28. Gott, *Guerrilla Movements*, p. 76.

29. Gilly, "Guerrilla Movement," p. 20.

30. Gott, *Guerrilla Movements*, p. 74.

31. Howard, *NYT Magazine*, p. 20.

32. Ibid., p. 7.

33. Dombrowski, *Handbook/Guatemala*, p. 4.

34. Robert L. Peterson, "Guatemala," *Political Forces in Latin America: Dimensions of the Quest for Stability*, ed. Ben G. Burnett and Kenneth F. Johnson (Belmont, CA: Wadsworth, 1970), p. 63.

35. Gilly, "Guerrilla Movement," p. 23.

36. Robert Moss, "Urban Guerrillas in Latin America," *Conflict Studies* no. 8 (October 1970):7.

37. Ibid. p. 10.

38. "Unity and Combat," *Fuerzas Armadas Rebeldes* (Guatemala City) no. 30 (March 1968):1–6; JPRS no. 69 (June 20, 1968):118.

39. Galeano, *Occupied Country*, p. 31.

40. Gott, *Guerrilla Movements*, p. 65.

41. Ibid. p. 77.

42. Ibid. p. 109.

43. Howard, *NYT Magazine*, p. 18.

44. Moss, "Urban Guerrillas," p. 5.

45. Ibid. p. 7.

46. Alejandro Portes, "Guatemala's Right Wing Terror," *Nation*, January 10, 1972, p. 48.

47. Galeano, *Occupied Country*, p. 155.

48. *NYT*, April 26, 1971.

# Uruguay

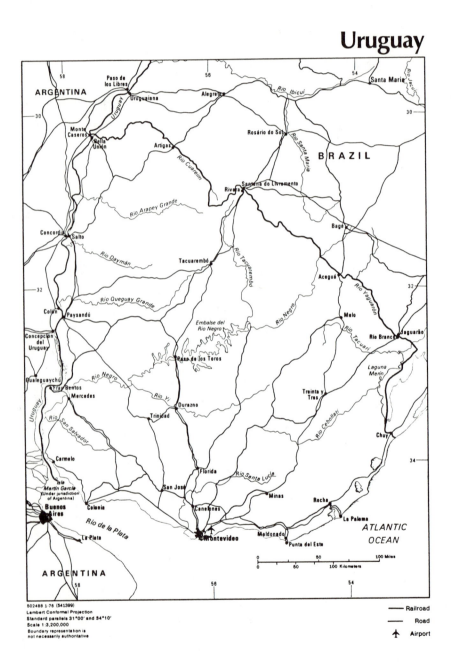

ARGENTINA

Paso de los Libres
Uruguaiana
Alegrete
Santa Maria
Rio Ibicuí
Rio Jacuí

Monte Caseros
Bella Unión
Artigas
Rosário do Sul
Rio Santa Maria

BRAZIL

Rio Cuareim
Rivera
Santana do Livramento

Rio Arapey Grande

Bagé

Concordia
Salto
Rio Daymán
Tacuarembó
Rio Tacuarembó
Aceguá
Rio Yaguarón

Colón
Paysandú
Rio Queguay Grande
Embalse del Rio Negro
Melo
Rio Tacuari
Rio Branco
Jaguarão

Concepción del Uruguay
Paso de los Toros
Laguna Merín

Gualeguaychú
Rio Negro
Rio Y.
Durazno
Trinta y Tres

Fray Bentos
Mercedes
Trinidad
Rio Ceballati
Chuy

Rio San Salvador
Florida
Rio Santa Lucia

Carmelo
San José
Minas
Rocha

Isla Martín García
(Under jurisdiction of Argentina)
Colonia
Canelones
La Paloma

Buenos Aires
Rio de la Plata
Montevideo
Maldonado
ATLANTIC OCEAN

La Plata
Punta del Este

ARGENTINA

0    50    100 Miles
0    50    100 Kilometers

502488 1-76 (541399)
Lambert Conformal Projection
Standard parallels 31°00' and 34°10'
Scale 1:3,200,000
Boundary representation is
not necessarily authoritative

——— Railroad
——— Road
✈ Airport

# 5
# Urban Terrorism in Uruguay: The Tupamaros

*James A. Miller*

## Introduction

In *The War for the Cities*, a very useful introduction to the worldwide phenomenon of urban insurgency, Robert Moss noted that as of the end of 1971 the Tupamaro urban guerrilla movement of Uruguay was the only such movement then in existence that stood any real chance of seizing power.[1] This, as well as the fact that the Tupamaro case is already a classic example of urban guerrilla strategy, tactics, organization, and activities – warrants inclusion of the movement in any volume on comparative insurgencies. Examination of the Tupamaro movement within a comparative framework can permit a relatively ready comparison between this movement and other urban- or rural-based insurgencies.

This examination of the Tupamaros will focus on the six major strategic variables or success factors explained in the framework for describing and analyzing an insurgency. The environmental variable will be treated first because comprehension of the environment in which the urban insurgents of Uruguay operate is essential to an understanding of the other variables. In addition, the discussion will generally be chronological. A chronological approach permits a clearer view of the rise and fall of the Tupamaro movement and of a weak government response that suddenly became extremely effective in 1972. In fact, the Tupamaros suffered such a blow at the hands of the government security forces in 1972 that the Tupamaro movement can be considered a past phenomenon. The overall ideology and strategy of the Tupamaros will be treated in connection with the strategic variables. The concluding portion of this chapter will include discussion of the major relationships or linkages between the variables.

Using the definitions set forth in the framework, one can readily identify the Tupamaro movement as an insurgency, i.e., "a struggle between a nonruling group and the ruling authorities in which the former consciously employs political resources and instruments of violence to establish legitimacy for some aspect of the political system which it considers illegitimate."[2] In this case, the regime was considered illegitimate. With regard to the Tupamaro movement, however, it is probably more accurate to say that the Tupamaros sought "to have the government replaced," to avoid the implication that the Tupamaros hoped to see their movement replace the existing regime; for, as will be noted below, the Tupamaros saw themselves as a catalyst to revolution and their movement would have comprised but a part of the ruling structure that would have emerged out of the Tupamaro-inspired revolution. Thus, in the sense that the ultimate goal of the Tupamaros was a fundamental alteration of the system by changing popular values and attitudes and by restructuring the political, economic, and social order, the Tupamaro movement can be viewed as a *revolutionary insurgency*.[3]

## Origins of the Tupamaros

The Tupamaro movement developed in Uruguay in the early 1960s as an outgrowth of the sugar workers' trade union movement.[4] In 1960, Raul Sendic Antonaccio, a member of the Uruguayan Socialist party, gave up his law studies in Montevideo and moved to the northern part of the country, where he began to organize first the sugar beet workers in the department (state or province) of Paysandu and later the workers in various sugar cane plantations in the departments of Salto and Artigas. Sendic created the Artigas Sugar Workers Union (UTAA), a well-organized and militant union that was initially successful in exacting respect and some concessions from the large Uruguayan sugar and rice companies that had largely been ignoring social laws designed to protect the rural workers. A massive march in 1962 by the cane workers, who trekked the length of the nation to reach Montevideo, highlighted the determination of these workers to end their poor living and working conditions. A female student marching with them was fatally wounded in a clash with police and members of a rival trade union; also, Sendic was imprisoned for several days. Despite the fervor of these activists, their goals were frustrated, including the aim of expropriating the large, practically abandoned, landholdings in the north. Many promises by the established political parties were made at this time, an election year, but few promises were kept.

During the years 1962 and 1963, the group which later came to be known as the Tupamaros was created. Sendic and other activists — from the Socialist party, from the sugar workers' trade unions with which Sendic had been affiliated, and from miscellaneous radical groups — joined together after deciding that Uruguay's liberal democratic system of government was unlikely ever to provide the benefits the poor were thought to deserve. Eschewing the peaceful route to power, these activists adopted armed struggle as their method and created the Movement for National Liberation (known by its Spanish initials, MLN). The first guerrilla act was the robbery on July 31, 1963, of 33 weapons from a private shooting club at Nueva Helvecia in the department of Colonia. Police soon identified Sendic as the ringleader and he fled to Argentina.

During the period 1963 through 1968, the MLN was a relatively anonymous grouping of miscellaneous radicals working to create an image, an ideology, and the organizational and material requirements for an intensive armed struggle against the government. Indicative of the movement's efforts to develop a favorable image was the hijacking of a delivery van at Christmas in 1963 and the subsequent well-publicized distribution to the poor in Montevideo of holiday food from the van. By virtue of such acts, the MLN acquired a "Robin Hood" image. The name Tupamaros and the movement's symbol, a five-pointed red star, surfaced for the first time in 1965 when the MLN publicized its bombing of the Bayer chemical plant in Montevideo as a protest against the Vietnam War. Even the name Tupamaro is reflective of the movement's concern for publicity and the desire to stress the liberty-seeking, anticolonial intentions of the movement. The name was originally used by followers of an Inca chief who revolted against the Spanish; later it was used by Jose Artigas, Uruguayan national hero of the wars of Uruguayan independence, 1818–20. During the Tupamaros' developmental years, many terrorist incidents were attributed to the MLN, including attacks and acts of sabotage directed at radio transmitters and Uruguayan and U.S. businesses, and various "expropriations" or thefts of weapons and explosives.

## Composition of the MLN

Most revolutionary movements in recent world history have been led by persons of bourgeois origin, despite the fact that most of the rank and file members have been either of the peasantry or the proletariat. The Tupamaro movement has been no exception with regard to the leadership; however, the composition of the rank and file Tupamaro membership was unique, as the following passage by Moss points out:

> first Tupamaros were of mixed background. Some were radical cane-cutters and frustrated unionists whom Sendic had brought with him from the plantations of Artigas. Other recruits were political leftists who joined the movement following a political schism within the Uruguayan Socialist Party and a humiliating defeat of the left-wing parties in the 1962 elections; as a result, a few young dissidents were converted to the idea of armed struggle. But from the beginning, the Tupamaros depended most heavily on support from students, professional men and low-grade civil servants and public employees. Police dossiers on the 150–odd Tupamaros arrested in the years since 1965 reveal the bourgeois origins of a majority of the guerrillas and the fact that several had led

double lives as highly regarded professional men. . . . It would be fair to generalize that the rank-and-file of the movement are young, with some university education, and of middle-class antecedents.[5]

The Tupamaros were overwhelmingly Uruguayan in national origin and citizenship. Of 648 Tupamaros captured between December 12, 1966, and June 22, 1972, only 1.8 percent were foreigners and each of them (12) had resided in Uruguay for some time.[6]

## Political-Military Analysis

Before considering the environmental variable, it is appropriate to look at the MLN's predominant emphasis on operation in metropolitan Montevideo. Why did they choose the city as the focus of revolutionary activity, instead of the countryside, as advocated by the Cuban guerrilla theoreticians? To answer this question, it is necessary to briefly reflect on the Cuban revolutionary heritage, and on insurgency developments throughout Latin America during the early 1960s.

In his monumental work, *Guerrilla Warfare* (1960), Ernesto "Che" Guevara, Fidel Castro's lieutenant and theoretician, noted that the Cuban revolution revealed three fundamental conclusions about armed struggle in the Americas:

1. Popular forces can win a war against an army.
2. One does not necessarily have to wait for a revolutionary situation to arise; it can be created.
3. In the underdeveloped countries of the Americas, rural areas are the best battlefields for revolution.[7]

With regard to the first two conclusions, Guevara commented as follows:

The first two conclusions refute the do-nothing attitude of those pseudo revolutionaries who procrastinate under the pretext that nothing can be done against a professional army. They also refute those who feel the need to wait until in some perfect way all the required objective and subjective conditions are at hand, instead of hastening to bring these conditions about through their own efforts. . . . Of course, not all the prerequisites for a revolution are going to be created solely by guerrillas. Certain minimum preconditions are needed to kindle the first spark. The people must be shown that social wrongs are not going to be redressed by civil means alone. And it is desirable to have the oppressor, wittingly or not, break the people first.

Under these conditions, popular discontent assumes increasingly positive forms, creating a state of resistance that, provoked by the attitude of the authorities, can easily lead to an outbreak of fighting.[8]

The necessity for certain objective and subjective conditions to exist in a nation before revolution should be initiated is a rather complex matter that involves interpretation of Marxist-Leninist, Maoist, and Fidelista dogma. While the various arguments are beyond the scope of the present discussion, certain aspects of this issue are being referred to here to place Tupamaro strategy in better perspective. Guevara commented further on his conclusions:

> The third conclusion is strategic, to convince those who want to center the revolution on urban masses not to overlook the tremendous role of rural people in underdeveloped America. We do not wish to underestimate the importance of armed resistence conducted by organized workers, but in the cities, armed revolt can all too easily be smothered when customary civil liberties are suspended or ignored, thus forcing resistance movements to act clandestinely, without arms, and against enormous dangers. This does not hold true in rural areas where guerrillas and inhabitants cooperate closely, beyond the reach of the oppressor forces.[9]

The most concise statement of the rural basis for revolutionary activity is *Revolution in the Revolution?* (1967), by Regis Debray, the French Marxist and Fidelista theoretician.[10] This book has been described as a more or less official statement of the Fidelista ideology, and it was disseminated by the Cuban regime throughout Latin America.[11] Debray discussed several concepts at variance with orthodox Marxist-Leninist doctrine, principally with regard to the strategy and tactics for attaining power. He stated that guerrilla war is the only effective way to attain a communist victory, at least in the underdeveloped countries. He argued that there is no need to wait for the maturing of certain objective revolutionary conditions before initiating a guerrilla struggle. Instead, a group of determined revolutionaries can establish *focos* (foci or nuclei) of revolution in isolated parts of the countryside and from there begin to undermine the authority of the ruling regime. In his most radical deviation from the Leninist viewpoint, Debray contended that there is no need for a party to assume leadership of the guerrilla struggle and that, to the contrary, the party will evolve out of the guerrilla army.[12]

Debray also viewed the leadership of the revolutionary *focos* as coming from middle- and upper-class youth. The armed struggle as the way to power, the lack of a need for objective revolutionary conditions, and the middle- or upper-class youthful leadership are all characteristics of the Tupamaro movement. The Tupamaros, however, rejected the primacy of the rural medium as advocated by Debray and Guevara. Debray said the following about guerrilla activity in an urban environment:

> Of course city terrorism cannot assume any decisive role, and it entails certain

dangers of a political order. But if it is subordinate to the fundamental struggle, the struggle in the countryside, it has, from the military point of view, a strategic value; it immobilizes thousands of enemy soldiers, it ties up most of the repres-sive mechanism in unrewarding tasks of protection: factories, bridges, electric generators, public buildings, highways, oil pipelines—these can keep busy as much as three quarters of the army. The government must, since it is the gov-ernment, protect everywhere the interests of property owners; the guerrilleros don't have to protect anything anywhere.[13]

Both Guevara and Debray were convinced that the cities were dominated by imperialism and its allies, the Latin American oligarchies, the proletariat, and the bourgeoisie. They believed that guerrillas from the urban areas could join the rural movement; but since the rural guerrillas were in the vanguard of the revolutionary movement, all action should be planned by the rural-based guerrilla leadership. These two Fidelista theoreticians stated that the revolu-tion must be victorious in the countryside before it can move on to capture the cities. And when insurgent activity in the cities begins, it will be directed by the rural leadership and will be aimed at destroying military targets to facilitate the advance of the rural insurgents.[14]

Guevara's exhortations to establish rural-based guerrilla cadres and the suc-cessful Cuban revolution inspired many Latin American revolutionaries in the early 1960s. Aided in many cases by material support and training from the Cuban regime, significant rural-based guerrilla movements developed in Colom-bia, Venezuela, Peru, Bolivia, and Guatemala. Even Guevara himself took to the hills in the ill-fated guerrilla venture in Bolivia, where he met his death in 1967.[15]

What happened when the other Latin American guerrillas attempted to ap-ply the Cuban revolutionary model to their own nations? After attempting to defeat the respective ruling regimes primarily through guerrilla warfare in the rural areas, the insurgencies in Colombia, Venezuela, Peru, Bolivia, and Gua-temala had all but collapsed by the late 1960s. With intensive training, arm-ing, and equipping of enlarged military and police forces, the governments of these nations either eliminated most of the rebels or drove them into hiding or virtual inactivity.[16]

During the middle and late 1960s, concurrent with the decline in the power and importance of the rural-based insurgencies, major urban-based insurgen-cies developed in Brazil, Uruguay, and Argentina. These nations were soon plagued by armed attacks, kidnappings, assassinations, and robberies. The adoption of the urban locale as the focus of revolutionary activity may be at-tributed to a combination of factors noted by Russell and Hildner:

Primary among these [factors] are an increasingly sparse rural population result-ing from continued and accelerated urbanization; the presence in most metro-politan areas of a growing, articulate, and quickly aroused cadre of students and young intellectuals willing to embrace terrorism and urban insurgency as the most effective means for toppling governments they consider corrupt and ineffective; the nonadaptability to urbanized societies of guerrilla tactics created, designed, and tested for use among a dense rural population; and the conspicuous failure of recent rural-based efforts at guerrilla warfare and the significant success achieved by urban terrorist groups.[17]

All contemporary urban guerrillas owe a debt to Carlos Marighella, the Brazilian guerrilla leader and author of the *Minimanual of the Urban Guerrilla* (1969). After Marighella was shot by Brazilian police in 1969, his "how-to-do-it" handbook provided considerable guidance to the Tupamaros and other urban guerrillas in Latin America. Urban guerrilla activities, or "action methods," described by Marighella and in which the Tupamaros have engaged include the following: attacks; entries or break-ins; occupations; ambushes; tactical street fighting; strikes or other interruptions of work; appropriation or "expropriation" of arms, ammunition, and explosives; liberation of prisoners; execution; kidnapping; sabotage; terrorism; armed propaganda; and "the war of nerves."[18]

Marighella saw the urban insurgency performing a revolutionary role. In his words:

> The urban guerrilla is an implacable enemy of the government, and systematically works against the authorities, and those who rule the country and wield power. His major job is to baffle, discredit and harass the military and other forces of repression, and to destroy or loot goods belonging to North Americans, the heads of foreign firms, or the Brazilian upper classes.
>
> The urban guerrilla is not afraid of dismantling and destroying the present economy, political, and social system, for his objective is to further the rural guerrilla war, and so contribute to the establishment of completely new and revolutionary social and political structures, in which the people will be armed and in power.[19]

It should be noted that whereas Marighella saw urban guerrilla warfare as an expedient means of diverting government forces while the guerrillas established themselves in the countryside, the Tupamaros saw the city as the focus of revolutionary activity through the duration of the struggle and most of their efforts in the countryside were designed to draw government security forces out of the city. In 1971–72, the Tupamaros undertook to establish bases in the rural interior of Uruguay. A document captured in 1972 described the Tupamaros' "Plan Tatu"—named after a species of burrowing armadillo—which called for the digging of underground hideouts, from which the guerrillas could operate in Uruguay's largely unmountainous and unwooded countryside. The document indicated that seven Tupamaro columns (see the section on organization) were operating in the interior by early 1972. This plan was clearly designed to weaken the control of the security forces in Montevideo.[20] (It should be noted that with the exception of a few unsuccessful attempts in 1970–71 to establish armed fronts in other urban areas outside the capital, the Tupamaros confined their urban operations to Montevideo.)[21]

In a document found in 1967, the Tupamaros expressed their reasons for emphasizing the urban focus for revolutionary activity. The document pointed out that the broad plain that covers most of Uruguay is unfavorable for guerrilla warfare because the government forces can maximize their use of vehicles and aviation. The modern trend toward the concentration of population, wealth, industries, and communications in the large cities, and the accompanying presence of many unemployed and hungry people in the cities, was described as demanding struggle in the cities and not in the countryside. The document further stated that in nations where the majority of the people are urban, as in Uruguay (84 percent), the revolutionary struggle should be in the urban areas because that is where the people are. The creation of incidents in the rural areas of low population density was, however, mentioned as an ideal way for guerrillas to cause the government to spread its forces thin. The struggle was to take place in both the countryside and the city, with the greatest emphasis being placed on the city. The document further suggested that the Tupamaros had noted well the failures of the rural insurgencies elsewhere in Latin America. And the decision of the Tupamaros to emphasize Montevideo was heavily influenced by the fact that half of all Uruguayans live in metropolitan Montevideo.[22]

Numerous advantages accrued to the Tupamaros operating in Montevideo (and, in most respects, to urban guerrillas operating in any large metropolitan area), including the following:[23]

*Terrorist Targets.* There is a ready availability of targets such as foreign embassies, diplomatic personnel, local government and police officials, business firms, vital communications lines, radio transmitters, etc.

*Funds.* Banks and domestic and foreign business firms as well as government enterprises provide a ready source of funds that can be stolen or "expropriated."

*Food.* The urban guerrilla is unlikely to see his movement on the verge of collapse for want of food, as has been the case with some rural-based insurgencies in Latin America.

*Medical Supplies and Services.* Pharmaceuticals and other medical supplies can be bought or stolen in the city, and perhaps surgical assistance may be found at a university when insurgent medical capabilities are inadequate.

*Arms and Explosives.* Like the rural insurgent, the urban insurgent can take weapons from dead government security personnel; the urban insurgent additionally has a large number of readily available sources of weapons and explosives such as police stations, armories, gun clubs, and stores.

*Hiding Places.* The intricate sewers in Montevideo, as well as the parks, plazas, alleys, and residential areas all provide a variety of meeting places, hideouts, and aids to clandestine communication.

*Intelligence.* Gathering intelligence on the government's forces is greatly facilitated as the guerrillas can observe without divulging their interest; also, they may have – through their middle-class connections – contacts inside the government structure capable of providing useful intelligence information.

*Vehicles.* The urban guerrillas have trucks, cars, motorcycles, etc., and possibly aircraft readily available for transport and escape. Vehicles can be stolen and disguised in special garages and paint shops.

*Educational Levels.* Working in an urban environment where the educational level is above that of the rural areas permits greater success in propagandizing and maximizes the possibilities of recruiting members through educated appeals.

*Recruitment.* This is aided by, in addition to the aspects noted above, the mere fact that there are thousands and thousands of persons speaking the same language in a small area. This is different from the situation faced by Guevara in Bolivia, where he was usually trying to recruit dialect-bound Indians who saw Guevara and his followers as foreigners. Similarity in language and culture is extremely important to guerrilla recruitment.

*Rest Areas.* The hideout aspect can be expanded greatly if the government respects the traditional autonomy (i.e., freedom from search) of the Latin American university.

This discussion of the Tupamaro reasons for concentrating on the urban milieu would not be complete without reference to the influence of Abraham Guillen, a Spanish veteran of Spain's civil war on the republican side who ultimately emigrated to Argentina in 1948. Residing in Argentina and Uruguay, Guillen became a prolific writer on revolution and has been called Latin America's first exponent and systematizer of the strategy and tactics of the urban guerrilla. Guillen's great influence on the writings and activities of Marighella has also been documented.[24] In his works Guillen dramatically noted the inapplicability of Guevara's approach to revolution in intensely urbanized Uruguay and Argentina. Guillen is especially important for this Tupamaro study because of his expressed belief in the possibilities of urban guerrillas' being able eventually to develop into an army of liberation. Their ability to do this is to be based on their ability to mobilize and arm the people against the repressive government hated by the people. In the urban guerrilla struggle, the "conquest of space is less important than the defeat of the enemy, the winning of more and more of the population by deeds, the force of example, to the point of converting the guerrillas into the armed fist of the people."[25]

Important to a revolutionary war is not a lightning victory when the people are not in the streets, but rather small and frequent guerrilla actions which prepare them for the moment at which they arise en masse like an enraged lion. The "strategy of the artichoke" is the most prudent or safe one for urban or rural guerrillas: to eat the enemy bit by bit, and through brief and surprise encounters of encirclement and annihilation to live off the enemy's arms, munitions, and paramilitary effects.[26]

The ultimate development in an urban guerrilla struggle, in Guillen's view, is the strategic paralysis of the enemy by an insurrectionary populace fighting at local, intermediate, and national levels of the society.[27]

## Environment

What is Uruguay's physical and human environment? After the Tupamaros decided to base their movement in Montevideo's urban environment, Uruguay's terrain (predominantly tall-grass prairies, with a considerable mixture of forests and some hills, 1,000–2,000 feet above sea level) and climate (temperature with rainfall distributed evenly throughout the year) had little bearing on the Tupamaro insurgency. The nation's good pattern of railways, all-weather roads, and electronic communications all converge on Montevideo, the capital and the center of the nation's commerce, manufacturing, fishing, and resort activities. The smallest nation in South America in area, Uruguay is still six times as big as Belgium. The total population of Uruguay was an estimated 2,800,000 in the mid-1960s; about 1,400,000 lived in Montevideo. The population is homogeneous, primarily white and European and nominally Roman Catholic. There is no population explosion – the rate of expansion of 1.4 percent is the lowest on the continent. There are no large uninhabited or undeveloped areas. The nation has the best public health record on the continent, and shares the highest literacy rate (91 percent) with Argentina. Living standards are high by South American terms, and there is a strong middle class with no pronounced extremes between rich and poor. The nation also had, until recently, a sound tradition of political democracy and stability.[28]

These are some of the major environmental characteristics of Uruguay in effect in the mid- and late 1960s, when the Tupamaros began their intensive campaign of violence directed against the government. Two additional environmental factors – economic conditions and attitudes of the population – are treated below.

## Popular Support

Popular support was crucial in determining the degree to which the Tupamaro insurgency was successful in attaining its goals. The Tupamaros were from the outset concerned with publicity and their public image, and they stated that popular support was essential to the success of their movement.

The Tupamaros had two types of popular support—active and passive. Active support refers to the actual participation of people who were engaging in MLN activities, either as combatants or as service personnel. Passive support included all of those engaged in such noncombative activities as logistics, intelligence, and propaganda. The distinction between combative and noncombative is artificial, however, because, for example, some types of logistics and propaganda activities were integral parts of armed operations. In any case, at its maximum strength, the MLN consisted of an estimated 3,000–4,000 combatants and service personnel.[29] In considering persons to be members, we assume they had acted on behalf of the movement and did not merely hold sympathetic views toward the movement.

"Passive popular support" refers to the persons who were either sympathetic to, indifferent to, or intimidated by the MLN, to the extent that their behavior either benefitted or failed to hinder MLN activities. What this means is—to use the distinction pointed out by Andrew M. Scott—what is crucial to insurgents is the behavior of the general populace and not their attitudes.[30] When the people look with favor on the guerrillas as romantic, Robin Hood–type individuals "expropriating" from a corrupt and inefficient government and its rich domestic and foreign business allies and passing proceeds to the poor, then these people are in effect passively benefitting the insurgency by embarrassing the government and by reducing the likelihood that individuals will report suspicious activities and persons to the authorities. Popular indifference can be especially valuable to an insurgent. The converse is of course true with regard to passive popular support. When people no longer marvel at insurgent activities but are instead repelled by them, when they stop pressing for changes in government leaders or policies and start pressing the government to fight the insurgents more aggressively, or when they begin actively to report suspected insurgent activity to the government and otherwise assist the authorities in counterinsurgency efforts, the lack of passive popular support takes its toll by diminishing the insurgency's chances of success.

The Tupamaros' attempt to gain active and passive popular support will be examined in terms of esoteric and exoteric appeals; demonstration of potency; terror; and provocation of government counterterror.

Although the Tupamaros themselves apparently never articulated a concise, internally consistent political ideology and strategy, they nevertheless sufficiently publicized their view of Uruguayan society and its ills, as well as ways in which the society could be transformed. Over the years a large number of Uruguayans were convinced by the esoteric and exoteric appeals

inherent in Tupamaro ideology to the extent that they at least passively supported the MLN.[31] Because Tupamaro views mirrored those held by the bulk
of the Uruguayan population, it is necessary to look at these views in order to
comprehend the widespread popular support the MLN once enjoyed.

Porzecanski has summarized the Tupamaros' views on what they saw as
Uruguay's crisis that justified resort to armed struggle to destroy the existing
government and society:

> The Tupamaros perceived Uruguay's current political and economic order
> to be at the very roots of the crisis. They blamed the economic structure
> for being traditional, inflexible, and unable to innovate and modernize the coun-
> try. They blamed the political system for being elitist and for favoring the inter-
> ests of the oligarchy to the detriment of the masses. They claimed, moreover,
> that it was not lack of skills or resources that created the inability of the system
> to introduce change; rather, it was the ideology underpinning the status quo
> that made it unable to devise adequate solutions.[32]

Besides having a view with respect to the ills of the society, the Tupamaros
also suggested the direction in which they wished the society to move. Basically they wanted the society to become more nationalistic and more socialistic, which would mean, to use Porzecanski's terms, "the adoption of policies
emphasizing national and regional cultural identity as well as policies leading
to greater economic centralization and control, planning for economic growth
and development, and income redistribution." Thus the solution to Uruguay's
socioeconomic problems would be undertaken within the context of nationalism and socialism.[33] Some of these ideas will be discussed below.

One of the most comprehensive statements available concerning Tupamaro
ideology, goals, and strategy can be found in an interview with an MLN
leader published in the Chilean periodical *Punto Final* on July 2, 1968. The
MLN spokesman stated the organization believed that revolutionary action
itself—the very act of becoming armed and of preparing for and carrying out
deeds that violated bourgeois legality—generates a revolutionary consciousness, the organization, and the conditions for revolution. Noting that "basically, it is revolutionary actions that create revolutionary situations," the
spokesman seemed to advocate violence for the sake of violence. He indicated
that once the revolutionary action had begun, the unity of the left could take
place within the struggle. Alluding to Raul Castro's relating of a guerrilla
group to "the small motor which starts the big motor of the revolution," the
Tupamaros expressed agreement with the thesis of Guevara and Debray in
the ability of a dedicated band of guerrillas to initiate the struggle without
waiting for any particular set of conditions to exist in the nation. The spokesman further stated that efforts to create a mass party or movement were useless without the launching of the armed struggle, but that the formation of the

mass movement would be greatly speeded by the armed struggle.[34]

When asked by the interviewer about the need of a revolutionary group for a platform, the Tupamaro stated as follows:

> Naturally, but one must not create confusion. It is not enough to work out programs in order for the revolution to take place. The basic principles of the socialist revolution are known and have been tried in countries like Cuba. There is no need to debate them further. It is sufficient to adhere to these principles and to indicate concretely the insurrectional path in order to see them become a concrete reality.[35]

The spokesman acknowledged that a revolutionary movement must prepare itself for the armed struggle at any stage in its development, even when conditions propitious for the armed struggle do not exist. This is the case because a leftist movement may be the victim of government repression at any point in its evolution and must be prepared to defend its existence. The spokesman also argued that if the guerrilla leaders did not instill a combative way of thinking in every militant from the very beginning, they would never be able to establish a true revolutionary movement, and they would only be creating small support groups for a revolution that others would carry out.[36]

Emphasizing that all of the militants—even those who worked within mass movements such as the trade unions—must be prepared at all times for revolutionary struggle, the MLN spokesman outlined the following objectives of the movement:[37]

1. To train an armed group which is as well prepared as possible and experienced in action
2. To have good relations with all popular movements that support this type of struggle
3. To create organs of propaganda in order to radicalize struggles and accelerate new awareness
4. To establish a system of recruiting militants with the possibility of giving them theoretical training
5. To constitute groups within the mass movements that will carry out these tasks

While stating that every armed movement must belong to a mass political apparatus at a certain stage in the revolutionary process, the guerrilla spokesman stated that existing Uruguayan political parties or a newly formed political grouping would not be appropriate. Uniting all groups in the struggle was to be the goal, "with or without a party" (the spokesman referenced a Fidel Castro quote).[38]

When asked about the existence of a detailed and definitive strategy, the

MLN spokesman stated the organization did not have such a strategy for taking power in Uruguay because its strategy had to be constantly worked out
based on "real facts." He stated that these facts change, usually independently of the will of the Tupamaros.[39] Several basic "real facts" were discussed by the guerrilla spokesman.[40]

*Worsening Economic Situation.* The MLN relies on popular discontent fed
largely by the growing economic crisis.

*Increasing Trade Union Militancy.* The economic crisis and the high degree
of unionization (in, e.g., the basic services, including banking, commerce, and
industry) permit the MLN to increase union militancy, to paralyze the nation
with strikes, and to maneuver the government into using harsh repressive
measures against strikers.

*Geographic Factor.* Although relying on an urban-based strategy centered
on Montevideo, the lightly populated countryside can be used at times to
provide temporary refuge for guerrillas; to provide food; to serve as the source
of small guerrilla *focos* in the isolated areas; and, if it is not possible to create
permanent *focos* in the countryside, at least organized guerrilla activities there
can force the government to split its forces.

*Forces of Repression.* The Uruguayan armed forces had 12,000 poorly armed
and ill-prepared men, and there were 22,000 Uruguayan police, of whom only
1,000 were trained and armed for a military-type struggle. Half of the soldiers
and 6,000 of the police were in Montevideo.

*Preparation of the MLN for Armed Struggle.* Any organization that plans to
resort to armed struggle must carefully prepare its material bases, and must
also create a vast support and cover movement in order to operate and maintain itself in the city.

*Possibility of Foreign Intervention.* The possibility of intervention, probably
by Argentina or Brazil, on behalf of the Uruguayan government against the
insurgents, would likely mean an initial military setback for the insurgents but
in the long run the public humiliation concerning the presence of foreign
troops in the nation would work on behalf of the rebel cause.

The spokesman summarized the main lines of Tupamaro strategy as follows:

> To constitute as rapidly as possible an armed force capable of meeting any
> favorable situation. To make the people aware that without revolution, there
> will be no change. To strengthen unions, radicalize their struggles, and bring
> them closer to the revolutionary movement. To establish the material bases for
> the development of the urban and rural struggle. To establish relations with
> other Latin American revolutionary movements for action on the continental
> level.[41]

By far the major focus of Tupamaro exoteric appeals to the Uruguayan populace was the nation's worsening economic situation. The overall decline in the standard of living since the early 1950s and the government's continued inability to solve Uruguay's economic ills resulted in a classic example of "relative deprivation" (to use Gurr's concept) being experienced by a significant portion of the populace.[42] When the largely literate, politically aware, and once prosperous middle-class Uruguayan populace became increasingly frustrated about the economic well-being of the nation, more and more Uruguayans became inclined to—at least passively, if not actively—support the Tupamaro movement, which promised changes for the better.

In 1950, when the Korean War was about to create a sharp upward boost to agricultural commodity prices, Uruguay was completing four decades of political stability, was enjoying satisfactory economic development, and had one of the most advanced social welfare systems in the world. (In the early twentieth century such benefits as workmen's compensation, unemployment insurance, retirement pensions, the eight-hour day, and free education up to the university level had been initiated.) The nation had the third highest standard of living in Latin America, and was first or second in the region in such statistical areas as life expectancy, newspaper circulation, and percentage of population enrolled in higher education. Uruguay was called the "Switzerland of South America." But the bubble broke after the Korean War and economic conditions steadily worsened.[43]

The steady decline of the world price of wool and the violent fluctuations in the price of meat, as well as the inability of Uruguayan agriculture to compete technologically with many other nations in agricultural production, led to a severe agricultural slump for the nation. By the late 1960s, the flight of local capital, the increasing foreign debt (over $530 million at the end of August 1970), the low growth rate (lowest in Latin America in late 1967), and the high rate of inflation (highest in the region in late 1967) were indications of the economic crisis. These problems, plus the continued economic decline, the lack of foreign investment, the constant wage demands of the private sector and the large government bureaucracy (some 300,000 workers), and the need to keep the highly advanced social welfare system operational, left most Uruguayans frustrated and susceptible to Tupamaro appeals.[44] The economic decline was also exacerbated by the terrorist activities of the Tupamaros. For example, they often carried out activities designed to scare off foreign ("imperialist") capital, and in 1971 they launched a campaign to scare away many foreign tourists who normally visited the Punta del Este and other summer resort attractions. Threatening letters to regular foreign visitors, especially Argentines, apparently had a great effect, as the number of tourists visiting the nation was said to have declined by over 40 percent over the first half of 1971.[45]

The Tupamaros promised wide-ranging economic and social changes if the revolution succeeded. For example, in a six-point program announced in

March 1971, the MLN presented proposals for land distribution; state takeover of commerce and industry; and seizure of foreign investments without
any compensation payments. The program was clearly designed to appeal to
both workers and farmers. Although this statement did not indicate what
type of political system the MLN favored, the Tupamaros did indicate that
the type of "justice" that would be put into effect would include such
elements as codes taking into account the essential human values instead of
maintenance of private property and the capitalist system; a review of the
past judicial decisions of the regime; and, prosecution and sentencing of those
who had served in "counterrevolutionary" capacities in support of the ruling
regime.[46]

Despite the presence in Tupamaro pronouncements and documents of statements concerning what reforms should be affected once the present government was overthrown, the Tupamaros did not see their movement as the
replacement for the old regime. Rather, as indicated in a captured document
dated in March 1972, the Tupamaros saw their movement as a catalyst to the
revolution and the creation of a new government in which the Tupamaros
would play a role. Three main objectives of the MLN as stated in the document were as follows:

> The MLN's minimum objective was said to create an undeniable state of revolu-
> tionary war inside Uruguay, polarizing politics (between the Tupamaro move-
> ment and the oligarchy). The medium objective would be (to) create a Frente de
> Liberacion Nacional (National Liberation Front), which would negotiate a series
> of minimum demands backed both by mass organizations (trade unions, etc.) and
> by the Tupamaros. This would have the effect of institutionalizing the guerrilla
> movement. The maximum objective would be to bring the government to the
> point of collapse with the subsequent installation of a coalition government in
> which the MLN would have "indirect participation." Such a government would
> be pressed to issue a general amnesty to all members of the MLN, which would
> then presumably operate openly like the Movimiento de Izquierda Revolu-
> cionaria (Movement of the Revolutionary Left) (MIR) in Chile.[47]

This captured document explicitly expressed the MLN's recognition that
popular support was required for the revolution to succeed. The document
reflected that the two greatest difficulties facing the MLN were how to
develop the struggle toward a final confrontation with the government and
how to win popular support. The response was to be a two-pronged effort to
build mass support through the creation of a national liberation front on the
one hand and, on the other hand, to increasingly direct the armed struggle toward direct confrontation with armed forces and police.[48] Thus, the Tupamaros attempted to create an urban *foco*, the military function of which would
be to slowly undermine, discredit, and eventually destroy the power of the

security forces. According to Porzecanski, the Tupamaros hoped:

> to facilitate a political process whereby the masses (and not just the guerrillas)
> would participate in a revolutionary uprising that would lead to power seizure.
> Guerrilla warfare was understood to be a temporary (although principal) stage in
> the ideological confrontation between the Tupamaro social movement and the
> ruling elite. The destruction of the government's forces was to be a necessary
> military step to allow a more strictly political battle against the power of
> Uruguay's oligarchy and the influence of neocolonialism to take place.[49]

Defined by Moss as "the systematic use of intimidation for political purposes,"[50] terror was the primary tool of the Tupamaros in attempting to gain
passive popular support and in undermining government authority and prestige. The use of terror by the Tupamaros will be discussed in terms of
demonstrating the potency of the MLN, in provoking government counterterror, and in otherwise increasing public support of the Tupamaros. An analysis of the use of terror by the Tupamaros will be included in the concluding
portion of this chapter.

Tupamaro operations will long comprise a classic example of the demonstration of potency of an insurgent group vis-à-vis the target government.
Whereas the framework distinguishes two dimensions of the demonstration
of potency—i.e., retaining the military initiative and meeting the needs of the
people through social services and a governing apparatus—the following
analysis of the Tupamaros includes only the former dimension. Operating
primarily in Montevideo, the Tupamaros never occupied territory long
enough to begin organizing, politicizing, defending, or providing services to
the people. Yet, as will be seen, the Tupamaros were well aware of the need
to retain the initiative in their struggle with the government.

Publicizing the insurgency to the populace was designed to prove to all,
through successful armed operations, that the government was weak and the
Tupamaros strong, and that revolution was a real possibility. Marighella
refers to the use of armed operations to demonstrate the credibility of an insurgency as "armed propaganda."[51] Violence, which was seen by the
Tupamaros as perfectly legitimate, was adopted by the Tupamaros as the
best tool for destroying the government's decision-making process, curtailing
the extent of its coercive powers, and cutting its ability to command loyalty
and respect.[52]

Activities of this nature include the above-mentioned "Robin Hood" policy
of distributing stolen food to the poor at Christmas in 1963, and the uncover-
ing of government and business corruption (see below). The image of the
MLN was enhanced in May 1968, when during a bank robbery, the
Tupamaros stopped to administer first aid to an elderly lady who had suffered
a nervous shock.[53] During 1963-69, the Tupamaros perpetrated 126 rob-

beries and seized an estimated $1.7 million. In 1969 seven Tupamaros, disguised as policemen, robbed the Casino San Rafael, the ultimate symbol of the rich life at the beach resort of Punta del Este, and took over $200,000. And in 1970, five men and four women from the MLN held the officers of Montevideo's Bank of the Republic at bay for over three hours while going through the vaults. They ultimately escaped with $6 million in jewels and cash.[54] Other notable acts included the destruction of a radio transmitter in April 1968, just before the president was due to defend his policies over the air; and the destruction of the main offices of General Motors, Uruguay, in July 1969, to protest the visit of President Nixon's envoy, Governor Nelson Rockefeller.[55] Besides embarrassing the government, the robberies had the additional important effect of financing future Tupamaro operations.

Publicizing the insurgency to the public was aided by "countermedia" tactics. Since the government for several years prohibited the media from referring to the Tupamaros by name, the MLN followed up its acts of selected violence with broadcasts over its own clandestine mobile radio transmitter; interceptions of regular government-sanctioned broadcasts; distribution of leaflets and other publications; and the temporary seizure of cinemas, workers' canteens, and other public meeting places where Tupamaros delivered impromptu harangues to captive audiences. They praised the "revolutionary justice" associated with their acts and labeled their thefts as "expropriations." Robberies uncovered records in 1969 and 1970 involving, respectively, the minister of agriculture, Carlos Frick Davies, and a tobacco magnate, Luis Mailhos Queiroio; disclosure of the records to the press indicated major financial wrongdoings on the part of each and the resultant scandals greatly enhanced the image of the Tupamaros at the expense of the government's reputation.[56]

The viability of the MLN was continually demonstrated in the Tupamaro efforts directed at the heart of the Uruguayan government's political control system, i.e., at the armed forces, the police, and the political-administrative structure.[57] The Tupamaros believed that the ultimate success or failure of their movement would depend in large part on their campaign to demoralize and subvert the forces of order in Uruguay.[58]

Tactics employed by the MLN to subvert the armed forces and police included bombings, assassinations, threats, and infiltrations. The Tupamaros had avoided killing security personnel until the late fall of 1969, and the only previous victims had fallen in gun battles. A shift in tactics was marked in November 1969, when Carlos Ruben Zambrano, a police agent, was shot on a bus, and in April 1970, when Hector Moran Charquero, a police inspector who had been accused of torturing prisoners, was gunned down on a Montevideo street.[59] A related subversive action was the temporary occupation of residences of officials and supporters of the regime. The guerrillas held a brief discussion with members of the family, explaining what the father or husband did to guerrillas and what would happen to him if he continued his behavior. This type of activity served as an effective means of nonviolent terrorism because most Uruguayans came to believe that the guerrillas were not making idle threats.[60]

In April 1971, the Tupamaros sent an "open letter" to the armed forces stating that every time soldiers "defend the regime, in one way or another, they are defending an antinational and antipopular policy."[61] The most effective propaganda the MLN had within the security forces was probably the general inability of these forces to capture Tupamaros or to free hostages who had been kidnapped. Tupamaro infiltration tended further to demoralize the armed forces and police. One Tupamaro agent, an Uruguayan marine, Fernando Garin, facilitated through his deceit the entry of a band of Tupamaros into Montevideo's naval training center on May 29, 1970. The guerrillas took everyone prisoner; gave speeches and harangued officers for alleged cruelty toward prisoners; and stole hundreds of rifles, some machine guns, and large quantities of ammunition and explosives.[62] Moss has pointed out that the Tupamaros actually used two apparently contradictory methods of subverting the government security forces: appealing to individual soldiers and policemen on the one hand, and issuing threats and carrying out selective terrorism or harassment on the other.[63] In spite of the attacks on the security forces, the Tupamaros avoided the complete alienation of the armed forces because they saw the possibilities of one day working with the armed forces to promote constructive changes in Uruguayan society; the police, however, never were seen by the Tupamaros as having a political role, but were instead seen as an obedient, coercive, armed branch of the government.[64]

A major example of the Tupamaros' ability to engage in well-coordinated, large-scale activities was the attack on the town of Pando on October 8, 1969, the second anniversary of Guevara's death. This attack demonstrated the credibility of "armed propaganda," the fruits of dedicated training and organization, and a major effort to undermine the government's political control. Simulating a funeral procession, a string of cars stopped in the middle of the town, less than 20 miles from Montevideo, and disgorged groups of armed men who joined others who had infiltrated the town. A total of some 40 men, probably supported by at least as many more in logistics and communications tasks, promptly seized the police and fire stations, the telephone exchange, the electric plant, and three banks. Even though the Tupamaros lost three dead and at least 16 captured during their retreat, they saw the attack as a successful show of strength, a strategic victory, and a qualitative leap forward in the level of their terrorist activity.[65]

The political kidnapping tactic was employed widely by the Tupamaros to undermine government authority and prestige. The kidnappings were used to gain publicity, to free political prisoners, to exact other concessions, and to create crises within the government. President Jorge Pacheco Areco, who had assumed office in late 1967, faced constant cabinet crises and confrontations with the national legislature over ways to respond to the kidnappings. His government was so deeply divided after a wave of kidnappings in August 1970 that he reportedly was on the verge of resigning before police captured several Tupamaro leaders (including Raul Sendic) in a lucky raid; also, the emergency security measures taken by Pacheco alienated large portions of Uruguayan society to the extent that in June 1971 an unsuccessful attempt to impeach Pacheco was made in the legislature.[66] A list of the major kidnappings follows:[67]

| | |
|---|---|
| July 1968 | *Ulises Pereyra Reverbel:* Head of government utility enterprise and close friend of President Pacheco. Released after five days. |
| September 1969 | *Gaetano Pelligrini Giampetro:* Leading banker. Kidnapped in sympathy for bank employees' strike. Released after ten weeks when large ransom was paid to charity. |
| July 1970 | *Daniel Peyera Manelli:* Magistrate who had tried MLN members. Released, August 1970. |
| July 1970 | *Aloysio Dias Gomide:* Brazilian consul. Released after ten months and payment by family of $250,000 ransom. |
| July 1970 | *Daniel A. Mitrione:* USAID police advisor. Shot by MLN when President Pacheco refused to release 150 prisoners. Body found August 1970. |
| August 1970 | *Claude Fly:* U.S. soils expert. Released in March 1971, after he had a stroke. |
| January 1971 | *Geoffrey Jackson:* British ambassador. "Operation Fan," government search of 300,000 homes in Montevideo, failed to locate Jackson. Released, September 1971. |
| March 1971 | *Guido Berro Oribe:* Attorney general. Freed after some two weeks and after admission regarding "wrongdoings" while in office. |
| March 1971 | *Ulises Pereyra Reverbel:* Second time kidnapped by MLN. Regime embarrassed as searches could not locate him and he had to be replaced as head of government-run utility. Rescued, May 1972. |
| May 1971 | *Carlos Frick Davies:* Former minister of agriculture. Rescued, May 1972. |
| February 1972 | *Nelson Bardesio:* Police photographer. Furnished MLN with |

information on repressive police tactics.

April 1972           *Hector Guitierrez Ruiz:* Legislative leader. Released after twenty-four hours.

The Tupamaros had much success in provoking government counterterror. Brian Jenkins has described how urban guerrillas attempt to force a government to assume dictatorial powers, declare martial law, suspend civil liberties, and resort to mass arrests.[68] Of course there is an inherent danger in that the insurgents can prompt such a strong reaction by the government that the very survival of the insurgent movement can be threatened or, in the Tupamaro case, virtually obliterated, regardless of how the general populace feels about the government's harsh methods.

Tupamaro terrorism, and the government's efforts to promote economic austerity and to control the public distrubances resulting from public dissatisfaction with the nation's continuing economic crisis, resulted in President Pacheco's instituting numerous security measures. The following are some of the major causes and/or indications of popular discontent that resulted in creating active and passive support for the Tupamaros.[69]

- Violent and lengthy strikes (1968) by private and public employees.
- Sympathy strikes and demonstrations by students and teachers.
- General unrest among pensioners because of late and deflated checks.
- Declaration in June 1968 of a state of emergency and the imposition of security measures that restricted some civil liberties that had been enjoyed by Uruguayans through most of the twentieth century. This condition lasted until March 1969, then was reimposed about four months later.
- Frequent freezing of wages, salaries, and prices.
- Eventual prohibition of strikes by public employees, and of private sector strikes unless advance government permission was received. Leaders of illegal strikes were subject to arrest without court order or warrant.
- Extended bank employee strikes were ended only after the government prepared to draft the workers and then court-martial them if they refused to work.
- Frequent closures of newspapers, some permanently.

A particularly significant government act was the violation of the autonomy of the University of Montevideo following the abduction of President Pacheco's close friend, Ulises Pereyra Reverbel, in 1968. When the police penetrated the campus, one student was killed and thereafter the student community became increasingly radicalized.[70]

Beyond the above-mentioned security measures resulting from the state of emergency that was in effect during most of the Pacheco presidency, the government also engaged in harsher methods that fall even more into the category of counterterrorism. In August 1970, following the kidnappings of Dias Gomide and the Americans Mitrione and Fly, and the murder of Mitrione, Pacheco gained from the legislature a 20-day suspension of all individual liberties to facilitate anti-Tupamaro measures. Another such suspension was granted by the legislature for 40 days in early 1971. A large number of Uruguayan liberals decried the moves away from the nation's longstanding and honored democratic traditions as the government operated under "emergency security measures" and occasional complete suspensions of civil liberties. Pacheco's actions resulted in regular battles with members of his cabinet and the legislature, where his partisans were in the minority.[71]

Liberal disenchantment with the Pacheco government was heightened greatly by the disclosures of a representative senate commission in 1970 to the effect that police torture of persons believed to be subversives was widespread.[72] Moss noted that the people came to be more concerned about the police and soldiers breaking down doors or torturing prisoners than the insurgents murdering policemen or abducting foreign diplomats.[73]

Several events occurred in September 1971 which were especially indicative of the types of embarrassment the Tupamaro caused the regime, and that were discrediting it and forcing it to assume a more repressive stance. The release of the British ambassador, Jackson, after he had been held underground in a "people's prison" despite massive search efforts by the security forces, highlighted the government's weakness. The escape through a tunnel of 106 prisoners, including Sendic, from the Punta Carretas prison in Montevideo was a severe blow to sagging government prestige.[74]

In late 1971, the Tupamaros publicly called off their terrorist operations and openly campaigned for the Broad Front, a coalition of radical political parties that included the Communist party of Uruguay, a legal party. Besides reflecting a high degree of doctrinal flexibility, this decision was also indicative of the desire of the Tupamaros to align themselves directly with those elements of the populace that were most discontented with the continued national economic crisis and the deplorable record of the Pacheco government. But the Broad Front coalition drew only 18 percent of the vote in the November 28, 1971, presidential election.[75]

The election results suggested that by the end of 1971 most Uruguayans still were not ready to accept radical solutions to the nation's ills—not the radical programs of the Broad Front or of the Tupamaros. It is also apparent that by this time a considerable number of Uruguayans had been repelled by the MLN's terror tactics. Probably a good bit of the Robin Hood image had worn off following the killing of Mitrione. The seizure of Pando by a large number of guerrillas, and the bloody conclusion of that incident, no doubt forced many Uruguayans to take note of the serious potential the MLN had for disrupting the lives of each and every citizen. And such measures as the efforts of the Tupamaros to disrupt the economy must have alienated many citizens. Besides the economic concerns of each Uruguayan, perhaps the most significant realization characterizing the popular consciousness through most of 1971 was that the nation's relatively violence-free political traditions, her democratic liberal institutions, and the very peaceful fabric of her life were being consistently and ruthlessly undermined by the Tupamaros.

One can only guess to what extent such perceptions characterized the average citizen. The election results of November 1971—in a nation where the vote is universal and compulsory for virtually all adults over 18 and where most do vote—had indicated a widespread rejection of radical solutions. But aside from the feelings of the general populace, it is now clear that by the end of 1971 there was growing support among leading circles in the nation, especially among the military, for stronger measures against the Tupamaros. The degree to which the Tupamaros had been successful in garnering popular support was indicated in the results of the military-led counterinsurgency campaign undertaken in 1972.

## Organization

The scope of the Tupamaro insurgency, i.e., the proportion of the population participating in the insurgent organization, was relatively broad when one considers that the 3,000–4,000 Tupamaro fighters and support personnel, located primarily in Montevideo, had a tremendous capability for perpetrating terrorist acts against the governing establishment on a rigorous and sustained basis. But the ability of these several thousand Tupamaros to have a continuing and significant impact on the government's ability to rule was based directly on the amount of passive popular support they retained among the rest of the population. As will be seen below, despite the expressed interest in building a large popular support base for the MLN, the Tupamaros very organizational structure was in many ways antithetical to the creation of such popular support. Another important point about the Tupamaros is that they do not appear to have been interested in engaging large numbers of persons in active support roles, i.e., as active Tupamaros performing combative or service roles.

The framework states that complexity or differentiation of an insurgent organization is necessary for the organization to attract and hold more and more members.[76] The Tupamaros certainly increased their membership greatly over the years, and they diversified their organization greatly in a military sense, but they had limited success in increasing the political complexity to encompass a large number of auxiliary organizations among such groups in

Uruguayan society as students, leftist political parties, the Church, the armed forces, and labor. Even though they spoke of the need to develop and maintain a positive relationship between the MLN and these groups,[77] the Tupamaros made very little progress toward their stated goal of organizing various opposition groups that would ultimately be linked together in the National Liberation Front. The Tupamaros' most significant activities in building up pro-Tupamaro and antigovernment support were in some of the trade unions where Tupamaro support committees (CATs) spread propaganda and fomented revolutionary fervor and militancy. The Tupamaros believed that massive strikes and militant activities by the workers would be integral elements leading up to and promoting the victory of the eventual urban uprising. But the banning of strikes and the arrest of many labor leaders by the government during 1968–72 sharply curtailed the unions and their activities. Also, the largest trade union federation, the National Confederation of Workers, with some 300,000 members, remained firmly under the control of the Communist party of Uruguay.[78]

Enroute to the urban uprising, the Tupamaros worked through their systematic use of violence to establish a "power duality," a condition which begins when guerrillas establish themselves in such a status and power position that they represent a real threat to the status quo and also command loyalty and adherence from significant sectors of the population.

> This allows the organization to be seen as a parallel government and provides it with four important advantages. First, such tactical operations as gathering of information and supplies are easier to conduct. Second, recruitment of new members is greatly facilitated, since the organization operates in the midst of its potential recruits. Third, it places the guerrillas in a position of power that enables them to function as a shadow government: it is possible for them to legislate, to make policy, and to administer justice. The kidnapping of a certain landowner, for example, will no longer be seen as just an ordinary criminal action but, rather, as the consequence of certain "wrong doings" committed by that person, for which the movement has now chosen to punish him. Fourth, power duality gives the masses an opportunity to visualize the eventual transformation of the guerrillas' localized de facto government into a generalized de jure one.[79]

But since the Tupamaros never occupied territory or parts of a city for extended periods of time, they were never able to create a parallel government in the sense of having freedom to organize and politicize the people within the framework of an insurgent political control system.

The Tupamaros did, however, diversify their internal organization greatly and created a relatively complex yet flexible organization to accomplish the necessary commando-type and service-type functions of the MLN. The organization the Tupamaros created focused on these two types of functions and was pyramidical in nature. The main operation units of the MLN were the cell, the column, the executive committee, and the national convention.[80]

The base elements of the organization were cells, usually containing two to six persons. In order to limit the effects of betrayal or police infiltration, each cell was compartmentalized—i.e., with the exception of the cell leader, each cell member was in theory familiar only with the members of his cell and no one else in the Tupamaro organization. Ideally each cell member used a nickname and false identification papers, and his real identity was to be unknown to his comrades. Other aspects of compartmentalization included limiting discussion of particular Tupamaro matters only to those persons with a direct requirement for the knowledge and sometimes blindfolding Tupamaros when moving from one hideout to another. The cell leader was picked by a higher body, normally the executive committee, and was the contact point with the higher levels of the pyramidical structure. Cells usually specialized in either commando or service operations, and within each cell individual members had assigned functions. The executive committee coordinated and supervised the activities of each cell.[81]

Between the executive committee and the cells were columns, which were largely administrative entities responsible for particular geographical or functional areas. By early 1972, there were reportedly seven columns operating in various areas in the interior. In Montevideo, some columns were responsible for such single functions as the maintenance of an underground medical facility. Columns were composed of several cells each, and the common functions of the column were conducted with the various cell leaders cooperating with one another. There was no column leader and action decisions were made by the executive committee and given to the cell leaders. In line with compartmentalization, the individual members of one cell did not know the members or leaders of the other cells in the column.[82]

The executive committee of the MLN was in effect the primary decision-making organ of the MLN and performed both political and military functions. Membership on the executive committee was confidential. A higher organ was the national convention, which was supposed to meet periodically and to deal with broad ideological and strategic issues. This body, however, apparently did not meet after 1970 and discussion of broad issues was undertaken through the circulation of various documents, essays, and working papers among Tupamaro leaders.[83]

The system operated quite well in insuring that a host of particular functions was performed. These functions included frontline terrorist and propaganda activities as well as the numerous service and logistics tasks such as obtaining meeting places, building hideouts, purchasing food and clothing, manufacturing explosives, gathering intelligence, providing medical treatment, obtaining and maintaining arms and ammunition, repairing and disguising vehicles, making uniforms, and preparing false documents. Besides performing various assigned functions, each cell and column were also to varying degrees engaged in intelligence and propaganda work and maintained links with such groups as unions, students, and the armed forces. Linked to, but outside, the columns were the Tupamaro support committees, which, in addition to their activities in the trade unions, also engaged in such tasks as minor logistical support and intelligence functions.[84]

Despite the rather elaborate structure and delineation of functions, a great deal probably existed only on paper.[85] Nevertheless, the Tupamaros were occasionally able to conduct operations with fairly large numbers, e.g., the attack on the town of Pando in 1969. The 40 or so Tupamaros participating represented many cells and were known to each other only by the white handkerchiefs affixed to each man's arm as the attack got underway.[86]

The Tupamaros consistently stressed the cohesiveness or the unity of their movement. This emphasis is evident in the following 1968 comments of a Tupamaro spokesman: "The armed struggle is a technical feat which obviously demands technical knowledge, training, practice, equipment, and the psychology of a combatant. In this area, improvization costs dearly in lives and failures. The spontaneity preached by those who speak vaguely about 'the revolution to be made by the people' can play only a dilatory role."[87]

The cohesiveness of the Tupamaro movement is exemplified in the fact that despite the arrest of Sendic and other MLN leaders in August 1970, the movement was still able to maintain its pace of terrorist operations. To some degree this was no doubt due to a bribery-aided courier system, but more than that it appears to be a manifestation of the fact that the MLN never had a single leader or small group of established leaders. Tupamaro interviews, pronouncements, and even internal documents refer to the movement as a whole and not to a particular leadership.[88]

Cohesiveness was facilitated because the Tupamaros had no significant rival guerrilla groups and they apparently did not suffer any major internal divisions until perhaps 1972 when their movement crumbled. The two main left-wing extremist groups that operated besides the Tupamaros were the Eastern Revolutionary Armed Forces (FARO) and the Popular Organization 33 (OPR 33). These groups, which cooperated at times with the Tupamaros, both engaged in robberies and kidnappings of their own in 1971 and 1972. There were also small extreme rightist terrorist groups whose activities included attacks on suspected Tupamaros and their families.[89]

MLN recruiting procedures and standards also enhanced the cohesiveness of the organization. Entry into the movement was based on a rigorous and lengthy procedure. Sponsorship, extensive background investigations, and careful consideration of physical, ideological, and psychological attributes all had the effect of improving the quality and loyalty of new recruits.[90] The recruiting process appears to have been purposely operated to maintain the MLN as a relatively small and cohesive group of activists performing combat-ant or service functions.

The degree to which the Tupamaro organization provided instrumental ser-vices and channels of expressive protest is difficult to analyze because of the clandestine organizational structure and practices of the insurgents. On the one hand, the Tupamaro organization did not differentiate itself greatly by creating a number of mass organizations that could attract adherents by pro-viding them with successful and desirable courses of action. On the other hand, the MLN was apparently quite successful through early 1972 in meeting the psychosocial needs of the existing Tupamaros. In other words, the MLN members received a sense of status, communality, participation, and progress by serving in the movement. The mostly youthful, idealistic, and educated Tupamaros maintained high morale and obtained considerable pleasure in demonstrating the strength of their own movement vis-à-vis the government. The Tupamaros also sensed for years that the public was behind them. But, after the vigorous counterterrorist campaign of 1972, the MLN suffered crippling losses and was increasingly faced with such problems as lowered morale, desertions, lack of popular support, treachery, and lack of new recruits.[91]

*External Support*

Despite its importance in many insurgencies, external support was of little importance to the MLN. Through 1972 there was no evidence that the Tupamaros ever received either money or arms from other countries or from other revolutionary movements.[92] The overwhelmingly Uruguayan-manned MLN was consistently able to obtain the weapons, ammunition, medical sup-plies and food, and other items it required through theft or through purchase, using stolen funds. And just as operating in the urban environment of Monte-video obviated the need for material support from outside Uruguay, hiding their forces within a clandestine, compartmentalized structure in Montevideo enabled the Tupamaros to prosper for years without having foreign sanctu-aries.

The MLN was able to go for so many years without external material or manpower support or the use of foreign sanctuaries because the movement re-mained relatively small and refrained from participation in large-unit warfare (the Pando raid was a notable exception). Had the Tupamaros ever decided to engage in large-scale guerrilla or conventional warfare, they may have had to rely on external sources for heavy weapons and they may have required foreign sanctuaries. (Despite the existence of favorable terrain in neighboring Argentina and Brazil, likely counterattacks launched by the military govern-

ments in both countries would have made the tenure of any Tupamaro sanctuaries very tenuous.) An interest in foreign support, however, was
evidenced in a document prepared in early 1972 wherein the Tupamaros discussed the creation of a committee on international affairs. The goals of this
body were to acquire arms and money from abroad, to facilitate the movement of members across borders, and to create a transnational intelligence
network. The Tupamaros were interested in ultimately establishing firm contacts with many foreign governments, including those of Cuba, Chile, Peru,
and Ecuador, as well as Algeria, the Soviet Union, and China. Thus early
1972 saw the Tupamaros beginning to create a policy of foreign relations.[93]

The Tupamaros also did not benefit from external political or moral support
of any significance from any foreign governments, with the exception of
Cuba, which voiced support for the MLN at times.[94] The Tupamaros remained ideologically aloof and were not tied to the dogma of Moscow,
Peking, or Havana, or to the policies and activities of the left-wing parties
sponsored by these communist capitals. The Communist party of Uruguay
adhered to the Moscow line and sought power through the ballot box. The
Tupamaros were able to remain aloof from the communist and other governments because of their virtual independence in terms of material and manpower requirements, and because external political and moral support were
not essential as the Tupamaros never approached creating an operational parallel government desirous of diplomatic recognition.

During their ascendency, the Tupamaros assisted terrorist groups, mostly
of the urban variety, in other parts of Latin America. They in fact saw themselves as the agents of a continental and global revolution and not just an
Uruguayan phenomenon. This sentiment motivated the Tupamaros to exchange cadres and information with similar groups in Brazil, Bolivia, and
Argentina. Especially close relations were maintained with insurgent and terrorist groups in Argentina. The People's Revolutionary Army (ERP) was pat-
terned after the Tupamaros and even has adopted the five-cornered red star
of the Tupamaros as its own symbol.[95] In August 1970 Tupamaro representatives reportedly met with members of Argentine and Brazilian guerrilla
groups to discuss joint revolutionary activity.[96]

*Government Response*

As with most cases of insurgency, government response was a primary
variable determining success or failure. The Tupamaros generally flourished
during the 1968–71 Pacheco presidency when the government was unable to
halt the insurgents' terrorist activities. The new president, Juan Maria Bordaberry, a conservative and wealthy rancher and minister of agriculture
under Pacheco, had stressed law and order in his campaign before the November 28, 1971, presidential election. By the time he assumed office on

March 1, 1972, Bordaberry had committed himself to following Pacheco's antiterrorist stance.[97] The new president was soon able, through a primarily military-oriented, coercieve counterinsurgency campaign, to inflict a crippling blow upon the Tupamaros.

Since the major aspects of the government's response to the Tupamaros during the years prior to 1972 have already been noted, this section will focus on the Bordaberry-initiated counterinsurgency campaign. First to be discussed will be the stages of the Tupamaro insurgency, the government's counterinsurgency organization and capabilities, and the major developments in the government counterinsurgency effort which began in April 1972.

The framework states that in general an insurgency presents the government with four types of threats, each of which corresponds to the four stages of the Maoist insurgency model.[98] Since the government combatting an insurgency must tailor its specific counterinsurgency measures to the specific threats being posed by the insurgents at each point in time, the present analysis of the government effectiveness in battling the Tupamaros will be facilitated by viewing the Tupamaro insurgency and the government response in terms of the stages of this insurgency. It should be noted at the outset, though, that there can be no firm cutoff points between the stages of an insurgency, and that activities initially associated with lower intensity stages will frequently also be prevalent in higher intensity stages of an insurgency.

Concerning the progression of insurgencies, the Maoist model sees an insurgency passing through organization, terrorism, guerrilla warfare, and mobile-conventional warfare stages, whereas the Cuban model suggests that insurgents, under certain conditions, may be successful if they immediately initiate a campaign of terrorism and small-scale guerrilla warfare. The Tupamaros followed Guevara and Debray in rejecting the idea that a guerrilla force should be subordinated to the party, and stressed the primacy of armed conflict.

The five-stage model of urban insurgency formulated by Brian Jenkins is relevant to the Uruguayan case.[99] Jenkins suggests that the tactics of an urban guerrilla struggle can be viewed as comprising two aspects: (a) the guerrilla warfare ("terrorist" in our terms) aspects—abductions, assassinations, bombing, raids—or what can be described as the tactics of the few; and (b) the mass movement aspects, such as strikes, demonstrations, and riots. The urban terrorist campaign is portrayed by Jenkins as increasingly attempting to coordinate the two aspects of the struggle, ultimately hoping to combine them in full-scale urban warfare or the urban uprising.[100] Thus, in describing the progression of the Tupamaro insurgency, it will be useful to keep in mind the distinction between the tactics of the few and the tactics of the many, or between terrorist warfare and mass organization. This distinction will be impor-

tant in the later analysis of the relationship between terror and popular support. What follows is a discussion of the Tupamaro insurgency in terms of
stages.

The most significant activity occurring in the first stage of an urban insurgency is likely to be military and not political. Jenkins used the term "violent
propaganda" to indicate that sporadic acts of terrorism such as bombings and
assassinations are designed primarily to demonstrate the existence and the
potency of the insurgent movement. The emphasis in this stage is on symbolic
targets, e.g., banks and officers of large corporations that serve as symbols of
economic exploitation, or government buildings as symbols of political repression. The small Tupamaro group followed this pattern during the approximate
1963–65 period when it developed the Robin Hood image by engaging in such
activities as distributing stolen materials to the poor. It was previously noted
how the Tupamaros attempted to link some of their terrorist acts to such
generally popular issues as opposition to government corruption and the Vietnam War. Organizational activity within the group of insurgents had begun
but, unlike that in the first (organizational) stage of the Maoist model, the emphasis was on military-oriented activities and not tasks of a more political and
organizational nature.

The second stage of Jenkins's urban insurgency model focuses on guerrilla
organizing efforts, whereas by the second stage of the Maoist model, the
guerrillas, having undertaken major organizational initiatives in the first stage,
are just now initiating significant terrorist activity. In any case, aside from the
fact that the urban insurgents will likely embark on terrorist activities and
concern themselves with organization later, the activities undertaken in the
first two stages of either the Maoist or the Jenkins models appear quite similar. By the end of the second stage, the insurgents are extensively involved in
recruiting, establishing cells, making esoteric and exoteric propaganda appeals, infiltrating agents into the government and society in general, gaining
publicity, and demonstrating the potency of the movement through the use of
selective terror. During this phase, for example, the Tupamaros (from 1965 to
about 1968) expanded their military-oriented activities but also stressed
organizational matters.

The Tupamaros expanded from small cells into the relatively elaborate,
compartmentalized, pyramidical structure containing a high command, columns, and cells. Training procedures, lines of authority, and discipline were
established. The terrorists adopted the nickname Tupamaros and the symbol
of the five-pointed star. They undertook concerted efforts to infiltrate the
government and to establish pockets of support in the trade unions, student
groups, and the armed forces. Militarily, the Tupamaros stepped up the intensity of their terrorist activities. Although Jenkins noted that abductions of
high-ranking personnel might well take place in the first stage of an urban insurgency, the Tupamaros completed their first successful abduction in the

second stage (Ulises Pereyra Reverbel, August 1968). Kidnapping is in itself an indication of improved organizational capability. One man can carry out a bombing or assassination attempt, but holding one or more persons hostage for an extended period of time will usually require careful planning, a good hiding place, and tight security.

In the third stage Jenkins saw the insurgents initiating an extended cam-paign to gain control of the streets. Government security forces become the main targets, and attacks on these forces are designed to demoralize them and to provoke repressive countermeasures that will further alienate the public. Jenkins noted that in this stage the insurgents might be able to take over par-ticular areas and begin collecting taxes, protecting supporters, and maintain-ing order. As noted above, the Tupamaros undertook an intensive terrorist campaign aimed especially at the Uruguayan security forces. By 1968, the Tupamaros had about 1,000 members, of which some 50 were actively en-gaged in military actions; the remainder were engaged in support roles.[101] The Tupamaros showed their strength and organizational talents as they briefly occupied the town of Pando in 1969 and Montevideo's naval garrison in 1970. But the Tupamaros did not permanently capture any territory in Montevideo. Thus, not having the equivalent of secure rural base areas, the Tupamaros did not have a captive segment of the populace which they could openly proselytize, enroll in insurgent-sponsored organizations, etc.

Jenkins's fourth stage, mobilization of the masses, follows when the efforts in the third stage to provoke government repression are successful. Once vio-lence forces the government to assume dictatorial powers, declare martial law, suspend civil liberties, and resort to mass arrests, the insurgents may be able to turn popular discontent—particularly among the youth and organized labor—into extended strikes and marches, and then rioting. According to Jen-kins, the judiciary is a primary target in this stage. Attacks on the judiciary, such as the kidnapping of the judge (Daniel Peyera Manelli, July 1970) who had sentenced many Tupamaros, plus the growth of the insurgent threat, saw the government ultimately shift the responsibility for trying of suspected political activists from the civil to the harsher military courts. Although the Tupamaros succeeded in provoking repressive measures, they did not succeed in mobilizing the public to protest the measures on a sufficiently large scale. Of course what happened was that the Tupamaros, lacking adequate popular support, were eventually decimated by the government repression they had incited.

The third and fourth stages of Jenkins's urban insurgency model roughly co-incide with the third stage of the Maoist model. The latter basically involves large-scale, well-coordinated guerrilla operations launched from secure guer-rilla base areas, coupled with intensive organizational efforts among the popu-lace in insurgent-controlled as well as contested areas. In both the Maoist third stage and the Jenkins third and fourth stages, the guerrillas are stressing the military- and political-organizational aspects of the insurgency, and in each they are attempting to secure territory but are avoiding large positional battles.

The Tupamaro insurgency did not reach Jenkins's fifth stage, the urban uprising. This stage, which is in essence the urban equivalent of the Maoist model's fourth stage (mobile-conventional war), involves the final assault on the government. In this stage, the tactics of the few—abductions, assassina- tions, and other terrorist acts—are combined with mass activities such as gen- eral strikes, demonstrations, and, ultimately, widespread rioting in the streets. (An example would be the Warsaw uprising in 1944.) Jenkins noted, however, that even if an urban insurgency did proceed as far as provoking an urban uprising, it is unlikely that the insurgents could win unless a portion of the army switched sides. A possibility, though, is that negotiating short of an insurgent takeover would take place, or the existing regime could be replaced by leaders more sympathetic to the insurgents' cause (or more hostile toward it).

Writing in early 1972, Jenkins related the Tupamaro experience to his five- stage model and commented that the Tupamaros appeared to have progressed into stage two and had occasionally advanced into stage three, e.g., during the larger terrorist activities of mid-1969.[102] The Tupamaro success in pro- voking government repression and adoption of dictatorial powers is another example of third-stage activity; had popular discontent with the government measures resulted in widespread strikes, demonstrations, and rioting against the government, the Tupamaro insurgency could have been considered to have entered Jenkins's stage four.

The Uruguayan government generally fared poorly in its anti-Tupamaro operations during the years prior to 1972 because it lacked proper organiza- tion and training to deal effectively with a large-scale urban insurgency and because the Tupamaros enjoyed widespread passive popular support while the government in general and its often repressive anti-Tupamaro tactics were largely unpopular. Moreover, the government was limited most of the time with respect to what actions it could take in combatting the Tupamaros. Despite the emergency security measures and two brief complete suspensions of civil liberties, the Pacheco government had consistently sought more powers.[103] Popular support for a government conducting any type of counterinsurgency campaign, rural or urban, is clearly essential. For without popular support—even passive popular support—the very existence of the government may be endangered. The Uruguayan government's difficulties in maintaining popular support primarily related to its inability to cope with the nation's economic problems.

The early years of government actions against the Tupamaros reflected that training was needed in such areas as intelligence, counterintelligence, crowd

and riot control, and psychological warfare. An efficient organizational structure for coordinating all aspects of the counterinsurgency effort, especially the
gathering and collation of intelligence information, was also required. Especially needed was a comprehensive and sophisticated intelligence program
capable of providing not only low-level, "listening post" information but also
capable of furnishing the information needed to penetrate the organization.[104]
Moss saw poor intelligence as the crux of the government's problem in dealing
with the Tupamaros.[105] The following description of those major Uruguayan
agencies engaged in counterinsurgency activities suggests that the government attempted to meet these requirements.

The constitution of 1967 gave the president of Uruguay the responsibility
for maintaining public order and internal security. His primary means for this
were the national police (under the Ministry of the Interior), the armed
forces, and the small maritime police organization under the Ministry of Defense.[106] In 1970 the national police organization, consisting of some 17,000
officers and men located throughout the nation, had four operating branches:
Montevideo Police, Interior Police, Highway Police, and the National Corps
of Firemen. In 1970 the chief of police of Montevideo and his deputy were
army officers who were also in charge of several special units that assumed increasingly important roles in the anti-Tupamaro struggle. The paramilitary
Republican Guard – a mounted, saber-carrying elite force of about 450
men – served as a back-up force for riot duty in addition to its guard and
ceremonial duties. The paramilitary Metropolitan Guard became the most important entity within the national police in the battle against the Tupamaros.
This organization was formed to help maintain public order, to take action
along with other forces to control disturbances, and to provide a ready
reserve for the chief of police. The Metros, numbering about 600 officers and
men in 1966, were equipped by 1970 with such items as machine guns, gas
weapons, and fire hoses. They had also been used to guard banks and large
stores. Also under the Montevideo chief of police were the Quick Reaction
Units which played a key role in counterinsurgency activities.[107] The Metros
and other counterinsurgency forces within the national police were
developed with assistance from AID in the form of advisers and equipment. Additionally, some Uruguayan police received instruction at U.S.
facilities in the Panama Canal Zone. The police counterinsurgency
capabilities were greatly enhanced through the addition of modern transportation vehicles and the improvement of communications facilities, patrol
capabilities, investigative procedures, and riot control methods.[108]

The military in Uruguay, through 1970, had generally been an apolitical,
respected, and popular national institution, and was able to obtain all the
recruits it needed through voluntary enlistments. Morale was usually high,
and despite the relatively low rates of pay, military careers offered many com-

pensatory benefits, such as medical benefits, housing, loans for private homes, pensions, and funeral costs. The military traditionally engaged in military civic action programs that benefitted the common Uruguayan and provided the military with favorable publicity. For example, in 1968 the army engaged in 22 projects, including the maintenance and improvement of roads, repair of broken telephone lines, building of additional classrooms for crowded schools, and construction of bridges and children's playgrounds. Air force participation in civic activities included provision of air transportation for emergency supplies, medical evacuees, and the like; and the navy engaged in numerous search and rescue and medical tasks. All three services operated public relations programs to enhance military-community relations.[109]

A major factor in determining the military's general popularity through the end of the 1960s and into the early 1970s was its overall apolitical nature. The military had played a relatively small role in Uruguayan politics in this century. Uruguay's only coup during the century (1933) had been civilian-initiated. As late as 1963, the military budget was only 1 percent of the total government budget. This was possible because of the lack of an external threat and because of the general lack of domestic violence. A 1962 study concerning the years 1946–60 noted that Uruguay had the lowest incidence of domestic violence in Latin America. But the budget and the role of the armed forces in meeting domestic violence and terrorism both sharply increased in the late 1960s. The visibility of the military and the police increased greatly in the Uruguayan political process.[110]

Operating under the Ministry of Defense, the army, the navy, and the air force totalled approximately 17,000 officers and men in 1970. The subordination of the services to the minister of defense was more an administrative relationship than a command relationship. The three services were able to exercise a great deal of independence. There was no overall joint services staff organization. The minister also exercised control over the maritime police, which had an authorized strength of 600 in 1970 and which was responsible for public order in the river and coastal areas. (The maritime police were also tied closely to the navy and its director general was usually the navy's second ranking officer.)[111]

In 1970, the army numbered 12,000 personnel; operated within four military regions for operations and internal security purposes; and had 9 horse and mechanized cavalry squadrons (with light and medium tanks), 6 infantry battalions, 6 field artillery battalions, and 6 engineer battalions. The navy had 2,500 personnel and was organized into an escort division of 2 destroyer escorts, a patrol division with several patrol craft, and a naval air arm with 14 aircraft primarily of a liaison nature. The air force consisted of about 1,700 men and 60 aircraft. Besides a training command and a materiel command, the tactical command was divided into 2 air brigades. The 1st Air

Brigade was located at Carrasco Airport near Montevideo and consisted of 2 transport groups, 1 fighter group, and 1 search and rescue group; and the 2nd Air Brigade was located at the departmental capital of Duranzo and included a tactical reconnaissance group.[112] Two air force UH–12 helicopters armed with machine guns were permanently assigned in late 1970 to standby duty at Carrasco Airport where they could rapidly transport troops to the sites of terrorist activities.[113]

In September 1971 the primary responsibility for the prosecution of the antiterrorist campaign was transferred from the police to the armed forces. A joint major staff, containing representatives from the army, navy, air force, and the national police, was created to coordinate the antiterrorist operations. The military and police had previously cooperated in anti-Tupamaro operations, but the police had been in charge. Intelligence became a major concern of the joint major staff, which coordinated intelligence inputs from the three services and the police. Reportedly, military control over the counterinsurgency campaign improved the quality and quantity of intelligence reports because the people had more faith in the armed forces and were more willing to report suspected persons and activities to the military.[114]

With this background information on the government counterterrorism capabilities in mind, what happened in 1972? By early 1972, the Tupamaros had become well-entrenched on the Uruguayan scene. Terrorism had become a regular occurrence. Despite occasional setbacks along the way, the Tupamaros now had 3,000–4,000 activists and had a lengthy record of successes against the government. The new Bordaberry government faced the difficult problem of locating fugitive Tupamaros, including Raul Sendic and the over 100 followers who had escaped from prison in September 1971, as well as identifying the large number of lawyers, electricians, tailors, and other common citizens who held regular jobs but were secretly MLN members. And even as the nation girded itself for a resumption of Tupamaro terrorist activities, which had been suspended before the November 1971 elections, the Tupamaros announced in February 1972 that they were resuming their terrorist offensive.

MLN commando units soon assassinated a prison officer accused of mistreating Tupamaro prisoners; wounded a police intelligence officer for allegedly supervising the torture of Tupamaros; and kidnapped the editor of the daily newspaper *Accion*, which was editorially supporting Bordaberry.[115] After assuming office in early March, Bordaberry sent to the general assembly a draft security law to replace the emergency measures first decreed by President Pacheco in June 1968. The draft law, which gave the executive stronger powers than those provided for under the emergency measures, was rejected by the general assembly, where Bordaberry's supporters were in a minority position in both houses.[116]

The legislature rapidly changed its viewpoint, however, when the Tupa-maros struck out violently and dramatically at government security personnel and ignited a multitude of gun battles throughout Montevideo. On April 14, 1968, the Tupamaros gunned down Professor Armando Acosta y Lara, a former undersecretary of the interior and a hardliner under Pacheco; Oscar Delega Luzardo, a senior police officer who was reportedly an expert in inter-rogating guerrilla prisoners; Delega's driver; and Ernesto Motta, a naval coun-terintelligence officer. Motta was the first officer of the armed forces to be killed by the Tupamaros in ten years of struggle against the government. These officials had been identified to the Tupamaros by a previously captured policeman as members of an antiterrorist "death squad" backed by the Minis-try of the Interior. The day's events included many unsuccessful Tupamaro attacks and many raids by security forces on suspected Tupamaro hideouts. Eight Tupamaros were killed and three were captured.[117]

Exacerbating the situation were many other incidents or disorders transpir-ing during the same general period, including two day-long general strikes; the escape on April 12 of sixteen Tupamaros from Punta Carretas prison; the involvement of right-wing extremists in twenty attacks against the homes and offices of Broad Front supporters; and the shooting by government forces of seven persons outside a communist club. After the three service commanders-in-chief went before the general assembly and stated that the government was being assaulted not by common criminals but by organized forces seeking to take power, President Bordaberry successfully pushed through the legisla-ture a declaration of a "state of internal war" and the suspension of civil rights.[118]

The new legislation, backed by implementing legislation and extensions, gave the army the power to hold suspects indefinitely, suspended the normal ban on searching homes without a warrant, and permitted the military courts to issue sentences of up to 30 years for subversive offenses. Large-scale security force dragnets were used in an attempt to round up all known or suspected Tupamaros. As the government counteroffensive continued into the summer and fall of 1972, the public, which had generally distrusted the police because of Tupamaro intimidation and infiltration, responded to the military's dominant role in the counterinsurgency campaign and rushed to military headquarters with information on suspected guerrilla personnel and activities.[119]

With the army leading the way, the security forces located 70 or more hide-outs, arsenals, caches of supplies, hospitals, and other secret sites. Many lists of names, addresses, and types of contributions from Uruguayan supporters of the MLN were found, as were large quantities of Tupamaro documents. The Tupamaros fought back with scattered "spectaculars," including the assassination on July 25, 1972, of Colonel Artigas Alvarez, army civil defense chief and brother of the commander-in-chief of the combined military and police forces that were combatting the Tupamaros. But with the capture on July 26, 1972, of leading Tupamaro Julio Marenales Saenz; the arrest on September 1, 1972, of Sendic; the death during 1972 of hundreds of Tupamaros; and the arrest of thousands of known and suspected Tupamaro personnel by the end of the year, the Tupamaro insurgency had been dealt a virtual death blow. The much publicized cell structure had been largely rolled up. And the discovery of security forces in late May 1972 of the Tupamaro's hidden "people's jail" and the release from the jail of Carlos Frick and Ulises Pereira Reverbel—who had been incarcerated for over a year—destroyed the legendary ability of the Tupamaros to kidnap (or "arrest") even the most prominent personalities, subject them to "trials," and condemn them to long prison sentences, all with total impunity.[120]

The exact plans of the Tupamaros in April 1972—when they struck out at the government "death squad,"—are still unclear, but it is apparent that they made a serious miscalculation. It has been speculated that the Tupamaros had planned to follow up the assassinations with a lengthy truce, during which they would have explained the reasons for their action and made political capital out of it. But the plan went awry when the armed forces reacted strongly and pushed the government and the legislature into declaring a "state of internal war." The Tupamaros had become overconfident and had underestimated the hostility in the armed forces toward their terrorist activities. The insurgents apparently had not expected that their multiple attacks on the security force personnel might be seen by the military as a direct challenge, nor were they aware that military intelligence had a detailed anti-Tupamaro contingency plan.[121]

The London-based weekly, *Latin America*, which regularly provides knowledgeable reporting on developments in the region, also noted that the Tupamaros blundered in intensifying their activities in the rural areas and in making political miscalculations. The attempt to establish guerrilla columns in the interior of the nation (*Plan Tatu*) was still in the developmental stage in early 1972. Lacking secure base areas, and operating out of their urban element in rural areas where they could be much more readily identified, the Tupamaros in the rural areas were virtually obliterated by the army in May and June of 1972.[122]

In the political realm, the Tupamaros miscalculated by striking only shortly after Bordaberry had taken office—during a honeymoon period when most of the public was still giving him the benefit of the doubt. Economic conditions might well have soon turned most of the populace against the new president. The economic squeeze and the wage freeze he imposed would likely have had a severe effect on popular support of the government. The cost of living increased by 11 percent in April alone. Some observers expected that by the fall of 1972, public opinion would have been enraged at the economic conditions.[123]

Before moving to the conclusion of this chapter, it is important to comment on political developments in Uruguay since the demise of the Tupamaros in 1972. These developments are relevant because they are a direct outgrowth of the successful counterinsurgency campaign.[124] The main political result of that campaign was the profound increase in the role of the Uruguayan military in politics. During the antiguerrilla campaign, the military discovered many Tupamaro documents, previously stolen, that disclosed widespread corruption in Uruguayan government and business circles. The military, dropping its long-held apolitical role, became as a whole greatly concerned with the same corruption and national economic decay that had troubled the Tupamaros. Despite considerable opposition from Bordaberry and supporters of the government in the business community, the military was able to retain most of the powers gained during the anti-Tupamaro campaign. The leaders of the military undertook an intensive war on "economic crimes."

Following a massive constitutional crisis in February 1972, in which the military refused to accept President Bordaberry's choice of a new minister of defense and put forth a list of proposed solutions to the nation's economic problems, the president averted possible bloodshed by agreeing to share power with a military-dominated national security council. Subsequent developments in Uruguay in 1973 included the June dissolution of the general assembly; the July dissolution of the communist-dominated CNT labor federation; the July arrest and imprisonment of former General Liber Seregini, who had been the Broad Front's presidential candidate in the November 1971 elections; the October closing of the national university; and the December outlawing of the previously legal Communist party of Uruguay and other leftist political parties.

It is beyond the scope of this chapter to treat further developments in Uruguay after 1973. But the upshot is that—largely as a result of the anti-Tupamaro campaign—the Uruguayan military assumed a dominant role in Uruguayan politics, a role which it has not relinquished. And while some Tupamaros remain in Uruguayan society, even engaging in sporadic and relatively minor acts of violence, the Tupamaro movement as a significant threat to the government was essentially eliminated in 1972.[125]

## Summary and Conclusion

Before the 1972 government counterinsurgency effort ripped apart the Tupamaro movement, the insurgents had been able to attain a position of considerable strength, even without external support, because the movement was virtually self-sufficient. This self-sufficiency—as well as the ability to remain strong without the use of foreign sanctuaries or secure bases in the Uruguayan interior—was made possible to a large extent by the operation of the Tupamaros within the environs of Montevideo and especially by the fact that the Tupamaros did not advance into the large-unit warfare which characterizes Jenkins's third and fourth stages of urban insurgency. If the Tupamaros had begun to occupy territory and engage the government forces in pitched battles, external support and sanctuaries might have proven vital to their ability to succeed in such activities. On the other hand, while there were indications in early 1972 that the Tupamaros were seriously considering acquiring various forms of external support, it is also quite conceivable that increased popular support of the Tupamaros, coupled with heightened government ineffectiveness, could have resulted in the Tupamaros' ultimately achieving their broad goal of overthrowing the existing government structure without ever receiving external support.

The environment gave the Tupamaro insurgency its setting and its fuel. Uruguay's particular environment, as viewed by the insurgents, led them to choose urban Montevideo as the focus of their revolutionary activity. By operating in the urban environment of Montevideo the Tupamaros obtained many advantages, such as hiding places, ready access to funds and weapons, and plentiful government and business community targets. But in the end the Tupamaros paid dearly for operating in Montevideo rather than out of secure base areas in the interior or from foreign sanctuaries. While in some respects the Tupamaro debacle was caused by deficiencies arising out of the MLN organizational structure, the major cause was the marked increase in government effectiveness in dealing with the insurgency. Despite the continuing economic crisis and no doubt considerable residual passive popular support for the Tupamaros, a suddenly well-organized and strongly committed Uruguayan government under the new president, Bordaberry, demonstrated that it had made substantial progress in improving its intelligence and other counterinsurgency capabilities; that it was willing to let the military forces and the military courts forcefully prosecute the anti-Tupamaro struggle; that it was sufficiently popular to obtain large numbers of voluntary reports on Tupamaro personalities and activities; and that it was willing to use any measures necessary, up to and including torture and the complete suspension of all personal civil rights, to gain victory over the insurgents. Once the government gained the upper hand in the intelligence area, the Tupamaros' concentration in Montevideo became a fatal liability.[126]

The government was able to gain detailed and accurate intelligence on the Tupamaros largely because of its stepped-up efforts in building up the intelligence capabilities of the security forces. Voluntarily offered intelligence from concerned citizens was also important during the anti-Tupamaro campaign. But major intelligence windfalls resulted from some deficiencies in the MLN organizational structure as it existed when the intensive counterinsurgency campaign began in April 1972. The organizational structure had been weakened greatly in 1971 and 1972 as a result of the escape from prison of some 180 captured Tupamaros. Although the jailbreaks were useful from a propaganda standpoint and in returning many fighters to the ranks of the MLN, ironically, they appear to have had very damaging effects in the long run:

> First, captured guerrillas obviously got to know one another well during their imprisonment. Hence, upon their release and reintegration into the ranks of the Tupamaro organization, the guerrillas' security network was unavoidably broken, because one of the basic operating rules of the Tupamaros was that members were not to know each other's true identity.
>
> When the military started to recapture some of these Tupamaros, it may have proven quite easy to extract accurate descriptions and true identities, and hence to obtain valuable information about individuals in different cells and columns. Second, the reintegration of freed guerrillas into the organization's ranks caused rivalries and some ill feelings. Indeed, among the escapees were many Tupamaro leaders and individuals with seniority who may have wanted or been granted leadership positions in detriment to those who had remained free. It is possible that these frictions may have accounted for more betrayals or quicker confessions than would otherwise have been the case.[127]

To a large extent, the success of the government security forces in breaking the back of the MLN in 1972 was due to revelations by Tupamaros like the high-ranking Hector Amodio Perez, who reportedly disclosed the location of some 30 hideouts, the "people's prison," a major field hospital, and a number of arsenals and documentation centers.[128] Although the number of hideouts and other Tupamaro facilities eliminated as a result of the disclosures of Amodio Perez was relatively small, what was most significant was the fact that he filled in the gaps in the security forces' knowledge of the key Tupamaro decision-making relationships. Compartmentalization is most effective at the cell level and possibly can limit the damage to the elimination of a cell when a single cell member is captured (assuming the cell leader is not captured and a confession extracted). Because compartmentalization can hardly exist at the highest levels of the organization. Amodio Perez's disclosures proved extremely valuable to the security forces.[129]

It should be emphasized that the effective government response to the Tupamaro insurgency was primarily military in nature. This expedient worked even as the nation's economic ills persisted and even as the bulk of the populace remained highly disenchanted with the performance of Uruguayan governments in coping with the economic crisis. But, just as generally sound and prosperous economy was not a contributing factor in the government's victory over the Tupamaros, its absence was probably the primary reason behind the initial popularity and successes of the Tupamaros.

For without a stagnant economy, it is unlikely that the Uruguayan people, who still enjoy one of the highest standards of living in Latin America, would have given much support to the Tupamaros or any similar group.

Some observers have stated that the key to the Tupamaros' success was a frustrated middle class.[130] The strong connections between the economic aspect of the environment and the popular support and government effectiveness variables are readily apparent. The persistent economic crisis and the government's inability to end the crisis prompted strikes and demonstrations that in turn prompted government countermeasures – in the name of law and order – and a government financial austerity program. The workers and other elements of the society became more dissatisfied and radicalized and even stronger government countermeasures were required. The Tupamaro insurgency benefitted tremendously from the intensifying spiral of violence and government countermeasures, and from its ability to express the economic, social, and political aspirations of a majority of the people.

There is a difference of opinion as to whether or not an urban insurgency like that of the Tupamaros requires popular support to attain victory. As we will see, the need for popular support depends on the ultimate goals of the insurgents. Russell and Hildner state that the urban guerrillas can remain very effective with a minimum of popular support:

> The need for popular support is not as critical to the urban insurgent as it is to the rural-based guerrilla. Since the urban guerrilla does not depend on the population at large to any great extent, its support is not a prerequisite for success. In fact, the urban insurgent may well be able to operate effectively even if the bulk of the urban population opposes him since it is as difficult for the population in any given urban area to determine who is a guerrilla as it is for the counterinsurgent forces. This has been evident in the inability of various Latin American nations to locate and rescue the victims of guerrilla kidnapings, despite the victim's and his captors' continued presence in the urban environment. Operational effectiveness in the absence of widespread popular support is illustrated by the Tupamaros in Uruguay, who draw their support primarily from intellectual, student, and upper-middle-class groups rather than from the middle and lower classes which constitute the bulk of the urban population.[131]

In contradistinction, Jenkins has noted the essentiality of popular support to success by urban guerrillas – it is a prerequisite for gaining political power. Although urban insurgents do not need popular support for sustenance, as do many rural-based insurgents, they must be selective in their terror and carefully avoid inflicting collateral damage – to avoid mass revulsion that could push the people to support the government, whatever the quality of its performance. Even though urban guerrilla warfare is often the expression of a minority that substitutes violence for a lack of widespread support it is not possible for urban guerrillas to keep a city paralyzed by fear forever. Jenkins noted that urban guerrilla warfare is above all a political and not a military campaign.[132] We can state that the importance of popular support to an urban insurgency depends to a large degree on the goals of the insurgents. If they aspire to going beyond terrorism and harassment of the government to the replacement of the existing regime with one that will pursue the insurgents' brand of political, economic, and social programs, then widespread active and passive popular support will likely be essential.

Passive popular support (i.e., sympathy, or at least indifference) was important to the Tupamaros, if for no other reason than to keep a large number of people neutral during the struggle with the government. The Tupamaros showed in their propaganda appeals, in their generally selective application of terror, and in several captured planning documents that they saw their movement as serving as the vanguard of a popular revolution that would erupt in the streets and cast out the ruling system. Based on available evidence, it seems that to a certain degree the Tupamaros actively sought widespread passive support. The vehicle for converting extensive passive support into support for the Tupamaro-inspired revolution was to be a national liberation front, in which both the Tupamaros and mass organizations such as the trade unions would cooperate in the armed struggle.

What is significant about the Tupamaro insurgency is that despite the various commitments to obtaining widespread popular support the Tupamaros, by their actions, actually enhanced the chances of their *not* receiving the degree of popular support the final victory required. This apparent ambiguity about the Tupamaro insurgency had its basis in the MLN's use of terror, and in the MLN's organization.

Terror, the major form of military activity used by the Tupamaros, proved to be counterproductive in spite of efforts to be selective in the choice of targets and complementary efforts to justify acts of terrorism as "expropriations," blows against "imperialism," etc. The Tupamaros avoided torture, massacres, mutilation, and indiscriminate bombings, and generally targeted individuals they believed were despised by the people.[133] But the Tupamaros lost their Robin Hood image when they began to systematically execute policemen and when they killed their American hostage, Dan Mitrione. The use of terror was successful in provoking government counterterror and the adoption of dictatorial methods by the government. But, although there was considerable public dismay at these developments, the reaction did not extend to the antigovernment demonstrations and violence envisaged by the Tupamaros.

Moss was prophetic when he noted in 1971, while commenting on the viability and successes of the Tupamaros, that in the rest of Latin America:

Urban guerrillas are learning to their cost that, if the government is sufficiently ruthless and can present a united front, effective repression is more likely than a popular uprising. The same is almost certainly true of Western societies. Modern techniques of police control rule out the possibility of a successful urban uprising unless a political crisis cripples the government or the loyalty of the security forces is in doubt.[134]

Jenkins provided very similar counsel in mid–1972 when he wrote:

Unless a portion of the army switches sides, however, or unless it is committed to battle elsewhere, the government will probably win any such overt contest for power [in reference to the urban uprising, or the "fifth stage" of his urban guerrilla warfare model]. Knowing this, urban guerrillas are sometimes willing to bargain with the government for a goal short of takeover. The government, long before its survival is threatened, may be willing to accede to certain demands by the guerrillas simply in order to end the violence.[135]

In retrospect, the comments of these two scholars seem very appropriate to the Uruguayan situation. The Tupamaro insurgency and the economic crisis with which it shared center stage in Uruguay can be held jointly responsible for fostering a predominant role for the Uruguayan military in the nation's politics.

Terror thus had the effect of provoking such a severe government—or military—reaction that the Tupamaros were decimated by the antiterrorist offensive. But, even before 1972, was the terrorism gaining followers? One will never know for sure, but the results of the presidential election of late 1971, in which the Tupamaro-backed candidate was soundly defeated, would seem to indicate that the general populace, despite the persisting economic crisis, did not see the Tupamaros' violent approach as being the answer to the nation's economic doldrums. The people may have tired of the terror, while seeing few if any appreciable improvements in their standard of living. Also, the fact that the Tupamaros continued to rely primarily on terror after a decade of struggle may have significantly tarnished the image of the MLN as a progressive organization continually strengthening itself vis-à-vis the government.

Besides the use of terror, the Tupamaros' organizational structure and practices also had the effect of limiting the amount of popular support enjoyed by the MLN. It is important here to recall the distinction between active and passive popular support. With an estimated maximum membership of some 3,000 to 4,000 members, including fighters and service personnel, the MLN was always a limited organization. Despite various attempts to garner additional passive popular support, the Tupamaros seemed content to keep the number of active MLN members small. The MLN was essentially an elitist, compartmentalized, and clandestine organization.

Although Tupamaro propaganda and documents did not appear to make a distinction between active and passive popular supporters, the distinction was nonetheless operational. Through their stringent recruiting criteria and practices and their vigorous training programs, the Tupamaros made every effort to insure that persons admitted to the inner movement were ideologically sound and not government infiltration agents. This recruiting process limited the number of incoming members, as did the existence of the highly compartmentalized cell structure. With compartmentalized cells comprising the greater part of the organization, the lack of contact with other cells, much less the public, meant that contact by Tupamaros was minimal with many citizens who might have been susceptible to Tupamaro recruitment approaches.

Most insurgencies require a differentiation of the organization, or the creation of structures through which political supporters in the population can be mobilized to assist in the insurgent effort. The Tupamaros were hindered in this regard by the lack of secure rural base areas in which they could develop such organizations. Even within the confines of Montevideo, they did not create significant followings within existing groups, nor did they develop front organizations. It is possible that they made every effort to create Tupamaro followings in such organizations as the trade unions through the use of the Tupamaro support committees or other measures. But, in light of the elitist nature of the organization and the apparent lack of concrete plans for building a mass national liberation front, it appears that the Tupamaros were less than fully committed to building an activist Tupamaro following among the general populace.

In their deviation from the more traditional guerrilla theory and from traditional Uruguayan and Latin American political patterns, the Tupamaros further limited their ability to attract popular support. Regardless of the respective merits of the Maoist and Guevara-Debray theses (as to initiating political activity or the armed struggle first), it seems apparent that in the case of the Tupamaros the failure to establish meaningful, broad-based, and ideologically committed mass organizations rendered the MLN vulnerable to strong pressure from the military. If the Tupamaros had ever articulated a coherent ideology and made it public, they might have attracted more followers, including many who might have hung on with the organization for ideological reasons and been less inclined to drop out when the militant aspects of the movement were successfully curtailed by the government. But the Tupamaros never publicly articulated a coherent ideology.[136]

Perhaps more important than the lack of coherent ideology—at least in the Latin American context, where ideology is of less importance than personalities—was the practice of not identifying the Tupamaro movement with a particular leader or leaders. Unlike other insurgents in Latin America, the Tupamaros had no single dynamic leader attracting followers, inspiring them to fight against overwhelming odds. There was no Tupamaro leader demonstrating great *machismo.* The ideal qualities of physical strength and dominance, courage, self-confidence, self-assurance, verbal facility, sexual prowess, and action-orientation that comprise *machismo* are more important in most Latin American nations, including Uruguay, than parties or ideologies.[137] *Personalismo,* or personalism, also traditionally plays a major role in Uruguayan politics. "Friendship, kinship, and loyalty to individual leaders have often overshadowed issues in determining the compositions of factions or coalitions."[138] Thus, the lack of charisma – or the lack of charisma actively applied – may have been a significant factor in the outcome of this insurgency. One can speculate what might have happened if Raul Sendic or some other Tupamaro had been suited for and/or desired to play a strong, publicly visible leadership role. It is possible that such a leader – through the persistent and public demonstration of his fighting skills, masculinity, courage, verbal facility, and other aspects of *machismo* – might have been able to facilitate the building of a broad mass following among the Uruguayan populace, had such a following indeed been desired.

In general, an insurgent movement needs less popular support when the government is weak and the army is demoralized. But when the government is strong and the army is confident, more popular support is needed by the insurgent movement.[139] When the Uruguayan government launched its intensive counterinsurgency campaign in the spring of 1972, the Tupamaros needed all the popular support they could obtain – using the term in the broadest possible sense. In the end they proved to be but several thousand very vulnerable guerrillas, unable to hide for long even in sprawling metropolitan Montevideo. There were many reasons why the Tupamaros were all but eliminated from the Uruguayan political scene. Among the major factors in the Tupamaros' demise were the deficiencies arising out of the MLN's compartmentalized organizational structure; the general lack of diversification or complexity of the MLN beyond the 3,000 to 4,000 activists; the ultimately counterproductive use of terror (either in terms of alienating the public or in provoking effective government countermeasures; and the emphasis on what Jenkins referred to as the tactics of the few (guerrilla warfare) and the relative lack of emphasis on the tactics of the many (mass organization).

Besides these contributing factors related to the popular support and organizational variables, government effectiveness was clearly the decisive factor in determining the outcome of the Tupamaro insurgency. The integral elements of the government's ultimate response to the insurgency were the expanded intelligence and other counterinsurgency capabilities; the assignment of the major counterinsurgency role to the military; the cooperation of significant elements of the population in the antiterrorist campaign; and the ability and willingness of the government to suspend civil liberties and carry out repressive measures. Regardless of the impact on the practice of democracy in Uruguay, the single most important reason for the downfall of the Tupamaros appears to have been the firm and sufficient application of forceful measures by the government.

## Notes

1. Robert Moss, *The War for the Cities* (New York: Coward, McGann, and Geoghegan, 1972), p. 247. This excellent volume is especially informative because it combines insightful discussion of such general topics as terrorism and the government response to urban insurgency with rather detailed case studies of urban insurgent activity in numerous locales including the United States, Ulster, Quebec, Brazil, and Uruguay. Some of Moss's earlier but still very valuable works in this area will be cited below. The significance of Moss's work and an overview of the literature on urban insurgency in Latin America are contained in Charles A. Russell, James A. Miller, and Robert E. Hildner, "The Urban Guerrilla in Latin America: A Select Bibliography," *Latin American Research Review* 9 no. 1 (Spring 1974):37-79. This review article includes text and 20 annotated references dealing specifically with the Tupamaro insurgency of Uruguay.

2. See the discusion in Chapter 1, this volume.

3. See Chapter 1 (this volume), p. 3.

4. The information in this and the next two paragraphs was compiled from the following works: "*Los Tupamaros y la lucha armada,*" *Punta Final* (Santiago, Chile), 58 no. 2 (July 2, 1968):1-8, passim; "*Uruguay: los Tupamaros en acción,*" *Tricontinental* (March–April 1970):45; Ernesto Mayans, ed., *Tupamaros, Antología Documental* (Cuernavaca, Mexico: *Centro Intercultural de Documentacion,* 1971), passim; Antonio Mercader and Jorge de Vera, *Tupamaros: estrategia y acción* (Montevideo: Editorial Alfa, 1969), pp. 9–11, 33–47, 145–161; Robert Moss, "Urban Guerrillas in Uruguay," *Problems of Communism* 20 no. 5 (September–October 1971):14-23; and Moss, *War,* pp. 211-217. The Mayans and Mercader–de Vera works are especially valuable references and contain fresh analyses as well as extensive chronologies of Tupamaro activities, and contain reprints of important Tupamaro documents and writings of other authors. With regard to the name Tupamaros, it can actually be traced to either one or both of two Inca chiefs: (a) Tupac Amaru, who harassed the Spanish near Cuzco in present-day Peru until killed by the Spanish in 1571; and (b) his lineal descendent, Jose Gabriel Condorcanqui, who used the name Tupac Amaru and revolted against the Spanish in 1780. See Thomas E. Weil et al., *Area Handbook for Uruguay* (Washington, D.C.: U.S. Government Printing Office, 1971), p. 380. Hereinafter identified as *Handbook/Uruguay.*

5. Moss, *Problems of Communism,* p. 17.

6. Arturo C. Porzecanski, *Uruguay's Tupamaros – The Urban Guerrilla* (New York: Praeger, 1973), p. 31.

7. Ernesto "Che" Guevara, *Guerrilla Warfare* (New York: Praeger, 1961), p. 3.

8. Ibid., p. 4.

9. Ibid., p. 5.

10. Regis Debray, *Revolution in the Revolution?* (New York: Grove Press, 1967), passim.

11. Robert J. Alexander, "The Communist Parties of Latin America," *Problems of Communism*, 19 no. 4 (July–August 1970):44–45. This scholar states he has no knowledge of any authoritative Cuban spokesman ever taking issue with Debray's book.

12. Ibid.

13. Debray, *Revolution*, p. 75.

14. Charles A. Russell, "Cuban Theories of Revolutionary War Examined in a Comparative Context" (unpublished Ph.D. dissertation, The American University, Washington, D.C., 1971), pp. 27–29. See also Guevara, *Guerrilla Warfare*, pp. 27–29; and Debray, *Revolution*, pp. 68–78.

15. Richard Gott, *Guerrilla Movements in Latin America* (New York: Doubleday, 1972), passim. While treating insurgency developments elsewhere in Latin America, this lengthy book focuses on the insurgencies that developed in Guatemala, Venezuela, Colombia, Peru, and Bolivia.

16. Ibid.

17. Charles A. Russell and Robert E. Hildner, "Urban Insurgency in Latin America: Its Implications for the Future," *Air University Review*, 22 no. 6 (September–October 1971):55.

18. Carlos Marighella, "Handbook of Urban Guerrilla Warfare," in Marighella's *For the Liberation of Brazil* (Harmondsworth: Penguin, 1971), p. 80. A version of Marighella's handbook, called the "Minimanual of the Urban Guerrilla" is an appendix to Robert Moss's "Urban Guerrilla Warfare," *Adelphi Papers* no. 79 (1971): 1–42.

19. Marighella, "Handbook," p. 63.

20. Porzecanski, *Uruguay's Tupamaros*, p. 16; and "Uruguay: People's War," *Latin America*, 6 no. 24 (June 16, 1972), pp. 189–190.

21. Porzecanski, *Uruguay's Tupamaros*, p. 16.

22. Mercader and de Vera, *Tupamaros*, pp. 15–16. For additional treatment of the Tupamaros' review of the Cuban experience and their decision to emphasize urban struggle, see also Porzecanski, *Uruguay's Tupamaros*, pp. 15–16; "*Los tupamaros y la lucha armada,*" *Punto Final*; and, "*Uruguay: los Tupamaros en acción,*" *Tricontinental*. The *Punto Final* article is translated in Joint Publications Research Service (JPRS), *Translations on Latin America* (Nr. 419, JPRS 51834, November 20, 1970, pp. 40–53). This translation is of the September–October 1970 issue of *Politique Aujourd'hui* (Paris) which was translated from the original Chilean article. Both the above cited Mercader and de Vera and Mayans texts contain transcripts of the important *Punto Final* article, but the JPRS text will be cited herein as it is the most available to English-speaking readers. The *Punto Final* article is important because it is based on an authoritative interview with a Tupamaro spokesman and includes the "Thirty Questions to a Tupamaro" dialogue.

23. The advantages to be derived from conducting an insurgency in an urban environment noted were based on a review of the following: Robert J. Black, "A Change in Tactics: The Urban Insurgent," *Air University Review* 23 no. 2 (January–February 1972):50–58; Debray, *Revolution*, pp. 68–78; Guevara, *Guerrilla Warfare*, pp. 19–20;

Mercader and de Vera, *Tupamaros*, p. 16; Marighella, "Handbook," passim; Porzecanski, *Uruguay's Tupamaros*, pp. 15–16; and Russell and Hildner, "Urban Insurgency in Latin America," pp. 56–57.

24. See the Introduction, entitled "The Social and Political Philosophy of Abraham Guillen," in Donald C. Hodges, editor, *Philosophy of the Urban Guerrilla—The Revolutionary Writings of Abraham Guillen* (New York: William Morrow and Co., 1973), pp. 1–55.

25. Hodges, *Philosophy*, p. 250.

26. Ibid., pp. 250–251.

27. Ibid., p. 250.

28. Preston E. James, *Latin America* (New York: Odyssey Press, 1959), pp. 366–380; and John Gunther, *Inside South America* (New York: Pocket Books, 1967), pp. 252–263.

29. As might be expected, strength estimates regarding the MLN vary. Mercader and de Vera, p. 95, state that in 1968 there were probably about 1,000 Tupamaros, of which 50–100 were engaged in commando actions, while the rest served in back-up and support roles. *Handbook/Uruguay*, p. 225, states that there were in early 1970 an estimated 500–1,000 fighters and an additional 2,000–5,000 collaborators. Moss, *War*, p. 211, notes that the movement, which probably contained less than 50 active members in 1965, contained an estimated 3,000 members by August 1970. Lewis H. Diuguid, "Guerrillas Weakening in Argentina, Uruguay," *Washington Post (WP)*, July 26, 1972, states that the Tupamaro movement at its peak contained 3,500 members. As we state that the MLN contained a maximum of 3,000–4,000 fighters and active supporters, we are assuming that the ratio between fighters and supporters was at least 1:5 and that some of the latter were less committed to the movement than the fighters.

30. Andrew M. Scott et al., *Insurgency* (Chapel Hill, N.C.: University of North Carolina Press, 1970), pp. 61–65. This volume offers a very useful dynamic model concerning the working of an insurgent movement and, despite its virtual neglect of insurgency that emphasizes the urban environment, is nonetheless must reading for any student of comparative insurgencies.

31. Moss, *War*, pp. 217–218, notes that the apparent Tupamaro indifference to ideology stemmed from "an emotional faith in the primacy of the deed as well as from the desire to appeal to as broad a range of public opinion as possible." Porzecanski, *Uruguay's Tupamaros*, Chapters 1 and 2, has been able, with the help of Tupamaro pronouncements, interview records, and documents captured in and before 1972, to piece together a view of Tupamaro political ideology, with political ideology being "a specific set of shared beliefs about what society is and ought to be, including a certain commitment to act" (p. 1). But since significant portions of Porzecanski's excellent ideological portrait of the Tupamaros were drawn from documents never made public by the Tupamaros, some aspects of their ideology did not serve as esoteric and exoteric appeals to people outside of the MLN.

32. Porzecanski, *Uruguay's Tupamaros*, p. 16.

33. Ibid., p. 9.

34. *Punto Final* (page references to the above cited JPRS trans.), pp. 45, 52.

35. Ibid., p. 46.

36. Ibid., pp. 46–47.

37. Ibid., p. 47.

38. Ibid., pp. 48–49.

39. Ibid., p. 49.

40. Ibid., pp. 49–52.

41. Ibid., p. 52.

42. Ted Robert Gurr, *Why Men Rebel* (Princeton: Princeton University Press, 1970). See especially p. 24 and the rest of Chapter 2.

43. Moss, *Problems of Communism*, pp. 16–17; David Reed, "Taps for the Tupamaros," *Reader's Digest* 101 no. 607 (November 1972):173–176, 183; and, Samuel Shapiro, "Uruguay's Lost Paradise," *Current History* 62 no. 366 (February 1972):98–99.

44. Moss, *Problems of Communism*.

45. Moss, *War*, p. 213.

46. Ibid., pp. 220–221.

47. "'Uruguay' Confrontation," *Latin America* 6 no. 20 (May 19, 1972):156–157.

48. Ibid.

49. Porzecanski, *Uruguay's Tupamaros*, pp. 14–15.

50. Moss, *War*, p. 32.

51. For treatment of the uses of "armed propaganda," see Moss, *Problems of Communism*, pp. 20–21, and Moss's other works cited in this chapter; Scott et al., *Insurgency*, pp. 92–102; Brian M. Jenkins, "An Urban Strategy for Guerrillas and Governments," RAND Paper P-4607-1 (Santa Monica, Ca.: The RAND Corp., 1972), pp. 4–5; and, Marighella, "Handbook," pp. 89–90.

52. Porzecanski, *Uruguay's Tupamaros*, p. 14.

53. *Punto Final*, p. 43.

54. Frances M. Foland, "Uruguay's Urban Guerrillas–A New Model for Revolution?" *New Leader* 54 no. 19 (October 4, 1971):9.

55. *Punto Final*, p. 43.

56. Moss, *Problems of Communism*, p. 20.

57. The term "political control system" is taken from the very useful discussion in Soctt et al., *Insurgency*, Chapter 6.

58. Moss, *Problems of Communism*, p. 21.

59. Moss, *War*, p. 230.

60. John Litt and James Kohl, "In the Mouth of the Monster–The Guerrillas of Montevideo," *Nation* 214 No. 9 (February 28, 1972):270.

61. Moss, *Problems of Communism*, pp. 21–22.

62. Ibid.

63. Moss, *Adelphi Paper* no. 79, p. 10.

64. Porzecanski, *Uruguay's Tupamaros*, pp. 20–21.

65. Maria Esther Gilio, *The Tupamaro Guerrillas* (New York: Saturday Review Press, 1972), pp. 125–233; and, Foland, *New Leader*, p. 9.

66. Moss, *Adelphi Paper* no. 79, pp. 9, 15.

67. Information compiled from the following sources: "Uruguay: Prison Visitor," *Latin America* 6 no. 17 (April 28, 1972):130, 132; Foland, *New Leader*, p. 9; Robert F. Lamberg, "*La guerrilla urbana,*" *Foro Internacional* (Mexico) 11 no. 3 (January–March 1971): 421–443, passim; Litt and Kohl, *Nation*, pp. 270–272; Mayans, *Antología,* especially the chronology, pp. 3-1 to 3-63; and, Mercader and de Vera, *Tupamaros,* pp. 145–173;

Moss, *Problems of Communism*, pp. 18–20; Moss, "Urban Guerrillas in Latin America," *Conflict Studies* no. 8 (1970), passim; and Moss, "Uruguay: Terrorism Versus Democracy," *Conflict Studies* no. 14 (1971), passim.

68. Jenkins, RAND Paper, p. 7.

69. *Handbook/Uruguay*, p. 226.

70. *Punto Final*, pp. 44–45; and Moss, *War*, p. 227.

71. Moss, *War*, pp. 217, 223.

72. "Torture Confirmed in Uruguay," WP, June 22, 1970.

73. Moss, *War*, pp. 217, 223.

74. "Uruguay: What Next?" *Latin America* 5 no. 37 (September 10, 1971):298–300.

75. "Uruguay: Cliff-Hanger," *Latin America* 5 no. 49 (December 3, 1971):385.

76. See pp. 11–13.

77. Porzecanski, *Uruguay's Tupamaros*, pp. 20–23.

78. *Punto Final*, pp. 49–52; *Handbook/Uruguay*, p. 223; Litt and Kohl, *Nation*, pp. 269–270; and Moss, *War*, pp. 219–220.

79. Porzecanski, *Uruguay's Tupamaros*, p. 17.

80. Porzecanski, *Uruguay's Tupamaros*, passim, provides the most concise view of Tupamaro organization. The Mayans and Mercader and de Vera works contain a wealth of valuable information, and Moss's various works touching on Uruguay also offer excellent treatment of major organizational aspects.

81. Porzecanski, *Uruguay's Tupamaros*, pp. 32–36; Mercader and de Vera, *Tupamaros*, pp. 97–100.

82. Porzecanski, *Uruguay's Tupamaros*.

83. Ibid.

84. Ibid. See also Litt and Kohl, *Nation*, pp. 268–270; and Moss, *War*, pp. 219–222.

85. Moss, *War*, p. 222.

86. Gilio, *Tupamaro Guerrillas*, p. 105.

87. *Punto Final*, pp. 47–48.

88. Moss, *War*, p. 222.

89. Ibid., and Porzecanski, *Uruguay's Tupamaros*, pp. 60–61.

90. Porzecanski, *Uruguay's Tupamaros*, pp. 34–35.

91. For example, see Porzecanski, *Uruguay's Tupamaros*, pp. 68–70; and the works cited in note 119, below.

92. Porzecanski, *Uruguay's Tupamaros*, p. 41.

93. Ibid., p. 23.

94. Russell and Hildner, "Urban Insurgency in Latin America," pp. 58–59.

95. Moss, *War*, p. 221.

96. "Los Principios Describes Guerrilla Meeting in Cordoba," Foreign Broadcast Information Service/*Latin America* (August 31, 1970):B-1. Similar to this meeting in Argentina was another meeting in early 1974. Following the meeting, representatives of the Tupamaros, the People's Revolutionary Army of Argentina, the Movement of the Revolutinary Left in Chile, and the National Liberation Army of Bolivia announced that the groups would pool their resources and support one another in unified operations in South America. The Tupamaros, apparently now short of weapons, funds, and other material needed to engage in combat operations, hoped to gain material and perhaps even manpower assistance through closer cooperation with other guerrilla groups.

97. "Hope in Uruguay?" *Christian Science Monitor (CSM)*, March 6, 1972.

98. The Maoist insurgency model is discussed in Chapter 1.

99. The following discussion of Jenkins' five-stage urban insurgency model is drawn from Jenkins, RAND Paper, pp. 4–8.

100. Jenkins, RAND Paper, p. 7.

101. Mercader and de Vera, *Tupamaros*, p. 95.

102. Jenkins, RAND Paper, p. 8. Jenkins noted that the Irish Republican Army was the movement which had advanced furthest toward the fifth stage, having definitely reached stage three and at times being able to mobilize mass movements behind it. All other urban guerrilla groups were seen in stages one or possibly two.

103. *Handbook/Uruguay*, pp. 211, 269–270, 319–320.

104. Russell and Hildner, "Urban Insurgency in Latin America," p. 60–63.

105. Moss, *War*, p. 232.

106. *Handbook/Uruguay*, pp. 371, 384.

107. Ibid., pp. 371–373.

108. Ibid., p. 225; Porzecanski, *Uruguay's Tupamaros*, p. 53; James Lingenfelter, "Uruguay: Urban Guerrillas and Counterinsurgency" (unpublished research paper, Air Command and Staff College, Air University, Maxwell Air Force Base, Alabama: April 1973), pp. 31–32.

109. *Handbook/Uruguay*, pp. 383, 393–394.

110. Ibid., pp. 217, 226, 261.

111. Ibid., pp. 374, 383–385.

112. Ibid., pp. 385–388.

113. Lingenfelter, "Uruguay: Urban Guerrillas," p. 31.

114. Ibid., pp. 23–27.

115. "Uruguay: New Leader, Old Policy," *Latin America* 6 no. 7 (February 18, 1972):50, 52.

116. "Uruguay: Playing Chicken," *Latin America* 6 no. 11 (March 17, 1972):84, 86.

117. "Uruguay: Country at War," *Latin America* 6 no. 16 (April 21, 1972):121–122, 124.

118. Ibid.

119. Issues of *Latin America, CSM, WP*, and *New York Times (NYT)* for the summer and fall of 1972 provide continuous coverage of the anti-Tupamaro campaign and its results. Some representative articles are: Lewis H. Diuguid, "Guerrillas Weakening in Argentina, Uruguay," *WP*, July 26, 1972; James Nelson Goodsell, "Uruguay, Guerrillas in Seesaw Fight," *CSM*, August 5, 1972; Goodsell, "Guerrillas Fare Poorly in Latin America," *CSM*, January 8, 1973; Juan de Onis, "Life in Uruguay Disrupted by Violence and Inflation," *NYT*, June 15, 1972; and Julio Villaverde, "Uruguay's 'Internal War' Routs Tupamaros," *WP*, July 2, 1972.

120. Diuguid, "Guerrillas Weakening."

121. "Uruguay: Confrontation," *Latin America* 6 no. 27 (July 7, 1972):213–214.

122. Ibid., plus "Uruguay: People's War," *Latin America* 6 no. 24 (June 16, 1972): 189–190.

123. "Uruguay: Confrontation," *Latin America*.

124. For material in the remainder of this paragraph and in the next two paragraphs, see the regular issues of the publications mentioned in note 119 above for the period concerned. Specific references are: "Military Revolts in Uruguay," *WP*, February 10,

1973; and, Lewis H. Diuguid, "Democracy Fades in Uruguay," *WP*, February 13, 1973.

125. "Police, Tupamaro Montevideo Clash Leaves Four Dead," FBIS, *Latin America* (April 22, 1974):K–1.

126. Lingenfelter provides a summary of the major reasons behind the government's success in its 1972 counterinsurgency campaign, "Uruguay: Urban Guerrillas," pp. 40–42.

127. Porzecanski, *Uruguay's Tupamaros*, pp. 69–70.

128. "Uruguay: Under Torture," *Latin America* 6 No. 35 (September 1, 1972):279.

129. Porzecanski, *Uruguay's Tupamaros*, p. 69.

130. James N. Goodsell, "Urban Guerrillas: Ebbing Influence or Wave of the Future?" *CSM*, December 3, 1971.

131. Russell and Hildner, "Urban Insurgency in Latin America," p. 60.

132. Jenkins, RAND Paper, pp. 8–10.

133. Moss, *War*, p. 223.

134. Moss, *Adelphi Paper*, no. 79, p. 3.

135. Jenkins, RAND Paper, p. 7. This statement was alluded to earlier in this chapter. The Tupamaros did attempt to negotiate with the armed forces in July 1972, several months after the intensive antiterrorist campaign had begun. They did not reach a satisfactory agreement and the talks ended when the Tupamaros assassinated Colonel Alvarez. In this regard, see "Uruguay: Military Mystery," *Latin America* 6 no. 31 (August 4, 1972):247.

136. See note 31 above.

137. *Handbook/Uruguay*, p. 183.

138. Ibid., p. 268.

139. See the discussion in Chapter 1.

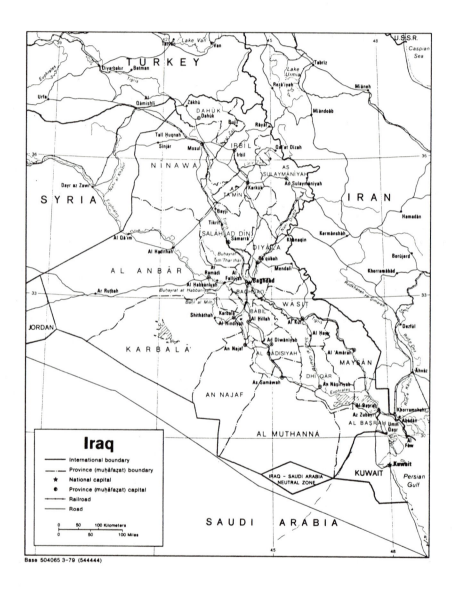

## Iraq

— International boundary
—··— Province (muḥāfaẓat) boundary
★ National capital
⊛ Province (muḥāfaẓat) capital
┅ Railroad
— Road

0   50   100 Kilometers
0   50   100 Miles

Base 504065 3-79 (544444)

# 6
# Iraq: The Kurdish Rebellion

*Paul R. Viotti*

Attempts to establish an independent or semi-autonomous homeland for Kurdish nationals have thus far met with failure. The most recent effort, an insurgency in northern Iraq led by Mullah Mustafa Barzani and his sons, Idris and Messaoud, collapsed in 1975 when the shah of Iran withdrew support for the movement. The Kurdish fighting forces (Pesh Merga) numbered on the order of at least 20 to 25 thousand and were under the direction of the charismatic septuagenarian leader, Barzani.

The ultimate aim of the Kurds may have been to establish a separate and autonomous Kurdish state, but the leadership of the insurgency was, in practice, willing to accept far less. Somewhat pragmatic in their dealings with Baghdad, Mullah Mustafa and his cohorts argued only that they should have greater control over Kurdish areas of the country, increased representation in the central government, and a more favorable allocation of economic resources. Thus, the thrust of the insurgency in practice was more reformist than revolutionary or secessionist – seeking merely to change the allocation of political and economic power within the Iraqi system rather than transform or fundamentally alter the system itself. On the other hand, the Baghdad regime never did see Barzani's movement as purely reformist. Instead, the Kurds were perceived as pursuing limited aims as a tactical first step toward their ultimate goal of achieving status as a separate nation-state, thus reestablishing a Kurdish political order with roots in ancient times.[1]

By late 1979 the Kurdish movement was best described as quiescent, although occasional clashes between Kurdish irregulars and government troops had been reported. The death of Barzani was an additional setback for the Kurdish movement. Moreover, the Baghdad regime has taken steps to relocate thousands of Kurds from settlements along the rugged Iranian border to areas more completely within Iraqi government control.[2] Nevertheless, political instability and alteration of the regime in Iran could well give impetus to a renewal of the Kurdish insurgency, perhaps within Iranian borders. Indeed, there have already been reports of uprisings in northwestern Iran, home of more than two million Kurds. Kurdish activity has also been noted in southeastern Turkey, perhaps with Syrian support. In any event, external support remains absolutely essential to any renewal of the insurgency. As noted above, termination of Iranian support for the Kurdish insurgency in Iraq forced the withdrawal of Barzani's troops, who had already suffered major losses in confrontation with the numerically and qualitatively superior Soviet-supported Iraqi forces. Assuming the Soviets do not shift toward support for the Kurds and assuming continuation of improved relations between Iran and Iraq and other states in the region, prospects for a successful Kurdish insurgency remain poor.

## Historical Aspects of the Kurdish Rebellion

The Kurdish peoples trace their history in the mountainous border area of present-day Iran, Iraq, the Soviet Union, Turkey, and Syria to more than two millennia B.C. Said to be descendants of the ancient Medes, the Kurds are of Aryan or Indo-European stock who later invaded or were invaded by several national groups including Persian Aryans, Turks and Turkomans, Mongols, Armenians, Arabs, and Assyrians. One observer has noted that "their physical characteristics vary according to the degree and kind of the admixture."[3]

Converted to Islam in the middle of the seventh century A.D. by invading Arabs, the Kurds made an impression on European history in the twelfth century through the successful campaign led by Saladin the Great, a Kurd, against Christian crusaders under Richard Coeur de Lion. Indeed, under Saladin, Kurdish influences spread to include large areas of present-day Iran, Iraq, Turkey, Syria, and the Soviet Union. Saladin, it should be noted, remains a Kurdish national hero to the present day.

The Mongols swept across Kurdish areas in the thirteenth and fourteenth centuries. The savage records of Hulago Khan (grandson of Ghengis Khan), Tamerlane, and others left their mark on Kurdish history. Nevertheless, the Kurds resisted the Mongol invaders through resort to defensive guerrilla warfare—a strategy that had a greater measure of success in the mountains than in the plains areas.[4]

Limited Ottoman control over Kurdish areas was established in the sixteenth and seventeenth centuries, following several hegemonic wars between Turks and Persians. As was true in so many other parts of the Ottoman Empire, considerable local autonomy was granted to the Kurds in exchange for tribute and soldiers to fight against Turkey's adversaries. The Ottomans attempted to establish greater control over the Kurdish tribes in the nineteenth century, but this policy was met by considerable Kurdish resistance and much blood was shed on both sides.

Ottoman rule, however limited it may have been, was ended by the Allied victory over the Central Powers in World War I. Kurdish fighting units had been established during the war to support the Ottoman cause—seen by at least some Kurds as another *jihad* or holy war. Kurdish elements reportedly fought well against the Russians and their Armenian allies. As the impending defeat of Turkey by the British became clear, Kurdish leaders sought to influence the latter in favor of a Kurdish national state. The result was the Treaty of Sevres in 1920, which provided for "a scheme of local autonomy for the predominantly Kurdish areas." A setback for Kurdish national aspirations followed, however, with the failure of the international community to ratify the Treaty of Sevres. The subsequent Treaty of Lausanne (1923), which established other states in the region, did not provide for a separate Kurdistan.

Assimilation or, more correctly, subjugation of Kurds in Turkey began in earnest under Mustafa Kemal Ataturk. Kurdish revolts in eastern Turkey in the 1920s and the 1930s were crushed by Turkish government forces. The Turkish government today refuses even to acknowledge the existence of a separate Kurdish nationality within its borders and refers to its more than two million Kurds euphemistically as "mountain Turks."

The more than 100,000 Kurds in the Soviet Union met a similar fate. Somewhat isolated from their brethren in neighboring countries since the post–World War I period, they have been firmly under Soviet control. It is important to note that both Turkey and the Soviet Union have been careful, particularly in recent years, to prevent active support by the Kurds in their territories for rebellions occurring in the more southern Kurdish-inhabited countries, notably Iraq.

With respect to Iran, military actions were undertaken by Reza Shah, who reigned in the pre–World War II period. Efforts were also made under Reza Shah to assimilate the Kurds by encouraging the nomadic tribes to settle in towns and villages. The Kurds resisted the Iranians as well as the Iraqis, who were under British mandate until 1932. Noteworthy were the efforts of the Barzanis under Mullah Mustafa's older brother, Sheikh Ahmed Barzani, and several other tribes to thwart British and Iraqi attempts to wrest control of Kurdish-inhabited areas of northeastern Iraq. During World War II, however, Soviet and British troops jointly occupied the Iran-Iraq border area in support of the Allied cause. The presence of Soviet forces in northwestern Iran gave considerable freedom of action to Kurdish nationalists. The Komula, later to become the Kurdish Democratic Party, was formed in 1942. The Kurdish national leader, Mullah Mustafa Barzani,[5] who had fought with Sheikh Ahmed in the early 1930s against the British-sponsored Iraqis, escaped in 1943 from Suleimaniya in northern Iraq where he had been living under surveillance since an abortive insurrection in 1932. Leading several hundred insurgents, Mullah Mustafa was successful in skirmishes with the Iraqi army and gained a reputation in the World War II period as a military leader. Another Kurd, Qazi Mohammed, emerged in 1944 as de facto leader of the Komula, then headquartered in the occupied town of Mahabad in the Soviet zone of northwestern Iran. In 1945 Qazi Mohammed ended the formal secrecy of the Komula and renamed it the Kurdish Democratic Party (KDP). Another Kurdish political organization, the Heva, was also formed in 1942, but it operated principally in Iraq. For his part, Mullah Mustafa joined neither organization, forming instead his own Freedom party in 1945. Under pressure from the Iraqi army, Mullah Mustafa finally withdrew to Iran with his armed followers and settled in Mahabad. In January 1946 Qazi Mohammed announced the formation of a separate Kurdish state and became its first president. Mullah Mustafa became the Mahabad Republic's first military leader with the rank of general, which he bore until his death.

Under Allied diplomatic pressure, the Soviets finally withdrew their troops from the region in the spring, a move that allowed Iranian military forces access to the area. By December 1946 forces of the neighboring Soviet puppet Azerbaijani state were defeated and Iranian troops entered the Mahabad Republic. Although Qazi Mohammed capitulated, he was later executed by the Iranians. Mullah Mustafa at first resisted the Iranian advance but ultimately began his long march, retreating across the mountains into the Soviet Union, which he reached in mid-June 1947.

The Iranian armed forces "pacified" the Kurds in the late 1940s and during the 1950s the Kurdish situation in both Iran and Iraq remained relatively quiescent. In the mid–1950s the new United Democratic Party of Kurdistan (UDPK) was formed in Iraq with Mullah Mustafa as its nominal head, even though he remained in exile in the Soviet Union and reportedly had no knowledge of his appointment. One of the UDPK central committee members was Jalal Talabani, a Kurd who would later become one of Mullah Mustafa's rivals. The UDPK at this time clearly had left-wing leanings and apparently maintained close contacts with the Iraqi Communist party.

A military coup in the summer of 1958 brought General Kassem to power in Baghdad. Pardon was granted to Mullah Mustafa and his cohorts, who then returned to Iraq, ending their eleven-year exile in the Soviet Union. Although there was considerable disorder and some civil strife in the first years of the Kassem regime, Mullah Mustafa and Kassem remained on generally good terms in spite of the fact that Kassem was somewhat wary of Mullah Mustafa's growing power position. The UDPK finally acquired legal status in 1960 and became known simply as the Democratic Party of Kurdistan (DPK).

Tribal infighting, encouraged by the Kassem regime to weaken Mullah

Mustafa's position, occurred between the Barzanis and rival tribes including the Zibaris, Baradostis, Surchis, Herkis, and Shaklawas. Although Mullah Mustafa remained titular head of the DPK, as a practical matter he had little control over the predominantly leftist organization. Indeed, Mullah Mustafa's power base rested with his Barzani tribe and its alliances with other Kurdish tribes in the mountain areas. Some of these alliances, it should be noted, were voluntary while others were forged through coercion by Barzani fighters. One commentator has described Mullah Mustafa's tactics as follows:

> He moved with what force he could muster against those tribes that would not ally themselves with him, burning their crops, killing livestock and destroying villages, as he drove the inhabitants either over the borders into Turkey or Persia or down onto the plains to the south. In this manner Mullah Mustafa soon dominated most of the smaller tribes in his area.[6]

Mullah Mustafa, of course, gradually built his appeal among Kurdish peasants as a national leader, which made such strong-arm tactics against "dissident" tribes increasingly less necessary.

The first of several Iraqi government offensives in the 1960s against the Kurds began in September 1961, marking the final break between Mullah Mustafa and Kassem. To counter Baghdad's forces, Mullah Mustafa organized his own fighting force known as the Pesh Merga. Throughout the 1960s a series of offensives, counteroffensives, and truces ensued that seemed to follow a general pattern.[7] The Iraqi armed forces, using conventional tactics, proved successful in the plains but became bogged down in the mountains where Kurdish defensive, small-unit guerrilla tactics prevailed.

The strife officially ended on 11 March 1970 with the signing of an accord by Mullah Mustafa's Kurds and the Baghdad government under President Ahmed Hassan al-Bakr and Baath Party Secretary Saddam Hussein Takriti. The agreement formally recognized Kurdish nationality and Kurdish as an official Iraqi language. Local control was to be held by Kurds over such social services as education and health. Government civil administrators in Kurdish areas were normally to be Kurds and representation of Kurds in the Iraqi legislature, judiciary, and executive organs was to be in accordance with the Kurdish proportion of the country's population. Freedom of the Kurdish press was to be maintained and political organizations such as the DPK were to be allowed to function. A general amnesty was granted: Kurdish "deserters" were to return to their respective Iraqi army and police units, other Kurds under arms were to return to civilian life, and civilian government workers were to return to their jobs. Restoring Kurdish sectors damaged or destroyed by war was to be the responsibility of the Baghdad government as was compensation to widows, orphans, and disabled veterans.[8]

A critical element of the agreement, necessary for its implementation, was a census to determine the actual Kurdish numbers in Iraq as well as the areas of their habitation. But the census was never taken and Kurds were forcibly resettled from disputed areas by the Baghdad government. These and other perceived breaches of faith led to the final breakdown of the peace accords and renewal of fighting in March 1974.[9]

## Political-Military Analysis

### Environment

The very rugged, mountainous terrain—largely impassable in winter months due to extremely heavy snowfall—is an ideally suited environment for the Kurdish insurgents. One of the best descriptions of these rugged mountains was set forth by a British engineer, A. M. Hamilton:

> Kurdistan is a country of high mountain ranges lying parallel to each other, approximately north-west to south-east. Beginning with the foothills near the Tigris each range rises higher than the last till finally the elevated Persian plateau is reached with its fringe of towering peaks. Between the ranges lie long valleys, down which run rivers and streams. But the really unique feature of these ranges is the number of mighty gorges that the rivers cut in their endeavours to escape from this mountain system to join the Tigris. Often enough these ravines are not straight clefts; they wind in the most curious fashion and have endless ramifications. The Rowanduz is the best known and perhaps the grandest of them all. It has not less than five branches through which tributary streams flow to join the Rowanduz River, and each of these is itself an imposing canyon.[10]

Until the 1974–75 campaign, the Iraqi army had not been able to gain a foothold in the mountainous areas, and the air force had not proven to be very effective there either. The Kurds operated from numerous mountain caves and other hideouts, trapping government forces attempting to penetrate the area. One observer, commenting on the Kurdish rebellion against the British in 1920, stated that the Kurds are as "elusive as the mountain ibex," adding that "they know every track and hiding place."[11] Further complicating efforts by the army was the lack of a good road network in the area, a factor that worked to the advantage of the insurgents who relied, for the most part, on irregular tactics. Nevertheless, in spite of these obstacles, the Iraqi armed forces were able to make considerable headway against the Kurdish insurgents in the 1974–75 campaign, but only because the Baghdad regime was able to concentrate superior numbers of troops equipped with Soviet-supplied modern tanks, aircraft, and other armament.

Although the Kurds and Iraqi Arabs are Muslims (most Kurds are Muslims of the Sunni sect,[12] as are most of the Arab power elite in Baghdad), the Kurds as a group are clearly the more religious, a fact that reflects vast cultural differences between mountain Kurds and lowland Arabs in Iraq. In addition to cultural differences, Arabs and Kurds represent separate ethnic groups.[13] As noted earlier, many Kurds claim descent from the ancient Medes who, in turn, are allegedly descendants of the Aryans.[14] (Iranians also claim Aryan lineage, but most are Muslims of the Shiite sect.) Concerning language, although many Kurdish dialects exist, there is apparently little difficulty in communication among the Kurds in Iraq and along the Iranian frontier.[15] By contrast, a severe language barrier exists between the Kurdish masses and the Arab-speaking majority in the country.

Thus, religious, language, cultural, and ethnic cleavages are wide. Moreover, the perception by Kurds of relative economic deprivation compared to Iraqi Arabs constitutes an additional irritant that contributes to insurgent efforts to forge a sense of Kurdish national identity distinct and apart from the Iraqi Arabs.

### Popular Support

Until its defeat in 1975, support for the Kurdish insurgency was widespread among the mountain tribesmen. Although some support was readily given to Mullah Mustafa, traditional hatreds for his Barzani tribe caused the Kurdish leader to coerce some tribes with military force to support the Kurdish national cause. As the years passed, tribal jealousies were not totally eliminated or forgotten, but they did come to take second place to Kurdish national interests. More than any other person, Mullah Mustafa promoted the idea of a common national identity among Kurds. His efforts were aided, of course, by common dislike for the Arabs, reinforced by their indiscriminate burnings and bombings of Kurdish villages.

Support was least from the urbanized Kurds, that is, those who had left their mountain tribes and settled in the cities away from the mainstream of Kurdish culture and tribal demands. Even many of these rallied to Mullah Mustafa's command, quitting their jobs and leaving the cities whenever renewed war with the Baghdad regime broke out or appeared imminent.[16] Those who rallied to Mullah Mustafa in early 1974, for example, included 2,000 Kurdish policemen, hundreds of civil servants, and the "entire staff of the University at Suleimaniya."[17]

The Kurdish insurgents did not use *esoteric appeals* very extensively; the focus was not on ideology or on any master plan for transforming Kurdish society from its present condition. Mullah Mustafa was thought by some to have been influenced by Marxist-Leninist thinking as a result of his eleven-year exile in the Soviet Union (1947–58), but contrary to such suspicions, Mullah Mustafa departed the Soviet Union unconverted. In fact, his experience in the Soviet Union, frequently cited by the Kurdish leader, convinced him that Marxism-Leninism was incompatible with the Islamic culture of the Kurds.

At first, Mullah Mustafa was only the nominal head of the Democratic Party of Kurdistan (DPK), but he seized complete control in 1968 and purged it of Marxist and other left-oriented elements not entirely loyal to his leadership.[18] The Kurdish intelligentsia, small as it was, belonged to the DPK or lived in Iraqi cities as "urbanized" Kurds or in Europe, notably Switzerland. For those Kurds under Mullah Mustafa, however, the only permissable ideology, if it can be called that, was commitment to Kurdish nationalism.

*Exoteric appeals,* by contrast, were more prevalent. Considerable emphasis was placed on abuses allegedly perpetrated by the Baghdad regime. Burning and bombing of villages, claims that the Iraqi armed forces used gas against the Kurdish positions, and the regime's failure to keep its promises were exploited by the Kurdish leadership, largely through radio broadcasts and less formal verbal communications. The Kurdish masses were certainly receptive to such appeals, given their firsthand experience with the anti-Kurd policies of successive Baghdad regimes. Indeed, government-inspired terror and counterterror directed against Kurdish peasants clearly generated support for the insurgents.

As noted earlier, the insurgents had to coerce some tribes into actively or, at least, passively supporting their activities. Although the necessity for such tactics diminished in the 1970s, tribal differences remained, and the Barzanis did resort on occasion to coercive action designed to secure compliance of some dissident (or independent) Kurdish tribes. Perhaps the strongest appeal was the repeated success of Mullah Mustafa's Pesh Merga against the better armed, more numerous government forces. Time and again, government offensives bogged down when regular troops had to confront the Pesh Merga in rugged mountainous terrain more suitable to the irregulars. The Kurds inevitably lost in the plains against the superior firepower brought to bear by the Iraqi army and air force, withdrawing instead to their mountain redoubts where they fought successful defensive guerrilla actions. Until they were finally defeated by overwhelming Soviet-supplied Iraqi army units, this pattern held. However, the Kurdish political and military control personnel were forced to withdraw when Iranian support was terminated. It was not simply a case of increased Soviet aid and Iraqi strength, but the lack of supplies and support from the Iranians coupled with the Iraqi strength.

Given their preoccupation with military activities, the insurgents were not very successful in improving the socioeconomic lot of the Kurdish peasant. In fact, the civil wars of the 1960s resulted in considerable suffering and economic deprivation for the Kurds. Accordingly, one of Mullah Mustafa's prin-cipal demands on Baghdad was for a greater share of Iraqi government funds for reconstruction and development of Kurdish areas. The fact that such monetary assistance was not forthcoming was a source of acute frustration for the Kurdish leadership. Although extensive social services were lacking, strides were made to establish some political and other administrative struc-tures. The DPK was still the most prominent political structure other than Mullah Mustafa's Pesh Merga, but structures to administer the Kurdish areas were gradually being established, particularly in the aftermath of the March 1970 cease-fire.

## Organization

Emergent national structures were, to a large extent, incongruent with traditional patterns that stressed tribal autonomy.[19] Nevertheless, Mullah Mustafa did assert his determination to establish "government departments to administer territory" he controlled.[20] According to an April 1974 report: "The Kurds . . . set up their own government and administration" under "an eight-man executive council . . . headed by Mullah Mustafa Barzani."[21] Nine administrative structures were reportedly established to handle such func-tions as finance, justice, the army, and internal affairs.[22] Nevertheless, the DPK, under Barzani control, was emerging as the core political structure adja-cent to (and maintaining control over) the administrative structures.

In the earlier years of the Kurdish rebellion, the movement was marked by considerable disunity. Not only were different tribes at odds with one an-other, but the military command under Mullah Mustafa operated separately from the DPK, which had its own military forces under Jalal Talabani. With the Kurds divided in this way, Baghdad was able to gain leverage by playing one Kurdish faction against the other. Most notable in this regard was Iraqi government support for Talabani against the Iranian-supported Mullah Mustafa. Talabani eventually lost his power position in the DPK as Mullah Mustafa took control and purged the organization in 1968 and 1969.

An important sidelight of the campaigns during the 1960s was the progress made by Mullah Mustafa in uniting the Kurds by overcoming opponent fac-tions. His most prominent competitor was Jalal Talabani, a member of the DPK central committee.[23] As noted above, Talabani organized his own Pesh Merga, which operated in the southern border area separately from Mullah Mustafa's northern-based forces. In July 1964 forces loyal to Mullah Mustafa moved against Talabani's elements, forcing the DPK headquarters to move across the border into Iran. Although the DPK remained in existence, its power was greatly diminished and Mullah Mustafa declared himself to be in charge of "both the political and military leadership of the Kurds."[24]

In subsequent years relations between Talabani and Mullah Mustafa re-

mained strained and marked by intrigue, even though Talabani represented
Mullah Mustafa on occasion in negotiations with Baghdad. Talabani's objective, as described by one author, was "to establish himself and his faction
firmly as an independent Kurdish political force with the ultimate aim of eclip-
sing Mullah Mustafa."[25]

Talabani ultimately was co-opted by the Iraqi government headed by President Bakr when in 1968 he received government assistance in fighting Mullah
Mustafa. Talabani and his cohorts were ousted from the DPK in 1968 as
Mullah Mustafa wrested direct control of the organization. According to one
source:

> During 1968 and 1969 there had been a complete reorganization of the political
> and administrative structure in Kurdish territory, and the nomenclature and
> jargon had been up-dated. The Executive Bureau of Kurdistan had evolved from
> the old Politburo of the DPK, from which all the traces of the Talabani influence
> had been eliminated, and the old DPK Central Committee had evolved into the
> Revolutionary Command Council of Kurdistan.[26]

It is important to note that Mullah Mustafa closed on Talabani and the DPK
with the support of many tribal chiefs who saw the leftist-dominated organization as a threat to their traditional authority patterns.

Strange as it may seem, however, Talabani's stated position in the spring of
1974 concerning the dispute between Mullah Mustafa and the Baghdad
regime was a moderate, generally pro-Barzani stand. Referring to the anti-
Barzani group, he stated:

> The mutiny of a small number—not more than ten—from the DPK does not
> mean that these represent the DPK or even a wing of that party. . . . The
> Lebanese press . . . published incorrect claims about the isolation of Barzani's
> leadership from the masses of Kurdistan. They forget its popular, political, and
> military might, which is now greater than at any time before. . . .
>
>    Efforts must be exerted . . . to avoid the detonation of the situation in Iraq and
> to continue the dialogue between the government and the Barzani leadership
> with the participation of good mediators in order to find a solution acceptable to
> both sides.[27]

Since the defeat of Barzani in 1975, his subsequent departure for the
United States, and his death, the Kurdish movement has remained divided.

Several factions have been identified—elements of Barzani's Pesh Merga
still claiming to represent the DPK (or KDP); guerrillas led by Talabani under
the banner of the left-oriented Patriotic Union of Kurdistan (PUK); factions
headed by an educator named Sayed Mohammed Nezami and by Mahmoud
Osman, formerly a Barzani supporter; and the KDP "government" faction that

includes Barzani's disowned son Ubaidalla but which is dominated by Iraqi Baathists.[28]

In terms of charismatic leadership, a possible substitute for Barzani is the Sheikh Hosseini, a religious leader among the Iranian Kurds. Although Hosseini and his followers supported the movement led by the Iranian Ayatollah Khomeini against the shah, Hosseini wants at least limited autonomy for the Kurds. Indeed, religious differences between the Sunni Muslim Kurds and the Shiite Muslim Iranians contribute to widening the nationalist cleavage between the two groups. In any event, Hosseini's aims do appear reformist rather than revolutionary or secessionist. He is quoted as stating:

> Of course it's a crime that eight million people who live in the same geographic area, speak the same language and have the same history and culture should be divided into five different countries (the USSR, Turkey, Syria, Iraq, and Iran) and oppressed by all of them. But we know we'll never have our own country. Look at the Kurds in Iraq. After so many years of fighting, they've achieved nothing. We must concentrate on gaining autonomy here. As for a separate Kurdish nation, we can't allow ourselves to think about it.[29]

*External Support*

The Barzani-led Kurds derived considerable support from the Iranians and reportedly from the Israelis, albeit to a much lesser extent. Both countries had interests served by Kurdish attacks on Iraqi military forces. From the Iranian perspective, such attacks tied down the Iraqi armed forces in the mountainous north and dissuaded Iraq from playing a substantial role in the Persian Gulf or stirring up new trouble along the disputed Shatt al Arab estuary between Iran and Iraq. Accordingly, Iran provided material aid, sanctuary, and moral support to Mullah Mustafa's Pesh Merga. By aiding the Kurds, Teheran also encouraged notions of Kurdish national autonomy on Iraqi and *not* on Iranian soil. For Israel's part, Iraqi preoccupation with the Kurdish rebellion lessened the likelihood of Iraqi military forces being sent to Syria or other Arab states bordering Israel to participate in some new anti-Zionist offensive.

In an earlier period, the Soviet Union was also an active supporter of Kurdish national autonomy, particularly if this resulted in an expansion of the Soviet sphere of influence. Moscow's support in 1946 for the short-lived Kurdish state—the Mahabad Republic—was certainly consistent with the objective of extending Soviet influence to the Persian Gulf. From Moscow's perspective, a Kurdish republic between the Soviet Union and the gulf would have served as a vehicle for such an extension of power. Pressure from Washington forced Soviet military withdrawal from northern Iran, thus reversing Moscow's plan for establishing hegemony in the region. Of course, Soviet withdrawal resulted in the collapse of the Mahabad Republic. Realiza-tion of the Kurdish dream of a national state appeared increasingly remote. For their part, the Soviets ultimately shifted the focus of their policy to sup-port for Iraq, becoming Baghdad's principal arms supplier. Relations between Moscow and Teheran improved somewhat in the period of détente between the United States and the Soviet Union, but Moscow's closest ties remained with the Iraqi regime.[30] Visits by Soviet Defense Minister Grechko and Soviet Interior Minister Schelokov in late March 1974 (at the same time that Baghdad was taking a hard line on the Kurdish question) certainly aroused Barzani's suspicions.[31] As if visits were not enough, a "cooperation protocol" was signed between the Iraqi and Soviet interior ministries providing for the "exchange of expertise and information."[32]

Turkey was also sympathetic to Baghdad's problems, given Turkey's own Kurdish minority—the "mountain Turks." Whenever fighting broke out in the 1960s in Iraq, Turkey quickly sealed its border, thus denying sanctuary or other assistance to the Kurds operating in Iraq.

Lack of significant external support other than that provided by Iran was a severe problem for Mullah Mustafa's command. The general appealed for U.S. support to counter Soviet assistance to Iraq, but such direct assistance was not forthcoming. Instead, the United States encouraged Iran to make arms shipments to the Kurds, at least until 1975. In that year, Teheran and Baghdad achieved a rapprochement that included settlement of the Shatt al Arab border dispute. The shah then proceeded to terminate all assistance to the Kurds. Not only were supply shipments halted, but the Iranian armed forces also ceased giving troop support and sanctuary to the Kurds. Within a fortnight, Mullah Mustafa ended the resistance and escaped to Iran with 200,000 or more Kurdish followers.[33]

The external support variable is central to understanding why the Kurdish rebellion failed. External support remains the sine qua non of a successful Kurdish insurgency. This dependence on external support stems from the fact that the Kurdish tribes and villages are surrounded by states with well-equipped armed forces and police prepared to suppress any insurrection with force. Successes achieved by the Barzani Kurds against the Iraqis depended upon continuation of Iranian support for the movement. When this support was withdrawn, the resistance failed.

### Government Response

Until 1975, when Iranian aid to the Kurds was terminated, the Iraqis had only limited success in attempts to extend their power from secure areas, converting contested regions into government bases—an undertaking that re-quired the government to convince and organize uncommitted people to support its cause. Moreover, there was no real attempt to undercut support for the insurgents by eliminating the concrete grievances of the masses. Promises of better representation, more local autonomy, and economic assistance more often than not were unfulfilled.

With respect to economic assistance to Kurdish areas, Baghdad reportedly trebled its effort in 1978 with expenditures increasing from about $715 million in 1977 to approximately $2.4 billion in 1978; however, much of this outlay was for roadbuilding that Kurds perceived as increasing the capability of Iraqi armed forces to penetrate Kurdish areas.[34]

The government in Iraq, dominated by Arab members of the Baath party that is formally committed to a kind of pan-Arab radical socialism, had little sympathy for Kurdish demands. Therefore, the regime lacked legitimacy among the country's more than two million non-Arabs, the Kurds (about 20-25 percent of Iraq's population).[35] Moreover, the Baath party itself was divided into warring factions, further weakening the government's political position. Thus, earlier Iraqi Baathist notions of unity with such Arab countries as Syria and Egypt took a back seat to more pressing domestic concerns. Although major military campaigns were launched against the Kurds during the 1960s, all failed to establish government control over Kurdish-inhabited areas.

Civilian moderates (a relative term) like Baath party Assistant Secretary General Saddam Hussein Takriti advocated compromise in dealing with the Kurds, reportedly to "save Iraqi strength for expansion in the Persian Gulf and to oppose Iran."[36] This strategy was opposed by Baathist factions within the military that favored a hard-line policy against the Kurds, including direct military action to terminate the Kurdish resistance. Iraqi President Hassan al-Bakr, a military man, was identified with the militant faction opposed to concessions made in the March 1970 cease-fire accords. In any case, at no time did any Baathist regime take serious steps to implement major socioeconomic development programs in Kurdish areas as the Iranians had done on their side of the border.

Literacy among the Kurds was less than 10 percent, and diseases such as trachoma, typhoid, and malaria were widespread.[37] Nevertheless, there was no effective civic action program of any significance in Kurdish areas to attack these rather basic problems. Moreover, attacks on Kurdish villages, often indiscriminate, further alienated the population. In addition, government efforts to rebuild villages following the March 1970 cease-fire were minimal.

Attempts to create a sense of loyalty and friendship between the government and the people were generally meager and short-lived. Baghdad paid the salaries of Kurds operating as border guards and serving police functions in Kurdish-inhabited areas, but each new outbreak of fighting nullified most gains from such organizational activity as the Kurds so employed often abandoned their government roles and returned to aid the nationalist cause. A growing number of Kurds had, of course, been detached from their mountain tribes and become "urbanized." Although these Kurds were offered by the Baghdad regime as "proof" of disunity in the Kurdish movement, they were not particularly useful as sources of information or intelligence concerning Kurdish insurgent plans. Indeed, the gap gradually widened between many urbanized Kurds and the mountain Kurds, particularly as the former became assimilated into the mainstream of Iraqi society.

Moreover, successive governments in Baghdad failed to keep promises made to Kurdish leaders, namely increased Kurdish representation in Baghdad and greater local autonomy for the Kurds. In fact, the renewal of hostilities in the spring of 1974 became inevitable when it became clear that Baghdad would once again fail to carry out an agreement. Indeed, the March 1970 cease-fire accord had provided for more Kurdish representation in the central government, more authority for Kurdish leaders over affairs in Kurdish-inhabited regions (including a local assembly with lawmaking power), and a share of oil earnings proportional to the Kurdish population in Iraq.

Original expectations included appointment of five Kurdish ministers as part of the Baghdad regime, a Kurdish vice-president (one of three vice-presidents), and a Kurdish army division commander or assistant army chief of staff. A new national council to include Kurds was to share power with the Baathist Revolutionary Command Council (RCC). A census was also to be taken to determine Kurdish-populated areas that would be part of the Kurdish autonomous sector of Iraq.[38]

The Baghdad regime continually delayed taking the census, using the time so gained to repopulate such cities as Kirkuk with Arabs to replace indigenous Kurds who were forcibly moved elsewhere or denied the right to return to their homes following the March 1970 cease-fire.[39] Idris Barzani accused Baghdad of "forcible Arabization" of Kirkuk and other Kurdish-populated areas by moving out more than 50,000 Kurds and replacing them with more than 10,000 Arabs.[40] The Kirkuk question was particularly sensitive since the city was claimed by the Kurds as a national capital and was, at the same time, the de facto Iraqi oil capital in the northeast.

A census was to have helped define those areas of Iraq that would have been part of the Kurdish autonomous region. The "forced Arabization" program was Baghdad's response to Kurdish claims to Kirkuk and other disputed areas. Such policies underscored the duplicity of the Baghdad regime from the Kurdish perspective. Although the Iraqis offered Arbil, located north of Kirkuk, as a Kurdish national capital, the Kurds rejected this proposal, insisting instead on "a temporary joint administration in the mixed towns such as Kirkuk, Sinjar, and Khanaquin on the Iranian frontier."[41]

The government's efforts were clearly hampered by disagreement within the ruling elite concerning the appropriate action to take in dealing with the insurgents. The de facto abrogation of the March 1970 accords, for example, reportedly was the result of pressure from Iraqi military commanders to renew the anti-Kurd campaign, using new, more sophisticated military equipment acquired from the Soviet Union. Throughout the antiinsurgent campaigns of the 1960s, Iraqi military doctrine had remained fairly rigid in its commitment to use of regular armies and conventional aerial and ground tactics in dealing with the Kurds.[42] Such measures were typically rather successful in plains areas, but failed miserably in the mountains. Small-unit actions in the mountains—sustained over a long period of time—would appear to have been a potentially more successful approach, but the Iraqi military command was not disposed toward organizing such units or implementing small-unit, counterinsurgent tactics.

Although there were occasional reports over the years concerning Iraqi use of (or plans to use) chemical (gas) warfare against the insurgents, there was never any clear evidence to substantiate these reports. Indeed, the reports appear to have been intended largely for Kurdish propaganda purposes.[43] Nevertheless, one of Barzani's spokesmen stated in an interview on French radio that "we know the Iraqis have these weapons [chemical and bacteriological] and we know in which camp they are storing them."[44]

Concerning Iranian sanctuary and material and moral support for the insurgents, the Iraqis were reluctant to take on the Iranians directly. Border clashes between the two countries were confined to the mountain areas and usually limited to involvement by police and Kurdish irregulars. Regular army units normally did not become involved.[45] Both Baghdad and Teheran saw a major Iran-Iraq war as contrary to their interests. Although Iranian forces appeared to be the militarily superior, both sides would have lost from such a war due to the inevitable disruption of mutually profitable oil extraction activities along the southern lowland sector of their common border.

Concerning the 1974 breakdown in the cease-fire, Baghdad offered a Kurdish autonomy plan on 11 March with the allowance of 15 days for compliance by the Kurds. As a practical matter, Baghdad's plan did not provide real autonomy and, in addition, did not give the DPK control over Kirkuk, nor was oil mentioned as a source of Kurdish revenue.[46] Aside from these factors, the general distrust of Baghdad was evident in the explanation by a Barzani spokesman for the Kurdish rejection of the Baghdad offer of "autonomy": "We have . . . no key positions" in the government and, moreover, "have no participation in the regime. We have participation only at the administrative level."[47]

## The Progression of the Insurgency
## in Kurdistan: A Summary

The Kurdish insurgency did not follow a neat Maoist scheme of an orderly progression through organization, terror, guerrilla, and mobile warfare stages. Indeed, the guerrilla phase seems to have come first, with attacks by a small band of Barzanis against the British in the 1920s and 1930s. Organizational activity—formation of the DPK and the development of cells—followed initiation of attacks against the government. The DPK as a political structure enjoyed only marginal legitimacy in the eyes of most Kurds. Legitimacy of the national movement was gained largely through repeated military successes by Mullah Mustafa that culminated in the formation of the Mahabad Republic in 1946. Although Mullah Mustafa was its nominal head, organization activity by the DPK during and after the days of the republic was secondary to the military organization of Mullah Mustafa.

Compared to other insurgencies, the Kurdish cadres did not have the usual task of separating the people from the government. Clearly, government influence in Kurdish areas had always been minimal. Instead, the task for Kurdish insurgents was to forge national unity in a sociopolitical system that had a segmentary structure (coequal tribal troups with no central political institutions).[48]

Concentration of superior Iraqi forces in the 1974–75 campaign combined with withdrawal of Iranian support to defeat the Barzani Kurds. In the years since this victory, Baghdad has consolidated its position in Kurdish areas through forced relocation of settlements and other tactics. Divisions within the Kurdish movement organization, exacerbated by competition among rebel leaders, make problematic any revival of the movement to the 1974 zenith of its strength. Of course, instability in Iran, Iraq, or other countries bordering "Kurdistan" might allow for such a revival. In any event, external support will continue to be essential if the Kurds are ever to realize success in armed insurgency against any of the governments in the region. Nevertheless, the governments will, at the very least, have to contend with sporadic uprisings and resorts to violence by nationalist rebels in Kurdish areas.

## Notes

1. See, for example, Arshak Safrastian, *Kurds and Kurdistan* (London: Harvill Press, 1948), p. 17. Safrastian asserts that "the few extant texts prove that as early as the twenty-fourth century B.C. or thereabouts, there was a kingdom of Gutium, which corresponds to the Kurdistan of today."

2. See the discussion in "Iraq," *Arab Report and Record,* May 1–15, 1978, p. 327 and

July 1–15, 1978, p. 473. Indeed, KDP guerrillas reportedly reacted against Baghdad's policies, clashing with Iraqi troops and inflicting "hundreds" of casualties.

3. Hassan Arfa, *The Kurds: An Historical and Political Study* (London: Oxford University Press, 1966), p. 1. The author was chief of staff, Iranian Army (1944–46) and ambassador to Turkey (1958–61).

4. The Mongolian invasion and subsequent Ottoman and post-Ottoman periods are covered in numerous accounts. Particularly useful to this writer, however, were Joseph H. Livernash, "Kurdish Nationalism: Strategic Implications to Middle East Security Pacts" (unpublished research report, Air War College, Air University, Maxwell Air Force Base, Alabama, 1967); and Hugh Fred Hutchinson, "Kurds in Turkey" (unpublished M.A. thesis, Columbia University, Faculty of Political Science, late 1960s).

5. The best single account of Mullah Mustafa's campaigns, starting in the 1930s and culminating in the March 1970 cease-fire agreements with the Iraqi government, is Edgar O'Ballance, *The Kurdish Revolt: 1961–1970* (London: Faber & Faber, Ltd., 1973 and Hamden, Conn: Shoe String Press, 1973). This writer has relied quite heavily on O'Ballance's historical account, particularly in this section of the article. Readers interested in a more detailed treatment should certainly consult O'Ballance.

6. O'Ballance, *Kurdish Revolt*, p. 82.

7. Ibid., pp. 74–163.

8. The "twelve points" of the agreement are contained in O'Ballance, *Kurdish Revolt*, pp. 179–180.

9. See, for example, Richard Johns, "No Peace for Kurdistan But Will There Be War?" *New Middle East* (January–February 1973), pp. 48–50; and Gabriel Mitchell, "Iraq's 'Battle of Endurance' Supported by Soviet Backers," *New Middle East* (April 1973), p. 42.

10. A. M. Hamilton, *Road Through Kurdistan* (London: Faber & Faber, 1937, 1958), p. 77.

11. Ibid., p. 62.

12. See Ralph S. Solecki, *Shanidar: The First Flower People* (New York: Alfred A. Knopf, 1971), p. 45.

13. According to Solecki: "The identification of a Kurd, apart from the chief distinguishing character of language, is not easy. Physically, there are tall Kurds and short Kurds, but few fat ones. Complexions can vary from a heavy tan to a light, rosy, English-type fairness; there are even redhaired Kurds." Ibid., pp. 39, 41.

14. Ibid., p. 41. "The Kurds, or at least the Kurds of Iran, believe that they are descended from the ancient Medes. The Medes were probably a powerful group of Aryan Kurds who . . . reached the high point of their existence about the seventh century B.C."

15. Ibid., pp. 42, 44. "Kurdish is . . . a member of the Aryan branch of the Indo-European language family. . . . Despite certain differences in the dialects . . . the Kurds from northwestern Kurdistan and southeastern Kurdistan find no real difficulty in communication. It is the southeastern dialect, however, which is the polished language of the present-day literature."

16. *Christian Science Monitor* (*CSM*), March 25, 1974. For example, it has been reported that "thousands of . . . Kurds, including Kurdish ministers in the Iraqi Cabinet,

governors, and civil servants, defected to the north to join General Barzani . . . when it became clear that General Barzani and Baghdad could not agree on terms."

17. *CSM*, March 19, 1974.

18. The DPK remains a haven for Kurdish mavericks. For example, Dara Tewfik, editor of the Baghdad Kurdish language newspaper *Al Taakhi*, has been described as "a leftist [who] represents some younger [DPK] leaders who have criticized General Bar- zani in the past." Even Tewfik, however, closed his newspaper operations in March 1974 and joined the reported "thousands" rallying to Mullah Mustafa in support of Kurdish national objectives. See *CSM*, March 25, 1974.

19. See C. J. Edmonds, *Kurds, Turks, and Arabs* (London: Oxford University Press, 1957), pp. 12–15. Edmonds states: "Outside the towns Kurdish society is essentially tribal. Each tribe is divided into clans and sections. Sometimes the whole of a tribe claims descent in the male line from a single ancestor. Sometimes it is the clan or sec- tion, or perhaps only the ruling family, that claims such descent, and the tribe is more a political or territorial unit. The tribal system is seen at its simplest among the true nomads, those who live throughout the year in black goat-hair tents, migrating with their flocks according to the seasons between the plains of Iraq and the highlands of Persia and Turkey. . . . But the majority of the Kurdish tribes are settled in villages and practice agriculture. In many places the tribal system is breaking down as the result of close Government control; even so it will be worthwhile to describe the typical tribal organization. . . . In every tribe there is a ruling family, the members of which bear the title of Agha (or Beg). . . . There may be one paramount Agha, or . . . two or more claiming the allegiance of different clans or sections. In each village within the sphere of influence of the tribes there may be some junior member of the family installed as the Agha, or squire of that village. The Agha is a kind of feudal baron who does not work with his hands; he lives on perquisites (such as taxation), which vary in different parts of the country."

20. *CSM*, March 19, 1974.

21. This is an AP citation of *Arab World*, a Beirut magazine, datelined Tehran, as noted in *Denver Post (DP)*, April 18, 1974.

22. *New York Times (NYT)*, April 1, 1974.

23. For details of the relationship between Barzani and Talabani during this period, see numerous references made in O'Ballance, *Kurdish Revolt*, and Dana Adams Schmidt, *Journey Among Brave Men* (Boston: Little, Brown, 1964).

24. O'Ballance, *Kurdish Revolt*, p. 122.

25. Ibid., p. 145.

26. Ibid., p. 158.

27. See *An Nahar* (Beirut), March 29, 1974, as cited in FBIS/*Middle East* (Foreign Broadcast Information Service), April 9, 1974.

28. *NYT*, March 1, 1979.

29. *NYT*, March 4, 1979. Although emergence of charismatic leadership would cer- tainly help the Kurdish cause, it is virtually impossible to predict whether Hosseini or some other figure will succeed in filling Barzani's role.

30. *CSM*, March 25, 1974. The reporter observes: "The Soviets have abandoned their past support to the Kurds and stepped up their military aid to Iraq, which has

become their strongest Arab ally. . . . [Moreover], on Soviet instigation, the Iraqi Com-munist Party has entered a national front coalition with the ruling Baath Party."

31. Significantly, this observation was made in Damascus on March 26 by the Mid-dle East News Agency: "Grechko's presence in Baghdad until 26 March, the deadline of the ultimatum given to Mullah Mustafa Barzani constitutes a hint to the Kurdish leader to accept the offer made by Baghdad and to Iran not to become involved in the Iraqi internal problem."

32. See Baghdad Radio, March 31, 1974, and Baghdad International News Agency, April 1, 1974, as cited in FBIS/*Middle East*, April 2, 1974, p. E3. Grechko and Bakr also agreed to denounce "continued intrigues woven by the forces of imperialism and reaction in the area," perhaps a veiled reference to Iranian support for the Kurds. Reference is Baghdad Radio of March 26, 1974, as cited in FBIS/*Middle East*, March 27, 1974.

33. President Nixon reportedly agreed in 1972 to join with the shah in supporting the Kurdish rebellion in Iraq. U.S. support was initially limited to supplying about $5 million in "captured Soviet equipment channeled through Iran." See William Safire, "Of Kurds and Kissinger, Carter and Conscience," *NYT*, December 19, 1977. According to another source, "the extent of U.S. assistance was somewhat greater, amounting to some $16 million worth of untraceable Chinese and Soviet weapons." In any event, U.S. assistance to the Kurds that began in 1972 was confirmed in 1976 by the House Select Committee on Intelligence. Cf. Jack Anderson, "How the Abandoned Kurds Lost Out," *Washington Post (WP)*, March 11, 1978, and "The CIA Report the President Doesn't Want You to Read," *The Village Voice*, February 16, 1976.

34. See Bob Reiss, "City of Exiles: Lion in a Cage," *WP Magazine*, July 23, 1978, and Joseph Kraft, "The Fall of an Insurgent," *WP*, April 24, 1975.

35. The total number of Kurds—including those in Iran, Iraq, Syria, Turkey, and the Soviet Union—is on the order of 8 to 10 million. See Solecki, *Shanidar*, pp. 39–40. For another estimate, see Edmonds, *Kurds, Turks*, pp. 3–4. Edmonds argues that there is "a grand total of between 4 and 4 1/2 million" Kurds.

36. *CSM*, July 5, 1973.

37. *NYT*, December 31, 1970.

38. *NYT*, April 2, 1970.

39. The "Arabization" program which led to the outbreak of fighting in the summer of 1973 between Kurdish and government elements is discussed in *WP*, August 29, 1973.

40. *CSM*, March 19, 1974.

41. Ibid.

42. Three regular army divisions (an estimated 48,000 troops) were reportedly com-mitted to the northeast. See *WP*, April 9, 1974.

43. According to one report attributed to Iranian sources: "The Iraqi armed forces are learning chemical warfare methods including use of Soviet-supplied gas." See *CSM*, March 20, 1974.

44. See Paris Radio, April 1, 1974, as cited in FBIS/*Middle East*, April 2, 1974, p. E1.

45. An exception may have been the fighting in early 1974 that reportedly involved tanks and artillery. See *Time*, February 25, 1975; *CSM*, February 13, 1974; and *NYT*,

February 12, 1974.

46. The "trappings" of autonomy included creation of numerous governmental struc'
tures, including a legislature, but none of these bodies was to have real power, given
their subordination to the "central authority" in all but very routine matters. See the
provisional constitution carried on Baghdad's International News Agency on March
11, 1974, as cited in FBIS/*Middle East,* March 12, 1974, pp. C11–C18.

47. Ibid.

48. Writing of experiences in Kurdistan in the period just prior to the outbreak of
World War I in 1914, G. E. Hubbard remarked that the Kurds "are divided into clans,
acknowledging the supremacy of chiefs, who are regarded with as much devotion and
followed with the same blind zeal, and all on the same grounds, protection, and kind'
ness in return for fealty and service. . . . The Kurd is a loyal clansman . . . and a born
fighter." See G. E. Hubbard, *From the Gulf to Ararat* (London: William Blackwood and
Sons, 1917), p. 216.

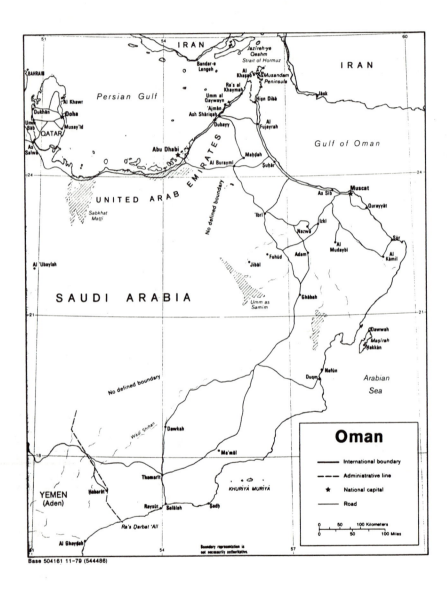

IRAN

IRAN

BAHRAIN

Al Khawr

Dukhan  Doha

Persian Gulf

Jazireh-ye
Qeshm
Strait of Hormuz

Bandar-e
Langeh

Al
Khasab  Musandam
Peninsula

Ra's al
Khaymah

Umm al
Qaywayn

Hisn Dibā

Jāsk

Umm
Bab
QATAR

Musay'id

Ash Shāriqah

'Ajmān

Dubayy

Al
Fujayrah

Gulf of Oman

As
Salwā

Abu Dhabi

Mahdah

Suhār

Al Buraymi

UNITED  ARAB  EMIRATES

As Sib  Muscat

Qurayyāt

Sabkhat
Matti

No defined boundary

'Ibri

Ibrā

Nazwā

Izki

Al
Mudaybi

Sūr

Al
Kāmil

Al 'Ubaylah

Fuhūd

Adam

Jibāl

SAUDI  ARABIA

Umm as
Samim

Ghābah

Dawwah

Maşirah

Hakkān

No defined boundary

Duqm

Nafūn

Arabian
Sea

Wadi Shihan

Dawkah

Ma'mūl

Thamarit

## Oman

——— International boundary

– – – Administrative line

★ National capital

——— Road

YEMEN
(Aden)

Haberūt

Raysūt

Salālah

Sadh

KHURIYĀ MURIYĀ

Ra's Darbat 'Ali

0  50  100 Kilometers

0  50  100 Miles

Al Ghaydah

Boundary representation is
not necessarily authoritative.

Base 504161 11-79 (544486)

# Revolutionary War in Oman

*Bard E. O'Neill*

Among the regions of the world, the Middle East has had more than its share of political violence during the past two decades. Though the Palestinian resistance has been well publicized in the West, lesser known but quite sanguinary internal wars have convulsed a number of states or areas such as Iraq, the Sudan, Spanish Sahara, Lebanon, the Yemen Arab Republic, Oman, and, more recently, Iran. Of these cases, the conflict in Oman should be especially interesting to students of insurgency inasmuch as it has been a protracted struggle in which all of the variables discussed in Chapter 1 have been important.

Oman, a state that has enjoyed the longest tradition of independence in the Arab world during the past three centuries, lies astride both the critical Strait of Hormuz and the Indian Ocean oil shipping lanes. It is this location, rather than its modest petroleum production, that has made Oman significant to the West. The principal concern of Western leaders is the possibility that a successful insurrection in Oman could demonstrate the utility of violence as a means to overthrow other, more important, traditional regimes in the vital oil producing states of the Persian Gulf. Longstanding ties between the insurgents in Oman and those in other sheikhdoms have added an element of credibility to such conjectures because they suggest that the insurgents in Oman would probably provide both sanctuary and training facilities for cohorts seeking to infiltrate the Union of Arab Emirates. Accordingly, the internal war in Oman has received more than passing notice from its neighbors.

Like most Arab states of the Persian Gulf, Oman has a patrimonial political system with a royal family at the apex. Unlike those states, however, the power of the monarch is absolute, in that other members of the royal family do not exercise the political influence that their counterparts do elsewhere. Although economic and social development has been stressed since 1970, no comparable effort has been undertaken in the political sphere. In the absence of a constitution, legislature, political parties, and suffrage, the level of politi-

cal institutionalization has remained low. Despite efforts to functionally differentiate, expand, and rationalize the administrative apparatus, the sultan
has personally held the reigns of power in his own hands, serving as his own
prime minister, minister of defense, minister of foreign affairs, and commander
in chief of the armed forces and the Royal Oman Police. Moreover, he continues to be the primary source of legislation and the highest judicial authority.[1]

Patrimonial monarchies, such as the one in Oman, have been under almost
constant attack in the modern era. Thus, it should come as no surprise to find
that the Omani regime also has its share of enemies. Since 1968 the most
prominent of these has been the Popular Front for the Liberation of Oman
(PFLO), a revolutionary insurgent movement that has sought, through
violent means, to supplant the traditional political values and structures of
the current regime with Marxist-Leninist ones. The strategy chosen to accomplish this ambitious task has been the familiar Maoist protracted revolutionary warfare approach that was successfully employed (albeit with local
modifications) in China and Vietnam.[2] Through a blend of political organization and propaganda, terrorism, and guerrilla warfare, the PFLO gradually has tried to erode the regime's will to resist, the morale of the Sultan's
Armed Forces (SAF), and what popular backing the regime enjoys. While
the influence of Maoist doctrine and strategy has been pervasive in all of this,
an examination of the origins of the violence directed at the sultanate reveals
other elements, such as strong tribal and religious identification, which
have had a major impact on the struggle. To better understand the interaction of Maoism and tribalism, as well as other aspects of the current insurgency, it is important that the conflict be placed in its historical context.

## The Legacy of the Past

Opposition to the sultan has been endemic for more than a century and has
reflected a basic societal cleavage between the conservative Ibadhi Moslems
of the interior and the rulers located in the coastal region of Muscat. The
Ibadhis, who settled in Oman during the seventh century, long have resented
efforts by Muscat to control them, in part because the sultans were perceived
as corruptors of the faith.

The spiritual and temporal leaders of the Ibadhis, known as imams, date as
far back as 1749, when the first was elected. Following the creation in the
seventeenth century of an Omani empire (which extended to the coast of
East Africa), civil conflict ensued between rival contenders for the office of
imam. The outcome was a victory for Ahmed bin Said, who was elected imam
in 1749, thereby establishing the Al Bu Said dynasty that has ruled all or part

of Oman until the present. Though the head of the Al Bu Said family took the title of sultan, he also was often the imam.

In 1786 the capital of Oman was moved to the coastal city of Muscat, a development that led eventually to a political cleavage between the interior and coastal areas that was reinforced by tribal and religious differences. As a result of the division of the empire into the sultanates of Zanzibar and Oman following the death of Sultan Al Bu Said, in 1856, and a reduction of revenues (due to a curtailment of the slave and arms trade), Oman entered a period of considerable violence and unrest. However, because of tribal rivalries and British assistance, the Al Bu Saids were able to maintain their rule.[3]

Nevertheless, the tribes of the interior increasingly had grown disaffected with the rulers in Muscat, who had established a hereditary basis for rule that contradicted Ibadhi traditions. In protest against the secularization of the imamate by the Al Bu Saids, the interior tribes elected another imam in the late eighteenth century. Although in the years thereafter the sultan occasionally was accepted as imam and sometimes there was no imam at all, the general pattern was to have an imam of Oman and a sultan of Muscat and Oman.

Whatever the case, distrust and tensions continued to be the hallmarks of relations between the regime and the people of the interior. These differences finally gave rise to a general revolt against Sultan Taimur bin Faisal Al Bu Said in 1913 that was triggered by tribal objections to cooperation with Great Britain and restrictions on the arms traffic in the area. When it became apparent that the sultan would be unable to maintain his rule without outside help, he turned to the British who promptly dispatched troops to Oman. Attempts to reconcile the differences between the two sides culminated in the Treaty of Sib (1920) in which the sultan recognized the imam's spiritual authority and granted him political authority over those who would accept his jurisdiction. The sultan, however, retained his claim to sovereignty and continued to control main posts and the coastal regions.

While tensions abated in the wake of the treaty, the gradual convergence of several developments over the next thirty years set the stage for a renewal of violence in the Jebal Akhdar (the Green Mountain) of Northern Oman in the mid-1950s. First of all, a new sultan, Said bin Taimur, came to the throne. Despite the fact that Said was cast in the same mold as his conservative co-religionists of the interior and notwithstanding his insistence on religious orthodoxy throughout the country, he was unable to divest himself of the image of corruption bequeathed by his predecessors. When a cooperative imam, Mohammad, died in 1955 and was replaced by Imam Ghalib bin Ali, the latter took advantage of the disenchantment with Said and instigated a campaign, backed by Saudi Arabia, to create a separate state in the interior where oil deposits had been discovered. This clashed with a campaign by Said to exert control over the area from which the sultan had been excluded by the Treaty of Sib.

The Saudis had entered the picture after World War II and King Saud's consolidation of most of the Arabian peninsula into a patrimonial theocracy under the rule of Wahhabi Moslems. Both religious and economic considerations inclined the Saudis to align with the imam. The strong conservative and puritanical outlook of the Wahhabis and the Ibadhis, both of whom despised the "corrupted" sultans of the coast, created an underlying mutual attraction upon which shared political and economic interests were superimposed. By the 1950s the belief that the Fahd area of Oman and the Buraymi Oasis contained petroleum deposits led the Saudis to seize or claim large parts of Oman and the nearby trucial sheikhdoms. Although Imam Mohammad had supported the sultan's resistance to the Saudis, his death paved the way for an alliance between Riyadh and his successor.

In the face of this new challenge, the sultan moved with alacrity to evict the Saudis from the Buraymi Oasis and the imam from the interior, thereby bringing the entire country under his rule. Tribal resistance ensued, and in 1957 the imam's brother returned to reopen a new phase of fighting in the Jebal Akhdar that ended in early 1959, but only after British military forces actively intervened on behalf of Said.[4]

With this pattern of internal discontent as a backdrop, a nationalist uprising gradually emerged from the shadows in the Western province of Dhofar, which had been under Oman's suzerainty since 1826. Once again the trouble pitted the jebalis (mountain people) of the interior against the sultan and his coastal supporters. Among other things, the jebalis were incensed by the maladministration, neglect, and discriminatory economic policies of the sultan.[5] Although any meaningful linkage between the Jebal Akhdar revolt of the 1950s and the Dhofari uprising generally is discounted, we do know that the Saudis aided the dissidents in Dhofar, that contacts were made between Imam Ghalib and Musselim bin Nuffl (leader of the rebellious jebalis), and that many Ibadhis appeared in the ranks of the insurgents.[6]

The hostilities in Dhofar, which commenced in the early 1960s, were conducted by the Dhofar Liberation Front (DLF), an offshoot of the Dhofar branch of the Arab nationalist movement. Although the DLF's manifesto stated that the poor classes would form the backbone of the organization and that the regime would be destroyed, it appeared that the leadership was, in reality, more interested in secession of Dhofar from the sultanate. Moreover, with the passage of time Musselim bin Nuffl acknowledged that he even would be willing to settle for a role in the government and an end to discriminatory policies, a position that amounted to political apostasy in the eyes of a number of Marxists who had joined the movement. Eventually, the leading Marxist, Ahmad al-Ghassani, aligned himself to tribal elements tradi tionally opposed to Musselim and seized the opportunity, with aid from Moscow and Peking, to consolidate his power while Musselim was convalescing from a serious wound.[7]

At the September 1968 congress of the DLF, the shift of power to the al-Ghassani faction was completed. New leaders were elected, a wider strategic objective was articulated and scientific socialism was adopted as the ideological rationale of the movement. A decision was made to pursue the unification of all the Arabian emirates into one socialist state; and the DLF appropriately was renamed the Popular Front for the Liberation of the Occupied Arab Gulf (PFLOAG).[8]

In June 1970 a new organization, the National Democratic Front for the Liberation of Oman and the Arab Gulf (NDFLOAG), backed by the Iraqi Baathists, appeared in the jebal northeast and southeast of Muscat. The NDFLOAG, which was composed of a number of small organizations, including tribal groups, announced its intention to supplement the revolutionary activity in Dhofar.[9] Within a year, however, its leaders were incarcerated, its urban terrorism campaign smashed, and its support from the people severely diminished. Subsequently, the NDFLOAG was absorbed by the PFLOAG and the latter changed its name (but not its acronym) to the Popular Front for the Liberation of Oman and the Arab Gulf.

In Dhofar, meanwhile, the PFLOAG extended its control over most of the jebalis by means of an active propaganda effort, organization, and terrorism. Its task was facilitated by what in the best of times was nothing more than an intermittent government presence.

As these events were unfolding, the sultan was overthrown by his son, Qabus, on July 23, 1970, an event that led a number of the nonsocialists in the PFLOAG, who primarily were interested in Sultan Said's ouster and who increasingly were resentful toward the severe regimentation imposed by the Marxists, to desert the struggle. The PFLOAG's problem further was compounded over the next few years as the new sultan moved to effectuate economic and social reforms, to buttress his military structure and to check insurgents attempts to extend their operations northward following a series of reverses in the south. Among those setbacks was an especially damaging military defeat at the town of Mirbat in July 1972. Within a year of that defeat, the movement of the political and military initiative to the government had become clear to most observers.[10]

Forced on the defensive, the PFLOAG convened its fourth congress in January 1974. A number of problems, including logistical shortages, communications breakdowns, and a high defection rate, were acknowledged. In response to these difficulties, the gradual success of the regime, and the emergence of dissention within its own ranks, the PFLOAG undertook a reappraisal of its strategy. This examination eventually produced a shift of emphasis from the military to the political struggle, especially in Kuwait, Bahrein, and Dubai. In addition, the insurgents began to focus almost exclusively on the situation in the Oman; therefore, the name of the movement was changed once more, this time to the Popular Front for the Liberation of Oman.[11]

Although the PFLO retained control over many parts of the jebal in 1974, the adverse trends set in motion by the sultan's reforms continued. The armed forces were augmented and generous military and material support was provided from a number of outside sources, including Britain, Jordan, Abu Dhabi, and, particularly, Iran. This enabled the Sultan's Armed Forces (SAF) to establish a permanent presence in several parts of the jebal and to build a barrier known as the Hornbeam line thirty-five miles from the coast to the interior. Besides cutting the insurgents' supply routes, the Hornbeam line provided an anchor for an effective territorial offensive that consisted of an admixture of patrolling and mobile air and ground operations. By early 1976 the PFLO's guerrilla units had been pushed against the western border with the People's Democratic Republic of the Yemen (PDRY), and a new sense of confidence emanated from Muscat as the government declared the war all but over. In reaction, the PFLO made frantic efforts in the Arab world to obtain the censure of, and support against, the regime by stressing the dangers to Arabism posed by Iran's intervention on behalf of the sultan. At the same time, limited hostilities broke out between Oman and the PDRY, a development that not only reflected the fact that the PFLO was bottled up near the border but also that the SAF saw the PDRY as the last obstacle to success. As could have been expected, recriminations and threats flew back and forth between Aden and Muscat.[12]

Over the next two years, the PFLO presence in Dhofar remained negligible. Despite its predicament, the PFLO leadership, which was located in the PDRY, pledged to continue "on the trail of struggle." As al-Ghassani put it during a major address on June 9, 1978, the thirteenth anniversary of the revolution, "we are committing ourselves to fight alongside our Omani people in the Gulf and the Arabian peninsula against the ambitions of imperialism and Iranian expansion."[13] In view of the existing state of affairs, however, the road back promised to be a long and perilous one. One way to understand why this was so and how it came about is to analyze the Dhofar insurgency systematically in terms of the factors set forth in Chapter 1.

### Political-Military Assessment

As noted above, the PFLO opted for a Maoist protracted warfare strategy as the best way to enervate and eventually defeat their opponent. Such a strategy was identified in Chapter 1 as a sequential one in which the insurgents lay the foundation for a violent campaign by creating a political party for the purpose of politicizing and organizing sizeable sectors of the population. Once this has been accomplished, violence in the form of gradually escalating guerrilla warfare is used (along with continued organizational efforts) against the regime. If necessary, a decision eventually may be reached to engage the enemy in direct conventional encounters. The successful evolution of such a strategy is, according to its proponents, heavily dependent on a favorable environment, the acquisition of popular support, the establishment and extension of a complex political organization, unity, and, to a somewhat lesser degree, external assistance. If the insurgents measure up well in terms of such criteria, it is assumed that the government's will and morale gradually will dissipate. Our examination begins with a consideration of the environment.

*Environment*

Oman is divided into several distinct areas, including the Musandam Peninsula in the north; the Batinah plain; the Muscat-Matrah coastal region; the Oman interior, composed of the Jebal Akhdar, its foothills, and deserts; the island of Masirah; and Dhofar Province in the south. Since the PFLO's activity has, for the greatest part, been centered in Dhofar, attention will focus there.

Dhofar is bounded by the PDRY in the west and Ras Sharbithat on the coast. A southwestern coastal plain that contains substantial vegetation extends about ten miles inland to the foothills of the Jebal al Qara, whose peaks reach as high as 4,000 feet. On their northern side, the mountains slope down to a rocky desert that is contiguous to the inhospitable Rub al-Khali (the empty quarter). With abundant foliage and boulder-strewn canyons, the jebal provided an excellent physical setting for the PFLO's base areas and guerrilla operations. Furthermore, in the early years of the insurgency the combination of the Indian Ocean monsoon between June and September and the poor road and communications system severely hampered the mobility of government forces, precluded the effective use of heavy weapons and limited the use of air power during those months.[14] Thus, the success that the insurgents enjoyed during the late 1960s and early 1970s was due in no small way to a physical setting that was conducive to guerrilla warfare.

Yet, upon closer inspection, the physical setting of Dhofar revealed some serious flaws with respect to the long-term ambitions of the PFLO. To begin with, the province could be isolated from the rest of the country because of the obstacles to transportation. While this may not have been a major problem for a reformist or secessionist movement, it was a notable impediment for an organization like the PFLO, whose revolutionary aims and protracted warfare strategy putatively encompassed all of Oman. Though it is true that the insurgents did manage to stage a brief, but ill-fated, terrorist campaign in the northeast, they never succeeded in linking their overall efforts. Even in Dhofar itself, the insurgents were hampered because the hot and inhospitable region to the north compelled them to restrict their camel supply lines to the jebal and its immediate environs. Following the Qabus coup, a reinvigorated SAF took advantage of the vulnerabilities inherent in this situation by building roads and extending lines of communications that, in turn, made it possible to establish permanent bases in the jebal. To add to the PFLO's woes, the SAF, along with its Iranian allies, constructed a series of fortified lines that bisected the supply routes and isolated guerrilla units. Consequently, what at first glance appeared to be an ideal area for guerrilla operations turned out to be something much less than that.

The human dimension of the environment was also a mixed blessing for the PFLO. On the one hand, ethnic, historical, and linguistic differences between the estimated 25,000–50,000 jebali tribesmen who were dispersed throughout Dhofar and their Omani neighbors constituted a situation that was conducive to the PFLO's policy of exploiting both religious and economic grievances in order to gain support.[15] On the other hand, while this conjunction of economic discrimination and societal cleavages paid dividends in the short-term quest for popular support, over the longer term it created difficulties for the PFLO because, once the insurgent movement took a Marxist turn and began to implement measures oppugnant to tribal values and customs, traditional resistance led to stresses in and defections from the PFLO. Moreover, in a larger sense, the PFLO's dependence on tribal minorities in an isolated region contradicted the logic of its revolutionary-Maoist strategy, which required at least some semblance of a nationwide base of support. In short, the reliance on tribal minorities and the geographic separation of Dhofar from the rest of the country, which were assets during the secessionist-reformist phase of the conflict, became a liability when the PFLO was transformed into a revolutionary movement that needed to create and sustain widespread popular support.[16]

*Popular Support*

The limitations on the PFLO in such a situation were further evident when popular support was analyzed. As students of insurgency are well aware, active popular support is the epicenter of the Maoist protracted revolutionary warfare model. Active popular support refers to the willingness of the people to risk life and limb in order to provide the guerrillas with the concrete assets (food, shelter, medical aid, hiding places, and information about the government's forces) necessary to compensate for the regime's military strengths. Insofar as the PFLO was concerned, the best estimates were that it was able to muster about 500–800 hard-core military cadres and a part-time militia numbering some 1,500; good estimates of the number of active noncombat supporters, on the other hand, have been elusive.[17]

What popular support the PFLO did acquire in Dhofar was due primarily to esoteric and exoteric appeals, demonstrations of potency, and terrorism. There was little to suggest that charismatic attraction was significant since there were no leading personalities in the movement who could galvanize emotional attachments that cut across tribal lines. Esoteric appeals, in the form of Marxist-Leninist ideology, were somewhat effective with respect to elite recruitment since they enabled the PFLO to obtain leaders and cadres from the small relatively educated strata. Intertwined with the Marxist class analysis propagated by these leaders was a heavy emphasis on nationalism that bore the imprint of Lenin's views on imperialism. In one statement, which typified the PFLO's propaganda, the armed struggle's aim was described as freeing the people from British imperialism and its agents, the Al Bu Said family. British, Iranian, and Jordanian forces in Oman were depicted as "war machines" that were being used to prevent the people from gaining real independence and liberating themselves from "the shackles of ignorance, poverty, disease and backwardness."[18] Though it is tempting to dismiss the PFLO's Marxist-Leninist ideology as a mask for personal interests, especially in a society such as Oman, the vigorous attempts to implement policies devised to actualize Marxist values in the liberated zones, as well as the considerable emphasis on indoctrinating the people, indicated that the ideology had been internalized by many in the leadership echelon. This is not meant to suggest that personal ambitions played no role. Quite the contrary, they obviously did, but in a mutually reinforcing relationship with ideology.

Support from the masses, by contrast, was acquired through the use of other techniques, the most prominent being the familiar emphasis on the concrete grievances of the people against the government, a theme that had many receptive listeners during the Said years. Not only did the PFLO dwell on the injustices and neglect of the regime and promise to rectify the situation, but it also took active steps to underline its sincerity by providing some essential services such as literacy training and health measures in the areas it controlled (the so-called "liberated zones").[19] Yet, at the same time, the PFLO was compelled to use terror against its own followers as well as recalcitrant tribesmen, because its ideological commitment to such goals as expunging the influence of Islam, emancipating women, and imposing stern political regimentation collided with the fierce individualism, elitism, and religiosity of the jebalis.[20]

Perhaps the best testimony to the failure of the PFLO to resocialize the jebalis and to maintain adequate support was the rather alarming defection rate in the wake of the Qabusian reforms (a reported 1,037 by 1975).[21] This strongly implied that for many the PFLO served as a vehicle for addressing grievances against the regime rather than as the beacon of a new, abstract, sociopolitical order. Nevertheless, it bears mentioning that it took the Qabus reforms to energize this basic division within the PFLO; without them the movement would no doubt have been able to retain the loyalty of its other-wise tepid followers.

### Organization and Unity

In spite of the problems that the PFLO encountered because of the Qabu-sian reforms, the fact remains that prior to the changes most jebalis either ac-tively supported or were passively subject to it.[22] Two major reasons for this were the implantation of elements of a parallel hierarchy or organizational structure, albeit inchoate, in the areas that the PFLO controlled, and the relative cohesion of the movement.

The central governing structure of the PFLO, as of 1974, consisted of a cen-tral committee of seven members that included al-Ghassani and Ahmed Ab-dul Samaid Daib, its president. Its political office, located in the PDRY, had various committees for information, finance, propaganda, and so forth. Inside Dhofar, the PFLO was organized both militarily and politically. For military purposes, the province was divided into three sectors, with each the respon-sibility of an undermanned regiment. Operational units were company-sized (100 men) formations that had commanders, political commissars, heavy weapons officers, platoons, and noncommissioned officer specialists. The key components of the political apparatus, meanwhile, were the people's councils that administered "liberated areas" and made efforts to provide some essential services. While this organizational presence was instrumental in gaining a modicum of popular support, there also is evidence that many of its policies (such as its declaration that all land in Dhofar was collective property and its efforts to give birth to communes) were, in spite of their rudimentary nature, anathema to many jebalis. Furthermore, on a more general level, it bears repeating that the failure to extend the parallel hierarchy beyond Dhofar meant that there was little in the way of the nationwide organizational ap-paratus deemed essential for a protracted revolutionary insurgency; hence, the PFLO organization basically was a localized one.[23]

Organizational deficiencies and the detrimental effects they had on popular support have been acknowledged by PFLO leaders like Said Masud. With the benefit of hindsight, Masud candidly has attributed the inability to mobilize the people to an overemphasis on military training and action.[24] This inclination toward the military sector, though not exclusive, was more reflec-tive of the Cuban "military foco" strategy than of the Maoist people's war ap-proach professed by the PFLO. Hence, it constituted a significant strategic shortcoming.

With regard to cohesion, there was a general consensus among the leaders dating back to the time of the Marxist consolidation of power in 1963. Though sharp differences over strategy and tactics occurred from time to time, they did not lead to the emergence of autonomous splinter groups opposed to the main organization as had happened, for instance, in the cases of the Palestinians, Eritreans, and Zimbabweans. Thus, in comparison to many other insurgent movements, the PFLO was relatively cohesive. Nevertheless, the fragile horizontal unity of the leadership was attested to by the disputes over the strategy that engulfed it in the wake of successful government reforms.

Even more important was the deleterious impact that the new counterinsurgency program had on vertical cohesion. As the lifting of the previous sultan's restrictions, civic action, administrative reform, economic changes, and an amnesty program began to transform the situation in Dhofar, defections from the lower ranks multiplied. This development, which was not altogether surprising in view of the rank and file's persistent identification with primordial tribal structures, was responsible for an intensification of disciplinary measures – murder and torture – by the Idhaara (execution squads), the bete noir of the jebal.[25] And, to the extent that such violence inside the PFLO continued, the underlying gap between the Marxist leaders and their tribally oriented followers was further accentuated.

## External Support

Though the PFLO had an uneven record with respect to popular support and organization, it fared quite well when it came to external support. Political, moral, and material backing was obtained, at one time or another, from a number of Marxist states, including the People's Republic of China (PRC), the Soviet Union, East Germany, Cuba, and the PDRY. Prior to the Marxist takeover of the Dhofar insurrection, limited assistance also was forthcoming from Saudi Arabia and Egypt; and, as of 1978, the PFLO had political offices in Algeria, Syria, Libya, and Iraq as well as ties with the Palestine Liberation Organization and Tudeh dissidents in Iran.[26]

Besides political and moral support, the PRC provided material assistance in the form of both military and ideological training (including some in China) and weaponry.[27] However, the winding down of the Cultural Revolution and increasing trepidations regarding a perceived Soviet strategy of encircling China by establishing "hegemony" in Asia led the Chinese leadership to search for new friends among old adversaries. A Yugoslav government previously castigated for the sin of revisionism was forgiven. NATO, which, in Peking's view, epitomized the militaristic aggressiveness of capitalism, was suddenly encouraged to strengthen itself in the face of growing Russian military might. The shah of Iran, who at one time was characterized as a feudal reactionary, became the target of friendly overtures. The basic shift in the PRC's foreign policy signified by these changes also had an effect on Chinese relations with both the PFLO and the sultan's regime. Material aid to the PFLO gradually dried up in the early 1970s and in May 1973 Peking established formal diplomatic relations with the Omani government.[28] Furthermore, there were unconfirmed reports in 1978 that the Chinese were training the SAF in counterguerrilla tactics![29]

Fortunately for the PFLO, the Soviet Union and its allies stepped into the breach with political, moral, and material assistance. Political and moral backing came primarily in the context of propaganda; material aid was both direct and indirect. The most significant direct assistance to the PFLO consisted of training in the Soviet Union for hard-core elements, and the provision of weapons (machine guns, 60-mm, 81-mm and 82-mm mortars, antipersonnel mines, antitank rockets, RPG-7 recoilless rifles, 122-mm katyusha rockets, and SA-7 antiaircraft missiles). Indirect aid came by way of Soviet assistance to the PDRY and encouragement of Cuban and Eastern European involvement, the latter mostly in a limited advisory, training, and indoctrinating capacity.[30]

Within the Middle East, the PDRY was, and continues to be, the main benefactor of the PFLO. Though it rendered consistent political and moral backing, the PDRY's main contribution was as a conduit for Chinese and then Russian aid, and as a sanctuary for planning, organizational activities, training, stockpiling of arms, and operational bases such as the major one at Hauf.[31] In fact, the PDRY role, which always was vital for the PFLO, became absolutely indispensable following the virtual expulsion of the insurgents from Dhofar by 1975. In recognition of this, the conservative Arab states, primarily Saudi Arabia, attempted to cultivate pragmatic circles in Aden through promises of financial aid and an end to Saudi backing for tribesmen who periodically harassed the PDRY.[32] However, this effort to sever the PDRY-PFLO connection and thus end the insurrection once and for all received a setback in June of 1978 when hard-line elements in the PDRY suppressed the more moderate faction led by President Salim Rubayyi Ali.[33] Shortly thereafter, Abdel Fattah Ismail, secretary general of the central committee of the United Political Organization, National Front (now known as the Yemeni Socialist party) dispelled whatever doubts there were regarding the PDRY's relations with the PFLO when he reiterated support for the struggle against Iran and the Qabus regime.[34] Although, as of the end of 1978, the PDRY remained fully committed to its client, it is quite likely that renewed efforts will be made by the Saudis and other conservative Arab states to undercut the PDRY-PFLO relationship because of their steadily increasing concern over the Soviet Union's presence in the Horn of Africa and perceived machinations in the destabilizing political turmoil engulfing Iran. If the Saudis are successful over the longer term, it will, of course, doom the PFLO.[35]

What all of the foregoing suggests is that external support has been critical for the PFLO. It played a major part in earlier achievements of the insurgents and in early 1979 was responsible for their continued existence. The importance of external support is also indicative of the strategic weaknesses of the PFLO since it has been necessitated by failures with respect to the most significant ingredients of the Maoist strategy, namely, popular support and organization.

## Government Response

Although many of the PFLO's shortcomings were self-inflicted, there is no gainsaying that the reinvigorated counterinsurgency effort under Qabus played a major, if not decisive, part in turning the conflict around. Indeed, it is more than coincidental that the PFLO's greatest success came during the moribund Said years whereas its greatest difficulties occurred under the reign of Qabus. A multifaceted array of political and military policy alterations accounted for this.

Under Said, it will be recalled, the neglect of the jebalis in Dhofar facilitated insurgent efforts to convince many tribesmen that they were deprived relative to their traditional rivals in the coastal areas. Furthermore, the near total absence of government administration in the jebal enabled the PFLO to implant at least a rudimentary political apparatus that signalled the possibility of effecting beneficial changes in Dhofar as time went on.

To meet this political and organizational threat, the Qabus government embarked on a major campaign to reduce the active popular support for the insurgents by, inter alia, bringing modern economic planning and techniques (especially with respect to animal husbandry) to the jebal, building schools, increasing health care, strengthening local administration, and promising the jebalis greater participation in running their own affairs. On a more general level, a policy of gradually staffing military and administrative offices with Omanis (the Omanization program) was instituted. A key role in the preparation for these developmental efforts was played by Civic Action Teams (CATs) that moved into newly secured areas and established the government's presence. Conceived for pacification activities, the CATs drilled wells and operated government centers with schools, clinics, stores, and the like. Compared to the neglect of the past, such attention hardly escaped the notice not only of the jebalis, but also of the rank and file fighters and cadres of the PFLO, many of whom responded to a government amnesty program by defecting and eventually assisting government counterinsurgency efforts.[36] When the PFLO reacted to these government inroads by intensifying coercive measures against suspect followers in the areas it controlled, its situation went from bad to worse.

The emphasis on social and economic development was facilitated greatly by the gradual shift of the military initiative from the insurgents to the government during the 1972–74 period. In the military sphere, the new counterinsurgency policy stressed police and intelligence work to apprehend terrorists and counterguerrilla techniques that included aggressive small-unit patrols and ambushes from secure areas, mobile assaults against insurgent bases, barriers (the Hornbeam and Damavand lines) across the PFLO's main supply routes, and air and artillery bombardment of guerrilla zones.[37] Once areas had been cleared, the government consolidated control through the use of local militias (*firqats*), half of whom were defectors from the PFLO.[38] From time to time, the military effort was made easier by insurgent blunders such as the previously cited July 1972 attack against the coastal town of Mirbat.

The sultan's far-reaching military campaign was not without costs. It required the expansion of the SAF from 2,500 to 15,000 and the purchase of new equipment, thus cutting deeply into new oil revenues.[39] To some extent, the situation was alleviated by generous inputs from Jordan, Saudi Arabia, Abu Dhabi, and, most important, Britain and Iran.

Britain not only provided field officers (both regular and contract), engineers, pilots, and an elite Special Air Services unit, but it also accepted overall military command responsibility.[40] Iran committed an estimated 3,000 combat troops, helicopters, and fixed-wing aircraft to the struggle. Notwithstanding the fact that their combat performance was at times described as lackluster, Iranian forces were instrumental in opening up transportation links with the interior by establishing forward helicopter bases and control over the road to the interior town of Midway; in seizing and holding the PFLO's self-proclaimed capital of "liberated Dhofar" at Rakhyut; and in building the Damavand line.[41]

Assistance from conservative Arab states was also helpful to the sultan. For instance, Jordan made available an engineering battalion and military training; Saudi Arabia contributed political and financial support as well as military equipment; and the Union of Arab Emirates provided garrison troops, monetary aid, and, in 1973, reportedly arrested and extradited to Oman a large number of Dhofaris opposed to the sultan.[42]

Though it is true that the Marxist takeover of the Dhofar insurgency no doubt influenced the decisions of Oman's Middle Eastern donors, it would be an oversight to ignore the impact of the new foreign policy orientation that Qabus adopted after his seizure of power. In contradistinction to the rigid isolationism of his father, the new sultan engaged in an active diplomatic effort to convince his richer neighbors that his struggle was as much in their interest as his.[43] As a consequence, Qabus was able to exploit the opportunity created by the Marxist coup within the PFLO. And, in retrospect, it is clear that this acquisition of outside assistance was a critical ingredient in the successful counterinsurgency program.

## Potential Problems

Although there is no question that the PFLO insurgency had been almost totally eliminated by 1977, there are a number of problems that, if not ad-dressed, could undercut stability. In the economic sphere, the cost of the military effort ($500 million per year) has left the Omani treasury overdrawn and has cast doubts on future economic projects, a situation that is exacer-bated by administrative corruption and inefficiency.[44] While Britain has sought to obtain more Arab oil money and promised technical assistance, it remains to be seen whether the new bureaucrats spawned by the Omaniza-tion program will be capable of managing the larger process of socioeconomic change in such a way as to continue meeting popular demands. If they are not, we may well see the emergence of a classic case of progressive relative deprivation, a social phenomenon that suggests the possibility of a resurgence and intensification of violence.[45]

In the political sphere, the regime may face pressures for more effective par-ticipation in the decision-making process from the newly educated strata. Like its patrimonial counterparts elsewhere in the gulf, the Omani government will have to fashion new institutions to cope with rising political aspirations if it is to preclude a renewal of revolutionary violence. The turbulent events in Iran during 1978–79 are instructive here for, in large part, they can be traced to the failure to give serious attention to creating adequate mechanisms for political participation and development.

In the more immediate future, the regime also faces problems in establishing an organizational presence throughout the country, due to the dearth of qualified personnel. In one analyst's view, a selective assassination campaign against officials could expose the shaky administrative structure as the Achilles heel of the regime.[46] Indeed, the government can scarcely afford to procrastinate on this matter, given the possibility that the PFLO may revert to terrorism in the aftermath of the defeats suffered by its guerrilla units.

In the military area, two problems stand out. One is the danger that without effective control from the top the *firqats* could easily transform their control over local grazing rights and essential services into an extortionary enterprise. The other problem is the presence of foreign military advisors and troops, which could have the longer term impact of alienating the people and providing the PFLO with continued grist for its propaganda mill. However, with the removal of Iranian forces in the wake of the Khomeini insurrection, a major precipitant has been removed. Whether or not Egyptian forces will, as rumored, replace the Iranians remains to be seen.[47] If they do, Oman will run the risk of making new enemies from among those who are bitterly opposed to Egypt's peace treaty with Israel. As a consequence, states that hitherto paid little attention to the situation in Oman might become benefactors of the

PFLO, not out of enthusiasm for the latter's purposes but rather out of an-
tipathy for "the friends of their enemy."

## Summary and Conclusions

The insurgency in Oman has been a particularly appropriate one for il-
lustrating the utility of the framework for analysis because the emphasis on a
Maoist strategy involves all of the major variables discussed in Chapter 1. By
carefully evaluating the progress of the PFLO in terms of those variables one
is better able to identify the reasons behind the early accomplishments of the
insurgents—i.e., favorable topography for guerrilla warfare in Dhofar, the exploitation of concrete grievances to obtain active popular support, the
emergence of at least a rudimentary organizational apparatus, relative cohesion, substantial external assistance, and an indifferent government that was
ill-equipped both intellectually and materially to cope with the threat. By the
same token, the framework for analysis called attention to some underlying
weaknesses of the PFLO that tended to be glossed over because of its initial
success, but that portended longer term difficulties. Among these were the
geographical isolation of the principal combat zone, Dhofar, and the potential
to interdict supply routes due to their constriction by severe climatic and
topographic features north of the jebal. With respect to popular support, the
tribal, cultural, and religious orientations of the jebalis were congruent with
reformist or secessionist overtures, but not with Marxist values and centraliz-
ing structures. In the area of organization, the confinement of the insurgent
apparatus to liberated areas in Dhofar was hardly compatible with the coun-
trywide requirements associated with a protracted people's war. As far as external support was concerned, the same revolutionary Marxism that brought
vital aid from the socialist states also provided the fillip for significant outside
countersupport for the regime. What stood out more than anything, however, was the reality that the exploitation of such insurgent weaknesses was
made possible only when Qabus devised and implemented new and
enlightened political, economic, and military policies that exemplified many of
the prescriptions set forth in the discussion of counterinsurgency in Chapter
1. Thus, the Oman case supported the proposition that government response
is the most critical variable in insurrectionary situations.

## Notes

1. For some more recent commentaries on the Omani political system see David E.
Long, *The Persian Gulf*, revised edition (Boulder, Colorado: Westview Press, 1976),
pp. 40–42; Michael Hudson, *Arab Politics* (New Haven: Yale University Press, 1977),
pp. 204–209.

2. On the adoption of the strategy of protracted revolutionary insurgency by the PFLO see, inter alia, the excerpt from the national action program, Aden Voice of Oman, August 9, 1974, in Foreign Broadcast Information Service/*Middle East and North Africa, Daily Report*, August 20, 1974, pp. C2–C3. Hereafter cited as FBIS/*ME*.

3. British influence in Oman dated back to 1789 and grew out of a desire to establish and protect trade routes to India. The sultans were favorably disposed and a long period of cooperation followed.

4. The reader who wishes to go beyond this brief historical synthesis of Oman should consult, inter alia, J. B. Kelley, "A Prevalence of Furies: Tribes, Politics and Religion in Oman and Trucial Oman," *The Arabian Peninsula: Society and Politics*, ed. Derek Hopwood (New Jersey: Rowman and Little Field, 1972), pp. 107–144; Richard F. Nyrop et al., *Area Handbook for the Persian Gulf States* (Washington: Government Printing Office, 1977), pp. 341–346; R. P. Owen, "Developments in the Sultanate of Muscat and Oman," *The World Today*, September 1970, pp. 379–383; Wendal Phillips, *Oman: A History* (New York: Revnal, 1968); George Rentz, "A Sultanate Asunder," *Natural History*, March 1974, pp. 59–60; Roberta Rubinacci, "The Ibadis," *Religion in the Middle East: Three Religions in Concord and Conflict, II: Islam*, ed. A. J. Arberry (Cambridge: Cambridge University Press, 1969), pp. 302–317; Ian Skeet, *Muscat and Oman* (London: Faber and Faber, 1974); and J. C. Wilkinson, "The Origins of the Omani State," *The Arabian Peninsula: Society and Politics*, pp. 67–88.

5. R. M. Burrell, "Rebellion in Dhofar: The Spectre of Vietnam," *The New Middle East*, March/April 1972, p. 56.

6. For varying views on the nature of the relationship between the Jebal Akhdar and Dhofar movements see D. L. Price, *Oman Insurgency and Development*, Conflict Study Number 42 (London: Institute for the Study of Conflict, 1975), p. 1; G. L. Bondarevskiy, "The Continuing Western Interest in Oman–As Seen from Moscow," *The New Middle East*, August 1971, p. 12.

7. Ranulph Fiennes, *Where Soldiers Fear to Tread* (London: Hodder and Stoughton, 1975), p. 56. For the Congress Manifesto of June 1965 see Appendix 1, Price, *Oman Insurgency*, p. 18.

8. Burrell, "Rebellion in Dhofar," p. 56; "Secret War in the Persian Gulf," *Atlas*, April 1972, pp. 46–47. PFLOAG was a Marxist-Leninist organization originating in Bahrein.

9. *NYT*, July 12, 1970; Price, *Oman Insurgency*, p. 5.

10. Price, *Oman Insurgency*, pp. 5–6.

11. On these events see *Christian Science Monitor* (*CSM*), July 1, 1974 and Price, *Oman Insurgency*, p. 6.

12. The serious situation that the PFLO found itself in at the end of 1975 was reflected not only in the SAF's positive statements but in the PFLO appeals for help directed to Arab states and the Arab League. The existing phase was described as the "hardest" in the struggle thus far and instructions were issued to make the supreme sacrifice, if necessary, to protect the political commissars against capture. On these points see Doha QNA, December 20, 1975 in FBIS/*ME*, December 2, 1975, p. C2; Baghdad INA, December 20, 1975 in FBIS/*ME*, December 23, 1975, p. C1; Paris AFP, October 27, 1975 in FBIS/*ME*, October 30, 1975, p. C2; Aden Domestic Service, October 18, 1975 in FBIS/*ME*, October 23, 1975, p. C1. Insofar as the charges surrounding border hostilities between Oman and the PDRY are concerned, see *Al-*

*Ahram* (Cairo), December 25, 1975, and Aden Domestic Service, December 24, 1975, in FBIS/ME, December 29, 1975, pp. C2 and C3.

13. *14 October* (Aden), June 9, 1978.

14. On these aspects of the environment and their impact see R. M. Burrell, *The Persian Gulf*, The Washington Papers, No. 1 (New York: The Library Press, 1972), p. 61; Burrell, "Rebellion in Dhofar," p. 55; R. Azzi, "Oman: Land of Frankincense and Oil," *National Geographic*, February 4, 1974; *CSM*, March 7, 1974.

15. The three most powerful tribes in Dhofar were involved in the insurgency. Two—the Mahrah and the Al Kathir—are culturally and socially akin to tribes in the PDRY, while the third— the Qara—is non-Arab. See Nyrop et al., *Area Handbook*, p. 354; Burrell, *The Persian Gulf*, p. 60; *CSM*, March 14, 1974.

16. Rupert Hay, "Great Britain's Relations with Yemen and Oman," *Mid East Affairs*, May 1960, pp. 142–146; J. C. Wilkinson, "The Oman Question: The Background to the Political Geography of South East Arabia," *Geographical Journal*, September 1971, p. 361; Fiennes, *Soldiers*, p. 56.

17. Price, *Oman Insurgency*, p. 7 and *Washington Post* (WP), December 16, 1974, generally agree on these figures. The latter is one of several insightful pieces of report-age by Jim Hoagland.

18. *14 October* (Aden), June 9, 1978.

19. Owen, *Muscat and Oman*, p. 381; Fred Halliday, "Oil and Revolution in the Persian Gulf," *Ramparts*, April 1971, p. 53.

20. Fiennes, *Soldiers*, pp. 85, 87, 132–133 and 171–172; Burrell, "Rebellion in Dhofar," p. 57. One very well-informed American official stationed in Oman in the early 1970s indicated to this writer that in his judgment the propaganda efforts of the PFLO never amounted to a real success because of the low literacy rate and poor com-munications in Dhofar. Price, *Oman Insurgency*, p. 11, has pointed out that interroga-tion of defectors revealed that political theory played a minor part in recruitment. The major reasons for joining the PFLO were tribal loyalties and intimidation.

21. *New York Times* (NYT), February 7, 1975.

22. Nyrop et al., *Area Handbook*, p. 390.

23. The limited organizational success of the PFLO was due, in large measure, to the absence of government administration. On the PFLO organization see Price, *Oman Insurgency*, p. 3; Nyrop et al., *Area Handbook*, pp. 390, 392–393. The official cited in note 20 stated that the PFLO organization had a diffuse, nonassertive, noncharismatic leadership, a lack of systematic structures, and a poorly conceived cellular makeup.

24. Interview of Said Masud by Eli Ramaro in *Afrique-Asia* (Paris) August 7 through September 3, 1978.

25. Price, *Oman Insurgency*, p. 5; NYT, April 15, 1973. Fiennes, *Soldiers*, pp. 144 and 167 ff, point out that the terror was often indiscriminate and based on old blood feuds. As such it constituted an inexcusable deviation from Maoist doctrine.

26. Besides providing financial help during the early, non-Marxist phase of the insur-rection in Dhofar, the Saudis also facilitated the movement of Musselim bin Nuffl to Iraq where he was trained in guerrilla tactics. Saudi monetary aid was terminated when the Marxists took over the PFLO, thus precipitating financial problems for the insurgents. See Price, *Oman Insurgency*, p. 4 and 17; Fiennes, *Soldiers*, p. 69.

27. On the various types of Chinese aid and their impact see, inter alia, Price, *Oman*

*Insurgency,* pp. 5 and 7; Fiennes, *Soldiers,* pp. 30–34, 69–70, 88, and 200; *The Econo-mist* (London), April 21, 1973; Nyrop et al., *Area Handbook,* p. 390.

28. *The Far Eastern Economic Review* (Hong Kong), June 23, 1978, reported that "a congruence of interest–the need to preserve Oman's national independence and to contain Soviet imperialist expansionism in Africa and the Middle East, notably the Arabian Gulf–[brought] Oman and China together."

29. *Middle East Reporter* (Beirut), August 22, 1978.

30. Soviet assistance to the PFLO is well known. See, for instance, Price, *Oman In-surgency,* pp. 6–7; Fiennes, *Soldiers,* pp. 67, 114, and 127; Nyrop et al., *Area Handbook,* p. 393. The Cuban and Eastern European connections are noted by *CSM,* November 18, 1967; interview of Said Masud, *Afrique-Asia* (Paris), August 7 through September 3, 1978; Price, *Oman Insurgency,* p. 7; and *NYT,* April 5, 1976.

31. *The Economist* (London), April 3, 1971, pp. 41–42; *NYT,* December 2, 1967, December 12, 1967, and December 10, 1968; Fiennes, *Soldiers,* pp. 144–146; Nyrop et al., *Area Handbook,* pp. 386, 390, and 398; Price, *Oman Insurgency,* pp. 7 and 17; and *CSM,* November 18, 1976. Occasionally, the PDRY supported the PFLO with air ar-tillery bombardment across the border. See, for example, *The Times* (London), No-vember 20, 1973.

32. *WP,* October 14, 1974.

33. A number of observers believe that the violence in the PDRY was partially due to fears on the part of hard-liners that Salim Rubayyi Ali was behind an effort to ameliorate relations with the Yemen Arab Republic and Saudi Arabia. Had this transpired, it may well have meant an end to the PDRY support for the PFLO. This in-ference may also be drawn from charges leveled against Ali to the effect that he had a "reactionary attitude toward Arab and world revolutionary movements." See Aden Domestic Service, June 28, 1978, in FBIS/ME, June 29, 1978, p. C10; *WP,* June 27, 1978.

34. Text of speech by Abdel Fattah Ismail, secretary general of the central commit-tee of the United Political Organization, *14 October,* June 22, 1978, Special Supple-ment. Also see, interview of Said Masud, *Afrique-Asia,* op. cit.

35. The precarious nature of relations with the Arab states following the govern-ment's successes was illustrated by the decision of Iraq, a former PFLO ally, to establish diplomatic relations with Oman in February 1976 and by its reported declara-tion at an Arab People's Conference held in Libya in June 1978 that the insurgency was over. The latter is noted by Sarkis Naum in "Secret Minutes of the Arab People's Conference in Libya," *Al-Nahar Al Arabi Wa Al-Duwali* (Paris), July 15, 1978.

36. On the political and economic policies inaugurated by Qabus see Price, *Oman In-surgency,* pp. 10–12; Nyrop et al., *Area Handbook,* pp. 373 and 402–404; *WP,* February 2, 1977; Detlev Rohwedder, "A Sultan Catches Up With the Times–Oman Is Not Building on Oil Alone But Is Nevertheless Making the Transition to Our Cen-tury," *Deutsche Zeitung* (Bonn), June 23, 1978; Udo Minne, "Dhofar Leaves War Behind–The Southern Region is Today a Key Development Area," *Deutsche Zeitung,* (Bonn), June 23, 1978.

37. The public security branch of the Royal Oman Police reportedly developed a sound capability for dealing with terrorism. See Nyrop et al., *Area Handbook,* p. 406. On the counterguerrilla campaign see Price, *Oman Insurgency,* pp. 5–7; Nyrop et al.,

*Area Handbook,* pp. 390–395; Burrell, "Rebellion in Dhofar," p. 57; *WP,* February 2, 1977. The reader who is interested in a less analytical but more detailed account of the day to day aspects of counterguerrilla operations in Oman should read the previously cited Fiennes volume. One feature of the military situation which could have caused problems was the substantial reliance on minorities and foreigners by the SAF. However, the use of foreign mercenaries had a long history in Oman and was sanctioned by traditional political arrangements, according to Nyrop et al., *Area Handbook,* p. 402. The present emphasis on Omanization is no doubt a response to fears that political development and increased nationalist sentiments would render such a situation increasingly illegitimate in the eyes of many Omanis.

38. The use of defectors is reminiscent of the effective use of former insurgents by the British in Kenya, Malaya, and elsewhere and thus was undoubtedly the result of British advice.

39. On arms procurement see Nyrop et al., *Area Handbook,* pp. 400–402.

40. On the British role see Fiennes, *Soldiers;* Nyrop et al., *Area Handbook,* pp. 387, 393, and 404; *NYT,* January 18, 1976; *CSM,* November 18, 1976; *WP,* February 2, 1977.

41. *WP,* December 16, 1974. This report, written by Jim Hoagland, indicates that the three to four month troop rotation policy, overreliance on firepower in lieu of pursuit, and general inexperience accounted for many of the Iranian difficulties. For information on the Iranian contribution see Price, *Oman Insurgency,* p. 9; Nyrop et al., *Area Handbook,* p. 395; *NYT* January 25, 1976.

42. On the assistance from the Arab states see *The Financial Times* (London), January 3, 1973. Jordanian and Saudi aid is, of course, well known. The assistance from the Union of Arab Emirates is noted by Price, *Oman Insurgency,* p. 14; *Deadline Data on World Affairs,* February 1973, p. 4 and March 1974, p. 5.

43. R. P. Owen, "Rebellion in Dhofar – A Threat to Western Interests in the Gulf," *The World Today,* June 1973, p. 271.

44. *The Economist* (London), May 20, 1972; *NYT,* February 15 and 17, 1975; *CSM,* September 15, 1975; *WP,* May 27, 1975.

45. Ted Robert Gurr, *Why Men Rebel* (Princeton University Press, 1970), pp. 52–56. As Gurr notes, progressive relative deprivation refers to a situation where there is a period of improvement in people's value positions which generates expectations about continued improvement. When value capabilities then decline or stabilize, progressive relative deprivation results, thus creating a propensity for revolutionary violence.

46. Price, *Oman Insurgency,* p. 7.

47. PFLO's newspaper *Sawt Ath-Thawrah,* Issue No. 175, for instance, emphasized the threat to the Arab region posed by "the Iranian invasion and occupation of Oman." See Aden Voice of Oman, October 25, 1975 in FBIS/ME, October 29, 1975, p. C1. Iran attempted to mitigate such criticism by stressing shared Islamic values, association with social reform policies, and the danger of communism in the gulf. See Teheran Domestic Service, October 20, 1975 in FBIS/ME, October 22, 1975, p. R4. Reports of Egyptian troops arriving in Oman were made by the newspaper *Al-Wahdah* (Abu Dhabi) on February 22, 1979. On February 25, the Foreign Ministry of Oman denied the presence of Egyptian forces in the country but left the future up in the air by in-

dicating that the government would consider "asking the support of its brothers if the need arises." See Baghdad INA, February 22, 1979 in FBIS/*ME,* February 22, 1979, p. C1; Manama Gulf News Agency, February 25, 1979, in FBIS/*ME,* February 26, 1979, p. C1. A high-ranking Egyptian officer acknowledged the presence of advisory personnel in Oman during a discussion with the author in Cairo in October 1979.

# Angola

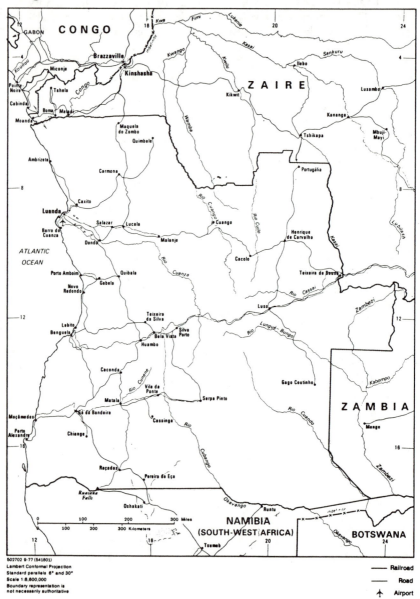

502702 9-77 (541801)
Lambert Conformal Projection
Standard parallels 6° and 30°
Scale 1:8,600,000
Boundary representation is
not necessarily authoritative

—— Railroad

—— Road

✈ Airport

# 8
# Armed Struggle in Angola

*Donald J. Alberts*

## Introduction

The primary purpose of this study is to examine the present insurgent war in Angola in light of the framework for analysis offered in this book. Those factors that will help us explain the present situation and anticipate the future will allow the reader to draw personal conclusions about the possibilities of eventual government or insurgent success.

One event dominates recent Angolan history – the 1975 civil war that came with the independence of Angola from Portugal. The insurgent movements existed before and after the civil war, but the enemies have changed. Complicating the issue is the paucity of reliable data. The Angolan insurgency was covered extensively during the civil war, but now much less is being reported. Available information in the journals and the press is largely biased toward one side or the other. Nevertheless, enough can be gleaned to get a fairly good idea of what is happening.

This analysis is directed to Angola proper, with only a very long note (62) focused on Cabinda. Cabinda is a very small piece of Angolan territory to the north of the country proper, separated from Angola by the Congo River and a portion of Zaire.

## Historical Background

The current insurgency in Angola can be viewed as a continuation of the war that started in 1961. An understanding of the relationships and the actors in that war against the Portuguese colonial government is necessary – if for no other reason than the degree of continuity of the players, organizations and other factors. Further, the fighting has never really stopped. The war started as one of national liberation against the Portuguese administration of the Angolan territory; it is now a war of one faction against another, both Angolan. The domestic and international environments have been altered in significant ways. The present war is between those who fought against the

Portuguese, although there was a considerable amount of conflict between the parties prior to national independence. Indeed, the roots of the war are found in the anti-Portuguese struggle.

Portuguese involvement in Africa started in the early fifteenth century as a result of the search for India, but penetration of the interior was slight until the latter half of the nineteenth century. Until then, the Portuguese were content to trade with the various tribal kingdoms of the interior. The main export from all of the Portuguese African territories was human beings. The slave trade was openly carried on from about 1510 until 1838, when the practice was declared illegal by the European powers. The Portuguese contented themselves with coastal trading posts until the turn of this century, when military conquest was undertaken.[1] The final boundaries of Portugal's African territories were set at the Congress of Berlin, and confirmed in the aftermath of World War I. Angola was the largest and potentially the richest of Portugal's African territories. The other territories of note were Mozambique and Portuguese Guinea, or Guinea-Bissau as it became known in revolutionary circles.

The armed independence struggle in Angola against the Portuguese started in 1961, led by a group that came to be known as the *Frente Nacional de Libertacao de Angola* (FNLA) under the leadership of Holden Roberto. Initial insurgent success, in a manner more reflective of ill-armed conventional war than guerrilla war, was followed by a fairly successful Portuguese counterattack. Stalemate set in, and other groups moved to create guerrilla forces to carry on the struggle. This pattern was essentially the same in all of Portugal's African territories; the Portuguese were fighting what amounted to a four-front war. In Angola, the three main insurgent groups that dominated the preindependence struggle were FNLA;[2] the *Movimento Popular de Libertacao de Angola* (MPLA), which is the current ruling government party; and *Uniao Nacional para Independencia Total de Angola* (UNITA). There can be little doubt that the original insurgent movement was a revolutionary insurgency, for all antigovernment groups involved sought to replace the Portuguese-dominated political values and structures with values and structures stressing nationalism, independence, "Africanness," and egalitarianism. The degree to which radical change was promised and hoped for beyond the granting of independence varied from faction to faction.

The Portuguese government and the colonial administrators of the African territories followed similar policies in each of the African territories. There were differences to be sure, but these differences derived more from the personalities and latitude allowed individual governors and generals than from any legal or constitutional differences in the manner in which the territories were treated. Of particular importance was the stated Portuguese view of race. The concept, termed "Lusotropicality," was one of equality on a theoretical level. This equal racial policy was not borne out by the dynamics and realities of life in the territories, especially in Angola. Lusotropicality was the combination of Portuguese culture and history with the Black African physique: a new race uniquely suited to build and develop the African territories into modern states, all part of a Greater Portugal. Putting a name on this policy was a relatively recent innovation, perhaps borrowed from Brazil, another former Portuguese colony (and one where substantial mixing of the races has occurred over time). But there were never any official distinctions among people in the Portuguese empire based on race. Rather, the class distinctions were based on levels of "civilization," that is, the speaking of Portuguese, education level, and other similar criteria. Natives of the territories were divided into two groups that were considered citizenship categories: the *assimilado* and the *indigena*. The requirements for *assimilado* status were the ability to speak Portuguese, income from a job, good character, age (over 18), and nonevasion of military or public service.[3] The *indigena* were all other native-born black inhabitants. Settlers from Portugal and those of mixed blood seldom had to meet the official standards of the *assimilado* class. The *indigena* class had no real political or economic rights, and *assimilado* status was restricted to a very small proportion of the population. While the *assimilado* was little better off than the *indigena*, he did share some of the rights of Europeans.[4] Like de facto segregation in the United States, class distinction was not on the basis of race, but rather on other factors that tended to break primarily on racial lines. Thus the Portuguese could claim that race was not a factor, while the insurgents could point to the obvious racial overtones of all the inequities of life. Both sides thus claimed a superior moral position. The race problem has not gone away with the Portuguese and continues to be an issue of great sensitivity for all the political factions in Angola.

Early nationalistic tendencies in the colony resided more in the European sector than in the indigenous sector. These tendencies were tied to the citizenship distinction described above, as well as certain political facts of life arising out of the Portuguese political system. Even whites from Angola were not treated as full citizens of Portugal. Portugal, prior to the coup in 1974, was an authoritarian state where little dissenting opinion was allowed to surface. The precoup regime was based on a blend of fascist political values and highly centralized, authoritarian, "nonpolitical," nationalistic, and bureaucratic organizational structures. Meaningful political participation, both in Portugal and in the overseas territories, was extremely limited. In an economic sense, the metropole can still be described as underdeveloped and backward, certainly by European standards. The Salazar regime (effectively ended in 1968 with the severe illness of Salazar) looked toward development of Portugal and the colonies, but in a very conservative manner. The cry for change was muted to begin with, and was allowed to circulate only within the very limited political circles of the territorial administration and the metropolitan governmental structures. While some liberalization occurred under Salazar's successor, Dr. Marcello Cataeno (1968–74), the overall picture regarding development did not change, although the pace accelerated somewhat–primarily in response to the insurgencies in the territories. In short, economic and social conditions were not that much different when comparisons were drawn between the metropole and the territories.[5] Education serves as a good example of the development problem, as well as an example of the de facto racial discrimination.

Free compulsory elementary education was the law of the land, both in Portugal and in the territories, but developmental constraints imposed by a lack of human and material resources tended to keep the actual number of schools and classrooms limited. In Angola, this limitation meant that schools were located primarily in the more developed urban areas, thereby automatically favoring the European and mixed population over the purely African, rural population. Since elementary education was a prerequisite for secondary and higher education, the lack of opportunity in elementary education translated into similar discrimination at all levels of education, becoming more pronounced at the higher levels. And, since education was the surest way to enter the *assimilado* class, the rural population had almost no chance of gaining such status.

To a certain extent, the Portuguese government tried to use the territories, and particularly Angola, as a place to solve the problems of the metropole. Rather than radically reform the landholding practices in Portugal, the government encouraged emigration to the territories. The unemployed, the landless, the tenant farmer, etc., were urged to move to Africa, thereby easing the economic pressure on the regime in the metropole as well as raising the proportion of Europeans in Angola.[6] Cape Verde, another Portuguese possession, also sent many people to the African mainland under similar conditions. The Cape Verde population was almost entirely *mestico*, or mixed.[7] Cape Verde is also poor in economic terms, but had the cultural values of rural Portugal. Emigration from Cape Verde into Angola relieved economic pressure in Cape Verde, helped transmit cultural values, and supposedly helped inculcate a more rational agricultural policy in the continental territories. Likewise, Africans in Angola and the other territories were encouraged to leave the bush and resettle in new villages in an attempt to change the system of land cultivation and meet the demands of both social mobilization and modernization.

In general, Portuguese economic and social reform measures were reflected throughout the system and they opened up the gate for revolutionary trends in that they were not accompanied by a corresponding liberalization in the political structure. As with many other insurgencies, those individuals benefitting from the early reforms and limited progress became the driving force and source of leadership for the liberation movements in Portuguese Africa. These elements were spurred on by the overall dissolution of the colonial system elsewhere in Africa. In the early stages, the authoritarian policies of the political system existing in Portugal and the territories served to inhibit the growth of organizational efforts of any antiregime force, be that force black African liberationists, liberal-democratic, or whatever. It made little difference to the Portuguese secret police what kind of subversion was being preached—antiregime activity of any kind was sufficient to bring rather violent repression, regardless of the color, creed, or location of the subversive. Consequently, nationalistic sentiment in the late 1950s was channelled into organizations such as labor unions that were allowed to exist by the regime for nonpolitical purposes. However, since these organizations, both in Portugal and in Angola, were heavily infiltrated and in many cases controlled by government agents, the true antiregime organizational efforts were exceedingly difficult and always clandestine.

The outbreak of fighting in Angola in 1961 and in Guinea-Bissau in 1962 led to the adoption in Lisbon in 1963 of The Organic Law of the Overseas Provinces. The effect of the law was to change the colonies from colonies to provinces—a cosmetic change at best. The Organic Law was an instrument of both integration and decentralization, attempting to bind the colonies more closely within an integrative whole, while at the same time allowing administrative decentralization and financial autonomy to the overseas provinces.[8] The Portuguese government also responded militarily and, as mentioned above, to some extent economically to the outbreak of fighting. Troops from the metropole were imported into Angola, natives were recruited into the Portuguese armed forces (speeding the *assimilado* process), and internal security measures were stepped up. The Portuguese responded quickly to the military demands of the situation. An attempt to establish "strategic hamlets" met with little success; the early resettlement program in Angola merely moved people into concentrated population points. There was little, if any, attempt made to better the social and economic opportunities of the populations. Their resettlement—or *aldeamento*—program, was given new life in the early 1970s, and seemed to be much more effective. The *aldeamentos* (where they were in fact new villages with schools, medical facilities, and economic incentives rather than mere resettlement centers) and the integration in the counterinsurgent military forces helped preclude a Portuguese defeat.

The insurgency in Angola, as in the other colonies, was stalemated. The insurgents did not seem to be making much progress although they controlled some territory. The Portuguese firmly controlled the cities and major population centers, and carried on operations in the field at the time and place of their choosing. There was no end or clear victor in sight. The Portuguese military was facing what seemed at the time a near impossible task; it was still a case where the Portuguese had to lose – the insurgents could not win. What the Portuguese did, of course, was quit! The magnitude of the overall task was simply too great. Of the three territories in Africa beset with anti-Portuguese insurgencies, Angola represented the biggest prize in terms of potential for the future. Portuguese counterinsurgent efforts in Angola seemed to be having effects conducive to long-term containment and control of the situation. However, if Portugal had withdrawn from her other territories to focus on Angola (a step that seemed absolutely necessary in order to achieve some form of long-term continued arrangement and political connection between the metropole and the overseas territory) she would have given up her last hold on legitimacy. By withdrawing from Mozambique and Guinea-Bissau and concentrating resources in Angola, Portugal would also be admitting that the ideals of a racially mixed, "new society," based on a fusion of African and Portuguese bloodlines and culture on an equal political basis was impossible and would therefore not work in Angola either. In a military sense, the job was just too demanding. Portugal's resources were too limited to sustain any significant level of effort for very long. As General Antonio de Spinola, the most successful of the numerous counterinsurgent military commanders and colonial governors, stated: "To want to win in a war of subversion by means of a military solution is to accept defeat in advance, unless one possesses unlimited capacity to prolong the war indefinitely. . . . Is that our case? Obviously not!"[9]

The physical characteristics of Angola, to cite an example, were such that no army of the size and technological state of Portugal's could hope to seal the borders. As long as insurgent organizations had external support, sanctuaries, and the will to continue, the insurgency could continue at some level. This is not to say that eventual victory for Portugal was an impossibility, but rather that its probability was very low and would have required decades of sustained effort. But prior to the 1974 military coup and fall of the semi-fascist regime in Portugal and the resulting civil war in Angola, the insurgent factions had not won, nor even been overly successful. The insurgents were still alive and carrying on operations; in insurgency warfare, there is always hope if the organization persists. The coup in Portugal was carried out by officers dissatisfied with the political response to the insurgencies – long-term victory was not possible without political liberalization, but political liberalization was the one thing the regime could not provide without liquidating itself and the political system upon which it was built. In short, the military was tired of fighting for a government system that was doomed to failure.

While the Portuguese did not withdraw from Angola suddenly following the coup in the metropole, their efforts at combatting the insurgent movements were dramatically reduced. A seemingly halfhearted attempt to create a federated system was rejected by all insurgents in the three territories. The insurgent groups quickly detected the obvious fact that the Portuguese had lost the will to continue fighting. The future of the Portuguese political system was itself highly uncertain. Hence, the Portuguese problem became one of finding someone to whom government could be entrusted.

In both Guinea-Bissau and Mozambique, the turnover of political power was facilitated by the existence of main insurgent organizations. In Angola, however, the process was complicated by rival claims to power on the part of the MPLA, FNLA and UNITA, none of which commanded sufficient popular support to legitimately represent all the Angolan people. The Portuguese army would not continue fighting to guarantee a democratic election in Angola, particularly when the prospect was very real that a civil war might also occur in Portugal. Had the Portuguese withdrawn immediately after the coup and ignored Angola completely, UNITA was perhaps in the best military-political position to take advantage of a political vacuum. However, the Portuguese set a date for independence in Angola (11 November 1975) and searched for a formula that would enable them to hand power over to a government that represented the majority of the Angolan people.

Two attempts to create a power-sharing transitional government came to naught and, as independence approached, it appeared that civil war was inevitable, especially since the contending groups were engaged in combat. As it turned out, the Portuguese did not turn the government over to anybody; they left.[10] The MPLA, originally an urban-based political party, had the capital city of Luanda and what levers of power still existed. From that point on, the three groups waged a primarily conventional form of warfare against each other. While factors dating to the preindependence period obviously affected the outcome, the civil war can best be analyzed in conventional terms. Intervention and support by outside forces were, in the eyes of most Western commentators, the decisive factors in the MPLA success.

From a strictly military point of view, more forceful or substantial aid by the United States to UNITA or FNLA[11] might have brought a different result. But there is evidence that the United States did not wish to win; it appeared Washington merely wanted to keep the MPLA from winning.[12] U.S. aid was small in comparison to Soviet aid; South African and Zairian troops were as much a political liability as a military asset to UNITA and FNLA respectively and, in any case, were outnumbered and outgunned by the thousands of Cuban combat troops dispatched to help the MPLA. It might best be said that neither side really planned for the civil war. The MPLA and the Soviet Union were more capable of instinctive reactions that proved correct in attaining the objective. As one U.S. official has stated: "Angola was a tragedy. It was a tragedy for moderate blacks, for radical blacks wishing to fend off alien influences, for whites in southern Africa, for Mobutu, Kaunda, Roberto, Savimbi, soldiers of fortune, Zairian infantrymen, and countless others."[13]

Soviet supplies, Cuban troops, control of the capital (with its inferred legitimacy), and eventual military victories in the field provided the MPLA a political victory. FNLA was shattered in the north of Angola; its leader and most of its survivors fled to Zaire. UNITA, small to begin with in terms of trained troops (although its ranks swelled noticeably in the period between the coup in Portugal and the outbreak of fighting at independence time),[14] was defeated in conventional combat and returned to the bush to carry on guerrilla warfare against the more numerous, better equipped MPLA/Cuban forces.

The MPLA, formerly under the leadership of Agostinho Neto, is in power. Cuban troops and Soviet supplies are the backbone of the MPLA army and the counterinsurgency effort. UNITA, under the leadership of Jonas Savimbi, continues guerrilla activity against the regime, primarily in southern Angola. FNLA, still under the leadership of Holden Roberto, exists but has been quiet since its crushing defeat in 1975. Under these circumstances, it is dif-ficult to classify the UNITA insurgency. Since it has been centered in the southern region of the country and since it has come to be identified over time with the Ovimbundu ethnic group, it is tempting to view the insurgency as a secessionist movement. However, indications from UNITA suggest that its aim is to force the MPLA to share power. If this is so, it would mean that UNITA is essentially reformist in terms of our definitions. However, the MPLA has not yet formed a concrete regime against which a revolution is possible. Should UNITA be able to wrest power from the regime, it would be just as revolutionary a process as is the MPLA attempt. To achieve its aims—however confused they may be—UNITA has proceeded to do what it knows best: namely, wage protracted guerrilla warfare against the MPLA. The general strategy invoked is the Maoist one that was followed against the Portuguese. To ascertain its utility, we shall examine the situation in terms of the environment, popular support, organization, external support, and the MPLA response.

## Political-Military Assessment

### Environment[15]

Four geographical regions can be distinguished in Angola: the coastal plain, the steppe-desert in the south, the central savanna, and the northern plateau rain forest. Each region has a different climate and vegetation pattern and therefore different potential for an insurgent guerrilla force.

The coastal plain was the first area settled by Europeans and is the area most economically developed. It changes from desert in the south to steppe in the north. Temperatures are moderate due to the presence of the Benguela current in the Atlantic. Vegetation is sparse. Rainfall increases from south to north and from west to east; the further east one goes, the hotter and more humid the climate becomes for the same degree of latitude. The southern steppe-desert is like most deserts, sandy and dry except along the water courses. The eastern half of this region is better watered, and the prevailing vegetation of elephant grass and scrubby forest reflects the better water condition. The northern tropical rain forest and tropical savanna region is rather difficult terrain, broken by hill and plateau formations. The valleys, particularly those close to the Congo River, are characterized by very dense rain forest, while the plateau areas are covered by tropical savanna. Precipitation varies between 40 and 60 inches of rain annually. Temperatures are fairly moderate, but humidity is quite high. The major geographical area of Angola is the central savanna plateau. The surface area is generally covered with savanna grass and occasional trees. Annual rainfall is between 40 and 60 inches. Relative humidity is fairly high, and temperatures are warmer than along the coast, despite the higher elevations. Hill formations, water courses, and altitude-temperature differences cause differing vegetation patterns. True deciduous forests are found on the western edges of the plateau. In short, geographical conditions are such that guerrilla warfare is clearly practical in most parts of the country, although the northern portion of the country—with its hills, karst-like rock formations, vegetation cover, and other such features—would seem better suited to guerrilla tactics than the central plateau.

FNLA has traditionally operated in the northern portion of Angola—in the areas that are best suited to guerrilla tactics from a strictly geographical viewpoint. UNITA's areas of operations (the southeastern quadrant of the country) are more neutral with respect to the geographical suitability. The terrain is not particularly difficult nor does it offer widespread cover and concealment possibilities. On the other hand, there are few roads. Other factors make this area of the country useful to UNITA.

Angola has 3,000 miles or so of border, most of which separates Angolan territory from neighboring states that previously harbored insurgents (Zaire apparently still does). To close the entire frontier would take perhaps as many as 250,000 troops devoted solely to this task. While a large portion of this border could be sealed as the French interdicted the Algerian border, the resources necessary for the task are clearly beyond the present regime's capabilities, just as they were beyond the capabilities of the Portuguese. Thus, infiltration cannot be stopped with the resources presently available or likely to be available to the MPLA.

There are three major rail lines in Angola. The most significant is the Benguela railroad, which runs from the port city of Benguela into Zaire, to Zambia, to Rhodesia, and on to Beira in Mozambique. Its Angolan length is 838 miles, with an additional 40-mile spur running to the copper mines at Cuima. The Luanda railway runs 373 miles between Malange and Luanda. There are also lines running inland from Lobito and Mocamedes.

In 1966, there was a 14,170–mile road network, of which only about 2,000 miles were paved. The best roads connect the cities on the coast; large areas of interior plateau are not accessible by road. The rivers are largely unsuitable for navigation; those that flow into the Atlantic are navigable from their mouths to the edge of the plateau, but this is a very short distance. The Congo, with portages, is highly navigable. Air transportation, at least under the Portuguese, was highly developed. In 1965 there were 30 airfields scattered throughout the country. This number was augmented steadily until the civil war, and did not include the number of small fields suitable for military resupply by light aircraft or helicopter traffic, a factor that the MPLA/Cuban counterinsurgent effort has taken into account.

The Portuguese, in their last years, were making a determined effort to improve the means of communication, although for the most part this effort seemed to be driven more by the imperatives of economic development than by the necessities of security. In the north, the road network is such that Portuguese troops were able to move into the general area quickly. The Cuban/MPLA forces now have this advantage. In the south and southeast, roads are still almost nonexistent. The Portuguese military efforts to find and dispose of bands of infiltrators or hidden base camps in the vast tracts of underpopulated territory were heavily dependent upon aviation, with its inherent limitations of range and loiter time. Evidence suggests that the MPLA/Cuban forces are following the pattern laid down by the Portuguese. However, the difficult terrain and lack of roads have rendered useless the most efficient weapon used by the MPLA/Cuban forces in the civil war—Soviet 122mm rockets.[16] It is almost impossible to bring the guerrilla units under fire. The converse is not true; guerrillas can set up and fire a weapon like the 122mm rocket quite easily at set targets.

As far as the human aspect of the environment is concerned, European and African residents have had different settlement patterns. The Europeans preferred the coastal areas and the urban areas, although over the years Africans have been migrating to the urban areas. The population of Luanda, the capital, grew from 61,028 in 1940 to 224,540 in 1960 and continued to grow at a high rate until the civil war. Of course, many of the white settlers have fled Angola; an exact count of those left is not available, but the number is reputed to have been as high as 300,000 at independence.[17] While the pre-

independence insurgency was partially responsible for the population movement toward the urban areas, much of the movement stemmed from the economic opportunities opening up in Angola as part of the development effort.
Other major cities of Angola are Huambo (formerly Nova Lisboa), Lobito,
Benguela, Malange, and San da Bandeira.[18] Though information gathered in
1966 indicated that urbanization was continuing at a very high rate, particularly near Luanda and Lobito, there is currently reputed to be a population movement away from the cities, which reflects a desire to avoid living
under the political-economic structure of the MPLA.[19] Population density
overall is fewer than 10 persons per square mile, making Angola one of the
least populated countries of the world. Densities in the pre–civil war guerrilla
operating areas varied. In the north, where FNLA operated, the range was
20–29 persons per square mile. In the east and southeast, where UNITA
now operates (in the past, along with the MPLA), the density varies between 0 and 10 persons per square mile.

The most significant aspect of the demography of Angola is without question its ethnic fragmentation. Ethnic groups are primarily determined by
language grouping and historic origins. There are approximately 100 tribes in
Angola, each sufficiently different from the others to be considered a separate
people. While the vast majority of languages spring from the Bantu root,
mutual intelligibility among languages of different regions is lacking. Portuguese still serves as the common medium of communication throughout the
country. Major tribal groupings and their general locations are: Ovimbundu
(western central highlands); Bokongo (extreme north of Angola, bordering on
Zaire); Ngangela (southeast and east); Nyganeka-Humbe and Chokwe-Lunda
(central). Each group is subdivided into several distinct tribes.

The Ovimbundu are the largest ethnolinguistic group, and, over time, have
become associated with UNITA. They are a fairly cohesive tribal group, who
adjusted well to the Portuguese presence and "benefitted from commercial opportunities created by it and maintained pride in their group."[20] While there
does not appear to be a legacy of deep animosity among groups (with the exception of the Bokongo versus everybody else), neither is there a great feeling
of unity. It is perhaps too early to tell how the various tribal groups relate to
the new MPLA government. The Bokongo have always been associated with
FNLA. In fact, FNLA has traditionally been almost exclusively Bokongo.
People from other tribal groups, while not unwelcome in the movement, were
discriminated against and most eventually left to join one of the other anti-
Portuguese groups. Further, the Bokongo indulged in a form of forced recruitment that caused whole villages to go into exile in Zaire. Other Bokongo fled
as the result of Portuguese counteraction against FNLA elements. (The tactic of forced recruitment by terror often used by FNLA operated along tribal
lines, and was very similar to the manner in which slaves were procured in

former times. This practice hardly endeared the Bokongo elements of FNLA to the other tribal groups.)

UNITA was not originally associated with any particular tribal group, having been created by refugees from FNLA and the MPLA. However, UNITA has most recently come to be associated with the Ovimbundu simply by the location of its area of operation and the ethnic makeup of the villages it controls. The MPLA also was not originally connected with a tribal group, deriving as it did from the Angolan communist party and the *mestico* urban intelligentsia. Yet there is some evidence that the MPLA is also taking on a perceived connection with certain tribal groups, in particular the Kimbundu.

There exists no sense of being "Angolan" that is shared by the African inhabitants. Though the Portuguese tried to create a sense of being Portuguese through several programs among those of the *assimilado* class, and did achieve some positive results, Portuguese efforts were not sufficient to mobilize the population. It is an open question whether the MPLA can mobilize the population fast enough to prevent tribalism from being an increasingly divisive factor, or whether UNITA can create or sustain what nationalistic feelings exist and turn them against the Cubans and the MPLA. Certainly, any government would have a hard time creating this feeling of nation, but the faction least associated with any particular tribe might have the best chance of doing so. At the time of the civil war, UNITA probably represented the "most national" of the three movements. It is doubtful that this is still true; the MPLA would seem to be the "most national" simply because it is the government. However, as will be discussed later, there are problems within the MPLA in this regard.

The environment offers opportunities to both sides, but the MPLA's advantages are not necessarily the same as those enjoyed by the Portuguese. The largest single advantage the Portuguese had was the potential to develop the country and employ a highly mobile fighting force in the guerrilla-dominated areas. The MPLA, due to the disruption caused by the Portuguese withdrawal, has fewer resources to develop the country. At present, the MPLA military ability depends largely upon Cubans and, ultimately, upon the Soviet Union. Thus the mobility of the counterinsurgent force is not inherent, but rather borrowed from the suppliers of men and material. The key environmental factors in the war today are ethnicity and the vast amount of territory. The side that first mobilizes and controls the most tribes and builds a political force that is truly multitribal will have a very decided edge.

*Popular Support*

The degree of popular support given to an insurgent movement is difficult to gauge; in absolute numbers of, say, men under arms or people under effective control, it is only a partial indication of overall support. There is no sure

way to ascertain the numbers of people who offer passive support to insurgent movements. A static figure of probable potential passive support can
be determined simply by looking at the number of people continuing to live in
an insurgent-controlled area, but such a figure should never be considered
definitive; there are many factors which could prevent flight from the area.
But, in general terms, staying must be taken as at least a willingness to exist
under the insurgent leadership.[21]

Active support, or at least a relative indication of it, can be more easily
determined if one has access to the insurgents. Units can be counted, as can
the number of people defecting. However, since this has not been possible in
Angola, and since accurate census figures have remained elusive, claims
regarding the degree of popular support have not been verifiable.[22]

Prior to independence and the civil war, all three major insurgent groups
espoused independence from Portugal as their primary *esoteric* appeal. Beyond
that, there was little congruence in the respective formulations of esoteric appeals. The MPLA was the outgrowth of the Angolan communist party and
generally espoused a Marxist-Leninist philosophy. However, the MPLA did
not often publicly enunciate specific doctrinal points; therefore it is difficult to
specify internal deviation from the major brands of communist ideology. From
available evidence, the MPLA has followed the Moscow version of communist doctrine fairly consistently in its outward behavior; but again, in only
a very general manner. The conduct of the regime since independence would
indicate that it does adhere to a Soviet-style ideological base, but such
adherence is by no means complete. In the period before the assumption of
governmental power, the analyst was faced with a typical problem of
ideological identification in that there was no sure way of determining how
"communist" a particular movement was. Esoteric appeals and exoteric appeals also constitute a tactic. The true ideological adherence might be judged
if one had access to the indoctrination and socialization systems a given group
used to prepare its cadres, something which is very difficult for an objective
outsider to do.

Both before and since the civil war, there were power struggles within the
MPLA between Neto and his followers and more radical communists. The
MPLA has traditionally found its basis of support in the *mestico* inhabitants
of the cities and in the intelligentsia. (The *assimilado* intelligentsia equates in
many ways to the *mestico* population.) The original leadership of the MPLA
was *mestico* and, at least before the civil war, the party did not appeal directly
to any particular tribal group, but rather to an ethnic minority that did not
subscribe to the Portuguese concept of multiraciality. This segment of the
population was discriminated against by portions of both the white and black
populations. This "neither white nor black" problem and the traditional appeal to the *mesticos* has plagued the government since independence, but was

temporarily resolved when a coup attempt was thwarted in May 1977. As one observer of the scene described Neto's overall policies:

> At various times since 1962, Neto has been criticized by his more radical col-
> leagues for political and economic policies that were considered too moderate,
> for alleged overdependence on *mesticos* and whites, and for generally ineffectual
> leadership. Neto has staked his political career on a stubborn commitment to the
> politics of nonalignment, multiracism, and socialism. His detractors within the
> MPLA have generally portrayed themselves as truer Socialists and the true
> choice of the black masses.[23]

Like the MPLA, both UNITA and FNLA espoused national independence as their primary cause prior to the civil war. FNLA has been relatively quiet since the war. UNITA has picked up the theme of nationalism, at least to the extent of trying to convince Angolans that they are Angolans and that the MPLA has merely exchanged the Portuguese for the Soviets and Cubans as the real power in Angola. The following statement by Jonas Savimbi, UNITA's leader, is typical of UNITA's esoteric appeals:

> Agostinho Neto came to power through Soviet tanks and not through people's
> choice. His decisive element of gaining power was the regular army from Cuba
> made up of 20,000 men who are still keeping Neto in power against the will of the
> people, against the effective and active guerrillas of UNITA, and even against
> growing dissatisfaction within the ranks of the Popular Movement for the
> Liberation of Angola. . . . We are determined to remain Africans whatever the
> odds against our temporary weaknesses. Yesterday we were slaves. Today,
> some still are slaves. Today, we want to free Africans on African soil. The price
> of true liberation and freedom is our own lives.[24]

Prior to the granting of independence, all movements used a variety of *exo-teric* appeals, mostly centered on the economic and educational deficiencies of the Portuguese regime. Since the MPLA regime has not completely taken shape, it is expected that UNITA will wait to develop specific themes until weaknesses are revealed. Two themes have already been identified for use. The first is propagandizing the population by calling attention to acts of misconduct perpetrated by Cubans and Eastern European nationals working for the government. Cuban soldiers, in particular, have been portrayed fre-quently as rapists.[25] The second theme is tribal in nature: Ovimbundu fear and distrust of the Kimbundu.[26] This particular theme would appear to be a counterproductive tactic in the long term, in that it contradicts any appeal stressing representation of all the people by UNITA.

The use of terror in the past appeared to be tied to organizational dif-ferences. FNLA indulged fairly heavily in terror directed against recalcitrant

Bokongo villages and the population in general. A typical tactic would be forced impressment or kidnapping of whole villages or at least of all men capable of military duty. UNITA, by contrast, eschewed terror as a means to mobilize support. Though some of UNITA's recent activity might possibly be classed as terrorism, it would be counterproductive and the type of mistake Savimbi would not condone or encourage.[27] As far as the MPLA is concerned, its resort to terrorism has been motivated by a need to provide internal control; it was not employed deliberately against the population as a device to generate support. It is too early to tell if terror is being used by the government as a mobilization and control device similar to the "Red Terror" used in other communist countries.

It is important to differentiate between two types of terror: indiscriminate and selective. Selective terror used against clearly identified enemies can best be evaluated in terms of the dynamics of the military effort. Its relationship to popular support is very general. It may generate support because it automatically demonstrates potency, competence, and success. Selective terror does not threaten the undecided population – in fact, it may contribute to an unwillingness to associate too closely with the government. Several students of violence have used different criteria to distinguish between the two types of violence. The difficulty stems from the fact that the intent to commit terror is obvious, but the intended target may be improperly defined or the means available to the guerrilla or terrorist may not be suitable for selective terror. A bomb placed in a theater is an obvious example of indiscriminate terror. There is no control over who will be killed. But if that theater happens to be the site of a political party meeting, the same bomb may in fact be a well-designed act of selective terror. Indiscriminate terror is counterproductive. In Angola, all three groups have used selective terror against the Portuguese and against each other. FNLA has been guilty of indiscriminate terror. The question for today's war is whether or not UNITA has switched from selective terror directed against the Cubans, Eastern Europeans, and the MPLA cadres to a more generalized terror against segments of the population.[28] Attacks against economic targets are ambiguous, unless further details about who was endangered by the action are known.

Attempts to provoke government counterterror do not seem to have been especially significant in Angola. The attacks on Cuban soldiers today would seem to be an attempt to provoke the Cubans into acts that can be used to generate exoteric appeals, although it is difficult to separate such attacks from the demonstration of potency or the more general form of guerrilla warfare. Merely continuing the guerrilla war can serve to provoke the MPLA into improper actions that would serve to alienate the population from the government. As pointed out in Chapter 1, success in this factor will be largely determined by the nature of the government response and ethnic considerations.

Certainly the potential for government irrationality and ethnic manipulation exists in Angola today.

Prior to the civil war, the primary demonstration of potency on the part of UNITA, the MPLA and FNLA was to remain in existence against Portuguese counteraction and each other. Both the MPLA and FNLA maintained their headquarters in exile, the MPLA in Congo (Brazzaville) and FNLA in Zaire. The MPLA also had a subsidiary headquarters in Zambia.[29] This is a fairly important point, for it suggests that neither movement had enough control or guaranteed popular support to maintain its headquarters inside Angola. UNITA, on the other hand, did maintain its headquarters inside Angola, albeit not necessarily by choice. Each movement had its area of operations. In the north, FNLA carried out sporadic raids against the Portuguese and frequent "recruitment" drives against villages. The locus of MPLA operations was in the east and southeast, out of Zambia. The MPLA had attempted organizational activity in the cities and had been forced out by Portuguese counteraction. In the north, FNLA action against MPLA forces drove the MPLA to another area. While the MPLA's immediate pre–civil war operating areas were contested with UNITA, UNITA seemed to have the upper hand. Finally, UNITA operated in the south and southeast of the country, with its area of control extending to the approximate geographical center of the country.

Prior to the coup in Portugal, the three groups combined had somewhere between 7,000 and 32,000 men under arms. Richard Gibson cited reliable primary sources and estimated 15,000 as the actual total.[30] Regardless of the estimated strength, all three groups could and did mount military operations. The Portuguese were incapable of preventing attacks, recruitment activities, or political organization efforts.

Since the civil war, FNLA has been relatively quiet within Angola proper. UNITA, however, has reverted to more or less continuous guerrilla warfare. While merely continuing in existence can be a demonstration of potency in its own right, it loses force as time goes on. UNITA has not been content with mere existence. It has repeatedly struck the Benguela railroad, thus undercutting ties with Zambia and, as mentioned above, has recently claimed responsibility for acts of industrial sabotage in the more populated areas.[31] The MPLA has admitted that such attacks have occurred – some fairly damaging attacks if government press reaction is any indicator.[32] As previously pointed out, UNITA does not have a history of terrorist activities that can be considerd indiscriminate. However, potency obviously has been demonstrated, and the reach of UNITA seems to be getting longer and stronger. If UNITA can bring its presence to Luanda or the other areas of population not previously under its control, this would represent a large step for the movement. If the MPLA cannot prevent UNITA from accomplishing such activities in the cities the MPLA, by inference, will show itself even less capable of stopping the insurgency than were the Portuguese.

No analysis of UNITA's quest for popular support would be complete without reference to the charismatic attraction of Savimbi, an attraction somewhat lacking in his opponents. As a number of observers have noted, Savimbi is an articulate, dynamic orator who has been able to relate to the people on an emotional level. Indeed, his popularity is such that many believe the insurgency would fall apart if he were eliminated.[33] Holden Roberto of FNLA also seems to possess a degree of charisma, at least of the type with which members of the Bokongo ethnic group can identify. Roberto's leadership has not been extended to non-Bokongo peoples however, and FNLA has been rent with sub-leader squabbles, often resulting in defection to other groups (and, in fact, the original founding of UNITA). Neto was a bland figure, neither dull nor able to excite the masses. Of the three, Savimbi seems to have proven most capable, on a personal basis, of reaching out to Angolans as a group.

Summarizing the situation with regard to popular support, all three groups had some basis of popular support in Angola before the Portuguese coup and the civil war, although the actual degree was impossible to calculate. FNLA might have been the biggest movement, but it did not have the largest amount of meaningful popular support. Popular support did not seem to have been a factor governing what measure of success the three movements had against the Portuguese, with the possible exception of UNITA. UNITA currently has sufficient popular support to be able to remain headquartered in Angola and carry on operations against the government. It still operates in a multitribal area, but it is becoming increasingly identified with one tribal group. Although this tribal group represents the largest single ethnic bloc in Angola, too close an identification would harm the ability to eventually extend the insurgency to the whole of Angola. The best that could be expected would be some sort of separatist or reformist movement.

### Organization

The importance of the organizational variable in protracted insurgencies cannot be overemphasized. Organization provides the vehicle for turning support and sympathy into action, be that action political, military, or further organization building. Angola, before the civil war, offered an example of a revolutionary movement characterized by multiplicity and disunity. The three major factions simply could not and did not coexist in a united front against the Portuguese.

UNITA, like its counterparts, took as the ideal form of organization the Leninist construct of a vertical party hierarchy tied in with mass, popular, horizontal organizations. At the same time, UNITA's civil-military-political organization was unique. Each district under UNITA control was considered to be a military region. Each region had a central military camp in the jungle or bush surrounded by a ring of controlled civilian villages. There were smaller satellite military camps in each region also surrounded by civilian villages. The main military camps contained UNITA's schools, hospitals, training areas, and political indoctrination centers. Each civilian village either elected representatives for local government or sat as a group to decide political matters. The large military camp served as a seat for a rudimentary local parliament consisting either of representatives from the circle of villages, or of a mass meeting of all the villagers. At the top of the organization, a central committee (in 1973 numbering 24 members) oversaw the peasant assemblies. A 10-member political bureau made the important decisions. In the past, there was a large overlap between the political bureau and command of the military organizations. One reporter who spent four months with the guerrillas to cover UNITA's third congress counted 5,000 civilians and 600 armed guerrillas present at various meetings. There were 221 representatives at the party congress itself.[34] Similar figures were reported for the most recent congress.[35] There is no indication that UNITA has changed its basic form of organization. It lives with and through the people it controls. Although UNITA's organization may appear rather rudimentary from the standpoint of complexity, its political work seems to be directly with the people, a factor that no doubt is a major reason for reported firm commitments to UNITA as an organization.

There is little to say about the government's other adversary at this point in time. FNLA has functioned largely as a government-in-exile, with people in all sorts of official organizational posts; however, there is little or no organization below the central level. In addition, FNLA is essentially a tribally based movement, with the vast majority of its support currently in exile in Zaire. The movement has always appeared to be the personal fief of its leader, Holden Roberto.

At present, both UNITA and the government are essentially involved in the political and military mobilization of the people. UNITA does not have quite the same problem that the MPLA has, simply because UNITA is not in power—what UNITA lacks in legitimacy, it makes up in not being held responsible for fulfilling promises of economic and social development of the whole of Angola. The MPLA must "produce" in order to sustain its claim to legitimacy.

UNITA appears to exercise some degree of control over substantial tracts of territory and people. And it is probably safe to say that the infrastructure that was established for the war against the Portuguese, as well as its internal cohesion, is one key reason why it has been able to continue its guerrilla operations against the government. Its military forces expanded significantly just before the civil war and, of the three movements, it seemed to do the best job of incorporating these additional members and training them into at least semieffective fighting forces.

## External Support

Prior to the civil war, external support was an absolute necessity for the continued existence of the MPLA and FNLA. This was the key factor that led to the MPLA victory in the civil war.

Moral support is the most difficult type of assistance to analyze, even though in our framework we stated that moral support is the least costly and risky for a donor because all it involves is public acknowledgment that the insurgent movement is just and admirable. When the struggle was against the Portuguese, it was very easy for a large number of countries, particularly African countries, to offer moral support for the insurgents. It is more difficult today, of course, since one of the insurgent groups is now the government and the other two have not made their peace with it. Factors that have little immediate relevancy to Angola become important and there has been a tendency to equivocate since the Portuguese left. For example, how can Zambia's president support UNITA, which has been linked with South Africa, or the MPLA, which is supported (some would say kept in power by) the Soviets and Cubans? Giving moral support to UNITA might imply tacit approval of South Africa's policies; not giving moral support to UNITA might imply tacit approval of Soviet encroachment into Africa.[36]

Political support is similar to moral support in this case. Before the coup, the insurgents enjoyed tremendous political support from Third World and communist-dominated governments. The prevailing conventional wisdom of the day considered colonialism an unsupportable evil. While this conventional wisdom did not automatically translate into positive support for the movements, it definitely translated into a lack of support for the Portuguese. Until recently, there was an almost universal international political climate that favored insurgent causes as automatically just.[37] The United Nations provided a propaganda platform for anti-Portuguese movements unmatched by opportunities for other insurgent movements then or now. Individuals belonging to anti-Portuguese movements were consistently given official status in various national delegations and could use these positions as a way to travel freely and propagandize the insurgent cause. The purpose of this activity was to arouse public interest and awareness and to incite public opinion against the policies of the Portuguese. Prior to the civil war, the effect of all of this activity was that the international perception of legitimacy rested with the insurgents, regardless of how they went about their liberating. This was a measure of support that even the NLF in South Vietnam or the FLN/ALN in Algeria never enjoyed.[38] Today it is different. FNLA has the political support of Zaire; UNITA seems to have Chinese political support and, by inference, that of the United States. However, most governments have recognized the MPLA as the government of Angola, which must be considered negative political support for the opposing groups.[39]

Material support is somewhat more easily defined than political or moral support, partially because the relationships since the civil war have been generally consistent, whereas before the civil war they were somewhat tenuous and shifting. Prior to the civil war, the Soviet Union and the People's Republic of China were the major suppliers of weapons and ammunition to all the anti-Portuguese movements.[40] The only group that did not directly receive arms from the Soviet Union and/or China in the three Portuguese colonies was UNITA. There was a short period of time early in UNITA's existence when the Chinese supplied some aid, but UNITA was judged to be "too capitalistic" by the Chinese and the connection was severed.[41] This connection was reopened just before the civil war. The Soviets had a particular affinity for supplying the MPLA, although support was given to other groups.

The standard armament of the insurgents before the war was the symbolic AK–47 submachine gun. The mode of warfare was such that the insurgents needed little else. Various photos released for propaganda purposes at the time, as well as numerous reports from individuals who had contact with the guerrilla movements in the field, indicated that units were well supplied with small arms and ammunition. The guerrillas thus did not have to depend upon captured arms and ammunition to carry out their operations, and could use monies derived from humanitarian groups for purposes similar to those for which the money was ostensibly donated rather than for the purchase of arms. Additionally, the ready availability of weaponry from the Soviet Union changed the tactics of guerrilla fighting substantially and made it less dangerous for the insurgent. The guerrilla forces did not have to attack armories, nor was it necessary to remain at the site of an ambush long enough to kill all the Portuguese soldiers to get their weapons and ammunition. Both the MPLA and FNLA normally carried all their combat requirements of food, ammunition, and weapons with them from their external sanctuaries. This made the Portuguese job more difficult in that the guerrillas were not tied to any specific arms dumps or sources of supply within the territory of Angola. Moreover, the Portuguese could not stop the supply of arms and munitions to the MPLA and FNLA, since the arms were delivered in neutral countries.[42]

The exception to this historical rule was UNITA. UNITA expressed great pride in the fact that the group received almost no external aid. UNITA portrayed itself as completely free of outside influence and dependency upon the good graces of other parties. However, UNITA did receive some money from humanitarian sources, and was the direct recipient of outside aid in the period between the Portuguese coup and the Angolan civil war.

There were other forms of material aid: money, medical supplies, and educational materials. The World Council of Churches supplied money for humanitarian relief to all movements involved in the anti-Portuguese wars of Africa, including UNITA.[43] The World Food Program, a UN arm, voted on 26 April 1974 to make food aid available to "peoples in the liberated areas in the colonial territories of Africa and their national liberation movements."[44] Sweden also recognized the movements and contributed cash, medical supplies, and other supplies.[45] The Organization of African Unity was, and is, a primary conduit of funds for anticolonial/anti-Rhodesian activity.[46] Private donations, primarily from Western (and black American) sources, were another source of money for the movements. Most of this aid from the West was channeled into nonmilitary areas such as refugee relief, medical expenses, educational costs, services, and the like. However, since the liberation movements did not have to pay for arms, an argument could be made that the wars were being paid for by the humanitarian donations. Today, most material aid goes to the MPLA as the recognized government of a war-torn nation. FNLA and UNITA probably still receive some money, but no estimate of the amount is possible.

The training of guerrilla fighters and cadres can also be considered a material benefit. Insurgent training can be broken down into three types: that provided to the guerrilla soldier, that provided to the cadre, and that provided to the leadership elements. Most of the guerrilla soldier training took place in the base camp countries, notably Zaire and Zambia. Some cadre training, particularly for the MPLA, took place in neutral countries under the reputed direction of Cuban and North Korean instructors with an occasional guest lecturer supplied by the North Vietnamese. Political leadership training had been provided for select students in almost every communist country in the world, plus Algeria and Egypt.[47] UNITA was generally not included in this aid, although some of the cadres, as defectors from other movements, undoubtedly had received some training. It would seem that the MPLA received the majority of such aid, followed distantly by FNLA and then UNITA.

After the coup in Portugal, the patterns of aid changed radically. The activity that occurred after the coup can be compared to that in Spain in 1936. Who started the rush to massive supply is open to question.[48] In the final analysis, there seems to be little doubt that the MPLA received massive amounts of material aid from the Soviet Union (sometimes via Cuba); FNLA received some aid from China, Zaire, and the United States (through Zaire); and UNITA received material aid from China, the United States (through South Africa), and indirectly (at least) from South Africa. As early as 1974, the MPLA started to receive weapons more slanted toward conventional armed conflict (as opposed to guerrilla activity) such as the SA-7, the Soviet hand-held surface-to-air missile.[49]

Soviet aid to the MPLA was relatively overt in nature. Cuban troops, technicians, arms in vast quantity, and other forms of material support were freely given to the MPLA forces. U.S. aid to FNLA and UNITA, by contrast, was covert and consisted of small arms and nonattributable support equipment funneled primarily through Zaire (the equipment was ostensibly to be used by the Zairian army).[50] FNLA was the primary Angolan recipient of U.S. aid, with UNITA almost an afterthought as a recipient. The most important elements of aid were undoubtedly the 30,000 or so Cuban combat troops and their equipment that the MPLA received.

The MPLA retains this aid advantage today. UNITA once again claims to be self-supporting; certainly continued UNITA tactical success against Cuban/MPLA army patrols and headquarters can lead to replenishment of arms and munitions in classic guerrilla style. However, it would seem an almost impossible task for UNITA to be able to take on the Cuban/MPLA army in conventional battle in the near future. This factor is a vital plus for the MPLA and there is no reason to believe the situation will change in the immediate future.

Another form of external support is sanctuary. In the wars against the Portuguese, all factions in all the Portuguese colonies enjoyed sanctuary most of the time. UNITA enjoyed such sanctuary only briefly, however. By performing the somewhat undiplomatic act of blowing up the Benguela railroad, UNITA alienated Zambia (the country which was granting the sanctuary).[51] Anti-Portuguese movements were sheltered in Congo (Brazzaville), Zaire, Tanzania, Guinea, Senegal, and, most important, Zambia. All factions, major or minor, from all the Portuguese colonies kept some sort of liaison in Zambia.[52] FNLA presently enjoys sanctuary in Zaire, but the recent agreement between the government of Zaire and the MPLA to control rebel forces attempting to cross the border between them might negate this advantage.[53]

The support of sanctuary is starting to present an interesting series of dilemmas in Southern Africa. Despite the open presence of guerrilla troops and publicly voiced support for guerrilla movements by Zambia's President Kuanda, the fiction is maintained that Zambia is not a base for aggressive attacks against neighboring states. Zambia currently hosts guerrilla groups acting against Rhodesia and Namibia, and it is occasionally reported that the country is not closed to UNITA. However, as might be expected, the MPLA has apparently extended a welcome to anti-Rhodesian and anti-South African (Namibian) revolutionaries. Rhodesia has added Angola as an air raid target in order to strike at guerrilla camps. Politically, UNITA does not seem to be in a position to take advantage of any ill effects suffered by the MPLA as a result of Rhodesian raids. But there may be some military spin-offs that will work to UNITA's benefit. One must also remember that if UNITA and the other antigovernment movements share the same territory, action against one will often be action against all in that the counterinsurgent force, whether it be Rhodesian or MPLA, acts on the material base. On the other hand, since it is the MPLA that is offering sanctuary, there is the increased possibility that action by Rhodesian or South African forces against "their" insurgents will also act against the host forces of the MPLA/Cubans, thereby weaken-ing them, perhaps at a time when UNITA can exploit the weakness without appearing to be allied with the white regimes.

At the moment, sanctuary is not a salient factor in the UNITA versus MPLA struggle, and while sanctuary gives FNLA life, it is a quiet life.

*Government Response*

While the MPLA has reflected the influence of the Soviet Union, there are some policies that are unique. Not surprisingly, the MPLA has attempted to socialize the economy. Many of the assets formerly belonging to Portuguese capitalists are now the property of the state. Likewise, many of the former large land tracts have been turned into communal agricultural collectives.[54] But certain industries have remained relatively untouched, some properties have not been collectivized, and a number of Marxist actions have not been taken. The MPLA does seem to be trying to mobilize the population along lines that might be predicted by adherence to a Marxist-Leninist party for-mat. But, as any student of authoritarian systems knows, mobilization is not exclusive to communist regimes, but rather is likely in any highly centralized system. The "democratic" content of such mobilization schemes is difficult to judge because it depends upon the amount of actual or implied coercion in-volved.[55] The MPLA also seems to be trying to build a bridge to the West, in particular the United States, although the United States has shown itself reluctant to reciprocate unless the Cubans remove themselves (or are re-moved) from Angola.

The presence of Cubans is a key feature of the whole Angolan scene. Without the Cuban help, the MPLA could not stand against UNITA. How-ever, without the Cuban presence, UNITA could lose its anti-Cuban appeal to the population.

In the military sphere, the MPLA/Cuban forces have tended to respond as though neither had ever heard of insurgency warfare. For two movements that came to power through guerrilla tactics in insurgency warfare, their counter to such warfare has been relatively unsophisticated and marked by errors one would not think possible for groups experienced in the art. There may be reasons, justifications, or rationalizations for this fact; the Cubans in Angola were not part of the guerrilla *focos* that helped cause Batista to flee, nor is the MPLA, a Moscow-type party, really versed in guerrilla mystique. But such justifications do not seem adequate in the face of what occasionally appear to be Cuban/MPLA blunders and their inability to defeat UNITA. There is evidence that Cubans have led search and destroy expeditions into UNITA-controlled areas.[56] Such activities have not led to increased allegiance to the central government in the past; there is little reason to suspect that they will now. UNITA has made some propaganda headway in being able to capitalize on Cuban activities that are contrary to good common sense. Cuban prisoners of UNITA have been tried and executed for raping women in UNITA areas of control; one would think that since Castro's forces made much of similar actions committed by Batista's forces in Cuba, the MPLA or the Cuban senior commander would publicly put their own soldiers on trial for any such alleged acts. In any case, mistakes are being made, mistakes that UNITA is capable of using to generate public support. Indeed, there is evidence that some degree of refugee activity is occurring because of MPLA programs and policies.[57]

There are reports that the MPLA is acting in a fashion often associated with radical regimes—jailings, executions, collectivization, nationalization of industry, and so on. Certainly the government has made military mistakes that have helped allow UNITA to continue to exist. Perhaps the major mistake is the massive overt reliance on Cubans and other outsiders. This presence automatically provides a focal point for nationalistic discontent, something that is real, demonstrable, and present that UNITA can exploit. Every failure to perform as advertised is a potential esoteric or exoteric appeal that UNITA or FNLA can use.

David Galula has argued that no truly authoritarian regime need worry about losing to an insurgency. This type of regime can be repressive without guilt or weakness; an insurgency does not become viable for that system, for any attempts at organization will be reported, infiltrated, rooted out, and crushed. Whether that statement is true or not is immaterial in this case. Any society that is trying to come to grips with some form of popular participation of democratic organization cannot be completely repressive. Mobilization of the population requires popular participation of some sort. In the MPLA's case, it does not have sufficient cadres, organizational apparatus, or technical expertise to instantly create a regime repressive enough to eradicate other insurgent movements.[58]

Thus the MPLA will continue—within the limits of its economic, political, and social power—to attempt to create a "socialist" state and, by doing so, continue to give some ground for UNITA to offer an alternative. This mobilization effort is not in direct response to UNITA's challenge; it is something the regime would do in any case. But it is through this type of organization that the regime hopes to control the country. "Counterorganization" has been known to be effective against counterinsurgency.

In this organization and mobilization attempt, the MPLA has involved itself in some forms of terrorism against those portions of the population not under its physical or attitudinal control (for example, the people of European stock remaining, former adherents of UNITA caught in MPLA territory, and recalcitrants of other sorts).

It is doubtful that the MPLA can afford to differentiate the threat posed by UNITA. When the Portuguese left, the economy – and to a great extent the society – disintegrated. If the MPLA does not perform propaganda-organizational activity, it will appear to be a puppet of its advisors; if it does not wage counterinsurgent warfare it will lose to UNITA. The MPLA has attempted to wage mobile-conventional warfare with the help of Cuban advisors in order to crush UNITA. The framework for analysis maintains that the "execution of a multifaceted counterinsurgency program obviously requires coordination of political, administrative, military policy and intelligence efforts." In this case, these are missing, either whole or in part, within the MPLA, although shortcomings are partially made up by help from Cubans, East Europeans or Soviets.

The MPLA is clearly deficient in the area of resources with which to build a society or solve the basic problems of the society it inherited from the Portuguese and the battlefield. Of course, neither FNLA nor UNITA has the resources either, but since they are not in power, they do not have to show concrete results to generate popular support. The MPLA must, or pay the price for failure in the erosion of popular support.

Personal security cannot be guaranteed by either side for its adherents at this point. UNITA's efforts in the more urban areas demonstrate its potency to harm MPLA adherents. Likewise, Cuban/MPLA military activities in UNITA-controlled territory show that UNITA cannot completely stand on its own in defiance of the government. The MPLA does not seem to have the strength to perform search and hold operations; rather the option has been for search and destroy. There is evidence that the MPLA has caused casualties and property losses among target area populations that have increased the ranks of the disaffected. People can and do move from one controlled area to another, which would seem to indicate that neither UNITA nor the MPLA exercises total control over their respective geographic areas.

Both UNITA and the MPLA "control" limited territory. UNITA's threat is geographically limited at this time, as its territory is increasingly seen as congruent with the traditional lands of certain tribes. However, the same can be said of the MPLA, in that control is strongest in the area around Luanda, a territory that can be associated with a certain group of tribes. Both factions, if either is to be ultimately successful, must strive to maneuver so as not to become too clearly associated with a given tribe, for to do so would forfeit all claim to being a "national" Angolan movement.

One other counterinsurgent tactic should be mentioned. Although the

MPLA is attempting to nationalize certain industries and collectivize certain agricultural areas, there is no evidence to support a hypothesis that the MPLA is forcing widespread resettlement. However, they and the Cubans have cleared a strip along the southern border to allow surveillance and hopefully stop any infiltration from Namibia.[59] This same strip is obviously useful to the South Africans in their counterinsurgent war against SWAPO (Southwest African People's Organization) attempts to liberate Southwest Africa (Namibia).

## Summary

Of all the factors considered in the study of Angola, the most important to the continued existence of UNITA is environment. The terrain, the population density, and the lack of roads in the guerrilla operating areas all point to a military inability for the government to stop the insurgency. However, environment alone never determines success or failure. UNITA's second greatest advantage is the patience that has been shown in building the organization and military forces capable of maintaining the movement in existence. This factor can probably be traced directly to the leadership skill exercised by Jonas Savimbi. The organization and its political functioning within the territory controlled by UNITA appear strong enough to build and sustain a base of popular support that will in turn sustain UNITA's armed forces indefinitely.

UNITA has disadvantages also. The surest disadvantage at this time is the lack of solid exoteric and esoteric appeals. The nationalist theme will quickly lose credibility if the Cubans withdraw and Soviet–East European presence is muted. The MPLA society is not yet firm enough for a "we can do it better" theme to be effective. UNITA can seize upon economic and social dysfunctions as they arise (as they surely will), but to a certain extent must wait for MPLA action to present such opportunities. At this time, UNITA's ultimate goal is unclear. There is evidence that power-sharing would be acceptable to Savimbi. A coalition government with the MPLA would seem the simplest solution to Angola's troubles. The MPLA has offered a coalition government, but UNITA refuses to accept until the Cubans leave and the Angolan government is completely Angolan. The MPLA, on the other hand, will not let the Cubans leave until the security threat to its existence posed by UNITA disappears. The result is political stalemate and a continuing guerrilla insurgent war. If the MPLA does not get too radical in its attempts to build a society—thus alienating a substantial part of the population—UNITA's ability to appeal to the people will wither. The Cubans are not a colonial power, and the population in the past did not exactly rush to throw the Portuguese out of Angola.

The second disadvantage – the claim of tribalism – might prove to be decisive to UNITA's ability to move from what is now a sectionalist-based movement. UNITA evolved, as did the MPLA, with the image of a national party, untied to any particular group. Neither faction can afford to be too closely identified with one particular tribal group, but as time passes, both are apparently being so identified. UNITA can afford such identification less than the MPLA, in that the "legitimate" government can more easily appear national and take overt steps to correct "false impressions."[60] The MPLA already may have tarnished itself to a certain extent with a class and race (*mestico*) image. If the MPLA is driven into reliance upon one tribe for support, it will greatly weaken its position, but by no means insure its defeat. FNLA has not been able to shed a tribal image and, in fact, seems not to care to do so. The pull of tribally based politics is tremendously strong and may prove irresistible over the long term for all parties. This could lead to a situation of almost permanent civil war, dismemberment of the present state of Angola in an effort to find peace, or grave injustice to one tribe or another.

In a military sense, UNITA seems to have the better discipline and competence when the forces of each movement are compared.[61] However, the presence of the Cuban forces changes the balance significantly. Even the critics of the Vietnam War admitted that it was unlikely that South Vietnam could ever be defeated if the United States continued to fight with and for it. Likewise, as long as Cuba and the Soviet Union are willing to supply men, money, and material to the MPLA, UNITA is unlikely to defeat the MPLA. The Cubans and Soviets might well have more staying power than the United States did in Vietnam.

Conversely, MPLA forces by themselves, or even in conjunction with the Cubans, have been unable to crush UNITA. Further increases in presence would substantiate UNITA claims. The prognosis is that the war will continue in Angola for an indefinite time, with neither side a certain victor. While FNLA cannot be completely disregarded, it seems to be a minor factor in the war in Angola.[62]

## Notes

1. See, for example, Roland Oliver and Anthony Atmore, *Africa Since 1800* (Cambridge: Cambridge University Press, 1979), pp. 15–42 and 66–78; also, Eduardo C. Mondlane, "FRELIMO: The Struggle for Independence in Mozambique," in Wilfred Cartey and Martin Kilson ed., *The African Reader: Independent Africa* (New York: Vintage Books, 1970), p. 343. Mondlane stated: "The Portuguese presence in Mozambique can be counted only from 1898, the year that the last of the African emperors was defeated." Reason tells us that presence must come before the ability to defeat.

2. The first colony to erupt was Angola, in 1961; the colony of Portuguese Guinea

(Guinea-Bissau) was next, in 1962; the movement in Mozambique erupted in guerrilla warfare in 1964. In Guinea-Bissau the dominant revolutionary party and present government was the *Frente de Libertacao de Mocambique* (FRELIMO), under the original leadership of Eduardo Mondlane. Neither Mondlane nor Cabral survived the war against the Portuguese, although it is unknown who was ultimately responsible for their deaths—the Portuguese or internal rivals. In Angola FNLA was previously known as the *Governo de Republica Angolana en Exilio* (GRAE).

3. Thomas Okuma, *Angola in Ferment* (Boston: Beacon Press, 1962), pp. 23–39; Allison B. Herrick et al., *Area Handbook for Angola* (Washington, D.C.: The American University, 1967), also known as DA PAM No. 550-50, available from the U.S. Government Printing Office. Hereinafter *Handbook/Angola*.

4. Prior to 1963 even the European colonial was not given the full rights of a Portuguese citizen when the colonial was in Portugal. There is no evidence in the literature that attests to the status of a white, non-Portuguese-speaking colonist in Angola.

5. Relative underdevelopment might be a better evaluative criterion than any attempt at determining absolute "underdevelopment." Portugal was (and is) underdeveloped by the economic standards of the 1960 world and the 1970 world. The colonies were even more so.

6. Angola had the highest proportion of whites in the three Portuguese colonies in 1960–3.7 percent of the population was white. Herrick et al., *Handbook/Angola*.

7. Ibid. Angola had only 1.1 percent *mestico* population in 1960. The significance of this small proportion is important in that it represents the MPLA's original power base.

8. Ronald H. Chilcote, *Emerging Nationalism in Portuguese Africa: Documents* (Stanford: Hoover Institution Press, 1972), pp. 10–12.

9. General Antonio de Spinola, quoted in *Newsweek*, May 6, 1974.

10. "Portuguese High Commissioner Cardoso had carried out his promise that if he could not hand over power to 'two or three' of the Angolan movements, he would 'just get on the plane and leave.' Neto's government in Luanda was therefore not officially given power." Daniel S. Papp, "Angola, National Liberation and the Soviet Union," *Parameters* VIII, no. 1 (March 1978): 33. The quote attributed to the high commissioner is from Godwin Matatu, "The Agony of Angola," *Africa* (November 1975): 14.

11. U.S. aid went primarily to FNLA through Zaire. An account of the transfers can be found in John Stockwell, *In Search of Enemies: A CIA Story* (New York: W. W. Norton, 1978). Stockwell was the chief of the Angolan Task Force for the CIA, by his account.

12. This is Stockwell's thesis, shared by others. Who did what, in what amount, when, and in what sequence is a matter of polemic controversy. A seemingly objective account is to be found in Nathaniel Davis, "The Angola Decision of 1975: A Personal Memoir," *Foreign Affairs* (Fall 1978): 108–124. See also, Charles K. Ebinger, "External Intervention in Internal War: The Politics and Diplomacy of the Angolan Civil War," *Orbis* (Fall 1976): 669–699.

13. Davis, "The Angola Decision," p. 124.

14. A 1974 observation put UNITA-trained troop strength at between 700 and 800. The movement has not, in contrast to others, indulged in gross exaggeration (although at the height of the civil war, exaggeration crept in, with ill results vis-à-vis

credibility). In any case, the difference between observations in, for example, Leon Dash, "Rebels' Congress Held in Wilderness," *Washington Post* (hereinafter *WP*), December 25, 1973, and Stockwell, *CIA Story*, indicates a large influx of potential guerrillas had occurred in a very short time. See also Kenneth Adelman, "Report from Angola," *Foreign Affairs* (April 1975): 62.

15. Unless otherwise noted, environmental data is taken from Herrick et al., *Handbook/Angola*, pp. 9–26; 35–98.

16. There is widespread agreement on this point. The range of these weapons compared to any artillery possessed by either UNITA or FNLA was great. The MPLA could plan artillery fire at such ranges that anti-MPLA forces could not return the fire, even if they knew the fire point location. However, these weapons–while extremely useful to a guerrilla force or any side that can plan the engagement–are relatively useless in a reactive counterguerrilla mode. The mobility advantage is important. See Rowland Evans and Robert Novak, "An Opportunity Ignored in Angola," *WP*, July 22, 1977.

17. Gerald J. Bender, "Angola, the Cubans, and American Anxieties," *Foreign Policy* (Summer 1978): 8. Bender's article seems pro-MPLA in tone; the figure might be viewed as a high-side estimate. The point is well taken, however–the economic glue of the old society is gone.

18. The population of Luanda was 61,028 in 1940 and had grown to 224,540 in 1960. In the latter year, Lobito had a population of 50,164 and Huambo, 38,745. No accurate census for the entire country has ever been achieved.

19. Bruce McColm and David Smith, "Angola: Behind the Lines," *Newsweek*, December 13, 1976, pp. 52–53. Also, "Guerrillas Growing Threat in Angola," *WP*, January 8, 1977.

20. Herrick et al., *Handbook/Angola*, p. 88. However, Bender paints the Ovimbundu as the most exploited and put upon by the Portuguese. The Ovimbundu, for some inexplicable reason, resent the MPLA and view it merely as a replacement for the Portuguese. Bender, "American Anxieties," p. 20.

21. Voting with the feet is a universal trait if the act is physically possible. The openness of the terrain in this case would seem to indicate a higher degree of possibility–and thus the voluntary nature of the act–than in other situations.

22. This is a purely subjective judgment. UNITA has traditionally encouraged visits by what seem to be objective Western newsmen and journalists. UNITA does not seem to hide much and, in the past at least, has taken pride in its lack of exaggeration in front of reporters. Speaking of exaggeration, Jonas Savimbi remarked to Leon Dash during the anti-Portuguese struggle: "If all three groups claimed to control a third of the country and did, the war with the Portuguese would be over by now." See Dash, *WP*, December 25, 1973.

23. Bender, "American Anxieties," p. 23.

24. Jonas M. Savimbi, "A Refusal to Become 'Black Russians' or 'African Cubans'," or an "open letter to the free peoples of the world." The letter was dated September 25, 1976, and excerpted and printed in *New York Times* (hereinafter *NYT*), December 8, 1976.

25. "Cuban Rapists; 17 Executed by Angolans," *Denver Post*, March 12, 1976.

26. Bender, "American Anxieties," p. 20.

27. "Angolan Leader Blames S. Africa for Bombings," WP, November 12, 1978. "Neto blamed UNITA guerrillas for attacks that killed 40 persons and wounded 120 in Huambo last week." Of course, Neto was not an unbiased observer.

28. For example, NYT, December 15, 1977, reported that UNITA claimed "it had killed a number of Cuban soldiers and East European technicians in a new offensive against Communist forces."

29. UNITA started with a headquarters in Zambia, but was expelled after UNITA demonstrated some potency by blowing up portions of the Benguela railroad. Unfortunately, Zambia's copper can only be gotten out on that railroad (unless it is shipped through Rhodesia—a somewhat unpalatable alternative). UNITA had no choice but to move into Angola if it were to continue.

30. Richard Gibson, *African Liberation Movements: Contemporary Struggles Against White Minority Rule* (London: Oxford University Press, 1972), p. 223. In the *Economist*, May 10, 1969, a special correspondent gave MPLA strength at 4,000 and FNLA strength at 8,000.

31. Marvin Howe, "Raiders Harass Angola Railroad," NYT, June 13, 1976; Bruce McColm and David Smith, "Guerrillas Growing Threat in Angola," WP, January 8, 1977.

32. "Angolan Leader Blames," WP, November 12, 1978.

33. See Basil Davidson, "Angola Since Independence," *Race and Class* (Spring 1977): 133–138. Davidson couples Savimbi's charisma with Ovimbundu nationalism. Davidson is somewhat of an MPLA apologist however; in 1972 he claimed that UNITA was a nonexistent force just as the MPLA did. It simply wasn't a fact. Other movements have survived the death of their founders, some have not. Savimbi's oratorical and leadership skills do seem higher than average, however.

34. Dash, WP, December 25, 1973.

35. Leon Dash, "UNITA: Self-Criticism Deep in a Hidden Forest," WP, August 13, 1977. The congress was held in March 1977. This article was part of a long series by Dash appearing in the WP, collectively entitled, "A Long March in Angola."

36. UNITA seems to have moved its external apparatus to Kinshasha, although this is by no means certain. The UNITA foreign minister, Mr. Sangumba, spends a lot of time on the road.

37. Perhaps a holdover from the two Vietnam wars and the Algerian war. Much of the press coverage and many journal articles researched for this analysis were decidedly prorevolutionary.

38. The process can continue. Mr. Sangumba, the foreign minister from UNITA, and Holden Roberto have frequent contacts with foreign journalists. Interestingly enough, a group or two of "Black liberation supporters" in the United States provide support for the antiregime insurgent groups in Rhodesia and Namibia, but urge recognition and aid to the MPLA. See Kevin Young, "Informal Channels of Black Civilian Input to the Process of Formulating U.S. Foreign Policy on Africa," (unpublished paper, University of the District of Columbia, 1979).

39. Support was split fairly equally at the time of the civil war. The recognized government has an automatic advantage in that legitimacy is acknowledged and known to be acknowledged.

40. UNITA's arms were rumored to have come from the Portuguese in order to counter MPLA influence in coincident operating areas. The source of these rumors is unknown. It would make sense to suspect the MPLA was the source of the rumors, with the obvious intent to discredit UNITA in nationalist eyes. UNITA established control in the southern and southeastern portions of Angola before the MPLA tried to work in those areas. The MPLA seems to have been the initiator of conflict between the two groups at that time.

41. *Foreign Report*, January 3, 1973, and February 5, 1973. Just prior to independence, China renewed contact with UNITA as a counter to Soviet support for the MPLA. Like U.S. aid, Chinese aid was almost insignificant in comparison to Soviet aid.

42. Zambia provided the base camp area for FRELIMO (operating in Mozambique), for the MPLA (after it moved its main headquarters there from Congo), for the two anti-Rhodesian movements, and for a time at least, for SWAPO operating in Namibia. Despite the open presence of guerrilla troops and publicly voiced support by Zambia's President Kuanda, the fiction is more or less maintained that Zambia is not a base for aggressive attacks. To recognize this would, of course, be to sanction a grave breach of international law. Thus, when Portugal raided such camps (as Rhodesia and South Africa do now), Zambia did not raise too great a fuss about it. One cannot raid what does not exist. See J. Bowyer Bell, "The Frustration of Insurgency: The Rhodesian Example in the Sixties," *Military Affairs* (February 1971):1–5; *Economist,* March 27, 1971.

43. Dash, Gibson, and others.

44. Eric Pale, "UN Agency to Give Food to African Insurgents," *NYT*, April 27, 1974.

45. Basil Davidson, "Arms and the Portuguese," *Africa Report* (May 1970):11.

46. See *Foreign Report*, January 10, 1973, and June 28, 1972. During the anti-Portuguese times, the OAU continually tried to bring the three movements together and create a united front. All such "alliances" proved illusory.

47. Among other sources (most admitted by the insurgents), see W.A.C. Adie, "The Communist Powers in Africa," *Conflict Studies* (December–January 1970–71): 4–18.

48. Davis, Stockwell, and Papp, although each has different views on the aid, agree that the Soviets and Cubans initiated the escalation. Apologists for the MPLA or Soviets disagree.

49. Evidence for the first arrival of the SA-7 in Angola is not available, but it was given to the PAIGC in Guinea-Bissau in 1973. Such weapons were rumored to be in the hands of all anti-Portuguese factions that also possessed Soviet backing. See *Newsweek*, December 10, 1973. However, the weapon identified in that article in a photo as a SAM-7 is *not* a SAM-7. Rather, it is a shaped charge launcher similar to the German WW II *Panzerfaust*. It is an antitank weapon, useful for hitting all sorts of things, even airplanes—on the ground. The Soviets stopped giving aid to the MPLA just before the Portuguese coup, but resumed it in October–November 1974. See Papp, "Angola, National Liberation," p. 29; John A. Marcum, "Lessons of Angola," *Foreign Affairs* (April 1976): 412–416; Colin Legum, "A Letter on Angola to American Liberals," *The New Republic* (January 1976): 17; and "National Liberation in Southern

Africa," *Problems of Communism* (January–February 1975):11–15.

50. Davis, "The Angola Decision," pp. 112–117.

51. See Note 30. UNITA did not seem to learn. One of its first acts upon reverting to guerrilla warfare after the conventional defeat at the hands of MPLA/Cuban forces was to blow up portions of the railroad, thereby alienating the Zambian government. Marvin Howe, "Raiders Harass Angola Railroad," *NYT*, June 13, 1976.

52. The following is a quick guide to who was where at the height of the anti-Portuguese fighting:

| Group | Primary Host | Secondary Host |
|---|---|---|
| PAIGC | Guinea | Senegal |
| FNLA | Zaire | Egypt |
| MPLA | Zambia | Congo |
| UNITA | | Zambia (unofficially) |
| FRELIMO | Tanzania | Zambia |
| ZANU/ZAPU | Zambia | |
| SWAPO | Zambia | Angola |

53. FNLA seemed to be in complete disarray in any case. See David B. Ottaway, "Angola: Charges Prompt New Look at U.S. Role," *WP*, May 10, 1978.

54. There is some evidence that coercion is in fact involved. See David B. Ottaway, "Angola, Its Economy Stalled, Begins Nationalizations," *WP*, May 7, 1976; "Angola Due to Move Toward Marxist Rule," *NYT*, December 5, 1977; Caryle Murphy, "Angolan Rulers Seen Planning Communist-Style Party," *WP*, November 5, 1976; Marvin Howe, "Angola Forging a Socialist State, But Leaving Door Open to the West," *NYT*, June 27, 1976; John F. Burns, "Refugees Describe Atrocities by Angolan Forces," *NYT*, November 13, 1976.

55. "Angolans Forcing Back Refugees, S. Africans Say," *WP*, November 9, 1976; Leon Dash, "A Long March in Angola" series, *WP*, August 1977.

56. Dash tells of some MPLA soldiers trying to go over to UNITA, but it is just as hard for deserters to make safe contact as it is for the MPLA to find UNITA.

57. There does not seem to be much choice at the moment. After all, the MPLA is the government and must provide some of the services expected of a government. If the Cubans pull out, UNITA might well win. If the Cubans stay, UNITA has a target.

58. This observation of Galula's in no way rules out spontaneous revolts. I suspect that Galula was less than correct here, because countergovernment movments have existed under some very repressive regimes. But, in terms of a mass-based political movement dedicated to guerrilla warfare, it may be very, very difficult under circumstances of severe repression. At the same time, other forms of counterregime activity, such as a coup or spontaneous uprising, might become more likely.

59. "Angola, With Cuban Help, Said to Clear Wide Strip Along Border in South," *NYT*, December 11, 1976.

60. UNITA is faced with a tremendous problem in this regard. Savimbi is Ovimbundu, as are the majority of his officers and men. Dash still reports a wide base of non-Ovimbundu support, but many other observers have begun to assume the identifica-

tion with the Ovimbundu. See Dash, "Colonialism Gone, Racism Remains," *WP*, August 12, 1977. Of course, outsider identification of the movement as tied to a given tribe is meaningless. What matters is the identification of nonmembers of that tribe inside Angola.

61. This was very true in 1973. The vast number of people coming into the movement during and since the civil war have reduced this factor. Dash reports that lack of discipline was a growing problem in 1977 and UNITA leadership was taking steps to correct the situation. See Dash's August 1977 series in *WP*.

62. The enclave of Cabinda lies to the north of Angola, separated by the Congo River and a strip of Zaire from the main portion of the country. Cabinda is a very small piece of territory that was part of the Portuguese colony of Angola and is now a part of the MPLA-controlled portion of Angola. Cabinda is interesting primarily because it is the location of working oil fields. These fields are presently operated by the Gulf Oil Corporation, headquartered in Pittsburgh, PA. By 1974, Gulf had invested more than $150 million in the oil wells. Approximately $33 million a year finds its way into the Angolan economy because of Gulf's operations. (John Marcum, "The United States and Portuguese Africa: A Perspective in American Foreign Policy," *Africa Today* [October 1971]: 35–36.) Cabinda has its own independence movement or two. The main group is known by the acronym of FLEC (Front for the Liberation of the Enclave of Cabinda). FLEC fought against the Portuguese, but without noticeable success. (See Gibson, *African Liberation,* p. 221; also A. J. Venter, *The Terror Fighters* [Capetown: Parnell and Sons, S.A. Pty, Ltd., 1969]. Venter is currently an editor of *Soldier of Fortune* magazine. It was in *Soldier of Fortune* that some of the Americans who fought in Angola as mercenaries advertised for their jobs. See also, Caryle Murphy, "Cabinda Rebels Harass Angola," *WP*, April 20, 1976.) The MPLA also tried to "liberate" Cabinda in the Portuguese era, but was fairly soundly defeated by the Portuguese, FLEC, and a general named General Apathy. The suspicion is that most inhabitants of Cabinda seemed to be doing fairly well in economic and material terms due to the working conditions and general prosperity of the enclave caused by Gulf's presence. Ironically, one now finds communist Cuban troops protecting a capitalist investment in a "socialist" state against the hordes of nationalist liberation formations. (*WP*, June 18, 1978.) In my opinion, as goes Gulf, so goes Cabinda. If Gulf gives encouragement to the rebels, who knows? Gulf has played it relatively safe in the past and, with good amoral business sense, will probably do so in the future. The oil represents the largest sure source of foreign currency in all of Angola. It is important to whomever wins the eventual victory.

9

Summary and Conclusions

The introduction to this book observed that while a macro theory of in-surgency does not exist, a clear, concise, and comprehensive framework for analysis may nevertheless enhance our understanding by identifying major variables and the interplay among them that significantly affects the progress and outcomes of internal conflicts. Such a framework was set forth in Chapter 1 and then applied to seven diverse cases. These case studies provided a rich source of comparable data. It is now time to summarize what we have learned with respect to the variables and the relationships among them.

### Environment

In Chapter 1 we called attention to the importance that many analysts ascribe to environmental factors in the genesis and progression of insurgent conflicts. Although our case studies confirm this general proposition, they reveal very clearly that while some aspects of the environment make a positive contribution to the development of an insurrection, others limit its growth. Moreover, the same aspect of the environment that is favorable dur-ing an insurgency's formative stage may actually become a hindrance at a later point.

The socioeconomic deprivation of minority groups in Thailand, Guatemala, Ulster, and Iraq provided a host of potential grievances that insurgent cadres could and did exploit successfully. In Uruguay a general downturn in economic development gave the Tupamaros grist for their propaganda mill, whereas in Angola tribal rivalries over political power did the same for UNITA. What the cases suggest, therefore, is that social, economic, and ethnic-religious aspects of the environment provided underlying causes for political violence. However, in the cases of Thailand, Guatemala, Ulster, and Oman the dependence on disadvantaged minorities to accomplish revolu-tionary aims was a long-term liability, given the resistance of the majority of the population. The pursuit of secessionist and then reformist aims by the Kurds also failed in the face of determined opposition on the part of the Arab government in Baghdad. Finally, the aims of UNITA to date have had little appeal to non-Ovimbundu elements that compose and sustain the present government in Angola. All told, then, a minority can provide a basis for generating a serious threat to the government, but is unlikely to galvanize sufficient resources for ultimate success.

With respect to the physical environment, events in Guatemala, Thailand, Oman, Kurdistan, and Angola support the proposition that rugged terrain in remote regions facilitates guerrilla operations and the creation of base areas. At the same time, the government's ability to use existing roads (e.g., Guatemala) or to build new ones, along with barriers and military camps (e.g., Oman) suggests that measures can be taken to neutralize or at least mitigate the advantages that the physical environment confers on the insurgents. It is important to bear in mind, however, that this penetration of remote regions is easier said than done, particularly when such regions are extensive and the population antipathetic toward the government (e.g., Southern Angola).

Like the rural areas, urban centers contain advantages and disadvantages for insurgents. On the one hand, they provide readymade soft targets for terrorists seeking to publicize their activity and gain support. On the other hand, the cities can be isolated and controlled by the government more easily than large rural areas. Furthermore, the terrorism that urban settings facilitate and encourage has not only failed to achieve notable success but it has also alienated former supporters when unduly prolonged (e.g., Ulster and Uruguay).

To sum up, while the environment remains an important explanatory factor behind insurgent success, the analyst must guard against the deception that can be engendered by early political and military achievements that are attributed to it. The principal danger here is that long-term problems associated with overlooked dimensions of the environment may be ignored. The antidote is, of course, a systematic appraisal that addresses the various aspects of environment and their relationship to other variables in terms of both their short- and longer-term implications.

## Popular Support

Like the environment, popular support traditionally has been viewed as a major determinant of insurgent fortunes. How much support is necessary, however, is difficult to say, inasmuch as it depends primarily on insurgent aims and the government's strength and will. Where insurgents seek to displace the regime—as in the case of revolutionary, reactionary, and restorational uprisings—and where the government's counterinsurgency program is initially effective, the acquisition of support from wide segments of the population (both geographically and demographically) has been deemed important by both analysts and practitioners. While this has been most evident in the context of the Maoist strategy, it presumably obtains for the urban terrorist strategy as well, since the latter involves the eventual transferal of violence and political activity to the rural areas.

The case studies underscore much of the conventional wisdom regarding popular support, albeit in different ways. In Iraq, the backing of Kurdish tribesmen, especially in the rural areas, was instrumental in the long defiance of the government by the Pesh Merga. Yet, as necessary as such support was to the Kurdish insurgents, it was insufficient for ultimate success against a government that possessed impressive military capabilities and drew its support from the much larger Arab population. To compensate for the limitations on popular support resulting from the demographic configuration of Iraq, the insurgents were compelled to seek external assistance from a number of sources. Once such outside aid was withdrawn and the government moved with substantial and ruthless force against the insurgents, popular support, though still strong, could not reverse government victories. Thus, the overriding lesson of the Kurdish case is that while popular support can provide a basis for effective resistance, the success of such resistance may be limited if it is based on a subnational minority group.

The Kurdish experience raises serious questions about the longer-term viability of the similar situations that exist in Thailand and Angola. In these cases a continuation of insurrectionary activity has been based on support from specific ethnic groups. A comparison of the two situations suggests that the long-term prospect of the insurgency in Thailand is inherently limited by virtue of the fact that the much greater Thai population has, on balance, remained indifferent to the appeals of a movement that is largely regarded as non-Thai. Under such circumstances, a vigorous and enlightened counterinsurgency effort would probably neutralize the insurrection.

The situation in Angola is more complex. Although the Ovimbundu, UNITA's source of popular support, are a minority when compared to other tribes taken in the aggregate, they nonetheless are the largest tribal group in the nation. Accordingly, as long as the MPLA government is unable to attract a wide following which significantly incorporates the various non-Ovimbundu peoples, UNITA would appear able to defy the government indefinitely. This leads to an important qualification of the proposition that insurgencies based on subnational groups are vulnerable over the longer term. Whereas this does seem to be the case when the government is controlled by members of a majority group, it may not hold true in multiethnic societies ruled by governments that, like the insurgents, draw their backing from a minority. Under the latter circumstances both the government and the insurgents will have a difficult time mustering adequate resources to defeat an adversary that demonstrates a reasonable degree of organizational effectiveness.

The studies of Oman and Ulster indicate the importance of popular support in a somewhat different way than the cases discussed above. In contrast to the Kurds, UNITA, and the Thai communists, there was a marked diminu- tion of popular support for the PFLO and IRA that could be traced to disen- chantment with excessive insurgent terrorism and positive responses to government reforms. In each instance, decreased popular support coincided with a diminished capability on the part of the insurgents to carry out acts of violence.

The Uruguayan and Guatemalan cases also shed light on the role of popular support. In these countries, the most salient aspect of popular support was its low level, rather than its narrow base or decline. Although the Tupamaro and Guatemalan revolutionaries acknowledged the importance of assistance from the people, they proved unable to acquire it. In Uruguay, the urban terrorist strategy and limited organization that accompanied it were largely to blame, whereas in Guatemala it was the indifference of the Indian population to in- surgent appeals that accounted for the failure. In each case, low popular sup- port prevented the insurgency from expanding and made the government's task that much easier once it decided to institute a major counterinsurgency effort.

Besides providing additional insights with respect to the importance of popular support in general, the seven studies yielded some useful observa- tions about the techniques for gaining popular support. In two cases – Angola and Iraq – charismatic leadership played an important role in attracting adherents. It was especially critical for the Kurds because it provided a unify- ing focus in an otherwise segmentary tribal society.

While esoteric appeals were evident in all situations, they differed in a number of ways. In Angola and Iraq, such appeals were primarily nationalist; while in Oman, Thailand, Uruguay, and Guatemala they were largely Marxist-Leninist. In Ulster, there was a split between the Provisional IRA, which emphasized Irish nationalism, and the Official IRA, which propagated Marxist ideas. In general, the nationalist appeals seemed to play an effective role in attracting both the intellectuals and mass followers, whereas the Marxist ideas were somewhat successful in attracting intellectuals into the movements. In all cases, Marxism appeared to have little appeal to the mass public. For the ethnic – and in most cases primitive – minorities of Angola, Oman, Iraq, and Guatemala, Marxism was irrelevant and incomprehensible. Nowhere was this more true than in Oman, where the attempt to impose Marxist values and structures on the mountain tribes stirred up substantial opposition because of the threat it posed to traditional values and modes of behavior. Elsewhere, the middle-class population and democratic ethos of Uruguay and the religiosity of the Catholic community in Ulster prevented Marxism from making much headway among the masses.

Where insurgents were able to gain support from the public it was largely on the basis of exoteric appeals. In Angola, Oman, Iraq, Thailand, and Ireland, the major theme struck by insurgents was that of political, social, and economic discrimination against minority groups. Grievances related to similar discrimination continue to be manipulated effectively by UNITA and the Thai communists. In Oman, and to some extent Ulster, reforms designed by the government to undercut exoteric appeals have been followed by a noticeable decline in popular support for the insurgents. In Iraq, the concrete grievances of the Kurds remained but are of little consequence in light of the demise of the Pesh Merga.

Although there seemed to be potential for using exoteric appeals in Uruguay and Guatemala, such endeavors met with failure because of organizational deficiencies (as in the case of the Tupamaros) or the indifference of the disadvantaged group (as in the case of Guatemala). What happened in Guatemala, namely the lack of response by the Indians, was interesting in that it confirmed the generally held view that it is deprived individuals with aspiration for a better life who engage in insurgent violence rather than extremely poor people who have no vision of a brighter future.

The use of terror in some form was noted in all cases. Ulster, Oman, Thailand, and Guatemala experienced a number of incidents where it was selectively applied. In the case of the Kurds, "coercion" against reluctant Kurdish tribes was undertaken to solidify the nationalist movement. In Angola, UNITA's primary targets to date have been non-Angolans working for the government faction. In Uruguay, the "nonviolent" terror was largely directed against those individuals who occupied high political or economic positions in the regime; the violent portion of the terror program was directed against internal security personnel of the police forces. Unfortunately, the sparse data available on selective terrorism's impact on popular attitudes toward insurgents precludes any strong conclusions. What little we do know contains no evidence that would seriously challenge the view that selective terrorism has at best a moderate influence on the acquisition of popular support. One reason for this is that not all targets of selective terror find popular approval. For example, although in Uruguay Tupamaro terrorist actions against the police and corrupt officials were welcomed, the public reacted negatively and seemingly approved of repressive measures when terrorism was directed at the military. The difference was that members of the police did not enjoy the respect of the populace that the military did. Whether selective terrorism can generate support for insurgents is therefore partially a function of the public's attitude toward the target.

In cases where terror was nonselectively applied, such as Ulster and Guatemala, the strength of the movement waned. In Guatemala, it led to both government counteraction and right-wing selective counterterror that helped crush the movement. In Ulster, popular support for the IRA appeared to decline after the initiation of random bombing attacks in the cities of Northern Ireland and in England. In Uruguay, the expansion of terrorist activities to the military – while still selective terror – helped drive support away from the Tupamaros. These illustrations reinforce our earlier conclusion that indiscriminate terror not only plays an insignificant role in the acquisition of popular supprt but it also can be counterproductive if prolonged.

With regard to the specific aim of producing government counterterror, we found this to be the case in Guatemala, Thailand, Uruguay, and Ulster. Two of the four situations backfired badly on the insurgents. In Guatemala, right-wing death squads operating outside the law eroded insurgent strength and drove the peasants into a neutral status. In Uruguay, the turn to more general violence brought the majority of the population fully behind the government's counteraction, thereby allowing the virtual elimination of the Tupamaros. Although an initial government overreaction helped the IRA in Ulster, the problem was solved through a combination of judicial reforms and increased military discipline. In Thailand, government blunders still seem to be bringing marginal increments of support to the insurgents in the areas considered to be non-Thai.

All acts taken against the govenment of a public nature are in effect a demonstration of potency.

Of the cases analyzed, "military" demonstrations of potency can be posited for Guatemala, Uruguay, Thailand, and Angola. The armed propaganda activities of the first three cases shows clear action by the armed insurgents wherein violence was not directly intended and the motive was to produce political and psychological effects in the target audiences. In Angola, attempts to cause economic disruption in the cities seems to have been motivated by a clear desire to communicate the strength and increasing power of the insurgent movement.

With regard to the other means of demonstrating potency – the provision of services – the insurgents in Oman, Angola, and Thailand made some progress. Their ability to provide services was indicative of organizational strength and seemed to engender passive and active support for the insurgency. Yet in one instance – that of Oman – the insurgents went too far in implementing radical policies and thus alienated their rank and file supporters.

Although, in the final analysis, demonstration of potency can be an important means of acquiring popular support, it is not without limitations. As far as violent acts are concerned, we have noted in a previous context that indiscriminate terrorism can be counterproductive. Likewise, the provision of services can have a negative impact if it is accompanied by doctrinaire policies that are anathema to the putative beneficiaries.

## Organization and Cohesion

Not surprisingly, the case studies confirmed the importance of political organization in insurgent conflicts. Any insurgent organization that is differentiated (complex) has the potential to reach wider segments of the population and to provide the instrumental services and channels for expressive protest that attract and sustain active popular support.

In Angola, the stubborn and effective resistance to the new MPLA regime on the part of UNITA has been closely associated with the existence of a parallel hierarchy in the southern region of the country and to a charismatic leader, two assets which enabled UNITA to survive and operate in the previous conflict against Portugal. With exiguous inputs from outside sources, UNITA was compelled to organize the population in order to resist the colonial power. While the situation regarding external assistance has not improved much under current conditions, UNITA has continued to oppose the government actively and effectively by relying on its organizational strength.

The insurgents in Thailand have also been able to maintain pressure on the government because, in part, they are well organized in several regions of the country and are relatively cohesive. Much the same could be said of the Kurds in Iraq and, to a lesser degree, of the PFLO in Oman and the insurgents in Guatemala.

While the organizational variable helps us explain the continued or temporary success of insurgents in the cases mentioned above, it also suggests shortcomings, particularly when it is related to their goals, strategies, and sources of popular support. In Angola, Thailand, Oman, and Guatemala the insurgent movements have had the ultimate revolutionary aim of transforming the regime through protracted armed struggle, an undertaking which normally involves the gradual extension of the organizational apparatus to major population groups and sections of the country. However, in each case, the insurgents have been constrained by their previously mentioned close identification with minority elements or particular regions—UNITA with the Ovimbundu, the CPT with non-Thai ethnic groups, the PFLO with the jebalis in Dhofar province, and the various Guatemalan groups with the Indians. Since the inability to extend the organizational structure beyond such narrow bases of support is a fatal flaw for a revolutionary organization that confronts a reasonably strong government, one can better understand the limits of UNITA's and the CPT's achievements, as well as the defeat of PFLO and the Guatemalan insurgents. The implications for UNITA and the CPT are that a meaningful political outcome would seem to depend on a goal transformation (i.e., from revolutionary to reformist) similar to that which occurred several years ago in the Sudan when secessionist aims were replaced by reformist ones.

As far as the Kurds are concerned, there seems to be little doubt that Barzani's ability to establish an administrative structure and unified command in an otherwise fractious society was a major reason for the successful resistance to Baghdad. The downfall of the Kurds, as Viotti notes, was primarily due to a withdrawal of vital external support, not organizational deficiencies. Whether the Kurdish nationalist sentiments that have been rekindled by the Iranian events of 1979 will be translated into renewed insurrectionary behavior remains an open question. If they are, the probability of success would seem low, not only because Iraq has placed the Kurds under close control, but also because the fragile cohesion of the Kurdish movement has been shattered in the wake of Barzani's exile and death.

The conflicts in Ulster and Uruguay differ from the ones considered thus far in terms of strategy and tactics. Whereas the Angolan, Thai, Omani, Guatemalan, and Kurdish insurgents adopted, in varying degrees, a strategy of protracted warfare that centered in the rural areas and relied on guerrilla attacks, those in Northern Ireland and Uruguay stressed urban terrorism. Of the two, the Tupamaros gave more systematic thought to long-term strategy, perhaps because the principal theoreticians of such an approach were Latinos. The IRA, by contrast, was divided. The Officials, who favored a political approach, appeared to engage in sporadic terrorism more out of fear of losing support to the rival Provisionals than out of a belief in its efficacy. The Provisionals, however, believed that terrorism was the only way to achieve their tactical aim of compelling the British to withdraw. In neither faction was urban terrorism rationalized by systematic theoretical considerations as it was in Latin America.

In Ulster and Uruguay the emphasis on urban terrorism led insurgents to create small-scale organizations. Though both the IRA and the Tupamaros had central political and military structures, the operational units were essentially compartmentalized cells. Moreover, as Mansfield and Miller point out, the organizations were far more impressive on paper than in practice. While the cellular organizations in Ulster and Uruguay proved capable of sustaining terrorism, they had little potential for sustaining larger-scale violence. In each case the governments were able (albeit with different approaches) to neutralize their adversaries, a task that was facilitated by the insurgents' lack of widespread popular support. This disadvantage, in turn, could be traced to the absence of organizational links with large segments of the populace. The ability of the IRA to gain popular backing for a brief period was due to the Catholic community's belief that it was the only defense against the British and Protestants. Once the British instituted reforms for dealing with the people, Catholic support for the IRA declined rather noticeably, particularly since the insurgents lacked the organizational structure necessary to mitigate such adverse trends. In Uruguay, the Tupamaros found that their limited organization denied them the opportunity to mobilize popular dissatisfaction in the face of a severe, violent, and extralegal response by the government.

The difficulties encountered by the IRA and the Tupamaros lend support to the general proposition that an urban terrorist strategy has little chance of success for revolutionary insurgents who face a determined government. In both cases, an underdeveloped organization could be identified as a major problem for the insurgents. Parenthetically, it should be noted that further evidence for the proposition has been provided by the recent events in Iran, where it was the effective mobilization of the people for continuous strikes and massive demonstrations by the Shia Moslems' organizational apparatus, rather than terrorism, that brought down the powerful and coercive Pahlavi regime. The government had proved it could contain terrorists, but it gradually disintegrated when confronted by a Moslem organization energized by an exiled cleric.

## External Support

As noted in the framework, external suport has received a good deal of attention from analysts of insurgency. While recognizing that some commentators believe it is necessary for success, we argued that the importance of external support depends on the situation vis-à-vis the other variables, particularly government response. Where the government's performance was poor, as in Batista's Cuba, there was little need for external support. Conversely, where the government demonstrated effectiveness, external support was important. When the government proved capable of destroying the insurgent organizational apparatus inside the country, external support was deemed essential for the continued existence of the movement. Not only do the case studies confirm these propositions but they also underscore the complexity surrounding this variable.

In Uruguay and Guatemala, the insurgent movements enjoyed little external material support. What's more, when the governments of the two countries began to invoke strong measures against the insurgents, the latter made little effort to compensate by obtaining outside assistance. Whether they would have been successful had they tried is purely conjectural. Consequently, the two cases do not provide a good basis for assessing our propositions.

Angola presents a case where external support has not been crucial. Though UNITA did benefit from the Republic of South Africa's backing during the continual fighting that took place in the wake of Portugal's withdrawal, external assistance has never been crucial for UNITA's viability during insurgent phases. Against both the Portuguese and the MPLA government, UNITA has relied primarily on a favorable environment, popular support, good organization, and the weaknesses of the government to preclude the government from extending effective control over the southern region of Angola. How far external assistance would lead UNITA beyond denying the MPLA control in the south is perforce a speculative matter.

Despite the fact that in Ulster, Thailand, and Oman external support has been an important factor behind insurgent achievements, its impact has been limited. In Ulster and Thailand, the constricted popular support for the insurgents reduced their potential for effectively using sizeable external assistance (even if it was available). In Oman, the significance of external aid has been undermined severely by a strong government response and insurgent blunders in the area of popular support. At one time external support was an important element behind a gradual increase in the success of PFLO operations; today it stands as the last obstacle to the total demise of the movement.

Finally, the Kurds represent a phenomenon which is generally overlooked, namely overreliance on external support. Aided by the former shah of Iran, they were emboldened to engage the Iraqi military in engagements that increasingly took on a conventional character. When that aid was terminated, the Pesh Merga found themselves vulnerable to an Iraqi crackdown. One underlying reason for this turn of events was the incompatibility of political aims between donor and client. Despite the stated reformist objectives of Barzani, Iran could never be sure that the Kurds might not achieve a major success leading to secession, a development that Kurds in Iran might seek to emulate. What Teheran did was modulate aid to Barzani as a means of putting pressure on Baghdad to make concessions on other issues of greater importance to Iran (e.g., the Shatt al-Arab question). The Kurdish-Iranian relationship implies that material support will be tenuous in situations where donor-client political aims are not in harmony.

It should not be inferred that stated, harmonious political aims will guarantee continued material assistance, for Chinese aid to the CPT and PFLO was either scaled back or discontinued despite the revolutionary Marxist aims of the insurgents. In both cases, the PRC's state interests simply took precedence.

In the final analysis, our case studies lead us to the conclusion that the significance of external support is all too often exaggerated. Though we still believe it can be very important in Maoist-type insurgencies that have progressed to either large-scale guerrilla warfare or the mobile-conventional stage, it plays a far more modest role in most other cases. What it can do is facilitate acts of violence or prevent the final eradication of insurgent movements. But, when the government manifests strength, such contributions are a long way from being decisive. Moreover, they can be offset by external assistance to the government.

## Government Response

The framework observed that the government response is the major variable affecting the outcome of an insurgency. Inasmuch as the insurgency arises because some aspect of the political system is considered illegitimate, the most effective response would be to restore legitimacy for those groups that have become disaffected. As demonstrated by our case studies, the government response is frequently somewhat less than this; that is, governments often rely on force rather than changing the political community, regime, authorities, or political-economic policies.

The first problem for the government is to identify the threat and devise an appropriate response. The framework identified four insurgent threats and stated that they could occur simultaneously. The threats include political organization, terrorism, guerrilla warfare, and mobile-conventional warfare. The government response must be geared to the actual situation.

The case of Oman is illuminating. The government combatted political organization through a series of administrative and economic reforms designed to eliminate the grievances upon which the insurgency was based, while at the same time taking appropriate military action against the insurgents. The insurgency was eliminated through a successful government strategy. In Northern Ireland, the British initially alienated the population through a rigid internment policy; however, once this policy was made more flexible, the British were able to partially undermine the popular support of the IRA while containing the level of terrorism. Yet, although terrorism in Northern Ireland has been reduced to considerable degree, the continuing religious and economic cleavages have enabled it to continue at a low level.

In Guatemala the insurgents launched military attacks before consolidating their political organization in the countryside. The insurgents were able to achieve little popular support among the various Indian groups in the rural areas. The Guatemalan authorities were able to exploit the apathetic character of the rural population in responding to the military threat of the insurgents without having to initiate political and economic reforms. A similar situation prevailed in Uruguay. The insurgency turned to terrorism without creating a broad base of organized popular support. This was clearly manifest when the MLN suffered severe setbacks in an election. The result was that the government was able to take military action against the insurgents without solving the economic problems that had contributed to the growth of the insurgency. Evidence from these case studies suggests that the government can conduct a successful counterinsurgency without implementing political reforms in situations where the insurgents themselves are not able to fully organize their potential supporters.

The government also enjoys an advantage when the insurgency is based on ethnic cleavages. In the case of Iraq, the Kurdish insurgents were successful in organizing themselves, but found little support among the Arabs of Iraq. Consequently, there were no voices speaking for the Kurdish minority among the larger Iraqi community. The result was that the majority of Iraqis were supportive of or indifferent to the government's policy of a military solution and forced resettlement of the Kurds. The Thai insurgents also labor under the popular perception that they are outside the mainstream of Thai culture. The government, even though it has been inept in the implementation of many counterinsurgency measures, has been able to limit insurgent growth by appealing to traditional values such as "nation, monarchy, religion."

The exception to this principle is, of course, when the government itself is based on an ethnic cleavage. The case in point is Angola. The government has increasingly narrowed its base of support to one tribal group even though it began with a potential multitribal base of support. Had the UNITA insurgents been capable of significantly expanding the base of their support beyond the single (though largest) tribal group in Angola, the MPLA government probably would have fallen. As things stand now, the MPLA has yet to organize an effective counterinsurgency; instead it has chosen to rely on Soviet and Cuban assistance. This assistance has been sufficient to contain UNITA but not to defeat it.

The Soviet and Cuban aid to Angola–as well as Soviet aid to Iraq and, to a lesser degree, U.S. support of Guatemala, Uruguay, and Thailand–demonstrates the importance of external support for the government. However, our cases indicate that where the government has relied extensively on external support the tendency has been for a primarily military response with little attention to political or economic reforms. In fact, in none of the cases mentioned above have the governments made serious attempts to deal with the economic and social causes of insurgency. With the support of foreign arms they moved against the insurgents. In cases where the insurgents have had a stronger organizational base, such as Thailand, foreign support has not brought about the defeat of the insurgents. In Angola, the presence of Cuban troops and Soviet advisors constitutes a major propaganda opportunity for UNITA. But in Iraq (after the Kurds lost the supprt of Iran), Guatemala, and Uruguay, where the insurgents did not have strong organizations, external support and a military response were sufficient to defeat the insurgents.

In Northern Ireland, external support for the government has been limited. The British derive moral and, to a lesser degree, political support from outside, but their policy is generally self-reliant. Concerning the use of judicial sanctions, the British in Northern Ireland have had the most far-reaching policy. Initially, the policy was unsuccessful because it lacked discrimination; when a discriminating judicial policy with regard to internment was restored, it created much more support for the government.

Interestingly, in two of our cases extralegal action outside the government played a role in undermining the insurgency. The right-wing terrorists and death squads in Uruguay and Guatemala were helpful to the government in that they sought out and destroyed some of the insurgents, thereby creating organizational and morale problems for the insurgency. However, since such vigilantism can ultimately turn on the government, the desirability of ex-tralegal action against insurgents remains questionable.

We must reemphasize our view that the government role is central in insurgencies. Although it normally enjoys an advantage at the outset of hostilities—because of the resources it commands—the government still must compete with its adversaries in terms of organization, cohesion, popular support, and external assistance. In those cases where the government response has been effective, it was largely due to outperforming the insurgents in terms of these factors. At times, this was the result of an effective counterinsurgency strategy (e.g., Oman). In other instances, it was because the government had massive external support (e.g., Iraq) or because the insurgent strategy and organization were notably deficient (e.g., Uruguay).

## Final Comments

By now, the reader will probably agree that insurgency is a complex phenomenon that defies easy generalizations. There is considerable variation with respect to causes, ultimate goals, strategies, tactics, and achievements. In view of this situation, students and analysts, whether civilian or military, must be prepared to examine given situations carefully and systematically. Although such an undertaking is normally frustrating because of the difficulty of integrating and synthesizing vast amounts of data and because of informational gaps in important areas, it is far more preferable to an unstructured, descriptive approach. In the case of the latter, the analyst is often tempted to fall back on unquestioned formulas and to let political biases affect prescriptions. To illustrate, we have observed that descriptive assessments often tend to overlook the important distinctions among insurgent movements. In conversations and seminars on the subject, one is struck by the tendency to assume insurgencies are revolutionary, Maoist, and rural-based, and that the appropriate response is to "win the hearts and minds of the people" through political and economic reforms. However, as our analyses show, many insurgencies are fundamentally different with respect to goals, strategy, and locus of operations. Moreover, the evidence suggests they can be contained, if not expunged, without political and economic reforms designed to gain the support of relatively deprived sections of the population.

The distinctions are very important in a practical sense because policies designed for dealing with prolonged Marxist revolutionary insurrections may be either inappropriate or unnecessarily costly for non-Marxist secessionist movements. The student or analyst who has recognized this will be led to inquire under what circumstances reform is or is not important and what it means for the situations he is examining.

We believe that our framework and case studies can be helpful in resolving questions such as this, since they have sought not only to arrive at general principles about many aspects of insurgency, but also to identify exceptions and reasons for the exceptions. In order to facilitate this task, we found our six variables and the complicated interplay among them to be most helpful. Although we are very much aware that our data are largely qualitative and, at times, somewhat soft, we hope that the propositions and hypotheses generated through use of the framework will make a modest contribution to the longer-term task of theory building; in the short term, we hope that we have provided insights that are useful to those working on their own case studies.

# Selected Bibliography

To aid in further scholarly inquiry we attach a list of significant secondary sources arranged alphabetically by chapter. These works give valuable historical insights into the countries studied or into insurgency in general. The authors of the case studies relied extensively on primary materials both in English and in foreign languages, including translations of radio broadcasts by Foreign Broadcast Information Service (FBIS), newspapers and magazines, journals, pamphlets, and other materials. Because of the often transitory nature of such material we do not restate it in this bibliography, but refer the reader to the chapter notes in which such sources are well documented.

## Chapter 1. Insurgency: A Framework for Analysis

Asprey, Robert B. *War in the Shadows*. Garden City, New York: Doubleday, 1975 (2 vols.).

Blaufarb, Douglas. *The Counterinsurgency Era*. New York: The Free Press, 1977.

Galula, David. *Counterinsurgency Warfare: Theory and Practice*. New York: Praeger Publishers, 1964.

Gurr, Ted Robert. *Why Men Rebel*. Princeton: Princeton University Press, 1970.

Johnson, Chalmers. *Revolutionary Change*. Boston: Little, Brown and Co., 1966.

Laqueur, Walter. *Guerrilla*. Boston: Little, Brown and Co., 1976.

McCuen, John J. *The Art of Counter-Revolutionary War*. Harrisburg, Pennsylvania: Stackpole Books, n.d.

Morales, Waltraud W. *Social Revolution: Theory and Historical Application*. Denver: The Social Science Foundation and Graduate School of International Studies, University of Denver, 1973.

Osanka, Franklin Mark, ed. *Modern Guerrilla Warfare*. New York: The Free Press, 1962.

Pustay, John S. *Counterinsurgency Warfare*. New York: The Free Press, 1965.

Rejai, Mostafa, and Kay Phillips. *Leaders of Revolution*. Beverly Hills, California: Sage Publications, 1979.

## Chapter 2. The Irish Republican Army and Northern Ireland

Barker, A. J. *Bloody Ulster*. New York: Ballantine Books, 1973.

Barry, Tom. *Guerrilla Days in Ireland*. Tralee, Ireland: Anvil Books, 1962.

Bell, J. Bowyer. *The Secret Army*. New York: John Day, 1971.

Coogan, Tim Pat. *The I.R.A.* New York: Praeger Publishers, 1970.

Hull, Roger H. *The Irish Triangle: Conflict in Northern Ireland*. Princeton, New Jersey: Princeton University Press, 1976.

Moss, Robert. *Urban Guerrillas*. London: Temple Smith, 1972.

Rose, Richard. *Governing Without Consensus*. Boston: Beacon Press, 1971.

———. *Northern Ireland: Time of Choice*. Washington, D.C.: American Enterprise Institute for Public Policy Research, 1976.

Rossiter, Bernard D. *Britain—A Future That Works*. Boston: Houghton, Mifflin Co., 1978.

Sellar, W. C., and R. J. Yeatman. *1066 and All That*. London: Methuen and Co., 1930.

## Chapter 3. People's War in Thailand

Armstrong, J. D. *Revolutionary Diplomacy: Chinese Foreign Policy and the United Front Doctrine*. Berkeley: University of California Press, 1977.

Blaufarb, Douglas S. *The Counterinsurgency Era: U.S. Doctrine and Performance*. New York: The Free Press, 1977.

Lovelace, Daniel. *China and "People's War" in Thailand, 1964–1969*. No. 8, China Research Monographs. Berkeley: University of California, Center for Chinese Studies, 1971.

Van Ness, Peter. *Revolution and Chinese Foreign Policy*. Berkeley: University of California Press, 1970.

Weatherbee, Donald E. *The United Front in Thailand: A Documentary Analysis*. Studies in International Affairs No. 8. Columbia, South Carolina: University of South Carolina, Institute for International Studies, 1970.

## Chapter 4. The Guatemalan Insurrection

Burnett, Ben G., and Kenneth F. Johnson, *Political Forces in Latin America: Dimensions of the Quest for Stability*. Belmont, California: Wadsworth, 1970.

Dombrowski, John, et al. *Area Handbook for Guatemala*. Washington, D.C.: U.S. Government Printing Office, 1970.

Galeano, Eduardo. *Guatemala: Occupied Country*. Translated by Cedric Belfrage. New York: Monthly Review Press, 1969.

Gott, Richard. *Guerrilla Movements in Latin America*. Garden City, New York: Doubleday, 1972.

## Chapter 5. Urban Terrorism in Uruguay: The Tupamaros

Gilio, Maria Ester. *The Tupamaro Guerrillas*. New York: Saturday Review Press, 1972.

Hodges, Donald C. *Philosophy of the Urban Guerrilla—The Revolutionary Writings of*

*Abraham Guillen.* New York: William Morrow and Co., 1973.

Labrousse, Alain. *Les Tupamaros: guerrilla urbain en Uruguay.* Paris: Seuil, 1971.

Mayans, Ernesto, ed. *Tupamaros, antología documental.* Cuernavaca, Mexico: Centro Intercultural de Documentacion, 1971.

Mercader, Antonio, and Jorge de Vera. *Tupamaros: estrategia y acción.* Montevideo: Editorial Alfa, 1969.

Moss, Robert. *The War for the Cities.* New York: Coward, McGann, and Geoghegan, 1972.

Porzecanski, Arturo C. *Uruguay's Tupamaros: The Urban Guerrilla.* New York: Praeger Publishers, 1973.

Weil, Thomas E., et al. *Area Handbook for Uruguay.* Washington, D.C.: U.S. Government Printing Office, 1971.

## Chapter 6. Iraq: The Kurdish Rebellion

Adamson, David. *The Kurdish War.* New York: Praeger Publishers, 1965.

Arfa, Hassan. *The Kurds: An Historical and Political Study.* London: Oxford University Press, 1966.

Eagleton, William Jr. *The Kurdish Republic of 1946.* London: Oxford University Press, 1963.

Edmonds, C. J. *Kurds, Turks, and Arabs.* London: Oxford University Press, 1957.

Gavan, S. S. *Kurdistan: Divided Nation of the Middle East.* London: Lawrence and Wishart, 1958.

Hamilton, A. M. *Road Through Kurdistan.* London: Faber and Faber, 1937, 1958.

Hubbard, G. E. *From the Gulf to Ararat.* London: William Blackwood & Sons, 1917.

Kinnane, Derk. *The Kurds and Kurdistan.* London: Oxford University Press, 1957.

O'Ballance, Edgar. *The Kurdish Revolt: 1961–1970.* London: Faber and Faber, 1973.

Safrastian, Arshak. *Kurds and Kurdistan.* London: Harvill Press, 1948.

Schmidt, Dana Adams. *Journey Among Brave Men.* Boston: Little, Brown and Co., 1964.

Solecki, Ralph S. *Shanidar: The First Flower People.* New York: Alfred A. Knopf, 1971.

## Chapter 7. Revolutionary War in Oman

Fiennes, Ranulph. *Where Soldiers Fear to Tread.* London: Hodder and Stoughton, 1975.

Hopwood, Derek, ed. *The Arabian Peninsula.* New Jersey: Rowman and Littlefield, 1972.

Phillips, Wendal. *Oman: A History.* New York: Revnal, 1968.

Price, D. L. *Oman: Insurgency and Development.* London: Institute for the Study of Conflict, 1975.

Skeet, Ian. *Muscat and Oman.* London: Faber and Faber, 1974.

## Chapter 8. Armed Struggle in Angola

Barnett, Don, and Roy Harvey. *The Revolution in Angola.* Indianapolis:

Bobbs-Merrill Co., 1972.

Carty, Wilfred, and Martin Kilson, eds. *The African Reader: Independent Africa*. New York: Vintage Books, 1970.

Chaliand, Gerard. *Armed Struggle in Africa*. New York: Monthly Review Press, 1969.

Chilcote, Ronald H. *Emerging Nationalism in Portuguese Africa: Documents*. Stanford: Hoover Institution Press, 1972.

Davidson, Basil. *In the Eye of the Storm*. New York: Doubleday and Co., 1972.

Gibson, Richard. *African Liberation Movements: Contemporary Struggles Against White Minority Rule*. Oxford: Oxford University Press, 1972.

Grundy, Kenneth W. *Guerrilla Struggle in Africa: An Analysis and Preview*. New York: Grossman Publishers, 1971.

Herrick, Allison B. *Area Handbook for Angola*. Washington, D.C.: U.S. Government Printing Office, 1967.

Marcum, John J. *The Angolan Revolution*. Cambridge, Massachusetts: The MIT Press, 1969.

Minter, William. *Portuguese Africa and the West*. New York: Monthly Review Press, 1972.

Okuma, Thomas. *Angola in Ferment*. Boston: Beacon Press, 1962.

Oliver, Roland and Anthony Atmore. *Africa Since 1800*. Cambridge: Cambridge University Press, 1979.

Stockwell, John. *In Search of Enemies: A CIA Story*. New York: W. W. Norton, 1978.

Valentim, Jorge Alicerces. *Qui Libere L'Angola*. Brussels: Michele Coppens, 1969.

Venter, A. J. *Portugal's Guerrilla War*. Capetown: John Malherbe Pty. Ltd., 1973.

Wheeler, Douglas L. and Rene Pelissier. *Angola*. New York: Praeger Publishers, 1971.

# Index